Schriften zur Restrukturierung

Institut für Interdisziplinäre Restrukturierung (iir) e. V.

Herausgegeben von

Dipl.-Kfm. Arndt Geiwitz
Dr. Frank Kebekus
Dr. Thomas C. Knecht
Prof. Dr. Christoph G. Paulus, LL. M.

Band 7

Annika Wolf

Promoting an Effective Rescue Culture with Debt-Equity-Swaps?

A Comparative Study of Restructuring Public Companies in Germany and England

Nomos

Die Deutsche Nationalbibliothek lists this publication in the Deutsche Nationalbibliografie; detailed bibliographic data is available in the Internet at http://dnb.d-nb.de

a.t.: Berlin, Humboldt-Universität, Diss., 2014
Original title: Progress Towards an Effective Rescue Culture in Gemany? A Comparative Study of Restructuring using Debt-Equity-Swaps in Germany and England

ISBN 978-3-8487-1535-0 (Print)
978-3-8452-5574-3 (ePDF)

British Library Cataloguing-in-Publication Data
A catalogue record for this book is available from the British Library.

ISBN 978-3-8487-1535-0 (Print)
978-3-8452-5574-3 (ePDF)

Library of Congress Cataloging-in-Publication Data
Wolf, Annika
Promoting an Effective Rescue Culture with Debt-Equity-Swaps?
A Comparative Study of Restructuring Public Companies in Germany and England
Annika Wolf
269 p.
Includes bibliographic references.

ISBN 978-3-8487-1535-0 (Print)
978-3-8452-5574-3 (ePDF)

1. Edition 2015

Foreword

The developments of the past twenty years have led to a rethinking of the purpose of restructuring and insolvency law. The primary objective in many jurisdictions, and the purpose of legislative action, is no longer the liquidation and market exit of companies in distress but the rescue of a going concern. England and Wales seemed to be better prepared to deal with distressed companies than Germany in the aftermath of the financial crisis – and one of the reasons given for this was the debt-equity-swap as a tool of financial restructuring.

The City of London has dominated the British economy since the 1970s and financial products have become the (almost) only relevant economic product of the nation. This may explain why the City wants to retain its position as forerunner in all financial products, precisely for financial restructuring. The anchored thinking of efficiency follows financial goals alone and is often exported to legal policy and legal doctrine. Most of continental Europe resisted this attack until the financial crisis. While other European countries then amended their restructuring and insolvency law, the German legislator acted with extreme caution at first, before introducing the debt-equity-swap into German insolvency law with the "Act to Further Facilitate the Restructurings of Companies (ESUG)".

In her dissertation *Annika Wolf* touches on the most current and competitive issue in the European legal order of restructuring and insolvency law. With a functional legal approach she has taken the logical point in comparing legal norms with regard to debt-equity-swaps in Germany and England, and whether the amendments in German law have (so far) succeeded in providing companies in financial distress with an improved legal environment for corporate rescue. The core question is whether the migration of German public companies to England for the purposes of a purely financial restructuring via a debt-equity-swap remains to be necessary.

Her analysis embraces the cultural differences between England and Germany with regard to rescue culture in general and corporate culture in particular. The debt-equity-swap may be a preferred option for a purely financial restructuring of public companies in distress, however, there are still other factors that affect the effectiveness of restructuring companies, such as a distinctive rescue culture and the influence of legal history, legal sociology and legal policy, the role of governments and national banks, the judicial infrastructure and access to finance.

The strength of her thesis is to provide the clear view of an economist on restructuring and insolvency law, as it provides an accurate presentation of the purely economic assessment of legal regulatory models. The emphasis is, thus, less on the detailed legal argumentation and more on the economic one.

With the discussion of these points, *Annika Wolf* provides valuable insight and promotes a deeper understanding of the obstacles and challenges for corporate rescue, and explains why the legal codification of the debt-equity-swap may not be enough to make progress towards a rescue culture in Germany. Her results will attract the attention of practitioners and researchers alike.

Prof. Christoph G. Paulus

Preface

Coinciding with the financial failure of Lehman Brothers in September 2008, I began working on distressed debt and was in the front line to experience the challenges financial institutions faced when companies began to fail, write-offs started to damage profitability and overall tightened regulations on capital requirements limited further financing. The market disruptions in the aftermath of Lehman initiated a market selection process in which non-viable companies eventually failed and exited the market. Since the global financial markets were shaken to their foundation, even viable companies began to become financially distressed, either because of the heavy burdens of debt carried forward from previous years or as a result of the effect of a general economic downturn in their industries.

When liquidity was withdrawn from the markets, the secondary market in which distressed assets were traded eventually dried up. With financial institutions no longer able to provide additional funds to their borrowers to finance them through the period of drought, the debt-equity-swap came under consideration as an instrument to provide for the rescue of companies, rather than their liquidation. This strategy seemed to work well in England, where the financial industry seemed better prepared to handle large-scale complex restructurings, and even German companies were attracted to being restructured under English law. The economic downturn resulting from the financial crisis and the forum shopping by German companies for English law has led to extensive reforms of the insolvency law in various countries. It was an exciting time to attend the discussions on whether Germany would need a pre-insolvency restructuring proceeding, and on whether the debt-equity-swap would be a godsend for companies in financial distress or whether state-owned banks should do their duty to society by rescuing insolvent debtors.

Having worked in both Germany and England, I was able to gather insight into the different legal frameworks and the factors affecting the effectiveness of restructuring companies. This motivated me to write this dissertation as I wanted to contribute to the existing literature and to foster the discussions on German and English restructuring and insolvency law.

The dissertation was accepted by the Law Faculty of the Humboldt-Universität zu Berlin in the winter term 2013/14. The text has been carefully revised and updated for publication; literature, case law and further developments were considered until December 2014.

My gratitude goes to my doctoral supervisor *Prof. Christoph G. Paulus* for his trust and encouragement during the past years, and for granting me a remarkable degree of freedom in defining my theme and pursuing my research; *Prof. Stephan Madaus* for being a critical and curious advisor and thesis referee. I would like to thank the editors of the "Schriftenreihe zur Restruktutierung" for including my work in their series.

A valuable contribution to this thesis was given by the many practitioners and lawyers in Germany and England, offering their time to discuss my questions and by providing an insight into the issues and challenges of restructuring and insolvency law cases. I thank them for the courtesy of sharing their experiences with me.

I would like to thank *Prof. Klaus J. Hopt* for welcoming me to the Max Planck Institute for Comparative and International Private Law in Hamburg. The atmosphere of high spirit, intellectual discussions and mutual support I experienced there, and for which I thank especially *Dr. Felix Steffek* and *Prof. Christoph Kumpan*, nurtured this thesis. To conduct most of my research in the Institute's library with its always committed and helpful staff was a fortunate circumstance.

My research was also conducted at the European University Institute in Florence. I followed an invitation by *Prof. Hans-W. Micklitz*, my advisor during my masters' studies, and to whom I owe my passion for restructuring and insolvency law. Later on, he also gave me the opportunity for a truly academic experience there by becoming my mentor at the Max Weber Fellowship Programme with an affiliation to the Department of Law.

My deepest gratitude goes to my family. Their continuous care and loving encouragement, patience and unconditional faith in me led to the genesis and completion of this doctoral thesis: Thank you.

Florence and Berlin, December 2014 *Annika Wolf*

Contents

Abbreviations

ABLJ	American Bankruptcy Law Journal
AG	Die Aktiengesellschaft
AG	Amtsgericht *(Lower District Court)*
AktG	Aktiengesetz *(Law on Companies Limited by Shares)*
AJICL	Arizona Journal of International and Comparative Law
ALER	American Law and Economics Review
Am. Bankr. L. J.	American Bankruptcy Law Journal
Aufl.	Auflage *(edition)*
BB	Betriebs-Berater
B.C.	Bankruptcy Code
BCC	British Company Law Cases
BCLC	Butterworths Company Law Cases
Bd.	Band
Begr.	Begründung *(Reasons Given)*
Beil.	Beilage *(Supplement)*
Berkley Bus. L. J.	Berkley Business Law Journal
BFH	Bundesfinanzhof *(German Federal Finance Court)*
BFuP	Betriebswirtschaftliche Forschung und Praxis
BGB	Bürgerliches Gesetzbuch *(German Civil Code)*
BGH	Bundesgerichtshof *(German Federal Court of Justice)*
BGHZ	Amtliche Sammlung der Entscheidungen des Bundesgerichtshof in Zivilsachen *(Official Journal of Decisions of the Federal Court of Justice in Civil Matters)*
BJIBFL	Butterworths Journal of International Banking and Financial Law
BKR	Zeitschrift für Bank- und Kapitalmarktrecht
BLJ	Business Law Journal
BLR	Business Law Review
BMJ	Bundesjustizministerium *(German Federal Ministry of Justice)*
BR	Bundesrat *(German Federal Council)*
BR-Drucks.	Bundesrat-Drucksachen *(Printed Items from the Federal Council)*
Brook. J Int'l Law	Brooklyn Journal of International Law
BT	Bundestag *(German Federal Diet)*
BT-Drucks.	Bundestags-Drucksachen *(Printed Items from the Federal Diet)*
BVerfG	Bundesverfassungsgericht *(German Federal Constitutional Court)*
c.	Cause
CA	Companies Act
CA 1985	Companies Act 1985
CA 1989	Companies Act 1989
CA 2004	Companies Act 2004
Cambridge L. J.	Cambridge Law Journal
CDDA	Company Directors Disqualification Act 1986
CFILR	Company Financial and Insolvency Law Review
CFS	Center for Financial Studies
Ch	Chancery
ChD	Chancery Division
CL	Company Lawyer
CLC	Commercial Law Cases
CLJ	Company Law Journal

Colum. L. Rev.	Columbia Law Review
COMI	Centre of Main Interest
CR&I	Corporate Rescue and Insolvency
CVA	Company Voluntary Arrangement
DB	Der Betrieb
DIP	Debtor-in-Possession
Disk-E	Diskussionsentwurf
DStR	Deutsches Steuerrecht
DZWIR	Deutsche Zeitschrift für Wirtschafts- und Insolvenzrecht
EA 2002	Enterprise Act 2002
EBLR	European Business Law Review
EBOR	European Business Organisation Law Review
EBRD	European Bank for Reconstruction and Development
EC	European Community
ECJ	European Court of Justice
ECFR	European Company and Financial Law Review
ECR	European Court Reports
eds.	editors
e.g.	example given
et al.	and others
et seq.	et sequentia
EIR	European Insolvency Regulation *(Council Regulation No. 1346/2000 on Insolvency Proceedings)*
ELJ	European Law Journal
ESUG	Gesetz zur weiteren Erleichterung der Sanierung von Unternehmen *(Act for the Further Facilitation of the Restructuring of Companies)*
EuR	Zeitschrift Europarecht
EuZW	Europäische Zeitschrift für Wirtschaftsrecht
EWCA	England and Wales Court of Appeal
EWHC	England and Wales High Court of Justice
EWiR	Entscheidungen zum Wirtschaftsrecht
EWS	Europäisches Wirtschafts- und Steuerrecht
FAZ	Frankfurter Allgemeine Zeitung
FG	Finanzgericht *(Taxation Court)*
FK	Frankfurter Kommentar *(Frankfurt Commentary)*
Fn.	Footnote
GG	Grundgesetz *(Basic Law of the Federal Republic of Germany)*
GmbHR	GmbH-Rundschau
GWR	Gesellschafts- und Wirtschaftsrecht
Harv. L. Review	Harvard Law Review
HB	Handelsblatt
HC	House of Commons
HGB	Handelsgesetzbuch *(German Commercial Code)*
HL	House of Lords
IA 1986	Insolvency Act 1986
IA 2000	Insolvency Act 2000
IBFL	International Banking and Financial Law
I.C.C.L.R.	International Company and Commercial Law Review
ICLQ	International and Comparative Law Quarterly
ICR	International Corporate Rescue
IFLR	International Financial Law Review
IL&P	Insolvency Law and Practice
InsVZ	Zeitschrift für Insolvenzverwaltung und Sanierungsberatung
Int'l Rev. L. & Econ.	International Review of Law and Economics
Int. Insolv. Rev	International Insolvency Review

IR 1986	Insolvency Rules 1986
IRLE	International Review of Law and Economics
InsO	Insolvenzordnung *(German Insolvency Statute)*
InsVZ	Zeitschrift für Insolvenzverwaltung und Sanierungsberatung
Iowa L. Rev	Iowa Law Review
Iss.	Issue
J. Appl. Corp. Fin.	Journal of Applied Corporate Finance
J.B.L.	Journal of Business Law
JBF	Journal of Banking and Finance
JCLS	Journal of Corporate Law Studies
J. Corp. Fin.	Journal of Corporate Finance
J. Corp. L.	The Journal of Corporation Law
J. Econ. Behav. & Org.	Journal of Economic Behavior & Organization
J. Econ. Persp.	Journal of Economic Perspectives
J. Fin. Econ.	Journal of Financial Economics
JIBL	Journal of International Banking Law
JIBLR	Journal of International Banking, Law and Regulation
J.L. & Econ.	The Journal of Law and Economics
JZ	Juristenzeitung
Kö-Ko	Kölner Kommentar *(Cologne Commentary)*
KredReorgG	Kreditinstitute-Reorganisationsgesetz *(Financial Institutions Restructuring Act)*
KSI	Zeitschrift für Krisen-, Sanierungs- und Insolvenzberatung
KTS	Zeitschrift für Insolvenzrecht
LBO	Leveraged Buy-Out
LG	Landgericht *(District Court)*
LR	Law Reports
LS	Legal Studies
LSG	Law Society's Gazette
Ltd	Limited
Mich. L. Rev.	Michigan Law Review
mn.	marginal number
MüKo	Münchner Kommentar *(Munich Commentary)*
N. C. L. Rev.	The North Carolina Law Review
NJW	Neue Juristische Wochenzeitschrift
No.	Number
Nw. U. L. Rev.	Northwestern University Law Review
NZG	Neue Zeitschrift für Gesellschaftsrecht
NZI	Neue Zeitschrift für das Recht der Insolvenz und Sanierung
OJ	Official Journal
OJLS	Oxford Journal of Legal Studies
OLG	Oberlandesgericht *(Court of Appeal)*
ORDO	Jahrbuch für die Ordnung von Wirtschaft
p.	page(s)
para	paragraph
paras.	paragraphs
Plc	Public limited company
Q. J. Econ.	Quarterly Journal of Economics
QREF	Quarterly Review of Economics & Finance
r.	Rule
RabelsZ	Rabels Zeitung
Rev. Econ. Stud.	Review of Economic Studies
RIW	Recht der Internationalen Wirtschaft
Sch.	Schedule
sec.	Section

ss.	Sections
Stan. L. Rev.	Stanford Law Review
SZ	Süddeutsche Zeitung
Tex. L. Rev.	Texas Law Review
UNCITRAL	United Nations Commission on International Trade Law
U. Chi. L. Rev.	University of Chicago Law Review
UK	United Kingdom
US	United States
Va. L. Rev.	Virginia Law Review
Vand. L. Rev.	Vanderbilt Law Review
VG	Verwaltungsgericht
Vol.	Volume
Wash. U. L. Q.	Washington University Law Quarterly
Western Econ. J.	Western Economic Journal
Wis. L. Rev.	Wisconsin Law Review
WM	Wertpapiermitteilungen – Zeitschrift für Wirtschafts- und Bankrecht
Yale L. J.	Yale Law Journal
ZaöRV	Zeitschrift für ausländisches öffentliches Recht und Völkerrecht
ZBB	Zeitschrift für Bankrecht und Bankwirtschaft
ZEuP	Zeitschrift für Europäisches Privatrecht
ZfB	Zeitschrift für Betriebswirtschaft
ZGR	Zeitschrift für Unternehmens- und Gesellschaftsrecht
ZHR	Zeitschrift für das gesamte Handels- und Wirtschaftsrecht
ZInsO	Zeitschrift für das gesamte Insolvenzrecht
ZIP	Zeitschrift für Wirtschaftsrecht und Insolvenzpraxis
ZRP	Zeitschrift für Rechtspolitik
ZP	Zeitschrift für Planung & Unternehmenssteuerung
ZVglRWiss	Zeitschrift für vergleichende Rechtswissenschaft
ZZP	Zeitschrift für Zivilprozess

Table of Cases

Germany

AG Charlottenburg, 36s IN 2196/13, 36i IN 2311/13
AG Köln, Beschl. v. 19.2.2008, 73 IE 1/08
BGH, Urt. v. 11.10.1961 – VII ZR 113/60
BGH, Urt. v. 29. 1. 1964 – Ib ZR 197/62, BGHZ 41, 98
BGH, Urt. v. 11. 5. 1978 – VII ZR 55/77, BGHZ 71, 309, 312
BGH, Urt. v. 24.5.2005 – IX ZR 123/04
BGH, Beschl. v. 17.7.2014 – IX ZB 13/14, ZIP 2014, 1442
BGH, Beschl. v. 7. 7. 2005 – IX ZB 266/04, BGHZ 163, 344, 347
BGH, Beschl. v. 22. 3. 2007 – IX ZB 10/06
BGH, Beschl. v. 29. 3. 2007 – IX ZB 204/05
BGH, Beschl. v. 26. 4. 2007 – IX ZB 5/06, NZI 2007, 521
BGH, Beschl. v. 10. I.2008 – IX ZB 97/07
BGH, Urt. v. 13. 10. 2009 – X ZR 79/06, WM 2009, 2330
BGH, Urt. v. 6. 10. 2005 – IX ZR 36/02
BGHZ 15, 52
BGHZ 54, 247
BGHZ 71, 40, 43
BGHZ 83, 319
BGHZ 83, 319, 321
BGHZ 90, 37
BGHZ 90, 370, 373
BGHZ 110, 47, 61
BGHZ 113, 335
BGHZ 116, 319 (Akkordstörer)
BGHZ 119, 305, 319
BGHZ 120, 140, 145
BGHZ 125, 141
BGHZ 125, 141, 145
BGHZ 125, 239, 241
BGHZ 129, 136
BGHZ 132, 141, 143
BGHZ 136, 133, 139
BGHZ 142, 167, 169
BVerfG, Beschl. v. 17.10.2013 – 2 BvR 1978/13
BVerfG. Beschl. v. 27.4.1999 – 1 BvR 1613/94, BVerfGE 100, 289

BVerfG, Beschl. V. 20.8.2000 – 1 BvR 68/95
BVerfG NJW 2007, 828 (Siemens Nixdorf)
BVerfG NJW 2007, 3266, 3267 (Wüstenrot/Württembergische)
BVerfG NJW 2007, 3268, 3270 (Edscha)
BVerfG ZIP 2007, 1261
BVerfG ZIP 2007, 2121
BVerfGE 14, 263, 276 (Feldmühle)
BVerfGE 25, 371, 407 (Rheinstahl)
BVerfGE 50, 290, 341
BVerfGE 102, 197, 211
FG Köln, EFG 2001, 588
LAG Rheinland-Pfalz Urt. v. 12. 10. 2006 – 4 Sa 281/06
LG Bielefeld, Beschl. v. 30. 11. 2001 – 23 T 365/01
LG Neubrandenburg, Beschl. v. 31.7. 2000 – 4 T 260/00,
LG Berlin, BB 1977, 213
LG Berlin, Beschl. v. 16.6.2014 – 95 O 52/13, ZIP 2014, 1388
LG Berlin, Beschl. v. 20. 10. 2004 – 86 T 578/04
LG Berlin, Bescheid v. 8. 10. 2004 – 86 T 588/04
LG Berlin, Beschl. v. 29. 10. 2002 – 86 T 534/02
LG Berlin, Urt. v. 10.12.2012, 99 O 79/11 = KG 23 U 186/12
LG Cottbus, Beschl. v. 17. 7. 2001 – 7 T 421/00
LG Frankfurt,/M., Urt. v. 13.11.2013 – 3-13 O 72/12
LG Frankfurt,/M., Urt. v. 20.3.2013 – 3-13 O 119/12
LG Frankfurt,/M., Urt. v. 13.8.2013 – 03-9O 78/13
LG Potsdam 22.10.2008 – 2 O 501/07
LG Rottweil, 17. 5. 2010 – 3 O 2/08
OLG Bamberg NZG 2005, 808
OLG Celle, Hinweisbeschl. v. 20. 11. 2006 – 4 U 166/06
OLG Celle, Urt. v. 8. 9. 2009 – Case 8 U 46/09
OLG Dresden, Beschl. v. 21. 6. 2000 – 7 W 951/00
OLG Düsseldorf, GmbHR 1992, 112
OLG Düsseldorf, NZG 2004, 328, 329
OLG Jena, Urt. v. 6. 2. 2002 – 2 U 1033/01
OLG Naumburg, Beschl. v. 2. 5. 2000 — 5 W 47/00
RG, Urt. v. 8.7. 1930 – VII 476/29
RG, Urt. v. 15. 12. 1899 – 240/99 III, JW 1900, 73

United Kingdom / United States / Canada

Anglo–Continental Supply Co Ltd, re [1922] 2 Ch 723
APCOA Parking (UK) Ltd & Ors [2014] EWHC 997 (Ch), EWHC 1867 (Ch)
Barclays Mercantile Business Finance Ltd & Another v Sibec Developments Ltd [1992] 1 WLR 1253

Bluebrook Ltd, re [2009] EWHC 2114 (Ch)

BNY Corporate Trustee Services Limited v Eurosail-UK 2007-3bl plc and others [2010] EWCA 2005 (Ch), [2011] EWCA Civ 227

Boys v Chaplin [1969] 2 All ER 1085

Broderip v. Salomon [1893] B 4793, [1895] 2 Ch 323, 337

Cavell Insurance Company 21.2.2005, re Ontario Supreme Court (unreported)

Cheyne Finance Plc (No 2), re [2007] EWHC 2402 (Ch)

Ci4net.com Inc, re [2005] BCC 277

Collins & Aikman Europe SA Collins and others, re [2006] EWHC 1343 (Ch)

Company, re a [1986] BCLC 261

Company (No 001418 of 1988), re a [1990] BCC 526

Connock and another v Fantozzi (Re Alitalia Linee Aeree Italiane SpA) [2011] EWHC 15 (Ch)

Countrywide PLC and others [2009] EWHC 1347 (Ch)

Damovo Group SA (unreported) re, 25 April 2007 (Ch D)

DAP Holding NV, re [2005] EWHC 2092 (Ch) B

Debtor (No. 64 of 1992), re a [1994] 1 WLR 264

Devi v Peoples Bank of Northern India Ltd. [1938] 4 AER 337

DKLL Solicitors v Revenue and Customs Commissioners [2007] BCC 908

DKLL Solicitors v Her Majesty's Revenue & Customs [2007] EWHC 2067 (Ch)

Eurofood IFSC Ltd, re [2006] Ch 508

European Directories v DH6 BV [2010] EWHC 3472 (Ch)

Equitable Life Assurance Society (No. 2), re [2002] EWHC 140 (Ch)

Hans Brochier Holdings Ltd v Exner [2006] EWHC 2594 (Ch), [2007] BCC 127 (Ch)

Hawk Insurance Company Limited, re [2001] 2 BCLC 450, CA, [2001] 2 BCLC 67

Hellas Telecommunications (Luxembourg) II SCA, re [2009] EWHC 3199 (Ch)

Heron International NV, re [1994] 1 BCLC 667

House of Lords [1897] AC 22

Jessel Trust Ltd, re [1985] BCLC 119

Johns-Manville Corp., in re 36 B.R. 727 (S.D.N.Y. 1984)

Kaupthing Capital Partners Master LP Inc (unreported), 31 March 2010 (Ch D)

La Seda De Barcelona SA, re [2010] EWHC 1364 (Ch)

Lennox Holdings Plc, re [2009] EWHC B11 (Ch)

Marconi Corp plc, re [2003] EWHC 1083 (Ch)

Minister Assets plc, re [1985] BCLC 200

MyTravel Group Plc, re [2005] 1 WLR 2365

NFU Development Trust Ltd, re [1973] 1 ALL ER 153

Olympia & York Canary Wharf Ltd (No.1) [1993] BCC 154

Olympic Airlines SA Pension and Life Assurance Scheme v Olympic Airlines SA [2012] EWHC 1413 (Ch)

Osiris Insurance, re [1999] 1 BCLC 182

Primacom Holding GmbH, re [2011] EWHC 3746 (Ch), [2012] EWHC 164 (Ch)

Prudential Assurance Co Ltd v PRG Powerhouse Ltd [2007] EWHC 1002 (Ch)

Rodenstock GmbH, re [2011] EWHC 1104 (Ch)

Sao Paulo (Brazilian) Rly. Co. Ltd. V. Carter [1896] AC 31
Savoy Hotel Ltd, re [1981] Ch 351, [1981] 3 All ER 646
Shierson v Vlieland-Boddy [2005] EWCA Civ. 974
Sovereign Marine & General Insurance Co Ltd and other companies, re [2006] EWHC 1335 (Ch)
Sovereign Life Assurance Company v. Dodd, re [1892] 2 QB 573
Stanford International Bank Ltd and others, re [2009] EWHC 1441 (Ch), [2010] EWCA Civ 137
T&D Industries plc [2001] 1 BCLC 471
The Atlantic Star [1972] 3 All ER 705
Texaco Inc., in re 73 B.R. 960 (S.D.N.Y. 1987)
Trimast Holding Sarl – and – Tele Columbus GmbH [2010] EWHC 1944 (Ch)
Truex v Toll [2009] EWHC 396
Uniq plc, re [2011] EWHC 749 (Ch)

European Union

ECJ, C–81/87 [1988] ECR I–05483 (Daily Mail)
ECJ, C–19/90 & C-20/90 [1991] ECR I–2691 (Karella and Karellas)
ECJ, C–381/89 [1992] ECR I–2111 (Syndesmos Melon)
ECJ, C–441/93 [1996] ECR I–1347 (Panagis Pafitis)
ECJ, C–212/97 [1999] ECR I–01459 (Centros)
ECJ, C–208/00 [2002] ECR I–09919 (Überseering)
ECJ, C–167/01 [2003] ECR I–10155 (Inspire Art)
ECJ, C–9/02 [2004] ECR I–02409 (de Lasteyrie)
ECJ, C–341/04 [2004] ECR I–3813 (Eurofood)
ECJ, C–411/03 [2005] ECR I–10805 (SEVIC)
ECJ, C–1/04 [2006] ECR I-701 (Susanne Staubitz-Schreiber)
ECJ, C–210/06 [2008] ECR I–9641 (Cartesio)
ECJ, C–396/09 [2011] ECR I–0000 (Interedil)
EJC, C–191/10 [2011] ECR I–13209 (Rastelli Davide)
ECJ, C–378/10 [2012] ECR I–00000 (VALE)

Chapter I Introduction and Background

1 Introduction

1.1 Setting the Scene

With the global financial and economic crisis causing uncertainties and disruptions in financial markets and provoking increased capital requirements for banks, corporate financial distress has been a great economic challenge.[1] In the past, companies were able to accrue massive funds on generous terms; now they suffer from these excessive burdens of debt.[2] The debts will have to be repaid or restructured in the near future in order to prevent the company suffering financial distress. With credit terms having changed and credit becoming harder and more expensive to obtain,[3] some companies will face fierce competition to finance their daily business – and will eventually fail. Distorted market conditions may also push companies with a viable core business towards insolvency,[4] leading to enormous losses that may cripple economies by suffocating any economic growth, harming the economic prosperity and the overall social welfare of a country.[5]

Insolvency law plays a fundamental role in credit societies and the economic concept of insolvency is an integral part of a market economy, providing an effective competitive mechanism for the survival of viable companies and the failure of unviable and inefficient businesses.[6] The legal framework ought to provide effective tools to either facilitate an orderly insolvency process or the restructuring of companies in financial distress.

---

1 *Laryea*, IMF 2010, p. 3.

2 *Bork*, mn. 1.10: Mezzanine financing in the years 2004 to 2007 in Germany alone amount to some EUR4.6bn, for leveraged buyouts USD72.61bn are required for refinancing before 2016. See also *Hölzle*, KTS 2011, 291, 300; *Sullivan / Warren / Westbrook*, 59 Stan. L. Rev. (2006-2007) 213, 220 for empirical evidence.

3 *Jostarndt / Rodt*, in FS Rudolph, p. 1100, 1101.

4 *Hommel / Knecht / Wohlenberg*, in *Hommel / Knecht / Wohlenberg*, p. 27, 30.

5 *Wood*, The Law and Practice of International Finance, mn. 1-23; *Easterbrook / Fischel*, viii.

6 See Chapter I 2.1.

The competitive race inherent in globalised markets has also led to competition between corporate legal entities[7] and, furthermore, to legal competition including the field of insolvency and restructuring law.[8] German companies such as *Deutsche Nickel*[9], *Schefenacker*[10] or *Brochier*[11] have engaged in forum shopping,[12] particularly in England. They have realised that migrating to a country with a legal framework favourable to restructuring can also be an important economic factor in the choice of location, despite the complexity and costs involved.[13] *Tele Columbus*[14], *Rodenstock*[15], *PrimaCom*[16] and most recently *APCOA Parking*[17] have found a way of benefitting from English restructuring law without fully moving to the country.

This legal competition has revealed an urgent need for reform in Germany.[18] The nation has lagged behind other European countries,[19] which have already pushed through such reforms over the past few years. The past English law reforms are believed to have established a rescue culture by offering legal proceedings to companies in financial distress that allow for regaining going concern status by restructuring as opposed to liquidation. As a result, the German legislature came under pressure to offer a more attractive restructuring and insolvency law[20] to prevent companies from relocating their businesses abroad, as this would result in an exodus of local businesses, endangering the national economy.[21]

---

7 *Eidenmüller*, ZGR 2007, 168, 170 et seq.; *Witt*, ZGR 2009, 872. 873.

8 *Eidenmüller*, ZGR 2006, 467 et seq.; *Eidenmüller*, Finanzkrise, Wirtschaftskrise und das deutsche Insolvenzrecht, p. 8; *Jacoby*, ZGR 2010, 359, 362 et seq.; *Bork*, ZIP 2010, 397, 398 et seq.

9 *Vallender*, NZI 2007, 129, 131 et seq.

10 *Windsor / Müller-Seils / Burg*, NZI 2007, 7.

11 *Hans Brochier Holdings Ltd v Exner* [2006] EWHC 2594 (Ch), [2007] BCC 127 (Ch).

12 *May*, ZInsO 2012, 165: „jurisdiction shopping".

13 *Eidenmüller*, ZIP 2010, 649, 650; *Eidenmüller / Frobenius / Prusko*, NZI 2010, 545, 546 et seq.

14 *Trimast Holding Sarl – and – Tele Columbus GmbH* [2010] EWHC 1944 (Ch).

15 *Re Rodenstock GmbH* [2011] EWHC 1104 (Ch).

16 *Re Primacom Holding GmbH* [2011] EWHC 3746 (Ch); *Re Primacom Holding GmbH* [2012] EWHC 164 (Ch).

17 *Re APCOA Parking (UK) Ltd & Ors* [2014] EWHC 997 (Ch.).

18 *Gebler*, NZI 2010, 665 ff.; *Jaffé / Friedrich*, ZIP 2008, 1849.

19 *Wessels*, ECL 2011, 27, 28.

20 *Schelo*, NZI 2006, VII, VIII; *Eidenmüller*, ZZP 2008, 273, 275.

21 *Vallender*, NZI 2007, 129, 130.

With the "Act for the Further Facilitation of the Restructuring of Companies" (*Gesetz zur Erleichterung der Sanierung von Unternehmen*)[22], the German legislature made amendments to the German Insolvency Statute (*Insolvenzordnung*)[23] to facilitate the restructuring of companies in financial distress. The shift was also motivated by a need to establish a culture in which insolvency is no longer seen as a stigma but rather as giving companies a real chance to survive. The German legislature recognised that changing debt into equity was an important restructuring tool for a company in financial distress[24] and anchored the measure as part of the insolvency plan proceeding in German law.

The legal uncertainties in a debt-equity-swap are reflected in the new legal rules.[25] In the future, a debt-equity-swap may even be implemented against the will of the shareholders.[26] Shareholders are integrated into the insolvency plan voting process as one or more independent voting groups and under certain conditions they cannot reject or prevent the validity of the insolvency plan. Regarding creditors, a conversion of debt into equity against their will is still not possible. Other measures in the ESUG include a modification of the insolvency plan proceeding, which had only very rarely been used as a restructuring tool in the past. One of the reasons for this was a strict separation between company and insolvency law measures, which caused uncertainties in insolvency plan proceedings. With ESUG, structural changes now interlink insolvency with company law, thereby lifting the neutrality of the Insolvency Statute and overcoming the separation between corporate and insolvency law.[27] German insolvency law should now be in a position to compete with other European jurisdictions.[28]

---

22 Gesetz zur Erleichterung der Sanierung von Unternehmen (ESUG), *herewithafter* ESUG.

23 Insolvenzordnung (InsO), *herewithafter* InsO.

24 BMJ, RegE-ESUG, BT-Drucks. 17/5712, p. 28.

25 *Ibid.* p. 27, 47 especially with regard to constitutional issues.

26 BMJ, Begr. DiskE-ESUG, ZIP 2010, Beil. 1, p. 2. Critical see *Kresser*, ZInsO 2010, 1409 et seq.; *Spetzler*, KTS 2010, 433, 444 et seq.

27 BMJ, RegE-ESUG, BT-Drucks. 17/5712, p. 26. The change in perception was likely due to the decision made by the BVerfG in Squeeze-Out-Proceedings, BVerfG, NJW 2007, 3268.

28 BMJ, RegE-ESUG, BT-Drucks. 17/5712, p. 1.

1.2 Definitions and Limitations

There are various definitions and limitations that apply to this dissertation.

Rescue culture has many different aspects. The basic concept aims to create a legal environment that favours the restructuring of a company in financial distress as opposed to liquidation.[29] A rescue culture is effective when it is fit for purpose and allows the rescue of the company in financial distress in a timely, low cost and constructive manner. *Financial distress*[30] is a situation where a company's cash flow is insufficient to meet current obligation,[31] which may eventually lead to *insolvency*.[32]

The term *restructuring*[33] is neither a legal term nor is there a generally accepted definition.[34] Restructuring generally includes the totality of "*organizational*[35]*, financial*[36] *and legal measures to lead a company out of an unfavourable economic situation*[37] *in order to ensure a continued existence; [... including the] conversion [...] of debt into equity*"[38]. Restructuring may cover any measures that give creditors access to the going concern value of the debtor's assets.[39] A restructuring is economically rea-

---

29 *Müller-Seils*, p. 20 et seq.

30 Compared to market distress or industry distress, see *Ofek*, 34 J.F.E. (1993), 3, 19.

31 *Wruck*, 27 J. Fin. Econ. (1990) 419, 421: financial distress "is not synonymous with corporate death".

32 *Altman*, p. 4 et seq., defining the terms failure, insolvency, default and bankruptcy and, despite that these terms are used interchangeably in this dissertation, they are distinctly different in their formal use; *Baird*, 54 U. Chi. L. Rev. (1987) 815, 829: default is not necessarily bankruptcy.

33 For distinctions between restructuring, turnaround and reorganisation, see *Holbein*, p. 65 et seq.

34 *K. Schmidt*, GmbH in Krise, Sanierung und Insolvenz, p. 148; *Belcher*, p.11 et seq.; *Bork*, ZIP 2011, 101; *Wellensiek*, NZI 2002, 233, 233; *Claussen*, ZHR 174 (1983) 195, 197; *Uhlenbruck*, KTS 1981, 531, 533 et seq.

35 *Wruck*, 27 J. Fin. Econ. (1990) 419, 420 et seq.

36 *Gilson / John / Lang*, 27 J. Fin. Econ. (1990), 315 et seq. For overview of equity and debt measure, see *Thierhoff et al.*, mn. 40 et seq.

37 *Wellensiek*, NZI 2002, 233; *Flessner*, ZRP 1982, 244; *Uhlenbruck*, KTS 1981, 513, 534.

38 *Flessner*, Sanierung und Reorganisation, p. 2; *Gless*, p. 44; *Wellensiek*, NZI 2002, 233, 234; *Ofek*, 34 J. Fin. Econ. (1993), 3; *Kilger*, ZIP 1982, 779, 781; *Uhlenbruck*, KTS 1981, 513, 533 et seq.

39 *Balz*, Sanierung von Unternehmen, p. 13.

sonable only if the business or the legal entity is worth preserving.[40] A company in distress decides whether to contemplate liquidation or restructuring[41] by establishing whether its going concern value is higher than its liquidation value.[42] This is its restructuring potential. With the successful implementation of restructuring measures, generally accompanied or followed by an operational restructuring,[43] the company will regain its competiveness and return on investment,[44] generating a surplus of revenues over expenditures.[45]

Extrinsic restructuring, as opposed to intrinsic restructuring,[46] deals with changes in the relationship between the company and its creditors and in the creditors' relationships to each other (financial restructuring),[47] focused on the law of obligation.[48] On the one hand, extrinsic restructuring can include the preservation of the business and the legal entity;[49] on the other hand, it can involve the preservation of the business in a new legal entity and the liquidation of the old legal entity through a business-asset sale,[50] allowing for a restructuring regardless of the approval of the shareholders.[51] However, some risks are involved[52] and in certain cases restructuring may be uneconomic or impossible.[53]

With regard to a company in *crisis*, there is no one definition provided by legislator or jurisprudence for the word. It generally indicates "*a time of great difficulty*"[54] for a company, a "*state of being in danger or difficul-*

40 *Hommel / Knecht / Wohlenberg*, in *Hommel / Knecht / Wohlenberg*, p. 27, 47 et seq.
41 *Wellensiek*, NZI 2002, 233 et seq.
42 *Körner*, p. 125; *Eidenmüller*, Unternehmenssanierung, p. 31.
43 *Laryea*, IMF 2010, p. 10.
44 IDW Anforderungen an die Erstellung Sanierungskonzepten (IDW 6), 2010; *Undritz*, Kölner Schrift zur InsO, p. 932, 933.
45 *Wellensiek*, NZI 2002, 233, 234.
46 *Eidenmüller*, Unternehmenssanierung, p. 262.
47 *Eidenmüller*, BB 1998, Beil. 10, p. 19.
48 *Eidenmüller*, Unternehmenssanierung, p. 262.
49 *Eidenmüller / Engert*, ZIP 2009, 541, 542; *Ehlers*, ZInsO 2009, 320, 322; *Fritze*, DZWIR 2007, 89 et seq.
50 *Schlegel*, MüKo-InsO / Länderbericht, mn. 5: "übertragende Sanierung" = business-asset sale.
51 *Ehlers*, ZInsO 2009, 320, 321.
52 *Ibid.* 322.
53 *Westpfal / Janjuah*, ZIP 2008, Beil. 3, p. 1, 13.
54 Oxford Dictionary, 1989.

ty and requiring help",[55] which endangers the company's ability to trade as a going concern.[56] This state is not static but rather dynamic: a development of a debtor through the pre-insolvency stages[57] of over-indebtedness and illiquidity into the opening of insolvency proceedings.[58] A corporate crisis[59] is not necessarily negative when the company recognises the prodromal warning signs.[60] As it is often too late once the over-indebtedness or illiquidity has occurred,[61] the company should initiate restructuring measures early, giving (although limited) time to create a viable restructuring plan to increase its probability of a successful recovery.[62]

The *debt-equity-swap*[63] is among the most important (and most discussed) restructuring instruments, "*in which creditors (usually, but not exclusively, lenders) exchange or convert a proportion of a company's indebtedness for one or more classes of its share capital*"[64]. The conversion can be achieved in various ways[65] and the agreed level of exchange will either reduce or eliminate the outstanding debt. A debt-equity-swap is a financial and legal measure implemented in a restructuring, highly encouraged to restructure over-indebted companies in the aftermath of 2008.

---

55 Oxford Dictionary, 1989.

56 BFH, BStBl. II 2004, p. 9. See also *Reinhardt*, in *Rattunde*, Fachberater für Sanierung und Insolvenzverwaltung, p. 13, mn. 13.

57 BGH, Urt. V. 23.2.2004 – II ZR 207/01 = NZI 2005, 284.

58 *Reinhardt*, in *Rattunde*, Fachberater für Sanierung und Insolvenzverwaltung, p. 14, mn. 15.

59 Distinction of crisis depending on the degree of threat, see *Kraus / Gless*, in *Buth / Hermanns*, Sec. 4 mn. 8 et seq.

60 *Fink*, p. 15.

61 *Braun / Uhlenbruck*, p. 284.

62 *Holzer*, NZI 2005, 308, 309. See also *Kraus / Knecht*, FS Wellensiek, p. 55 et seq. for a holistic approach to restructuring a company in financial distress.

63 There is no legal definition, see *Cohen / Maclennan*, CRI 2009, 91.

64 *Chatterji / Hedges*, p. 246.

65 See Chapter III 8.2.

This dissertation concentrates on *single companies*[66] in Germany and England and it proceeds on the assumption that the company is in a *crisis* situation. The cause or stage of the crisis is irrelevant to the discussion. Despite the fact that the restructuring of companies involves various legal challenges[67], this dissertation only focuses on German and English[68] corporate and insolvency law[69], and the implementation of a debt-equity-swap in a viable company worth preserving. The debt constitutes corporate credit owed to financial institutions.[70]

1.3 Research Question and Course of Examination

The core issue of the discussion focuses on the question whether the debt-equity-swap, provided for by the adjustments to the provisions for the German Insolvency Statute made by ESUG, facilitates a progress towards an effective *rescue culture* in Germany. As the question mark at the end of the title suggests, the discussion includes the challenges and obstacles of an effective (English) *rescue* or (German) *insolvency* culture and analyses

---

66 In accordance to the Second Council Directive 77/91/EEC of 13 December 1976 on coordination of safeguards which, for the protection of the interests of members and others, are required by Member States of companies within the meaning of the second paragraph of Article 58 of the Treaty, in respect of the formation of public limited liability companies and the maintenance and alteration of their capital, with a view to making such safeguards equivalent Official Journal L 026, 31/01/1977, p. 0001 – 0013, "relating to the following types of company: [...] in Germany : die Aktiengesellschaft; [...] in the United Kingdom : the public company limited by shares, the public company limited by guarantee and having a share capital".

67 For an overview of legal challenges with regard to capital markets, antitrust or taxation issues, see *Schleusener*, p. 84 et seq.; *Thierhoff et al.*, mn. 35; *Born*, BB 2009, 1730 et seq. See also *Kahlert*, ZIP 2014, 1101 et seq. on the necessity to have both insolvency and tax law work together to foster restructurings.

68 The rules differ partly between rules for England and Wales as such for Scotland. For the purpose of this dissertation, the law for England and Wales applies and is subsumed under English law or the law of England.

69 It will only regard valuation issues from a legal and not from a financial perspective as far as it is necessary for the understanding of the implementation of a debt-equity-swap.

70 The dissertation excludes the restructuring of bonds or regarding investors as debt providers.

whether such a culture has already been established, and whether or not Germany is only now on the way towards one just yet.

In order to properly understand insolvency law, a study of the underlying theoretical and legal policy considerations is necessary to capture the meaning and principles of the rules and understand them as a process than rather a merely set of rules.[71] Whether or not a legal framework provides for proceedings facilitating restructurings as opposed to liquidations and thereby establishing or having established a rescue culture may be part of the overall reasoning for insolvency law in a national economic system. Chapter I provides an introduction and background on the topic of this dissertation. The background focuses on the reasons for insolvency law and its regulatory function in an economy by weighing the various economic and legal interests with a view to the overall result.[72] It leads to the discussion of different theories on the purpose for insolvency law: either arguing that the insolvency law serves to achieve the best possible outcome for (secured) creditors, or that insolvency law should not only consider creditors, but all parties affected by the failure of the debtor follows. Based on these theories, the importance of insolvency law in a market economy and the market conformity of insolvency law are analysed.

Chapter II explores the factors, which affect the effectiveness of restructuring companies in Germany and England. It begins with the general attempt to gather the roots and aspects of the term *rescue* or *insolvency* culture, the aspects of legal competition versus legal harmonisation, stigma and forum shopping, how history and legal reforms have shaped the legal framework and why both countries may have developed a different approach towards dealing with companies in financial distress. A nation's approach does not only depend on its effective legal framework but may also be attributed, among others, to the role of its government and national bank, the judicial infrastructure and the access to financial markets and corporate finance.[73]

Subsequently, Chapter III analyses the legal framework for debt-equity-swaps in Germany and England. It regards the question whether a company should be restructured in an informal or statutory proceeding. A background of the different proceedings in restructuring and insolvency law in both countries is provided as far as it is necessary for understanding

71 *Finch*, p. 28.

72 *Finch*, OJLS 1997, 227, 234 et seq.

73 The thesis neglects behavioural/psychological aspects.

the consideration of a debt-equity-swap as a restructuring tool to rescue a company in financial distress. The obstacles arising from the implementation of a debt-equity-swap have been much deeper imprinted in the legal framework in Germany where the debt-equity-swap is now codified in the Insolvency Statute. In England, however, there is no codification of the debt-equity-swap but the measures to implement one are a matter of company law and case law. The chapter aims to distinguish these challenges.

Chapter IV is a combination of law and practice since it focuses on the aspects of legal competition with regard to company law and insolvency law. It discusses the case law of previous years that have led the German legislator to rethink the dealing with companies in financial distress.

The conclusion is dedicated to the general observations and will address whether Germany has made progress towards an effective rescue culture, and whether the debt-equity-swap has become an effective tool in the German insolvency legal framework to achieve that goal.

1.4 Research Methodology

Whether Germany promotes an effective *rescue culture* by allowing for debt-equity-swaps in restructuring of public companies is analysed by using the method of comparative law[74], considering German and English corporate and insolvency legal norms.

---

74 *Zweigert / Kötz*, p. 2 et seq.: comparative law is differentiated between *macro-comparison* and *micro-comparison* but (p. 5) "one must often do both at the same time, for it is only by discovering how the relevant rules have been created and developed by the legislature or the courts and ascertaining the practical context in which they are applied that one can understand why a foreign legal system resolves a given problem the way it does and not otherwise". See also *Watson*, Legal Transplants, p. 2: a comparison has to, by nature, examine "the equivalent rules and procedures in at least one other legal system". See also *Ewald*, 143 U. Penn. L. Rev. (1995) 1889, 1956: "comparative jurisprudence raises important questions for legal philosophy", however, legal philosophy and legal theory in depth would be beyond the scope of this dissertation.

The dissertation focuses on the comparison of the rule of law[75] and the law as an institutional normative order[76]. The question as a matter of legal theory is of whether the comparison of any law to any other law[77] will lead to results that are not only valid but also serve some useful[78] purpose, which, "*in national legislatures [...] can be law reform or [...] enhanced knowledge of legal solutions in other legal systems*"[79]. Especially in a distressed economy, feeding the financial distress of companies,[80] every society gives its law the same problem to solve: viable companies in financial distress should be given the opportunity to restructure rather than to liquidate. The approaches of solving this issue, however, are very different. Comparative law evaluates these approaches and the institutional factors.[81] The solutions for achieving a specific goal[82] in accordance to the

75 The rule of law is the underlying framework of rules and rights that make prosperous and fair societies possible. See definition http://worldjusticeproject.org/what-rule-law, accessed 12.10.2012. See also *Fleischer*, RabelsZ Bd. 75 (2011) 700, 726.

76 *MacCormick*, p. 11 describing that the institutional factors presuppose a "body of legal or other rules"; for more details, see *Del Mar / Bankowski*, Law as an Institutional Normative Order.

77 *Reitz*, 100 Mich. L Rev. (2002) 1453, 1457 that "comparative work has been chided for the tendency to reduce law [...] by being satisfied with simple comparisons of a statutory scheme from one country with that of another".

78 *Zweigert /Kötz*, p. 34; see also *Platsas*, EJCL 2008, 1, 5 et seq.: on the problem of defining *useful*.

79 *Platsas*, EJCL 2008, 1, 6; also *Zweigert / Kötz*, p. 15 stating that "the primary aim of comparative law is knowledge" whereas the "political aim" is the international unification of law, reducing or eliminating "so far as desirable and possible, the discrepancies between the national legal systems by inducing them to adopt common principles of law", (*Ibid.*, p. 23). See also *Watson*, Legal Transplants, p. 16, 17 with reference to bankruptcy law.

80 *Korobkin*, 91 Colum. L. Rev. (1991) 717, 766; *Rasmussen / Skeel*, 3 Am. Bankr. Inst. L. Rev. (1995) 85, 88.

81 *Zweigert / Kötz*, p. 30: "often it is the feeling of dissatisfaction with the solution in one's own system which drives one to inquire whether perhaps other legal system may not have produced something better".

82 *Hyland*, in *Patterson*, p. 189.

societal and economic requirements[83] are also "*the mirror of society*"[84]. However, law is not always capable of solving the problem effectively[85]; since "*Law is power [,] Law is politics*"[86], the political power and the influence of interest groups should not be underestimated in making law.[87]

Usually, law equivalents are compared.[88] However, as long as the laws in question fulfil the same function[89] and display similarity of the factual needs, they are comparable.[90] One may argue that using a debt-equity-swap for restructuring companies in Germany and England may not be a useful comparable equivalent since the laws belong to different legal systems, civil law jurisdiction[91] as opposed to a common law[92] jurisdiction. However, in both jurisdictions, the debt-equity-swap serves the purpose[93] of allowing companies in financial distress to restructure with codified

83 *Graveson*, ICLQ 1958, 649, 650 et seq.; *Örücü*, in *Örücü / Nelken*, p. 50 et seq.; *Watson*, 131 U. Penn. L. Rev. (1983) 1121, 1134 et seq.: "all legal rules are created by a cause; and this cause of creation is commonly, but not always, rooted in social, economic, or political factors important to the life of the society or its leaders". *Watson*, however, recognised that once legal rules have been created, they will continue to exist, disregarding the changing environment for some time until the "law [again catches] up with broader societal change". In addition, *Watson*, Legal Change and Society, p. 8: "one of the most striking features of legal rules is their power of survival". For more detail on the characteristics of legal rules, see *Watson*, Cambridge L. J. 1978, 313, 314 et seq.; *Nelken*, in *Harding / Örücü*, p. 25, why conflicts of law develop with no input from society.

84 *Brand*, 32 Brookl. J. Int'l. L. (2007) 411, 416. See also *MacCormick*, p. 12, describing the recognition of institutional factors as "omnipresent and inherent elements of social reality". See also *Watson*, Cambridge L. J. 1978, 313 that "Law [..] exists in society and for society's needs". For critical discussion, see *Nelken*, in *Harding / Örücü*, p. 25 et seq.

85 *Brand*, 32 Brookl. J. Int'l. L. (2007) 411, 415.

86 *Watson*, 131 U. Penn. L. Rev. (1983) 1125.

87 *Watson*, Society and Legal Change, p. 9 whereas "various interests of groups and individuals" may be "very active in preserving [rules suiting them]". The political dimension will not be further discussed.

88 *Zweigert / Kötz*, p. 37.

89 *Ibid.* p. 31: "always in comparative law one must focus on the concrete problem". See also *Örücü*, in *Örücü / Nelken*, p. 29: "[f]unctional inquiry also suits the utilitarian approach to comparative law". Critical see *Pieck*, ZEuP 2013, 60, 62.

90 *Zweigert / Kötz*, p. 37.

91 *Milman*, p. 10.

92 *Ibid.*, p. 9.

93 *Cotterell*, in *Harding / Orücü*, p. 38: an analysis should focus on similarities between both legal systems rather than only differences.

provisions as a matter of company law, hence, the institutional factors in both countries are the same.[94] In addition, both laws' legal norms are distinct enough to be compared. A theory emerging from comparative law as a theory of law should be about legal change and about the relationship between legal structures and rules and the society in which it operates.[95] Therefore, there must be a correlation between law and society.

Although in the discussion on how to foster debt-equity-swaps in German law with the general example and the view to English law, the debt-equity-swap is neither a new concept[96] nor is it a legal transplant or legal borrowing[97] from English law. It attracted only more attention when German companies actually took their chance to apply English law to implement one. In light of the recent past developments where English courts sanctioned the restructurings of German companies and the on-going debate about a rescue culture, the dissertation takes the approach not to initiate reforms since that has already been done by the ESUG in 2012 but rather to see whether the reforms fulfilled the very purpose they were aiming at and whether the debt-equity-swap with the measure of cutting shareholder rights is a fit to the German rule of law.

---

94 *MacCormick*, p. 11, 12: "[i]nterpretation of the things and their use in the light of the relevant rules is what makes such […] objects have the meaning they have".

95 *Watson*, Cambridge L. J. 1978, 313, 321.

96 United Nations Centre on Transnational Corporation, giving an overview of the different debt equity conversion programs of developing countries post-1982 debt crisis and (iv) stating that "[e]ven in cases where debt equity conversion programmes are clearly appropriate, they are likely, by themselves, have only limited impact and should, therefore, be seen as only one of a number of options, the debtor […] ought to consider." See also *Paulus*, DZWIR 2008, 6.

97 *Watson*, Legal Transplants, p. 21 et seq.; *Watson*, Cambridge L. J. 1978, 313, 316 et seq. that a *legal transplant* is "moving of a rule or a system of law from one country to another or from one people to another". Due to historical research, Watson concluded that in the Western world, the borrowing of foreign legal concepts with subsequent adjustment was the usual way of legal development. So if *legal borrowings* happened beyond space and time, then the law would not be considered a local phenomenon, which is functionally linked to the living conditions of an existing society. On the contrary: the law, created by *legal borrowing* and developed through processes within the legal culture exists largely autonomous from society and, therefore, does not necessarily satisfy their needs or solve their social problems. See also *Ewald*, 43 Am. J. Comp. L. (1995) 489, 492 et seq.; *Nelken*, in *Harding / Örücü*, p. 25.

The research of this dissertation is primarily based on library conducted research, focusing on a comprehensive review of existing legal[98] and economic literature as well as official legislative documents, case law and journalistic articles from the internet.

2 Background

This section provides an overview of the general purpose of insolvency law in a market economy and discusses the various insolvency theories.

2.1 Insolvency Law in a Market Economy

"*Bankruptcy is a backup*"[99] since "*[t]he rule must still be that debts are meant to be repaid in full*"[100]

The existence of credit inherits the concept of debt and consequently insolvency.[101] Insolvency, having been around since Ancient Greece,[102] is an aspect of debt, being defined as over-indebtedness[103] or the inability to pay debts[104]. While people were held personal liable and may lose a limb

98 While writing this dissertation, *Reinhard Bork* published 'Rescuing Companies in England and Wales' (2012), focusing more on procedural issues in both jurisdictions. The dissertation 'Der Debt-Equity-Swap' (2012) by *Ann-Kathrin Schleusener* focuses on the various legal challenges of debt-equity-swaps in Germany. The book 'Corporate Rescue Law – An Anglo-American Perspective' (2008) by *Gerard McCormack* provides a critical comparative evaluation of US and UK law. The question on "[w]hat values and purposes are served by reorganisation proceedings" was kept in mind for this dissertation.
While updating the book for publication, *Sebastian Hagemann* published 'Debt Equity Swap nach englischem und deutschem Recht unter Berücksichtigung des ESUG' (2014), and *Michael Burkert* 'Der Debt-to-Equity Swap im Spannungsverhältnis von Gesellschafts- und Insolvenzrecht' (2014). These publications reinforce the importance in dealing with and discussing the challenges of debt-equity-swaps in general and for corporate rescue in particular.

99 *Easterbrook*, 27 J. Fin. Econ. (1990) 411, 416.

100 *Cárdenas*, in: *Buljevich*, xx.

101 *Wood*, The Law and Practice of International Finance, mn. 1-23; *Paulus*, in FS Görg, p. 363, 365.

102 *Paulus*, JZ 2009, 1148, 1149 et seq.; *Bridge*, p. 37 et seq.

103 See Chapter III 7.1.3 for grounds in German law to open insolvency proceedings.

104 See Chapter III 7.2.3 for grounds in English law to open insolvency proceedings.

for failure to repay their debt, the introduction of the limited liability company[105] provided limited liability to shareholders of a company. With the notion of limited liability, creditors also accepted the fact that not all corporate debt would necessarily be repaid.[106] While someone must bear the losses,[107] creditors still need to be willing to take that risk of default since an economy will only flourish when liquidity is provided to nourish entrepreneurial spirits.[108] The financial crisis in the aftermath of *Lehman* has shown that a market inherits certain vulnerabilities, especially when markets are prone to exaggeration due to the irrational behaviour of market participants. In this situation, corrective intervention and an appropriate legal framework by governments and legislators seek to mitigate the effects[109] and lower the risks and costs[110] to an economy arising from insolvent companies[111] by providing effective tools to either facilitate an orderly insolvency process or the restructuring of companies in financial distress.[112]

---

105 The law of limited liability companies includes provisions for the establishment, rights and duties, especially capital requirements and capital maintenance for the protection of creditors and shareholders. While in German law, these provisions are codified in a single piece of law, the Aktiengesetz, in English law, the Companies Act 1985 is heavily complemented by case law. See also *Milman*, p. 3 et seq.: "the artificial legal person known as the company".

106 *Bridge*, p. 31. Corporate limited liability for joint stock companies was first introduced in the UK by the Limited Liability Act of 1855. The restriction to apply limited liability to insolvent debtors in liquidation was defeated in [1897] AC 22 by the House of Lords, overturning the judgements by the High Court (*Broderip v. Salomon* [1893] B 4793) and the Court of Appeal (*Broderip v. Salomon* [1895] 2 Ch 323, 337). Although the decision by the House of Lords was not the first in this regard (*Sao Paulo (Brazilian) Rly. Co. Ltd. V. Carter* [1896] A.C. 31), the decision in Salomon v A Salomon & Co Ltd clearly extracted the dogmatic principles of the legal independence of the company, followed by the discussion on the theory of legal separation and theory of economic entity especially for holding structures.

107 *Easterbrook / Fischel*, p. 44, 48.

108 *Armour / Cumming*, ALER 2008, 303, 304.

109 *Balz*, 23 Brook. J. Int'l L. (1997) 167, 171.

110 *Wood*, The Law and Practice of International Finance, mn. 1-23.

111 *Bigus / Eger*, 5(2) Perspektiven der Wirtschaftspolitik (2004) 193 et seq.

112 Among others *Paulus*, in FS Görg, p. 363, 368.

The question is whether insolvency law should create a market-compatible legal framework[113] within which all the creditors of the debtor may be able to maximise the value of the debtor's assets and to decide rationally whether this is better achieved by the liquidation or restructuring of the company's legal entity or the restructuring and going concern of the company's business.[114]

Corporate insolvencies have a negative impact on a country's economy by being value destructive[115] and, in accumulation, may cause serious economic damage.[116] Effective insolvency laws should therefore minimise the damage caused by insolvent debtors.[117] On the one hand, it should provide effective and efficient remedies and legal certainty to creditors, enabling them to assess their risk more accurately and thereby increasing their willingness to lend. On the other hand, it should also protect the rights of the debtor, retaining him to borrow for financing his business operations. Insolvency laws "*are the cornerstone of sustainable economic development and provide a safety valve for financial failures*"[118] by promoting fairer and more efficient recapture of assets from failed businesses and also a "*test of a jurisdiction's ability to realise its own views of fairness, equity and legal civilisation*"[119]. At their inception, insolvency laws provided rather an orderly framework of a terminal liquidation proceeding; in recent times, however, and against a wider backdrop of evolution in the nature of insolvency law,[120] the nature of insolvency proceedings has shifted to foster potential business rescues.[121] In addition, there has also been a tendency to use insolvency law to deal with emerging social and economic problems.[122]

---

113 *Harvit-Segal*, 2 Berkley Bus. L. J. (2005) 357 et seq., discussing the justification for any bankruptcy law.

114 *Balz*, Sanierung von Unternehmen, p. 2; *Bigus / Eger*, 5(2) Perspektiven der Wirtschaftspolitik (2004) 193-194.

115 *Jaffé*, ZGR 2010, 248, 250.

116 *Cork / Graham*, ZIP 1982, 1275, 1279.

117 BMJ, "Recht" Informationen des BMJ, Nr. 3, 1978, 21, 23.

118 ERBD, Homepage Insolvency Law, http://www.ebrd.com/pages/sector/legal/insolvency.shtml, accessed 6.7.2013.

119 *Cárdenas*, in *Buljevich*, xvi.

120 *Bridge*, EBRD, p. 39.

121 *Mucciarelli*, EBOR 14 (2013) 175, 178.

122 *In re Johns-Manville Corp.,* 36 B.R. 727 (S.D.N.Y. 1984); *In re Texaco Inc.* 73 B.R. 960 (S.D.N.Y. 1987).

Since national economic interests vary from country to country, there are different approaches to insolvency law.[123] In a market economy, based on the power of division of labour in which the prices of goods and services are determined in a free price system set by supply and demand[124] and where the market allocates resources primarily through the interaction of individuals and private firms,[125] insolvency law should also constitute the concept of market laws and the private autonomous decisions of stakeholders in insolvency proceedings.[126] This goal of market conformity has been incorporated in the German Insolvency Statute.[127]

In the competitive environment of a market economy, some companies will eventually fail as only the continuous selection process[128] guarantees an economically rational allocation of resources to a more productive use and, therefore, for future economic growth.[129] An effective and functioning insolvency law is essential for a market economy.[130] It should be incorporated into the existing legal and economic order,[131] ensuring that unviable companies in financial distress are forced to exit the market, especially if the value realised in liquidation is greater than its value going

---

123 *Omar*, ILP 2001, 138; *Rajak*, p. 10; *Bigus / Eger*, 5(2) Perspektiven der Wirtschaftspolitik (2004) 193, 200 et seq., discussing alternatives to insolvency law.

124 http://www.princeton.edu/~achaney/tmve/wiki100k/docs/Market_economy.html, accessed 15.11.2013.

125 *Stiglitz*, A9.

126 BMJ, Begr. RegE-InsO 1992, BT-Drucks. 12/2443, p. 76. See *Balz*, 23 Brook. J. Int'l L. (1997) 167, 171.

127 BMJ, Begr. RegE-InsO 1992, BT-Drucks. 12/2443, p. 77 et seq.; *Balz*, Neuordnung des Insolvenzrechts, p. 2 et seq.; *Ibid.*, ZIP 1988, 273, 277; *Ibid.*, 23 Brook. J. Int'l L. (1997) 167, 171.

128 *White*, J. Econ. Persp. 1989, 129: "[e]conomic theory suggests that bankruptcy should serve as a screening process designed to eliminate only those firms that are economically inefficient and whose resources should be better used in some other activity". See also *Balz*, 23 Brook. J. Int'l L. (1997) 161, 171: "that insolvency law should not supersede market processes […] but rather stimulate and, wherever necessary, stimulate efficient market exchange".

129 *Frost*, 74 N. C. L. Rev. (1995) 75, 130, "[..] liquidation may harm the community served by the closed enterprise, it may benefit a distant community served by a competing enterprise.".

130 *Eidenmüller*, Finanzmarktkrise, Wirtschaftskrise und das deutsche Insolvenzrecht, p. 9; *Eidenmüller / Frobenius / Prusko*, NZI 2010, 545, 546.

131 *Engelhardt*, ZIP 1986, 1287, 1288.

concern,[132] while viable companies should be rescued,[133] thereby constituting the penalty function of insolvency law in a market economy.[134]

By rescuing inefficient companies that should be allowed to fail, the intervention into the market avoids efficiency, thereby hindering the markets to run towards a state of long-run equilibrium.[135] The result is that the economy will stack up with progressively weaker business models, leading to the adverse effect whereas economic growth will go into reverse.[136] Another challenge attached to the alternative of introducing restructuring and the rescue mechanism as opposed to liquidation is adverse selection.[137] Some failing companies may be rather liquidated even though their resources are most valuable when continuing operating while others continue to operate despite their previous losses and their resources could be better employed in some new use.[138] One should keep in mind, however, that even the best insolvency law cannot increase the restructuring potential of an unviable company.[139] And the question remains why viable companies do not initiate a restructuring at an earlier stage after having recognised financial difficulties.

The decision on the route to take, either liquidation of unviable or restructuring of viable companies, is often difficult to determine for stakeholders in a company due to the lack of information. While management generally has that information, liquidation may be against their own inter-

---

132 *Chatterji / Hedges*, p. 14.

133 *Balz*, Neuordnung des Insolvenzrechts, p. 2, 4; *Stürner*, ZIP 1982, 761, 762 et seq.

134 *Flessner*, Sanierung und Reorganisation, p. 177.

135 *White*, J. Econ. Persp. 1989, 129.

136 *Pym*, BBC News online, 13.11.2012.

137 *Easterbrook*, 27 J. Fin. Econ. (1990) 411, 415 which refers to the decision-making of managers and the conflict between debt and equity for the "right" time to make the decision. See also *White*, J. Econ. Persp. 1989, 129, 133 et seq. arguing that there are different (coalition) models that will lead to economic efficiency when making the bankruptcy or reorganisation decision. Economic efficiency and "the coalition's choice between liquidating and reorganizing [affects the] level of debt forgiveness under which the coalition has an incentive to make economically efficient choices". In addition, *White*, J. Econ. Persp. 1989, 129, 142: If the economically efficient choice is chosen, there is no adverse selection. However, the model is based on the assumption of rationale decision making and not under the aspects of behavioural economics of law.

138 *White*, J. Econ. Persp. 1989, 129, 130.

139 *K. Schmidt*, Insolvenzrecht der Unternehmen, p. 11.

est. The information asymmetry between the stakeholders and management leads to even more uncertainty in the company's state of financial distress. The question now is whether the interests of the stakeholders, especially with different ranks, should be pooled together in a common pool. In the case of uncertainty, stakeholders likely to suffer a shortfall in their claims in liquidation may engage in competing with other stakeholders to realise assets or to withdraw their stake from the company. Those actions could precipitate a crisis, causing even a viable business to fail.[140]

Whether insolvency law should balance the conflicting interests by the various stakeholders with a view to the broader interests of society and the economy as a whole[141] has been discussed in the various insolvency theories.

2.2 Insolvency Theories

Different normative theories[142] have evolved over the years on the purpose and objectives for a corporate insolvency system. Although these are mainly from American scholars on US Bankruptcy Law,[143] some distinctions of the discussion mirror the interests of German and English[144] insolvency law. The purpose of corporate insolvency law may either be

140 *Chatterji / Hedges*, p. 14-15.

141 *Raiser*, ZGR 2006, 494 et seq. that the law should not only balance the different interests of all parties involved but rather carries also a symbolic character, more see Chapter II 3.1, 3.2.

142 *Korobkin*, 82 Iowa L. Rev. (1986) 75, 76 on the unique value of normative theory and normative requirements are often overlooked as rationality is often thought to consist in acting for reasons; following normative requirements is also a major part of rationality. A normative requirement is a relation: one thing normatively requires another. *Example* Sec. 16 InsO: "The opening of insolvency proceedings shall require the existence of a reason to open such proceedings."

143 Chapter 11 of the Bankruptcy Code (B.C.) in the US law has served as a blueprint for the insolvency law reform, both in Germany and England. Since most of the theories have been developed in the US, the term "bankruptcy" in the context of this paper is used with regard to corporations, although the English and German law refer to insolvency. See *Keay / Walton*, p. 12.

144 For further detail, see *Finch*, p. 32 et seq.; *Keay / Walton*, p. 25 et seq.; *Goode*, mn. 2-02 et seq.; *Copp*, JCLS 2001, 1, 3 et seq.

the maximisation of the debtor's economic[145] value for the benefits of the creditors or the protection of the debtor's diversified values.

145 The creditor' bargain theory is an approach to apply economic analysis to law. The positive economic analysis of law concentrates on "the making and content of law" as opposed to the normative or prescriptive analysis of law with its "impact of law on conduct generally", see *Michelman*, 46 U. Ch. L. Rev. (1979) 307 et seq.). The *economic analysis of law* is based on the assumption "that people involved with the legal system act as rational maximisers of their satisfaction" (*Posner*, 53 Tex. L. Rev. (1975) 757, 761) thereby in their "self-interest" (*Posner*, 46 U. Ch. L. Rev. (1979) 281, 302) although "[t]he logic of rational maximisation is subtle, frequently complex, and very often counterintuitive" (*Posner*, 53 Tex. L. Rev. (1975) 757, 762). The individual in law and economics is reduced to its economic interests in the markets where actions are driven by capital and economic efficiency as the initial distribution of rights (*Posner*, 46 U. Ch. L. Rev. (1979) 281, 291) and where legal system is expected to "duplicate the results of competitive markets" (*Posner*, U. Ch. L. Rev. (1979) 281, 288). Since there is more to rational maximisation involved in behaviour of people (*Posner*, 53 Tex. L. Rev. (1975) 757, 773), which has led to the field of behavioural economics of law (*Jolls / Sunstein / Thaler*, Stan. L. Rev., 1471 et seq., *Rasmussen*, 51 Vand. L. Rev. (1998), 1679 et seq.) The legal system itself has been influenced by a concern with promoting efficiency (*Posner*, 53Tex. L. Rev. (1975) 757, 764), however, if the legal system would be designed to maximise economic efficiency, there would be no room for normative economic analysis anymore. Nowadays there is a distinction between the "new" law and economics as the application of the theories and empirical methods of economics to the central institutions of the legal system without limitations (*Coase*, 3 J. Law & Econ. (1960) 3 et seq. as the first attempt to economic analysis in a systematic way to areas of law that did not regulate economic relationships) and the "old" law and economics focused on laws governing explicit relationships, applied only to a limited subset of laws (*Posner*, 53 Tex. L. Rev. (1975) 757, 759). Although the economic analysis of law has limits, based on the unrealistic assumptions of human behaviour (*Posner*, 46 U. Ch. L. Rev. (1979) 281, 303) it also has benefits: studying the legal system may be fruitful (*Posner*, 53 Tex. L. Rev. (1975) 757, 765), may increase the knowledge about the legal system (*Ibid.*, 768.) and may eventually help in designing reforms of the legal system. (*Ibid.*, 764). Also *Raiser*, ZGR 2006, 494, 496 on limits / critics of economic analysis of law.

2.1.1 Creditors' Bargain Theory

The creditors' bargain theory[146] has been widely adopted as the theory providing normative reasons for bankruptcy law,[147] based on maximising the debtor's overall economic value by avoiding individual debt-collection[148] and minimising costs and risks. It is, also, much debated.[149]

The theory is based on the notion that creditors as a group[150] have agreed upon the proceeds in liquidation at the time of signing the contract,[151] which is used to maximise the debtor's economic value for their satisfaction in insolvency. The theory relies on an efficient insolvency law,[152] performing beyond normal requirements. Efficiency, however, is not achieved when creditors feel insecure and monitoring the other creditors' behaviour[153] incurs high administrative[154] and strategic costs[155].

---

146 *Jackson*, 105 Yale L. J. (1982) 857; *Jackson*, 36 Stan. L. Rev. (1984) 725; *Baird / Jackson*, 51 U. Chi. L. Rev. (1984) 97; *Baird*, 54 U. Chi. L. Rev. (1987) 815; *Rasmussen*, 71 Tex. L. Rev. (1992) 51; *Bebchuk*, 101 Harv. L. Rev. (1988) 775. See also *Goode*, p. 41: *proceduralists*; *Korobkin*, 82 Iowa L. Rev. (1986) 75: *free-market critics*.

147 *Jackson*, 105 Yale L. J. (1982) 857, 868, 907.

148 *Jackson*, 105 Yale L. J. (1982) 857, 862 et seq.

149 *Warren*, 54 U. Chi. L. Rev. (1987) 775 et seq.; *Warren*, 92 Mich. L. Rev. (1993) 336, 366 et seq.; *Scott*, 53 U. Chi. L. Rev. (1986) 690, 692 et seq.; *Korobkin*, 91 Colum. L. Rev. (1991) 717, 722 et seq.; *Skeel*, 1993 Wis. L. Rev., 465, 471; *Carlson*, 85 Mich. L. Rev. (1987) 1341.

150 *Jackson*, 105 Yale L. J. (1982) 857, 864 collective scheme results in an increased aggregate pool of assets than individual enforcement of claims. See also *Flessner*, in *Ziegel*, p. 19, 23 describing the common pool approach as the *capitalist philosophy*.

151 *Jackson*, 105 Yale L. J. (1982) 857, 860: bankruptcy law exists "as a system designed to mirror the agreement one would expect the creditors to form among themselves were they able to negotiate such an agreement from an *ex ante* position". See also *Flessner*, in *Ziegel*, p. 19, 26: "it might be wise to respect pre-bankruptcy rights as much as possible but there is nothing to preclude new considerations, peculiar to the situation, being added in the search for appropriate solutions to this kind of business failure. There is no 'logic of bankruptcy' to be derived exclusively from the pre-bankruptcy situation".

152 Critical *Carlson*, 85 Mich. L. Rev. (1987) 1341, 1343: "the contractarianism is not an effective tool to pursue economic efficiency".

153 *Jackson*, p.16; *Jackson*, 60 Am. Bankr. L. J. (1986), 399, 402.

154 *Jackson*, 105 Yale L. J. (1982) 857, 866.

155 *Ibid.,* 861 et seq.; *Ibid.*, p.15; *Ibid.*, 36 Stan. L. Rev. (1984) 725, 730. See also *Baird*, 64 U. Chi. L. Rev. (1987) 815, 816 stating that wealth distribution is "a

Risk adverse creditors, therefore, prefer statutory provisions, enabling them, with a high probability, to anticipate their recovery rate[156] rather than a provision with greater risk[157].

The creditors' bargain theory does not prefer either restructuring or liquidation.[158] As long as secured creditors are satisfied with their position in a collective proceeding in comparison to their position previously negotiated with the debtor[159], they would have no reason to object to a collective proceeding. This also includes minimisation of the costs[160] incurred in the process, which are generally to the detriment of the creditors.[161]

2.1.2 Bankruptcy-Policy Theory

The response[162] to the creditors' bargain theory was the bankruptcy-policy theory[163], criticising the theory as negating "*a realistic appraisal of the bankruptcy system*"[164] since economic value enhancement[165] is only a par-

---

question of the law generally" and not only a question "peculiar to the bankruptcy law"; *Ibid.*, 822 "[l]egal rights should turn as little as possible on the forum in which one person or another seeks to vindicate them. Whenever we must have a legal rule to distribute losses in bankruptcy, we must also have a legal rule that distributes the same loss outside of bankruptcy".

156 *Jackson*, 105 Yale L. J. (1982) 857, 863: The advantage of the bankruptcy law is, by defining the distribution, reduce the distribution risk, and, thus, adjust for the more risk-equivalent interest rates, benefitting both the debtor and the creditor.

157 *Ibid.,* 863.

158 *Ibid.,* 864 et seq.

159 *Jackson*, 105 Yale L. J. (1982) 857, 868.

160 *Rasmussen / Skeel*, 3 Am. Bankr. Inst. L. Rev. (1995) 85.

161 *Jackson*, 105 Yale L. J. (1982) 857, 866.

162 *Warren*, 54 U. Chi. L. Rev. (1987) 775, 811: "a dirty, complex, elastic, interconnected view of bankruptcy from which I can neither predict outcomes nor even necessarily fully articulate all the factors relevant to a policy decision". See also *Korobkin*, 91 Colum. L. Rev. (1991) 717, 719 et seq.

163 *Warren*, 92 Mich. L. Rev. (1993) 336, 338.

164 *Ibid.*: "bankruptcy policy becomes nothing more than a debate over the allocation efficiency, it will pass over crucial elements of the policy scheme that cannot be so neatly tied up in economic models. An approach that eschews any role for efficiency analysis suffers a similar fate, creating an economic versus noneconomic dichotomy that negates a realistic appraisal of the bankruptcy system".

165 *Ibid.,* 373: "the value-enhancement principle is sufficiently well accepted [...], however, a more complete elaboration of a bankruptcy policy may change how a problem is framed or what solutions are proposed".

tial purpose of insolvency law.[166] The law in general should protect the various parties[167] and value affected through specific distribution rules.[168] These rules also recognise the distributional effects of a business failure on unrelated parties with no formal legal rights to the assets of the business.[169]

The bankruptcy-policy theory argues that, due to fact that there are various kinds of defaults[170], insolvency law differs in its "*central policy considerations because they rest on fundamentally different premises*"[171], which may result in competing-and sometimes conflicting distributional values.[172] The bankruptcy-policy theory may have "*identified the distributional rationale of bankruptcy*"[173], providing useful assistance to the legislative and judicial decision-making[174] in order to solve the conflict between the various distributive goals,[175] however, there is still a need to explore the detailed policies or normative basis of an optimal insolvency distributional scheme.[176]

---

166 *Ibid.*, 368 on the four principal goals of bankruptcy law.

167 *Baird*, 54 U. Chi. L. Rev. (1987) 815, 825 et seq. special protection may be granted to employees' claims whereas labour law provides for provisions of preferred claim for employees'.

168 *Warren*, 54 U. Chi. L. Rev. (1987) 775, 777: "Bankruptcy encompasses a number of competing-and sometimes conflicting-values in this distribution. [...] no one value dominates, so that bankruptcy policy becomes a composite of factors that bear on a better answer to the question, 'How shall the losses be distributed?'".

169 *Warren*, 92 Mich. L. Rev. (1993) 336, 354 et seq; *Baird*, 54 U. Chi. L. Rev. (1987) 815, 825 et seq.

170 *Warren*, 54 U. Chi. L. Rev. (1987) 775, 781: "two prototypes of default: first, the single default where only one creditor complains about repayment and the remaining creditors are evidently (even if only temporarily) content with their repayment prospects; and second, the debtor's widespread default and collapse in which every creditors' prospects for payment are sharply diminished".

171 *Ibid.,* 784.

172 *Ibid.*, 777.

173 *Ibid.,* 790 et seq.: e.g. favouring creditors whose ability to bear the cost of default is relatively weak, preventing pre-bankruptcy transactions based on perverse incentives, treating like creditors alike, forcing shareholders to bear the loss of business failure, benefiting the whole bankruptcy estate by helping the business to survive.

174 *Ibid.,* 775, 795.

175 *Warren*, 92 Mich. L. Rev. (1993) 336, 352 et seq.

176 *Warren*, 54 U. Chi. L. Rev. (1987) 775, 785: "Distribution is not incidental to other concerns; it is the center of the bankruptcy scheme".

2.1.3 Value-Based Theory

The value-based theory asserts that problems arising from financial distress are complicated and ambiguous.[177] Solutions depend on the specific historical context,[178] the particular questions[179] and the parties' values involved. The goal of insolvency law is the protection of all the debtor's values[180] affected in every specific business failure case. However, bankruptcy law should be given the means to alter rights as to respond appropriately to the problem of financial distress.[181] Under the value-based theory, insolvency decisions are the result of a "*rational debate*"[182] among all parties, including formal investors and non-investors, supporting the alteration of non-insolvency rights, protection of non-investors and wealth redistribution in insolvency.[183]

2.1.4 Team Production Theory of Bankruptcy Reorganisation

The team production theory of bankruptcy reorganisation[184] builds on the team production theory of corporate law.[185] Team members may include stockholders, creditors, executives, other employees, suppliers, customers, local governments, regulatory agencies, and others.[186] With an hypothetical team production contract[187], the team of a public corporation has the

---

177 *Korobkin*, 91 Colum. L. Rev (1991) 717 et seq.

178 *Ibid.,* 766 et seq.

179 *Ibid.,* 744 et seq., 768.

180 *Ibid.,* 745: beyond the economic value, the debtor has moral, political and social values.

181 *Korobkin*, 91 Colum. L. Rev (1991) 717, 768.

182 *Ibid.,* 789.

183 *Ibid.,* 788 et seq., discussing why bankruptcy policy is still an issue to write about.

184 *LoPucki*, Vand. L. Rev. 2004, 741. *Note*: The team production theory of bankruptcy reorganisation is only a theory explaining the bankruptcy reorganisation of public corporations and is not a theory concerning the whole bankruptcy law.

185 On the team production theory of corporate law, see *Blair / Stout*, 85 Va. L. Rev. (1999) 247 et seq.

186 *LoPucki*, Vand. L. Rev. 2004, 741 749.

187 *Ibid.,* on the difficulties to deal with these matters through explicit contracts in the changing and uncertain everyday business environment.

ultimate power to steer the company by distributing power among team members, especially to the board of directors.[188]

In insolvency, the board of directors enjoy complete freedom on dealing with the creditors' and shareholders' entitlements,[189] changing and amending their entitlements, redistributing wealth and protecting non-investors[190] "*to serve the interests of all team members*"[191]. The team production theory criticises the creditors' bargain theory especially with regard to the objective of the bankruptcy law being "*solely for the benefit of creditors and sharehol-ders.*"[192]

2.1.5 Risk-Sharing Theory

The risk-sharing theory expanded the creditors' bargain theory[193] not only aiming for the maximisation of the debtor's overall value but also forcing all claim holders to "*share (at least in part) the 'common' risks of business failure*"[194]. The risk-sharing agreement would, therefore, provide provisions equal to the insolvency wealth redistribution provisions.[195]

Common risks[196] may be mitigated by an *ex ante* agreement for the benefit of all parties whereas the risk-allocation has been negotiated among the creditors[197]. The risk-averse groups benefit from the reduced variance of future payments, contributing to their wealth status.[198] Since

---

188 *Ibid.*, 778: "The theory is based on a wholesale grant of unfettered power to directors [...]. Power corrupts, and absolute power corrupts absolutely".

189 *Ibid.*, 749 et seq.

190 *Ibid.*, 766: "bankruptcy's service of a broad range of interests".

191 *Ibid.*, 769.

192 *Ibid.*, 766.

193 *Jackson / Scott*, Virg. L. Rev. (1989) 155, 158: "the inherent incapacity of the legal system to specify ex ante rules for implementing *ex post* distributional principles".

194 *Ibid.*, 164.

195 *Ibid.*, 156 et seq.

196 *Ibid.*, 164, 168: Common risks are the risks of loss from "exogenous" sources beyond management's control while particular risks are the risks from "endogenous" sources.

197 *Ibid.* 165 et seq. redistributing the risk according to the different risk preferences of creditors: riskier creditors or shareholders bear higher risks in comparison to the more risk-averse investors.

198 *Ibid.* 166.

the contractual allocation of risk usually fails due to the prohibitively high cost of identifying common risks, bankruptcy law may offer advantages by specifying a risk allocation key, ensuring that each party has a higher probability of incurring a smaller loss,[199] resulting in an advantageous risk capital allocation of common risks for all creditors.[200] In agreeing to share common risks, parties may be obliged to relinquish their strict legal position, thus, their relative position of wealth, in order to engage in risk sharing.[201] However, changes in the relative wealth positions of parties by bankruptcy law may provide incentives to follow perverse actions and adverse selection in initiating the insolvency proceedings. The debt-collection process results in indifferent behaviour where the assets cover the liabilities. However, at the edge of insolvency, there is usually already an impairment of debtor's assets, ultimately borne by creditors and shareholders.[202] A risk-sharing agreement may, therefore, streamline actions to preserve the debtor's economic value for the benefits of all parties.[203] The risk-sharing agreement should also include firm-specific investments by shareholders or managers, which cannot be evaluated but are required for a successful restructuring.[204] Non-investors like employees should also participate in the wealth distribution as they are generally not able to protect themselves with security, "*they 'deserve' a distribution of the assets in bankruptcy*"[205]. Taking into account the investments and all parties involved, the risk-sharing theory may lead to a behaviour beneficial for the

199 *Ibid.* 167 et seq.
200 *Ibid.* 169, 171; *Scott*, 53 U. Chi. L. Rev. (1986) 690, 700 et seq.
201 *Jackson / Scott*, Virg. L. Rev. (1989) 155, 185 et seq.
202 *Jackson*, The Logic and Limits of Bankruptcy, p. 198 et seq.
203 *Jackson / Scott*, 75 Va. L. Rev. (1989) 155, 169 et seq. See also *Jackson*, 105 Yale L. J. (1982) 857, 867. There is always the threat by creditors to engage in an insolvency proceeding rather than in an out-of-court restructuring to support their individual wealth position.
204 *Ibid.*, 175.
205 *Ibid.*, 177, 178: "in some sense, these claimants are analogues to the victims of a common disaster, such as a flood" and "share an important quality with the victims of true disasters", "it may in some sense be analytically correct to suggest that the problems that animate distribution to nonconsensual victims of common disasters are not 'bankruptcy' problems." "[T]he individual participants in the creditors' bargain would presumably be as willing to support these claimants as they would any other charitable cause. From the perspective of the collective [...] these forms of redistribution will be seen as costs of bankruptcy that will undermine [...] the primary objectives of collectivisation".

"*wealth of the claimants as a group*"[206], however, "*ultimately leaves unresolved the on-going normative debate concerning the proper role for bankruptcy in the resolution of creditor claims.*"[207]

2.3 Summary

In a market economy, the competition for resources will lead to a selection process, in which some companies will eventually fail. Insolvency law provides for an effective framework to deal with companies in financial distress. While the stigma of insolvency may prevent companies from encountering restructuring action at an early stage of distress, insolvency law provides for proceedings either to restructure or liquidate a company. Whether to accept any of the above mentioned theories depends on the economic rationale of a nation laid upon the purpose of insolvency law, which is reflected in the reason for a company's being and the creditor's reason for lending in a market economy: making profit. A company goes through a life cycle, which also includes the death of the company. The creditors' bargain theory suggests that all moral, political and social values are by-products of a company's profit-making activity, with only the economic value being the determining value to be protected in a bankruptcy proceeding.

The legal framework for a collective insolvency proceeding[208] or the objective of *par condicio creditorum* used to maximise the debtor's economic value for satisfaction of the creditors in German[209] and English[210] law suggest that the normative theory for insolvency law in both countries is foremost the creditor's bargain theory. This is also supported by the fact

206 *Ibid.*, 202.

207 *Ibid.*, 203.

208 *Harviv-Segal*, 2 Berkley Bus. L. J. (2005) 355, 382 et seq.

209 BMJ, Begr. RegE-InsO 1992, BT-Drucks. 12/2443, p. 77 et seq.; Stürner, MüKo-InsO 2007, Introduction mn. 1, 20.

210 On the collective nature of English insolvency proceedings, see *Goode*, p. 4 et seq.

for the case of default the terms have been negotiated beforehand,[211] providing an answer to the ranking of interests in insolvency.[212]

There is another aspect to be included in the discussion. While insolvency theories focus on stakeholders, the aftermath of the financial crisis revived the debate about the purpose of companies and whose interest companies should serve.[213] The shareholder or stockholder theory[214] believes that the sole purpose of the company was to use its resources to maximise the shareholders' returns; contrary is the stakeholder theory[215] whereby the company serves those that are a vital part for and to the survival and success of the company. It was argued that companies following the shareholder theory fail to recognise and respect the needs of those, contributing to their existence. This would eventually result in self-destructive behaviour through negligence and selfishness. Therefore, one may draw the conclusion that the stakeholder theory is superior to the shareholder theory,[216] leading to the result that shareholders' do crystallise their position in insolvency as the economic owner of the company.[217]

211 *Kraakman et al.*, p. 7, acknowledging that insolvency legislation providing a standard form of default terms in contracts of certain creditors or when collective action problems prevent creditors from obtaining terms that might benefit all creditors ex ante". The risk of shareholder opportunism is particularly likely when the corporate debtor approaches insolvency.

212 *Finch*, 3 J.B.L. (2012) 190, 207 et seq.

213 The Economist, 22.4.2010 online. Also *Coase*, Economica 4 (1937), 386; *Teubner*, ZHR 148 (1984), 470 et seq. on discussion whether the company should have an organisational interest in itself.

214 *Jensen / Meckling*, J. Fin. Econ. (1976) 305; *Dodd*, 45 Harv. L. Rev. (1932) 1145. See also *Friedman*, p. 6: "there is one and only one social responsibility of business--to use its resources and engage in activities designed to increase its profits so long as it stays within the rules of the game, which is to say, engages in open and free competition without deception or fraud".

215 *Freeman*, p. 112–122.

216 *Bowie*, Business Ethics Quarterly (2001), 225.

217 *Nietsch*, ZVglRWiss 112 (2013) 45 et seq. on the position of the shareholders in European law.

Chapter II Factors Affecting the Effectiveness of Restructuring Companies

Introduction

This chapter regards the factors affecting the effectiveness of restructuring companies in Germany and England beyond the scope of their legal framework, analysing the roots and aspects of the term *rescue* or *insolvency culture*, the role of a country's government and its national bank, the judicial infrastructure and the access to financial markets and corporate finance.

3 Rescue Culture versus Insolvency Culture

> "*The term 'rescue culture' has become a fashionable* [218]*epithet in international insolvency circles. It represents a belief that the insolvency process should be seen as a value-added commercial process rather than a merely legalistic burial of the business.*"[219]

When companies with complex structures and various layers of debt,[220] held by global creditors, became financially distressed in the aftermath of 2008, it seemed that England was better prepared to comply with the restructuring of such companies than Germany was.[221] This was mainly attributed to the *rescue culture*, which England was perceived to have already well-established.[222] The different attitudes to how to deal and proceed with companies in financial distress is already seen in the terms used

218 *Wells*, BLR 2012, 156: "Corporate rescue became a fashionable topic".

219 *Nigel / Jones*, p. 138.

220 *Baird / Rasmussen*, 119 Yale L. J. (2009-2010) 648, 651.

221 *Balz*, 23 Brook. J. Int'l L. (1997) 167, 167 "rescue Neanderthals"; *Vriesendorp / Gramatikov*, 19 Int. Insolv. Rev. (2010) 209, 223: providing data that the importance of rescue as a primary goal was declining after 2008 in Germany while England was pre-crisis compared to post-crisis rather stable.

222 *McCormack*, p.1, administration is a "dedicated rescue procedure".

to discuss the problem: while in England reference is made to a *rescue culture*, in Germany the term regularly used is *insolvency culture*.[223]

While *rescue* may be defined as an act of saving or being saved from danger or difficulty,[224] in the case of corporate rescue it is a major intervention[225] to avert a corporate failure.[226] In this sense, as already stated in the introduction, *rescue culture* is understood as providing a legal environment where a company is restructured as a going concern rather than being liquidated in cases where the company's assets are more valuable on a going concern basis than in dissolution. Such an environment, which England is believed to provide, may be a mere perception rather than reality.[227] In reality, however, the trust in the legal framework and the business environment, whether justified or not, leads the perception to be a self-fulfilling prophecy.

This also accounts for the contrasting case of the *insolvency culture*, where the goal for all the parties involved is to maximise the satisfaction of creditors' interests – which may be reached, among others, by a restructuring of the debtor.[228] Germany prefers to use the instruments provided in an insolvency to be used for restructuring. These may be facilitated via an insolvency plan proceeding, increasing the chances of a successful restructuring, which may be even higher than in an informal restructuring.[229] The focus, therefore, is not on the rescue of the company itself but on the restructuring being rather a means for the sa-tisfaction of the creditor. Whereas a positive perception of restructuring may be a self-fulfilling prophecy, this also accounts for the negative case. The *Adam Opel GmbH* could have been restructured in an insolvency plan proceeding.[230] The application, however, was avoided by rather giving state subsidies.[231] The

223 *Priebe*, ZInsO 2012, 1589. See also *Braun / Heinrich*, NZI 2011, 505: *insolvency plan culture*.

224 Oxford Dictionary 1989.

225 *Finch*, 6 J.B.L. (2010) 502, 503.

226 *Belcher*, p. 36; *Wells*, BLR 2012, 156.

227 *Walters / Smith*, 19 Int. Insolv. Rev. (2010), 181, 203: "the perception that the English insolvency system facilitates efficient outcomes".

228 *Vallender*, NZI 2010, 838.

229 *Heinrich*, in FS Greiner, p. 111, 113.

230 *Geldmacher*, p. 29, 30: *Adam Opel GmbH*.

231 *Weiland*, Spiegel online, 30.5.2009: Chancellor Angela Merkel described the risks of another solution – the insolvency – "as politically irresponsible". See also Reuter, INDat-Report 01-2006 online: The former Chancellor *Schröder* inter-

interventions of the German legislature were perceived that the government did "*not trust its own law*"[232] to provide the company with a successful restructuring or an adequate insolvency proceeding.

The questions remain of how a *rescue culture* is established and whether a developed *rescue culture* is more civilised than an *insolvency* or *liquidation culture*.[233] Only in the case where the restructuring of a company as opposed to liquidation provides for maximal creditor satisfaction, do *rescue culture* and *insolvency culture* overlap. However, it should be kept in mind that liquidation as an option in an insolvency proceeding "*is not an economic ill or a 'destroyer of wealth' [but r]ather, reallocating the assets amidst the drama of bankruptcy [...] to the economy because idle factors of production can be put to use more efficiently*"[234].

The aspects to consider for a *rescue* or *insolvency culture* are the general evolution of a legal culture, the stigma of insolvency, the influence of legal competition and legal harmonisation, and forum shopping. Furthermore, it could also have an implication to what is rescued in a company's restructuring: the business or the legal entity.

3.1 Legal Culture

> "*What is legal culture, we do not exactly know – or believe to know it.*"[235]

Since the term *legal culture* is not uniformly defined,[236] dividing it into *law* and *culture* may help.[237] While the term *law* clearly applies to positive

---

vened into the self-administration of *Philipp Holzmann AG*. See also *Peters*, Spiegel online, 18.11.2008: *Schröder* provided the construction company with a state guarantee of EUR 100 million to save it from insolvency and to ensure that the workers "have something under the Christmas tree".

232 *Haarmeyer*, in *Jacobsen*, ZEIT ONLINE, 30.5.2009. See also *Geldmacher*, p. 27: It is a "declaration of bankruptcy". In addition, see *Paulus*, WM 2011, 2205, 2209.

233 *Balz*, 23 Brook. J. Int'l L. (1997) 167.

234 *Ibid.*, 169.

235 *Mankowski*, JZ 2009, 321.

236 *Skouris*, ZEuP 2012, 1: there is no consensus of a definition of 'legal culture', it is "a framework that goes beyond a given legal system and encompasses it, that affects the operation of this legal system, which in turn reflects a given legal culture. Legal system and legal culture interact."

237 *Von Münch*, p. 52.

law, habitual law and case law,[238] the term *culture* is more difficult to isolate. In its etymology from the Latin word *cultura*, it refers to care or education,[239] based on history and traditions,[240] the relative national and societal values and roots,[241] and the nation's economic development. Law is, therefore, also a part of culture[242] and a nation's legal framework originates back to its legal culture.

A nation's legal policy is either aimed at the preservation or the modification of existing law.[243] Legal culture could be seen as a foundation of the applicable law and legal policy; on the other hand, legal policy shapes legal culture.[244] It is also influenced by other legal cultures.[245] Legal culture changes; it is dynamic.[246] The liberality of a legal culture[247] is very much shown in how it responds to new needs and changing circumstances[248] and, thus, also allows the desire for change.[249] More important, legal culture also implies the reliability of law and public confidence in the law.[250] In this sense, legal comparison also has a cultural mission in raising awareness of the advantages and disadvantages of different legal systems and traditions.[251] German law is intended to be "*predictable, affordable and enforceable*"[252].

The understanding of legal culture in continental Europe differs from the use of *legal culture* in the Anglo-American jurisdiction[253], being further developed on the basis of values.[254] The fundamental differences between Germany and England are partly rooted in legal structures derived

238 *Ibid.*
239 Oxford Dictionary, 1989; *Griffiths / Hellmig*, NZI 2008, 418.
240 *Vallender*, NZI 2010, 838, 839; *Mankowski*, JZ 2009, 321, 324.
241 *Lechner*, AJICL 2002, 975, 977.
242 *Von Münch*, p. 53.
243 *Ibid.*
244 *Ibid.*, p. 52, 53.
245 *Mankowski*, JZ 2009, 321, 322 et seq.
246 *Ibid.*, 324: a missing dynamic may also be an attribute of a certain legal culture.
247 *Ibid.*
248 *Vallender*, NZI 2010, 838, 839.
249 *Mankowski*, JZ 2009, 321, 324.
250 *Von Münch*, p. 132; *Vallender*, NZI 2010, 838, 839.
251 *Von Münch*, p. 132, *Mankowski*, JZ 2009, 321, 324 et seq.
252 *Zypries*, Ein Rechtssystem mit Qualitätssiegel, in FAZ Nr. 251, 27.10.2008, p. 10.
253 *Jayme*, RabelsZ Bd. 67 (2003) 211, 212.
254 *Von Münch*, p. 52.

from their historical contexts, attitudes and values.[255] This is already shown in discussing of whether a nation needs an *insolvency culture*[256] as opposed to a *rescue culture*. It is unquestionable that a nation's cultural understanding imprints the thinking of its members and steers their beliefs into a specific direction. This leads to the effect that the same approach towards an issue may be recognised, realised, evaluated and understood[257] differently by members of different cultures.

3.1.1 Germany

Due to the overall economic development[258] and the increased complexity of companies, the Bankruptcy Code (Konkursordnung) from 1877 and the Vergleichsordnung of 1935 were almost inoperable.[259] The German Insolvency Statute came into force 1 January 1999.[260] The legislature had identified an urgent need to encourage the restructuring companies in financial distress. This was seen as a "*stark paradigm shift*"[261]. An *insolvency culture* may be shaped by social and economic understanding,[262] however, no law is able to create it.[263] This is reflected in the use of restructuring instruments such as the insolvency plan and self-administration proceeding as opposed to business-asset-sale[264] or liquidation since the focus of the insolvencyproceedings continues to be the maximisation of assets to satis-

255 *Vallender*, NZI 2010, 838, 839; *Finch*, 6 J.B.L. (2010) 502, 521.
256 *Vallender*, NZI 2010, 838.
257 *Kaufmann*, p. 245 et seq. also for the different aspects of "understanding".
258 This especially applies to the development if the global financial markets with structured finance, leveraged buyouts and derivative business.
259 BMJ, Begr. RegE-InsO, BT-Drucks. 12/2443, p. 72. For historical background, see *Altmeppen*, in FS Hommelhoff, p. 1, 2 et seq.; *Madaus*, p. 60 et seq.; *Paulus / Berberich*, in *Faber / Vermunt / Kilborn / Richter*, p. 313 et seq.
260 *Balz*, Brook. J. Int'l L. 1997, 167, 168: the law was "considered so radical that is was thought wise to postpone [it from its enactment in 1994] until its entry into force in January 1, 1999".
261 *Vallender*, NZI 2010, 838, 840.
262 *Ibid.*
263 *Ibid.*, 838.
264 *Ibid.*, 841.

fy creditors.[265] Since the instruments did not serve their purpose, the legislature put forward legal changes with the ESUG to make progress towards a *rescue culture*.[266] This especially since it was repeatedly discussed whether Germany already has an *insolvency culture*[267] that would shift from the liquidation of the debtor's assets towards the going concern of the debtor company.[268] The successful restructurings by usage of the creative restructuring instruments of the Insolvency Statute would also counteract the stigma of insolvency.[269] The restructuring opportunities within the insolvency plan were, however, seldom applied.[270] The shortcomings became apparent especially with the forum shopping of some German companies and with the financial crisis. Calls for reforms, especially for a pre-insolvency proceeding became louder.[271]

3.1.2 England

Due to its importance in the global financial markets as a system of law "*universally seen to be fair and consistent*"[272], English law and the English courts with their case law have been and continue to be a vital part of successful corporate restructurings.[273] Post Second World War,[274] English

---

265 *Eidenmüller*, Unternehmenssanierung, p. 50: as long as the insolvency plan or self-administration does not supply the same proceeds as the liquidation, they will not be the choice of proceeding.

266 *Moldenhauer et al.*, September 2013: the progress is rather hesitant. See also *Gravenbrucher Kreis*, ZIP 2014, 1262, pointing out where ESUG needs further adjustments, rather now than after the evaluation period of five years' time.

267 *Vallender*, NZI 2010, 838, 840; *Braun / Heinrich*, NZI 2011, 505, et seq.

268 *Vallender*, NZI 2010, 838, 842.

269 See Chapter II 3.2.1; also *Undritz*, ZGR 2010, 210, 216.

270 See discussion on *Adam Opel GmbH* in the previous section.

271 *Paulus*, WM 2010, 1337 et seq.; *Beissenhirtz*, ZInsO 2011, 57 et seq.; *Frind*, ZInsO 2010, 1426 et seq.; *Geldmacher*, ZInsO 2011, 353 et seq.; *Hölzle*, NZI 2010, 207 et seq.; *Jacoby*, ZGR 2010, 395 et seq.; *Jaffé / Friedrich*, ZIP 2008, 1849, 1856 et seq. Contrary *Pape*, ZInsO 2010, 1582, 1583 et seq.; *Uhlenbruck*, NZI 2008, 201 et seq.

272 *Mellon / Waisman*, p. 1. See also *Paulus*, DZWIR 2008, 6.

273 *Perry*, Steward, ECL 04/ 2010, 77.

274 For more historical background, see also *Goode*, mn.1-05, *Keay / Walton*, p. 7 et seq.; *Finch*, p. 10 et seq.; *Mellon / Waisman*, p. 1 et seq.; *Omar*, 18 (4) I.C.C. L.R. (2007) 127, 128 et seq.

insolvency law was more of an "*ancient philosophy*"[275] with a penalising effect on the debtor. The social and economic environment in the late 1960s led to reforms and some "*revolutionary*"[276] changes to the insolvency law[277] – and the *rescue culture* was developed as an alternative to liquidation.[278] The insolvency of a debtor not only has an influence on the creditors but also affects public interests and, therefore modern insolvency law should provide a framework to preserve viable companies that would contri-bute to the economic life and development of the country.[279] *Rescue culture* has a positive and protective role as well as a corrective and a punitive role, and it not only refers to the legal aspect of insolvency but also regards the economic impact.[280] The effects of *rescue culture* were not as effective as implied since the underlying attitude towards insolvency has not fundamentally changed.[281]

Two main reforms in the last twenty-five years further shaped the English insolvency law, creating the confidence[282] in the legal environment that "*enterprises worth saving, will live on, to fight and trade and enrich the nation*"[283]. The Insolvency Act 1986 (IA 1986),[284] prompted by the

275 For development of English bankruptcy and insolvency law, see *Hunter*, J.B.L. 1999, 491 et seq.

276 *Hunter*, J.B.L. 1999, 491.

277 *Keay / Walton*, p. 52: corporate insolvency law "is not equipped, except in a very small degree, to address wider economic or social problems [...but should be subordinated] to economic interests that are considered to require a higher priority".

278 *Hunter*, J.B.L. 1999, 491, 492: Schemes of arrangement were already possible, however, not used due to their complexity and difficulties in acquiring the required majority consent; *Ibid.*, 497 whereas the consideration "of what reforms were necessary or desirable" as well as suggesting "possible less formal procedures as alternatives to bankruptcy and company winding-up proceedings in appropriate circumstances" are the "first official signpost" of the English rescue culture.

279 *Cork Report*, Chapter 4, para. 198.

280 *Hunter*, J.B.L. 1999, 491, 498 et seq.: on the principles governing rescue culture.

281 *Ibid.*, 519 with reference to *Rt. Hon. Peter Mandelson*, former Secretary of State for Trade and Industry and M.P.

282 *Ibid.*

283 *Ibid.*, 520.

284 *Milmann*, in *De Lacy*, p. 415, 417 explaining that the corporate rescue procedures were originally introduced in the Insolvency Act 1985, which was, however, immediately overtaken and replaced by the consolidating Insolvency Act 1986. The 1986 Act is supplemented by a set of detailed Insolvency Rules 1986 (SI

recommendations of the Cork Committee[285], introduced administration as a formal corporate rescue procedure into English law[286] to facilitate restructuring rather than the liquidation of insolvent or nearly insolvent companies.[287] The Insolvency Act 2000 (IA 2000)[288] made a number of important amendments to IA 1986, mainly focusing on streamlining the court-based administration procedure and restricting the use of administrative receivership.[289]

The Cork Committee had concluded that the proceedings within IA 1986 still caused too many companies to fail while instead "*all insolvency schemes must be aimed at saving a business*"[290]. The Enterprise Act 2002 (EA 2002) sought to have radically reshaped corporate insolvency law,[291] establishing a *rescue culture*[292] whereas the insolvency practice moved from an *ex post* (reactionary) to an *ex ante* (anticipatory) approach to facilitate corporate restructurings.[293] Creditors received more influence on the appointment of the insolvency practitioner, thereby having a choice of

---

1986/1925) (Insolvency Rules 1986). These principal Rules are amended by the Insolvency (Amendment) Rules 2010 (SI 2010/686) and the Insolvency (Amendment) (No.2) Rules 2010 (SI 2010/734) (together, the 2010 Rules), both in force from 6 April 2010. See *Goode*, mn. 1-06.

285 *Cork*, Insolvency Law and Practise, Report of the Review Committee (Cmnd. 8558, 1982). See also *Keay / Walton*, p. 11: "a critical development of modern insolvency law in the UK".

286 *Milmann*, in *De Lacy*, p. 415, 417.

287 *Cork / Graham*, ZIP 1982, 1275 et seq.; *Finch*, p. 15 et seq.

288 The IA 2000 was the result of a review process which began with the publication in September 1999 of a joint Treasury and DTI (now BIS) working group consultation paper, setting out proposals for corporate insolvency law reform (A Review of Company Rescue and Business Reconstruction Mechanisms). The proposals were then subject to a further review and the report of the review group was published in November 2000 (The Rescue Green Paper). *See also Goode*, mn. 1-09, *Keay / Walton*, p. 7 et seq.; *Finch*, p. 10 et seq.

289 *Keay / Walton*, p. 11: "the legislation was intended to address a number of matters that affect commercial life in today's Britain".

290 *Cork*, K Cork on Cork, Macmillan, London, 1988.

291 *Wells*, BLR 2012, 156.

292 *Hunter*, J.B.L. 1999, 491; DTI, Productivity and Enterprise, 2001, Foreword; *Armour / Hsu / Walters*, ECFR 2008, 148, 155 et seq.; *Müller-Seils*, p. 170; *Lieder*, p. 179; *Mokal / Armour*, ICR 2004, 13.

293 *McCormack*, J.B.L. 2007, 701 et seq., 732; *Finch*, 8 J.B.L. (2008) 756; *Franken*, EBOR 5 (2004) 645, 653 et seq. on the *ex ante* and *ex post* efficiencies of different insolvency regimes.

preference, facilitating rescue arrangements.[294] The Cork Committee also recognised that in order to maximise the success of the corporate rescue procedures, directors would have to be given an incentive to have recourse to these new options. That incentive took a negative form in the shape of a harsher legal environment to be imposed on directors of struggling businesses through the agency of the wrongful trading sanctions and the director disqualification regime embodied in the Company Directors Disqualification Act 1986[295] (amended by the Insolvency Act 2000).[296]

Despite the fact that the European High Yield Association wanted to introduce a separate restructuring proceeding,[297] it is felt that the English insolvency framework is fit for purpose.[298]

3.1.3 Summary

A legal culture needs to evolve to develop certain perception about the law; the law itself will not be able to create a culture.[299] Both Germany and England have made efforts in the last century to amend their insolvency laws. While the EA 2002 sought to have established a rescue culture, which was already perceived to exit prior to the enactment, Germany has made progress to initiate a legal change, however, the perception needs to change as well.

---

294 *Frisby*, in *Ringe / Gullifer / Théry*, p. 45.

295 *Goode*, mn. 1-06.

296 *Milmann*, in *De Lacy*, p. 415, 417.

297 *Vickers*, CR&I 2009, 262-26, the UK should move more towards the US Chapter 11. See also *Evans*, IFLR 2008, 56: "The problem with the UK's law is not legal but psychological".

298 *Wells*, BLR 2012, 156, 158. See also *Finch*, J.B.L. 2003, 527, 528, discussing the implications and objectives in government reforms on the *rescue culture*.

299 *Paulus*, WM 2011, 2205.

3.2 The Stigma of Insolvency

> *"Bankruptcy is perhaps the greatest and the most humiliating calamity which can befall an innocent man. The greater part of men, therefore, are sufficiently careful to avoid it."*[300]

Although more than 200 years have passed since this quote was written, the attitude towards insolvency has not entirely changed.[301] The stigma of insolvency has been around throughout history[302] and is still valid in some countries today.[303] In order not to concede to the financial failure, debtors will try to avoid insolvency as long as possible,[304] sometimes through the manipulation of annual accounts. The delay to initiate restructuring measure is then too long delayed, eventually resulting in the failure of most companies.[305] In comparison to Anglo-American investors, German companies did not have the mind-set to see insolvency as an opportunity to restructure the company and, after a successful restructuring, to return to profitability.[306]

3.2.1 Germany

With the implementation of the Insolvency Statute, the law shifted towards providing debtor with the opportunity to restructure rather than to liquidate.[307] This should change the perception that insolvency is rather seen as the beginning of the end than an opportunity for a new beginning.[308] There could be various reasons for the German attitude. One may be the German mentality of caution and defensiveness towards entrepreneurial risk. This approach is regularly seen in cases of companies in financial distress, with the parties involved generally not being willing to grant them a second chance. Another reason lies in the history of insolv-

---

300 *Smith*, Wealth of Nations, p. 282.
301 *Sullivan / Warren / Westbrook*, 59 Stan. L. Rev. (2006-2007) 213, 233.
302 Chapter I 2.1. See also *Bridge*, p. 37.
303 *Leutheusser-Schnarrenberger*, ZInsO 2011, 2078, 2079.
304 *Richter*, p. 148 et seq.
305 *Hingerl*, ZInsO 2008, 404.
306 *Flessner*, Sanierung und Reorganisation, p. 139; *Smid*, WM 1998, 2489, 2506; *Smid / Rattunde*, Der Insolvenzplan, 2005, mn. 2.37 et seq.
307 BMJ, Begr. RegE-InsO 1992, BT-Drucks. 12/2243, p. 77.
308 *Heinrich*, FS Greiner, p. 111, 113; *Tashiro*, Recovery, Winter 2009, p. 23.

ency law in general. The Bankruptcy Act *(Konkursordnung)* tended to imply automatic liquidation.[309] Politically, corporate restructurings were only pursued in election campaigns and to save jobs.[310] The implementation of the Insolvency Statute made a technical shift in the law,[311] but even more than ten years later insolvency proceedings are still seen as a nightmare[312] for most companies and the stigma of insolvency is still present.[313] It is hoped that this attitude will change with ESUG and the amendment it made to the Insolvency Statute, providing a more suitable legal environment for restructurings.

3.2.2 England

England has a rather long tradition to provide a legal environment that supports a fresh start after a distressed period for a company. Prerequisite for a successful restructuring is the professionalism and effectiveness of all parties involved.[314] With the financial crisis, especially banks used a proactive approach to respond to corporate troubles at a far earlier stage of development than before.[315]

Bringing upon independence and trust among the various stakeholders, it has become common that the creditors' committee or the management hires a Chief Restructuring Officer (CRO)[316] to serve on the company's board when it is on the threshold of insolvency.[317] Especially the uprising of distressed assets investors has also driven new players[318] onto the market, having the restructuring experience to facilitate the successful

---

309 BMJ, Begr. RegE-InsO, BT-Drucks. 12/2243, p. 73; *Undritz*, Kölner Schrift zur InsO, 2009, p. 936.

310 Examples in Germany include the public involvement of politics in *Philip Holzmann AG* and *Adam Opel GmbH.*

311 BMJ, Begr. RegE-InsO, BT-Drucks. 12/2243, p. 77.

312 *Heneweer*, p. 13.

313 *Jaffé*, ZIP 2001, 2302; *Paulus*, ZGR 2005, 309, 310 et seq.; *Undritz*, ZGR 2010, 201, 202.

314 *Hunter*, J.B.L. 1999, 491, 498 et seq.

315 *Finch*, J.B.L. 2008, 756, 758.

316 *Rajan / Dettbarn / Kroner*, eurofenix, Summer 2014, 24: the concept started in the US.

317 *Pinfield*, ICR 2006, 111; *Jeffrey*, LexisNexis Restructuring & Insolvency, 6.

318 *Baird / Bernstein*, 115 Yale L. J. (2005-2006) 1930, 1947.

turnaround of the company.[319] Whether installed by management or by creditors, mainly banks,[320] these professionals negotiate an informal restructuring rather than a statutory proceeding.[321] The players include consulting companies, which now all have established special restructuring units, either providing the consultancy service or becoming part of the management of the company in the position of a CRO.[322] Most CROs already have experience and the appropriate skill-set to deal with distressed companies.[323] Especially in those cases, insolvency is not seen as much as a stigma but rather a valuable experience that solid managers should have: strong and collaborative leadership,[324] acquired by accompanying a company through its whole life cycle from establishment to death.

3.2.3 Summary

Germany and England have a different attitude towards insolvency. While Germany seems to be sticking to the stigma of insolvency, it is rather seen as a valuable experience having experience with companies in financial distress and the consequences of insolvency in England. The effects of insolvency, and in particular, the (social) stigma have also been noted by the European Commission.[325]

---

319 *Finch*, J.B.L. 2005, 690, 693 et seq.

320 *Rajan / Dettbarn / Kroner*, eurofenix, Summer 2014, 27: 28% are appointed by the company, 47% by lenders (source Deloitte European Restructuring Outlook 2014.).

321 *Finch*, J.B.L. 2008, 756, 759.

322 *Schleusener*, p. 23 et seq. e.g. Alix Partners; *Jeffrey*, LexisNexis Restructuring & Insolvency, 6: on the role of the CRO.

323 *Jeffrey*, LexisNexis Restructuring & Insolvency, 7; *Rajan / Dettbarn / Kroner*, eurofenix, Summer 2014, 25, quoting a survey by Deloitte (European Restructuring Outlook 2014) on the skills most required for a CRO: financial advisor, management, all-rounder and operational change.

324 *Pinfield*, ICR 2006, 111, 113.

325 Commission Recommendation of 12.3.2014 on a new approach to business failure and insolvency, C(2014) 1500 final, Recital 20, http://ec.europa.eu/justice/civil/files/c_2014_1500_en.pdf, accessed 30.6.2014.

3.3 Legal Competition versus Legal Harmonisation

> "*To advertise for one's own legal system, is not to be considered questionable. In a globalised world, the legal system – including the protection of constitutional rights – is a positive factor for location and it seems natural to communicate the benefits of your own system.*"[326]

While financial and economic markets have evolved to a global level, law is not only an instrument for the control of competition, but has become a marketable good itself.[327] Law is nowadays subject to global competition and needs to be commercially competitive[328], referring especially to choice-of-law[329] and choice of jurisdiction[330].

Corporate law and insolvency law are subject to that competition, which both increases the economic efficiency of a system and leads to welfare gains, or, in a *race to the bottom,* leads to market failure.[331] Law is thus increasingly economised.[332] In particular, the economic effects of corporate and insolvency law must be observed. They are about "*solid political and commercial interests [in which the] export of law [also serves] the re-import of investment*"[333]. A perceived advantage of another legal system allows for its influence on the legislature in other nations. This mostly benefits the exporting nation. It has further fuelled the legal competition in insolvency law that "*an insolvency process in Germany would be likely [to] lead to very substantially less recoveries on behalf of the*

326 *Hans Jürgen Papier* (former president German Federal Court of Justice), in *Von Münch*, p. 132: German players need to engage more in the competition and market German law on a global level.

327 *Eidenmüller / Frobenius*, WM 2011, 1210; *Milman*, Preface*:* "the UK system of corporate law might be viewed as a commodity to be sold to the international business community".

328 *Milman*, Preface.

329 *Basedow*, RabelsZ Bd. 75 (2011) 32 et seq. discussing choice-of-law and party autonomy.

330 *Eidenmüller*, ECFR 1999, 1, 2. *Piekenbrock*, NZI 2012, 905; *Hölzle*, KTS 2011, 291, 304.

331 *Eidenmüller*, in *Simon*, p. 83.

332 *Mankowski*, JZ 2009, 321, 324. See the footnotes on law and economics in Chapter I 2.2.

333 *Von Münch*, p. 136.

broad constituencies of creditors than would be available if a scheme is successfully promulgated under the provision of the English statute"[334].

As "*bankruptcy is a big business*"[335], the English financial and consulting industries as well as the judiciary have done a great deal to show to the rest of Europe the benefits of its rescue culture and how companies may be restructured more effectively in English courts than in other countries.[336] Overall, does it make much difference to the company or its stakeholders whether a German company with German employees would be restructured under German or English law as long as the advantages of a different legal system and its approach outweigh the disadvantages for all parties involved? On the corporate side, England may have benefitted at the expense of Germany[337] and considering the outcry by insolvency administrators in Germany seeing their business going abroad could lead to a different presumption. However, one has to ask whether the outcry was for the benefits of the company and its stakeholder or the self-interest of the insolvency administrators.[338]

It is important to differentiate that legal competition in corporate law leads to overcoming unnecessary bureaucracy and outdated regulatory approaches, while competition in insolvency law usually takes place in situations of existence-threatening crisis, in which a company in financial distress is already controlled by certain influential creditors and the management.[339] Adaptation of (parts of) a different legal culture as a result of legal competition, however, may not lead so much to legal harmonisation[340] in which the best of both worlds – the German and the English law – are chosen,[341] but rather to tragic choices when the adaptation of legal

334 *PrimaCom Holding GmbH and others v Credit Agricole and others* [2011] EWHC 3746 (Ch), para. 8.

335 *Altman*, p. vii.

336 *Walters / Smith*, 19 Int. Insolv. Rev. (2010) 181, 203: London is "the restructuring capital of Europe".

337 *Rutstein / Bloomberg*, CR&I 2010, 158.

338 See Chapter II 5.1.2.

339 *Eidenmüller*, in *Simon*, p. 83.

340 *Von Münch*, p. 136. See also *Basedow*, ZEuP 1996, 379, 381: "overarching European legal culture". See also *Jayme*, RabelsZ Bd. 67 (2003) 211, 213: the cultural dimension of law rather limits (European legal) harmonisation.

341 *Griffiths / Hellmig*, NZI 2008, 418, 420: the development of choosing the appropriate law for a case should not lead to a competition of law or legal cultures but rather pave the way towards a European insolvency law. See also *Wessels*, ECL 2011, 27 et seq.

rules does not interact with or respect the traditional national legal (constitutional) values. Harmonisation of certain areas as transparency of the administrative process and equitable treatment of creditors may proof to be beneficial for both debtors and creditors, increasing predictability and legal certainty of the process.

European Insolvency Regulation

In order to encounter legal competition, the adoption of the European Union Regulation on Insolvency Proceedings (EIR)[342] met the need for effective and efficient legislation to administer cross-border insolvencies within the European Union, including provisions on jurisdiction, recognition and applicable law, which was hard to achieve on the national level.[343] The EIR has been a major step forward[344] to establish the internal market[345].[346] The Regulation came into force on 31 May 2002 and contains the framework for cross border insolvency and is directly effective[347] within the Member States of the European Union (except Denmark).[348] As a regulation, the EIR is directly applicable in the Member States; it does not replace the national insolvency regimes.[349] The objective of the EIR is to introduce uniform conflicts-of-law rules, not substantive rules, for

342 Council Regulation (EC) No 1346/2000 on insolvency proceedings, Official Journal L 160, 30.6.2000 p.0001-0013. *Hereinafter* the Regulation; Articles and Recitals without any notation refer to this Regulation. The Regulation excludes from its scope insolvency proceedings concerning insu-rance companies, credit institutions, investment undertakings holding funds and securities for third parties, and collective investment undertakings (Article 1(2)). *See also* Fletcher, in *Moss / Fletcher / Stuart*, mn. 3.08.

343 Recital 2 EIR. See also *Wolf*, Cross-Border Insolvencies, 2006, p. 16 et seq. for the European Initiatives that have led to the European Insolvency Regulation. In addition, see *Ehricke*, EWS 2002, 101.

344 *Paulus*, NZI 2012, 297.

345 Treaty of Amsterdam, Article 65, Council Regulation (EC) No 1346/2000, Recital 1.

346 *Walters / Smith*, 19 Int. Insolv. Rev. (2010), 181, 183.

347 Recital 8 EIR.

348 Recital 33 EIR: Denmark [...] is not participating in the adoption of this Regulation, and is therefore not bound by it or subject to its application.

349 Recital 15 EIR.

insolvency proceedings and judgements.[350] The EIR addresses difficulties that arise when an insolvency case involves a number of different European jurisdictions.[351] It designates the state whose courts may open insolvency proceedings in respect to the debtor's centre of main interests (COMI), and is an instrument to mediate between potentially competing courts of each Member State in order to determine which country has jurisdiction over the insolvency of a particular debtor.[352]

In 2012, the European Commission decided to review the EIR ten years after its enactment as it was found[353] that the EIR would not sufficiently reflect the EU current priorities, among others, "*promoting the rescue of enterprises in difficulties*"[354]. The review process examines the EIR's operation and application in all Member States and found that "*in general, the Regulation functions in a sound and satisfactory manner*"[355]. It was also noted that the Commission will not propose amendments with regard to the applicable law in the EIR, keeping the conflict-of-law rules in place until further examination has been conducted.[356]

The Commission has also initiated "A new European approach to business failure and insolvency"[357], as the consequences from the economic

350 Recital 12 EIR.

351 Recital 11 EIR.

352 Recital 12 EIR.

353 *Paulus*, NZI 2012, 297; *Reinhart*, NZI 2012, 304; *Bufford*, IILR 2012, 341; *McGormack*, IILR 2011, 121; *Ibid.*, Legal Studies March 2010, 126.

354 Proposal for a Regulation of the European Parliament and of the Council amending Council Regulation (EC) No 1346/2000 in insolvency proceedings, COM(2012) 744 final, p. 2, http://ec.europa.eu/justice/civil/files/insolvency-regulation_en.pdf, accessed 30.6.2014.

355 *Ibid.*, p. 17.

356 *Ibid.*, p. 18.

357 Communication from the Commission to the European Parliament, the Council and the European Economic and Social Committee – A new European approach to business failure and insolvency, COM(2012) 742 final, accessed 30.6.2014; Report from the Commission to the European Parliament, the Council and the European Economic and Social Committee on the application of Council Regulation (EC) No 1346/2000 of 29 May 2000 on insolvency proceedings, COM(2012) 743 final, http://ec.europa.eu/justice/civil/files/insolvency-report_en.pdf, accessed 30.6.2014. See also *Marks*, ICR 2012, 227 et seq.

crisis have led to a major increase in failing companies.[358] The recommendation[359] proposes

> "*to ensure that viable enterprises in financial difficulties, wherever they are located in the Union, have access to national insolvency frameworks which enable them to restructure at an early stage with a view to preventing their insolvency, and therefore maximise the total value to creditors, employees, owners and the economy as a whole. The Recommendation also aims at giving honest entrepreneurs a second chance across the Union.*"[360]

This will put considerable pressure on the Member States to modernise their national insolvency law, where appropriate[361], as the Commission deemed it necessary to

> "*encourage greater coherence between the national insolvency frameworks in order to reduce divergences and inefficiencies which hamper the early restructuring of viable companies in financial difficulties [...] to lower the cost of restructuring for both debtors and creditors. Greater coherence and increased efficiency in those national insolvency rules would maximise the returns to all types of creditors and investors and encourage cross-border investment. Greater coherence would also facilitate the restructuring of groups of companies irrespective of where the members of the group are located in the Union.*"[362]

While the Member States are invited to implement the principles, the Commission will assess the implementation within 18 months of publication and decide "*whether additional measures to consolidate and strength-*

358 Communication from the Commission to the European Parliament, the Council and the European Economic and Social Committee – A new European approach to business failure and insolvency, COM(2012) 742 final, p. 2: "From 2009-2011, an average of 200,000 firms went bankrupt per year in the EU. About one-quarter of these bankruptcies have a cross-border element. About 50 % of all new businesses do not survive the first five years of their life. 1.7 million jobs are estimated to be lost due to insolvencies every year".

359 Commission Recommendation of 12.3.2014 on a new approach to business failure and insolvency, C(2014) 1500 final, http://ec.europa.eu/justice/civil/files/c_2014_1500_en.pdf, accessed 30.6.2014.

360 *Ibid.*, Recital (1).

361 *Paulus*, NZI 2012, 297, 298.

362 Commission Recommendation of 12.3.2014 on a new approach to business failure and insolvency, C(2014) 1500 final, Recital (11), http://ec.europa.eu/justice/civil/files/c_2014_1500_en.pdf, accessed 30.6.2014.

en the approach [...] should be proposed".[363] While the European Union itself respects different legal traditions and values,[364] this is a clear statement towards more harmonisation in the area of restructuring and insolvency law within the European Union. Overall, the (new or amended) legal rules should shift the focus away from liquidation to develop a new approach to helping businesses overcoming financial difficulties, all the while protecting creditors' right to get their money back[365] where appropriate[366], in the best case towards a harmonised European rescue culture.[367]

However, we are not there yet and as long as the substantive corporate and insolvency laws are not (nearly) harmonised so long will legal competition encourage forum shopping.[368]

3.4 Forum Shopping

> "*Forum shopping is merely the optimisation of procedural possibilities and it results from the existence of more than one available forum, which is in no way unlawful. However, where forum shopping leads to unjustified inequality between the parties to a dispute with regard to the defence of their respective interests, the practice must be considered and its eradication is a legitimate legislative objective.*"[369]

Forum shopping is generally any action before a particular court or in a particular jurisdiction where the plaintiff (debtor or creditor) expects a decision in his favour.[370] This approach is well established in England, which "*is a good place to shop in, both for quality of goods and the speed*

363 Commission Recommendation of 12.3.2014 on a new approach to business failure and insolvency, C(2014) 1500 final, Nr. 34, 36, http://ec.europa.eu/justice/civil/files/c_2014_1500_en.pdf, accessed 30.6.2014.

364 *Jayme*, RabelsZ Bd. 67 (2003) 211, 214; *von Bogdandy / Schill*, ZaöRV 70 (2010) 701.

365 European Commission Justice / Insolvency Proceedings, http://ec.europa.eu/justice/civil/commercial/ insolvency/index_en.htm, accessed 30.6.2014.

366 *Paulus*, NZI 2012, 297, 298.

367 *Konecy*, NZI 2008, 416.

368 *Walters / Smith*, 19 Int. Insolv. Rev. (2010) 181, 183.

369 Case C-1/04, *Susanne Staubitz-Schreiber*, Advocate General Opinion, 6 September 2005, paras. 72-73.

370 *Ringe*, EBOR 9 (2008) 579 et seq.

of service"[371]. Divergent legal systems, especially in the European Union, offer a variety of opportunities for forum shopping,[372] and these aspects have particularly been discussed for corporate and insolvency law in recent years.[373] In insolvency law, the proceedings vary between jurisdictions, depending on whether they are *debtor- or creditor-friendly*[374] or *rescue-friendly*[375]. In corporate law, different countries take different positions as missing initial capital requirements.[376] When making the decision whether and where to litigate, favourable legal conditions and the predictability of law and costs[377] are undoubtedly desirable objectives to achieve.[378] Timing is also an issue to consider.[379]

England has been a popular choice of venue[380] because its judges have a significant degree of discretion in certain cases.[381] With their precedents in restructuring, English courts have and will continue to play a crucial role in the European Union.[382] Forum shopping will always exist as long as there are general and special international jurisdictions where debtors and creditors see advantages for their respective positions. Only exclusive jurisdiction would be an effective way to completely prevent a party choosing between different forums,[383] however, this could clearly complicate international and cross-border restructurings. It is not the forum shopping itself but its misuse that have been criticised and ought to be prevented in future.[384] Restructurings and insolvencies of companies have a

---

371 *The Atlantic Star* [1972] 3 All ER 705.

372 *Reuss*, p. 8; *Walters / Smith*, 19 Int. Insolv. Rev. (2010) 181, 202 on good and bad forum shopping. See also *Siehr*, ZfRV 25 (1984) 124, 125; *Eidenmüller*, ECFR 2009, 1, 27; Mankowski, WM 2011, 1201, 1209.

373 *Jasper*, p. 18.

374 See Chapter II 3.5. See also *Jasper*, p. 20 et seq., 93 et seq.; *Boys v Chaplin* [1969]2 All ER 1085.

375 *Armour / Hsu / Walters*, ECFR 2008, 148, 149.

376 *Reuss*, p. 8.

377 *Jasper*, p. 25: proceedings in an English court are not necessarily more cost effective than a proceeding in a continental court.

378 *Dickinson*, in *Vareilles-Sommières*, p. 115, 135.

379 *Rasmussen / Thomas*, 94 Nw. U. L. R (1999-2000) 1357 et seq.

380 *Heneweer*, p. 14; *Walters / Smith*, 19 Int. Insolv. Rev. (2010) 181, 191 et seq.

381 See Chapter II 5.2.1.

382 *Jasper*, p. 139; *Rutstein / Bloomberg*, CR&I 2010, 158: English courts are a "brothel for bankruptcy".

383 *Jasper*, p. 139.

384 *Ibid.*

great impact on the economic performance of a country,[385] therefore, forum shopping may be problematic.[386]

Freedom of Establishment and Centre of Main Interest

Within the European Union, the freedom of establishment enables companies to decide on where to (re-)locate and, therefore, which Member States' law is applicable. However, with regard to insolvency proceedings, especially in a cross-border context, the EIR explicitly seeks to prevent forum shopping since

> "*it is necessary for the proper functioning of the internal market to avoid incentives for parties to transfer assets or judicial proceedings from one Member State to another, seeking to obtain a more favourable legal position (forum shopping)*"[387].

The EIR directs the opening of a main proceeding with universal scope but leaves room to open secondary proceedings.[388] The main insolvency proceeding is opened by the court in the Member States where the debtor has the centre of main interests (COMI),[389] hence *lex concursus* is applicable.[390] Once a main proceeding has been opened in one Member State, further proceedings in other Member States can only be secondary proceedings.[391] Secondary proceedings may be opened in one or more other states to protect the diversity of interests arising in the context of cross-border insolvencies.[392] The EIR principally assists in those cases where a company or business has an establishment[393] or significant assets[394] in more than one Member State. Secondary proceedings tend to be only liquidation or winding up proceedings[395] and are limited in scope to the

385 See Chapter I 2.1.
386 *Reuss*, p. 3.
387 Recital 4 EIR.
388 Not only insolvency procedures (Article 1(1)) are available but supplemented by other proceedings (Article 2(a)) in Annex A.
389 Recital 13, Article 3(1).
390 *Lechner*, AJICL 2002, 975, 980.
391 Article 3(2)(3) EIR.
392 Recital 12 EIR.
393 Article 2(h) EIR.
394 Article 2(g) EIR.
395 Article 3(3) EIR.

realisation of the debtor's assets within that jurisdiction.[396] The law applicable to secondary proceedings is the law of that Member State opening those proceedings.[397] One of the principal facets of the EIR is that it provides that any judgement opening main or secondary proceedings is to be recognised automatically[398] in other Member States without the need for further formalities, unless the Regulation provides otherwise, or a secondary proceeding has been opened in the jurisdiction in question.[399] There is also a residual public policy exception that gives a Member State the discretion to refuse to recognise proceedings brought in another Member State if to do so would be "*manifestly contrary to the State's public policy*"[400].

When the EIR came into force, COMI was not a new concept[401] but not defined yet. While many countries in Europe, including England, followed the *command and control approach*[402], the European Court of Justice (ECJ) and various national courts have developed criteria to determine a company's COMI. A company's COMI is described as "*the place where the debtor conducts the administration of his interests on a regular basis and is therefore ascertainable by third parties*"[403] and "*in the case of a company or legal person, the place of the registered office shall be presumed to be the centre of its main interests in the absence of proof to the contrary*"[404]. However, the EIR did not provide further criteria for estab-

396 Article 27 EIR.

397 Article 28 EIR.

398 Article 17 EIR.

399 Article 16 EIR.

400 Article 26 EIR.

401 United Nations Commission on International Trade Law (UNCITRAL) Model Law adopted the Model Law on Cross-Border Insolvency, 2012, p. 22; see http://www.uncitral.org/pdf/english/texts/insolven/V1188129-Judicial_Perspective_ebook-E.pdf, accessed 13.6.2014.

402 *Rutstein / Bloomberg*, CR&I 2010, 157.

403 Recital 13 EIR.

404 Article 3(1) EIR.

lishing a company's COMI,[405] and consequently the lack of definition led to legal challenge.[406]

The ECJ laid out that the factors to determine COMI must be "*both objective and ascertainable to third parties*"[407]. In the view of the High Court, ascertainable to a third party means what is in public view and what a typical party would learn in the ordinary course of business with the company.[408] The Court of Appeal added that COMI must refer to where the company's head office functions[409] are carried out and there is principally only one objective head office.[410] The ECJ held that instead of the registered office "*greater importance*" must be given to the place where the company conducts the administration of its interests, which may be located in a different Member State than the registered office.[411] The administration as an establishment requires the presence of a structure consisting of a minimum level of organisation and a "*degree of stability*" necessary for the purpose of pursuing an economic activity.[412] The requirement for stability has not to be necessarily permanent but rather focused on the relevant economic activity not being carried out only on a transitory basis.[413]

---

405 The factors also apply to companies with their COMI in a Member State despite being incorporated or registered outside the EU, *Re BRAC Rent-A-Car International Inc* [2003] EWHC (Ch) 128. The applicability of English law to non-English companies, having their COMI in England is primary provided for by the EIR and subsidiary in accordance to the Cross-Border Insolvency Regulations 2006, implementing the UNCITRAL Model Law on cross-border insolvency. See *Fletcher*, Insolvency in Private International Law, mn. 3.03, 3.17 et seq., 323 et seq.

406 *Fletcher*, in *Moss / Fletcher / Stuart*, mn. 3.10 et seq.

407 *Re Eurofood IFSC Ltd (Case C-341/04) [2006] Ch 508*. See *Bachner*, ECFR 2006, 311 et seq.

408 *Re Stanford International Bank Ltd and others* [2009] EWHC 1441 (Ch)*;* *Kaupthing Capital Partners Master LP Inc (unreported*), 31 March 2010 (Ch D).

409 *ReCi4net.com Inc* [2005] BCC 277*; Re Damovo Group SA* (unreported), 25 April 2007 (Ch D*); Re Lennox Holdings Plc* [2009] EWHC B11 (Ch). See also *Re Collins & Aikman Europe SA Collins and others* [2006] EWHC 1343 (Ch), for background see *Deadock*, ICR 2006, 88.

410 *Re Stanford International Bank Ltd* [2010] EWCA Civ 137.

411 Whether the company's administration refers to the head-office functions laid out before was not clarified.

412 *Interedil Srl (in liquidation) v Fallimento Interedil Srl and another* [2011] EU-ECJ C-396/09. See also *Omar*, ICR 2012, 349 et seq.

413 *Re Ci4net.com Inc* [2005] BCC 277*; Olympic Airlines SA Pension and Life Assurance Scheme v Olympic Airlines SA* [2012] EWHC 1413 (Ch).

Especially for key third parties like the company's creditors, COMI must be objectively ascertainable. However, even though the presence of the debtor's assets or contracts in a Member State may be objective and in public view,[414] it is not enough to rebut the assumption that COMI is at the registered office in another Member State. Without any economic activity, no insolvency proceeding can be opened.

The ECJ held that COMI is to be determined on an entity-by-entity basis. Even if a number of companies operate as a single enterprise across borders, the assumption of the COMI being at the company's registered office is not rebutted.[415]

Especially in the aftermath of the financial crisis, the English courts have placed considerable weight on where restructuring negotiations have taken place to determine COMI "*to enable creditors in particular to know where the company is and where it [...] may deal with the company*"[416]. A German court has made the distinction on whether the shift of COMI was to evade creditors' protection or is in the interest of creditors to restructure a company and thereby preserve value for the creditors.[417] The ECJ ruled that COMI is determined on the date that the application of the insolvency proceeding is filed[418] and not when the court is required to decide whether to open insolvency proceedings at the date of the hearing[419] since this would give the company a window of opportunity to relocate its COMI from one Member State into another Member State.[420]

In order to take advantage of the insolvency law of another jurisdiction, the company must achieve a genuine shift in COMI by either migrating or

414 *Re Stanford International Bank Ltd and others* [2009] EWHC 1441 (Ch).

415 *Rastelli Davide e C. Snc v Jean-Charles Hidoux [*2011] EUECJ C-191/10 (15 December 2011*).*

416 *European Directories v DH6 BV* [2010] EWHC 3472 (Ch); *Re Hellas Telecommunications (Luxembourg) II SCA* [2009] EWHC 3199 (Ch), see *Dakin et al.*, CR&I 2012, 120, 125 on details of the restructuring.

417 *PIN Group*, AG Köln, Beschl. v. 19.2.2008, 73 IE 1/08. See *Schwemmer*, NZI 2009, 355, 358.

418 *Re Staubitz-Schreiber (Case C-1/04)* [2006] E.C.R. I-701. See *Duursma-Kepplinger*, ZIP 2007, 896; *Knof*, ZInsO 2005, 1017, 1024; *Schwemmer*, NZI 2009, 355, 357 et seq. on *perpetuatio fori*.

419 *Shierson v Vlieland-Boddy* [2005] EWCA Civ. 974.

420 *Mankowski*, BB 2006, 1753, 1756.

relocating the COMI from one Member State to another Member State.[421] This is consistent with the principle on the freedom of establishment enshrined in European law.[422] There are different ways on how COMI may be shifted. A company could relocate its registered office, however, that does not necessarily result in a genuine shift of COMI.[423] By registering a legal entity in another Member State and subsequently transfers its assets and liabilities to that company,[424] a company could thereby shift its COMI from one Member State to another Member State.[425] The cross-border merger under the "Directive 2005/56/EC on cross-border mergers of limited liability companies" can also facilitate a change in COMI where two companies from different Member States merge and then decide in which Member State the COMI of the merged company is to be located.[426] Due to the various registration and formal requirements, such a merger might be too time consuming and costly in a restructuring scenario. The migration of assets and liabilities as well as a cross-border merger both need extensive preparation, time and funds in order to meet the formal requirements. Time and funds are generally restricted for a company in financial distress.

A legal shift of the registered office may not be achievable. In order to relocate its COMI, a company must then demonstrate that the administration of interests is being conducted elsewhere in order to rebut the presumption that the Member State where the registered office is located is the company's COMI. This can be achieved by moving head office functions including to board meetings to a different jurisdiction and by establishing economic activity (including assets), opening bank accounts, and

421 *Eidenmüller*, ECFR 2009, 1, 11 et seq., 16 et seq., evaluating the abuse of COMI shifts in general, before and after the insolvency petition. See also *Werlauff*, ECL 2008, 136; *Walters / Smith*, 19 Int. Insolv. Rev. (2010), 181, 188 et seq.

422 Article 49, 58 Treaty on the Functioning of the European Union (TFEU). For case law on the mobility of companies, see Guide to the Case Law of the European Court of Justice on Articles 49 et seq. TFEU, http://ec.europa.eu/internal_market/services/docs/infringements/art49-establishment_en.pdf, accessed 10.8.2013.

423 *Re Eurofood IFSC Ltd (Case C-341/04) [2006] Ch 508; Re Stanford International Bank Ltd and others [2009] EWHC 1441 (Ch).*

424 The transfer of assets and liabilities must be valid under the laws of both the emigrating and immigrating Member State.

425 *Deutsche Nickel Schefenacker,* in contrast *Hans Brochier Holdings Ltd v Exner* [2006] EWHC 2594 (Ch), see Chapter IV 9.

426 *Werlauff*, ECL 2008, 136, 138 et seq.

informing suppliers, creditors and counterparties of the new address. The factual relocation must comply with the criteria set for determining COMI.[427]

Shifting COMI is not always abusive but may ultimately preserve value for the creditors by leading to the rescue of an insolvent company, or a higher return by maximising the debtor's assets. However, the courts have been mindful of the possibility of a debtor reducing or avoiding payments to creditors by attempting a shift.

There are, however, also various risks involved in shifting COMI that need to be considered. A company in financial distress is unlikely to be able to provide the funds[428] for relocating and/or reincorporating the company's COMI in another Member State. The situation of financial distress may trigger default clauses in commercial contracts (termination rights) or loan/intercreditor agreements (change-of-control clause), prohibiting the company from changing its legal status or jurisdiction. The shift will probably involve a change in fiscal jurisdiction with the elimination of the right to utilise tax losses. Especially for multinational groups, it is important that the main insolvency proceeding is recognised in the various Member States, however, also in any country having operations (business, affiliates, subsidiaries) outside of the scope of the EIR. Even though COMI has been genuinely shifted, it does not prevent secondary proceedings at the former COMI from being opened when assets are involved as long as an establishment remains. These assets are then not being included in the main proceeding.[429] A company moving its COMI from Germany to England may consider that the company's employees will not receive the three months' salary state funding (*Insolvenzgeld*) to keep the company operational through any restructuring negotiations.

Some Member States' national law may prohibit companies from relocating their COMI.[430] The ECJ[431] has delivered several judgements in

---

427 *Re Damovo Group SA (unreported),* 25 April 2007 (ChD)*; PIN Group,* AG Köln, Beschl. v. 19.2.2008, 73 IE 1/08.

428 Total advisory costs of relocating and reincorporating *Schefenacker* plc exceeded EUR40 million.

429 *Connock and another v Fantozzi (Re Alitalia Linee Aeree Italiane SpA)* [2011] EWHC 15 (Ch).

430 *Drinhausen / Gesell*, BB 2006, Beil. 8, p. 3 et seq. for discussion on corporate mobility in Europe.

431 *Grohmann*, DZWIR 2009, 322, 323 et seq. for discussion the various aspects of the EJC case law.

recent years covering various aspects of freedom of establishment for companies on the valid immigration,[432] emigration[433] and cross-border merger[434].

Another aspect to consider is the creditors' perception about the debtor's COMI. Creditors generally base their credit decision on various factors, one being the COMI and the associated insolvency law the debtor had at the time of the decision. On the one hand, creditors have no way of knowing where the debtor may decide to move its COMI.[435] This uncertainty may cause credit to become more expensive, an even higher challenge for companies in financial distress.[436] On the other hand, the jurisdictional awareness could lead creditors supportive of a financial restructuring together with the management to engage proactively in forum shopping.[437]

3.5 Company Rescue: Business or Legal Entity?

"*Does this company have a reason for being?*"[438]

When considering the aim of any corporate rescue proceeding, the question is to what is actually rescued: the company's business or the com-

432 Case C-208/00, *Überseering B.V. v Nordic Construction Company Baumanagement GmbH (NCC)*, Judgement of the Court of 11 May 2002, ECR 2002, p. I-09919; Case C-167/01, *Kamer van Koophandek en Fabrieken voor Amsterdam v Inspire Art*, Judgement of the Court of 30 September 2003, ECR 2003, p. I-10155; Case C-212/97, *Centros Ltd. v. Erhvervs-og Selskabsstyrelsen*, Judgement of the Court of 3 September 1999, ECR 1999, p. I-01459; Case C-378/10, *VALE Építési Kft*, Judgement of the Court of 12 July 2012, ECR 2012, p. I-00000; Case C-210/06, *Cartesio Oktató és Szolgáltató bt.*, Judgement of the Court of 16 December 2008, ECR 2008, p. I-09641. See also *Knop*, DZWIR 2009, 147 et seq.

433 Case C-81/87, *The Queen v. H.M. Treasury and Commissioners of Inland Revenue, ex parte Daily Mail and General Trust plc.*, Judgement of the Court of 27 September 1988, ECR 1988, p. I-05483; Case C-9/02, *Hughes de Lasteyrie du Saillant v Ministère de l'Économie, des Finances at de l'Industrie*, Judgement of the Court of 11 March 2004, ECR 2004, p. I-02409.

434 Case C-411/03, *SEVIC Systems AG*, Judgement of the Court of 13 December 2005, ECR 2005, ECR p. I-10805.

435 *Rutstein / Bloomberg*, CR&I 2010, 158.

436 *Paulus*, DZWIR 2008, 6, 12.

437 *Patel / Fennessy*, ICR 2006, 255, 256. See Chapter IV 9 et seq.

438 *Schuppe*, ABIJ (March 2005) 52.

pany's legal entity.[439] One of the aspects to consider when to decide whether to restructure the business or the legal entity is in whose interest the process is carried out. Statutory frameworks differ significantly from each other, generally being oriented either *pro-debtor* or *pro-creditor*.[440]

3.5.1 Pro-Debtor or Pro-Creditor

In a *pro-creditor* jurisdiction, creditor rights are paramount,[441] protecting the creditors by security or set-off in order to avoid losses resulting from a debtor's default.[442] As the opening of a formal insolvency proceeding may create unpredictable risks for creditors with no chance of recovering their claims, control over all the company's assets is taken away from its management and shareholders and given to an administrator, who takes responsibility for and on behalf of the (secured) creditors.[443] The administrator usually realises the assets and the proceeds are distributed among the creditors; this may also mean that a secured creditor will not lose his security simply because of an insolvency filing, but it may have to accept losses in its position because the debtor's assets are usually available for equal distribution among all the creditors.[444] In the past, the focus in a *creditor-friendly* regime was more on asset realisation and maximising value on behalf of the creditors than on restructuring the debtor pursuant to the debtor's interests. Countries with an English law tradition are considered to have strongly *pro-creditor* insolvency regimes,[445] while countries with

---

439 *Balz*, Sanierung von Unternehmen, p. 1; *Ulmer*, ZHR 149 (1985) 541, 544, 566.

440 *Lechner*, AJICL 2002, 975, 97; *Fletcher*, Private International Law, mn. 4-5; *Wood*, Principles of International Insolvency, 3 et seq. Other jurisdictions are mainly former communist states, fundamentalist Muslim States and states without a commercial tradition have no distinct insolvency law. See also *Chatterji / Hedges*, p. 17 for "creditor- and debtor-friendly insolvency regimes"; *Nigel / Jones*, p. 134 et seq.; *Vriesendorp / Gramatikov*, 19 Int. Insolv. Rev. (2010) 209, 214.

441 *Nigel / Jones*, p. 134.

442 *Wood*, Principles of International Insolvency, p. 3-4; *Mucciarelli*, EBOR 14 (2013) 175, 179; *Löffler / Maurer*, 35 JBF (2011), 3351, 3353 on default risk and default prediction.

443 *Chatterji / Hedges*, p. 17; *Franken*, EBOR 5 (2004) 645, 653 et seq.

444 See Chapter I 2.1.

445 *Nigel / Jones*, p. 135, stating that the UK moved towards a more pro-creditor position with the administration proceeding. Also *Vickers*, CR&I 2009, 262; *Evans*,

German law traditions also have *creditor-friendly* regimes, although less so than the English ones.[446]

In contrast to a *pro-creditor* legal framework, a *pro-debtor* one supports the rescue of a debtor in the event of default.[447] The debtor will remain in control of its day-to-day operations, which gives it some negotiating power with respect to the treatment of creditors through the insolvency process; some form of debt forgiveness or forbearance as part of a financial restructuring is generally encouraged.[448] The debtor uses the insolvency proceeding as a shield against the influence of creditors.[449] Examples of such legal frameworks are the United States and France.[450]

3.5.2 Germany

While it has already been the ambition of the last insolvency law reform in Germany prior to ESUG to allow for a long-term going concern of viable but insolvent companies[451] by means of an insolvency plan proceeding and self-administration by interfering in the capital and management structures of a company,[452] progress has been slow. Looking back at restructuring practice in Germany over the last 20 years, the business-asset deal[453], subsequently leading to liquidation and dissolution of the legal en-

---

IFLR 2008, 56.Critical *McCormack*, 18 Int. Insolv. Rev. (2009) 109, challenging the perception that the UK is 'pro-creditor' while the US is 'pro-debtor'.

446 *Chatterji / Hedges*, p. 17.

447 *Franken*, EBOR 5 (2004) 645, 654 et seq.

448 *Chatterji / Hedges*, p. 17.

449 *Nigel / Jones*, p. 135.

450 *Chatterji / Hedges*, p. 17.

451 Erster Bericht der Kommission für Insolvenzrecht 1985, Sentence 2.1.1, para. 1, p. 162: "The aim of the restructuring is to ensure the survival of the debtor company and ensure sustainable profitability", however, restoring the competitiveness of the company in the long-term can neither be foreseen nor guaranteed in a dynamic market environment. See also *Balz*, Sanierung von Unternehmen, p. 18: It may well be in the economic interests of creditors to allow the company to continue trading for a while despite a lack of profitability in the case the company carries high sunk costs.

452 Erster Bericht der Kommission für Insolvenzrecht 1985, p. 152. The Insolvency Commission considered it of particular importance for a modern social-market environment to preserve viable companies from unnecessary destruction by insolvency.

453 See Chapter III 7.1.4.3.

tity, has been the major proceeding to rescue the company's business for going concerns instead of liquidation.[454]

The question remains whether the aim of the insolvency proceeding ought to be to restructure the legal entity and not the business.[455] The Insolvency Commission of the last reform did not provide any reason whether preference was given for restructuring the legal entity prior to restructuring the business,[456] however, it did not recognise the business-asset deal as a restructuring alternative.[457] In the legal-political discussion, the restructuring of the company's legal entity was preferred over the business-asset deal.[458] This aspect is surprising. The decisions to be made in a restructuring process regularly lead to a conflict between the management of the debtor[459] and the creditors when they do not agree on legal measures, e.g. having the creditors intruding into the corporate structure of the company by implementing a debt-equity-swap.[460] Such a conflict regularly leads to suboptimal creditor satisfaction while it is the primary objective of the Insolvency Statute to fully serve the interests of creditors and their satisfaction in the insolvency proceedings.[461] It is therefore not enough for a company to be viable, they have to be restructured in a reasonable way for creditors.[462] Otherwise, creditors could take the decision to realise the going concern value of the company by enforcing their claims, which may not necessarily lead to the survival of the company's legal entity.

One may argue that there could be economic reasons for preferring the restructuring of a company's legal entity over a business-asset deal.[463] However, this cannot be a justification for the continuation of the com-

---

454 *Ulmer*, ZHR 149 (1985) 541, 544.
455 *Balz*, Sanierung von Unternehmen, p. 14, 15; *Madaus*, p. 29.
456 *Balz*, Sanierung von Unternehmen, 1986, p. 2, 21.
457 *Ulmer*, ZHR 149 (1985) 541, 544.
458 *Balz*, Sanierung von Unternehmen, p. 1.
459 *LoPucki,* 57 Vand. L. Rev. (2004) 741,767: "the members of the board of directors, acting as fiduciaries, decide which of these claims to recognise and how much to pay the claim holders".
460 *Balz*, Sanierung von Unternehmen, p. 5. Comparison was always especially made with U.S. bankruptcy law, whose goal is not the restructuring of the debtor by courtesy of the financiers but rather the acquisition of its assets by the creditors, who seek to satisfy their claims in the going concern of the company as part of a debt-equity-swap.
461 *Berges*, KTS 1955, 49, 51.
462 Erster Bericht der Kommission für Insolvenzrecht 1985, p. 152.
463 *Balz*, Sanierung von Unternehmen, p. 21.

pany' s legal entity. Especially in a market economy, this approach cannot be followed because otherwise the law intrudes too far into the market forces that ensure that companies are run by the most efficient corporate legal entity.[464] The liquidation of a business with the concurrent dissolution of its legal entity does not comply with the forces of a dynamic market economy, especially if the assets of the company rated stand-alone carry a higher value than the company as a whole and thus there is no market-based interest in the going concern of the company's legal entity.[465] A new corporate legal entity for the business may be particularly a solution when the creditors are not otherwise willing to participate in a restructuring.

Despite the fact that creditor satisfaction is the main goal of the Insolvency Statute, the first insolvency reform discussed whether and how much participation in decision-making the existing shareholders of the company should have or even is required, or whether it is just that they should be ignored.[466] Since the shareholders were granted the right to obstruct any legal measures that would violate or intrude into their own rights[467] and were not made a party involved in the insolvency plan proceeding, one could argue that it was the aim of the legislator to rather restructure legal entities in appropriate cases in a commercially reasonable manner.[468] The literature also disagreed over whether restructuring by means of a business-asset deal would suffer a legitimacy deficit because it would preclude the creditors from the success of the restructuring,[469] or not, because the proceeds from the sale of the company in a business-asset restructuring would flow into the insolvency pool and would therefore be available for creditor satisfaction.[470]

The success of the business-asset deal as a form to encourage the restructuring of the business rather than the legal entity was foremost due to the fact that the creditors were able to implement restructuring measures

---

464 See Chapter I 2.1.

465 *Balz*, Sanierung von Unternehmen, 1986, p. 23.

466 *Ibid.*, p. 4.

467 BMJ, RegE-InsO, BT-Drucks. 12/2443, p. 78 et seq. This was contrary to the suggestions of the Insolvency Commission, *see* Erster Bericht der Kommission für Insolvenzrecht 1985, p. 282 et seq. allowing for the intrusion into the shareholder structure of the company.

468 *Balz*, Sanierung von Unternehmen, 1986, p. 18.

469 *Schmidt*, ZIP 1980, 328, 337 et seq.

470 *Stürner*, ZZP 1981, 263, 285; *Stürner*, ZIP 1982, 761, 771.

after the business was transferred to a new entity and did not have to deal with obstructing shareholders, which generally is time-consuming and thereby value destructive. Although some restrictions may apply in business-asset deals with reference to certain rights,[471] it allows companies to restrict liability to the old legal entity, which is especially important for the recognition of unknown future claims.

With ESUG, shareholders are now a party involved in insolvency and are not able to obstruct legal measures anymore for the case that the company is insolvent.[472] This could lead to the conclusion that the focus of restructuring now may has shifted from restructuring the business after a business-asset deal to restructuring the legal entity in an insolvency plan proceeding.[473] The insolvency plan may include the temporary going concern of the company being as well as partial liquidations and restructuring or complete restructuring, implementing a debt-equity-swap at the old or a new corporate entity. Therefore, the focus is yet not on the restructuring of the company's legal identity.[474]

3.5.3 England

There is no evidence in England whether the rescue of companies refers to the business or the legal entity, however, the process to facilitate restructuring is leading towards the conclusion that English law is rather focusing on saving businesses than corporate shells.[475] Most restructurings include a new corporate structure whereas debt-equity-swaps are regularly not implemented within the existing legal entity but rather carried out by setting up another (holding) company, which sells the shares to a new company by the creditors in exchange for their debt.[476]

---

471 See Chapter III 7.1.4.2.
472 See Chapter III 7.1.4.3, 8.2.4.
473 *Brinkmann*, WM 2011, 97, 99.
474 *Balz*, Sanierung von Unternehmen, 1986, p. 12.
475 *McCormack*, 18 Int. Insolv. Rev. (2009), 109, 132; *Finch*, Legal Studies 2012, 302, 303.
476 *Howard / Hedger*, mn. 6.97 et seq., for a corporate structure after a consensual debt-equity-swap; mn. 6.114, for a corporate structure after an enforcement process.

3.5.4 Summary

Whether or not the rescue of a company refers to the business or the legal entity of the company is only important when considering the goal of the restructuring proceeding for a company in financial distress, which is rather the going concern of the viable business for the benefit and satisfaction of the creditors.

With ESUG in Germany and the limitation of obstruction potential for shareholders in implementing any legal measures to change the corporate structure in an insolvency plan proceeding, creditors are encouraged to engage in debt-equity-swaps. This would rather lead to the restructuring of the legal entity now and, in the next step, the restructuring of the company. Despite the fact that this may be carried out in a timelier manner than a business-asset deal, new liabilities arise from future unknown claims, endangering the validity of the insolvency plan proceeding *ex post* when enforced. In England, the corporate structure is rather a means to an end to implement a debt-equity-swap for the benefits of the creditors. The holding structures provide for a new start of the business whose rescue is the focus of restructuring.

4 Role of Governments and National Banks

The government of a country generally sets the monetary policies for its economy, carried out by the national/central banks. An efficient national banking system secures the financial stability of a country's economy by providing liquidity necessary to foster the growth of an economy.[477] In the aftermath of the financial crisis, some governments intervened in the market mechanisms[478] to support non-viable corporate businesses for national economic stability.[479] They had the intention to protect the economy from long-term economic damage, thereby gaining considerable influence over the country's economic affairs after intervening to bail-out financial insti-

---

477 *Rajak*, p. 236: when intervening in market performance, economic interests are always closely related to political interests.

478 *Spindler*, AG 2009, 601, 603: the government and the regulator theoretically have the power to intervene into the market, however, these interventions have proven not to counteract systemic risks.

479 *Paulus*, in FS Görg, p. 361, 363 et seq.

tutions.[480] These rescue measures as well as the initiation of insolvency reforms to encourage corporate rescue had the objective to re-establish trust in the market and to avoid negative social, political or financial consequences.[481]

4.1 Germany

There is no evidence that the German Federal Bank (*Deutsche Bundesbank*) as the national bank of Germany has ever directly or indirectly intervened in the markets by providing liquidity directly or indirectly to companies in financial distress. This is not part of its defined duties.[482]

4.2 England

The governing statutes of the Bank of England do not limit its activity to a narrowly defined role.[483] Rather, the Bank of England still sees that its core purpose is "*maintaining financial stability and seeking to ensure the effectiveness of the UK financial system*"[484], as "*[w]ithout a framework that is predictable, equitable and transparent, designed to maximise value for all interested parties, the costs and wider economic disruption from unnecessary corporate liquidations may be enormous*"[485].

As a response to the recession in the UK in the mid-1970s,[486] the Bank of England formulated the guidelines as a response to the recession that had led to large numbers of non-performing loans on bank balance sheets, leading banks into financial difficulties[487] due to the out-dated insolvency

---

480 Short-term government intervention in free market activities were to improve the macroeconomic situation and to enable the best possible economic outcome for society as a whole by aiming towards a social and economic optimum.

481 *Chatterji / Hedges*, p. 18.

482 http://www.bundesbank.de/Redaktion/DE/Standardartikel/Bundesbank/Aufgaben_und_Organi- sation/aufgaben_der_deutschen_bundesbank.html, accessed 17.5.2013.

483 *Buljevich*, p. 5.

484 *Clementi*, Deputy Governor or the Bank of England, Speech 19.7.2001, p. 1.

485 *Ibid.*

486 *Buljevich*, p. 4-5.

487 *Howard / Hedger*, mn. 1-21.

law[488] not providing the necessary tools for voluntary restructurings to facilitate the rescue of companies in financial distress[489]: the *London Approach.*[490]

The *London Approach* refers to a set of non-binding guidelines[491] which may be

> "*summarised as a non-statutory and informal framework introduced with the support of the Bank of England for dealing with temporary support operations mounted by banks and other lenders to a company or group in financial difficulties, pending a possible restructuring*"[492].

The Bank of England as "*keeper of the London Approach*"[493] intervened in the markets[494] by providing liquidity for companies in need[495] and actively persuading banks to behave in a utilitarian way,[496] not adopting deconstructive measures by strictly enforcing their legal entitlements but rather engaging in the concept of an informal restructuring, thereby protecting the going concern value of the company by guiding agreements on

---

488 *Milmann*, in *De Lacy*, p. 415, 417: "the overriding impression was rather that English law was not interested in constructively engaging in the problem of offering solace to distressed businesses".

489 *Ibid.*, p. 416: "corporate rescue was largely a barren landscape as far as legislation is concerned".

490 *Armour / Deakin*, JCLS 2001, 21 et seq. on the normative aspects of the *London Approach*.

491 For a detailed overview of the guidelines, see *Buljevich*, p. 8 et seq.; also British Banker's Association, *London Approach*, online, 16.2.2004, http://www.bba.org.uk/policy/article/london-approach/fx-and-money-markets-policy, accessed 16.4.2013.

492 *Ibid.*

493 *Clementi*, Deputy Governor or the Bank of England, Speech 19.7.2001, p. 1.

494 *Buljevich*, p. 10: "[The] *London Approach* was indeed very much embedded in a set of cultural, economic, and social institutions and organisations that were peculiar to the United Kingdom in those days [and...] relied primarily on a set of incentives to cooperate and to reach a solution that were linked to several specific elements of the UK corporate and financial sector at that time, including a culture of cooperation, [...] the existence of a legal framework for bankruptcies and insolvency, and the presence of an efficient judicial system that could implement and enforce the legal framework. The particular trust placed by all actors in, and the authoritative leadership of, the Bank of England was also critical to the success of corporate debt restructurings in the United Kingdom".

495 *Ibid.* p. 4, especially liquidity to pay off overdue wages and suppliers to keep the business running. See also *Clementi*, Deputy Governor or the Bank of England, Speech 19.7.2001, p. 2.

496 *Keay / Walton*, p. 195.

new money financing, standstill and forbearance agreements, or special arrangements for the prioritisation of certain debts.[497] The approach towards corporate workouts was welcomed by banks, since a restructuring of companies' debts and nurturing them towards going concern would also limit losses throughout the financial system.[498] One of the aspects of this policy was clearly to minimise the losses of banks arising out of unavoidable company failures and avoid unnecessary liquidations of viable companies facing short-term financial problems despite having a viable future in the long run.

Briefly, the *London Approach*[499] allows for a company experiencing financial distress to initiate a "*workout*" with its major banks, trading the company out of its financial difficulties. The banks involved collectively agree a form of moratorium, not to take any enforcement actions against

---

497 *Buljevich*, p. 5.

498 *Clementi*, Deputy Governor or the Bank of England, Speech 19.7.2001, p. 2.

499 The *London Approach* is also referred to as the *London Rules*. However, see *Clementi*, Deputy Governor or the Bank of England, Speech 19.7.2001, p. 2: "rules" is not the appropriate term for characterising the framework "since the *London Approach* had no legal or statutory backing – it is merely an informal codification of a set of practices that had come to be widely accepted in the vast majority of large corporate workouts undertaken in the United Kingdom in recent years." See *Buljevich*, p. 7: the Bank of England always refrained from having the guidelines as means of a formal policy document to not have these rules challenged in court, wanting to keep these rules as flexible as possible to encourage voluntary acceptance of the restructuring community. This is why it is still referred to the *London Approach*. See also *Howard / Hedger*, mn. 1-22: "they are not rules and they are not prescriptive"; *Armour / Deakin*, JCLS 2001, 21: "social norms".
From a legal theory point of view, one may argue that even though the *London Rules* are no legal rules in a normative order or legal system and have, therefore, no validity in the sense of being authorised and sanctioned by an authority or enforced if necessary, they have established rather a moral obligation, relying upon the honour of the parties involved for its fulfilment. The *London Approach* is more like a gentlemen's agreement: an informal agreement, rather oral than written, which codify and approach, widely accepted between the lenders in the London market ("The City") and the UK in general on how to deal with companies in financial distress by following a standardised process structure. This ensures their effectiveness. It is fair to say that the *London Approach* fulfils the aim of addressing both efficiency and ethics. See *Wood*, Philip, The Law and Practice of International Finance, mn. 1-23; *Easterbrook*, 27 J Fin. Econ. (1990), 411, 413: "laws also may have a moral bases but there are unlikely explanations for the rules governing corporate bankruptcy".

the company and to keep the existing lines of credit open. Further working capital may need to be provided to keep the company trading as a going concern. Any such new money is given priority status over existing debt. During this *workout* period, a team of accountants investigates the company's position and the team's findings are used collectively by the banks to decide on the next steps. If the business has a viable business model and can be saved, a restructuring is initiated. If the business cannot be saved, the costs incurred up to this point are shared pro rata between all the participating banks and the company is dissolved. If a rescue is feasible, one bank will lead the restructuring negotiations. The lead bank will act as the intermediary between the parties involved. The ultimate result may typically be a debt compromise or some form of debt-equity-swap. The banks share the financial benefit of allowing the company to avoid formal insolvency. The *London Approach* is a collective procedure which benefits all the participants. This is because, although a particular bank may benefit from sitting on its legal rights in certain situations, over a period of time adoption of the *London Approach* prevents any huge losses to any particular bank at any particular time and leads to many businesses being turned around. All the investigations and negotiations are kept secret so as not to destroy confidence in the company involved.[500]

Market interventions and the supply of liquidity under a favourable credit climate led to a rather positive attitude in the London market towards corporate debt, where companies stocked massive bank borrowings[501] and lenders did not have much control over how the money was spent. However, when the economic downturn began at the beginning of the 1990s, companies were not prepared to service the unsustainably high level of debt financing. At that time, the Bank of England reviewed its former approach and, this time, let the private sector parties[502] develop and

500 *Keay / Walton*, p. 196: there are no official figures available, however, the relatively small number of large companies which enter formal insolvency proceedings may be viewed as success.

501 *Buljevich*, p. 6: companies benefitted from more favourable, flexible lending terms, driving the innovation / development of hedging instruments, the emergence of complex syndicated facilities with different tranches and leverage buyout schemes. See also *Milmann*, in *De Lacy*, p. 415, 417, fn. 14.

502 *Buljevich*, p. 13: private sector engagement "provides better incentives for recovery and for avoiding future losses of banks [...and] it encourages banks participating in the process to provide additional financing" and "it reduces the influence of political considerations in debt restructuring decisions".

consummate restructuring approaches.[503] The Bank of England reformulated its guidelines for lenders to create their own workout proposals and to govern multi-bank restructuring situations.[504]

The drawbacks of the *London Approach* include the need for unanimity, which may easily be achieved within a small group of creditors but it becomes challenging within a large diversified group,[505] thereby delaying or impairing the workout process, since it gives holdout lenders, no matter how insignificant, an effective veto power. In addition, a company in financial distress cannot benefit from a formal moratorium or stay to protect it from outside creditor pressure or attacks during the workout process. This is because although the *London Approach* generally entails an informal standstill granted by creditors during the initial stages of a restructuring, it does not necessarily afford the firm a formal moratorium over part or all of the restructuring process. The lack of automatic stay protection can make it more difficult to protect a distressed company from the attacks of unwilling creditors, who can sometimes endanger or undermine the workout effort.[506]

Over the last two decades the *London Approach* has served as a source of inspiration for the way different countries have tackled the problem of massive corporate debts in distress.[507] Because many countries' institutional and legal frameworks were inadequate to overcome the complexities of widespread insolvencies, many nations[508] have adopted principles

503 *Ibid.,* p. 6. See also *Howard / Hedger*, mn. 1-21.

504 *Buljevich*, p. 6-7.

505 *Clementi*, Deputy Governor or the Bank of England, Speech 19.7.2001, p. 3: insurance companies, institutional investors, bond holders, hedge funds and secondary market debt providers.

506 *Buljevich*, p. 9.

507 *Ibid.,* p. 13, 14 :"governments may need to recognise the peculiar links between corporate and financial sector distresses when dealing with policy decisions for overcoming a systemic distressed debt situation. Corporate and financial sector restructurings generally are two sides of the same problem in a country facing a systemic financial crisis". See also *Clementi*, Deputy Governor or the Bank of England, Speech 19.7.2001, p. 3.

508 As such, the *London Approach* guidelines inspired such local variants as the *Bangkok Rules*, the *Jakarta Initiative*, and the *Argentine Approach*, see *Buljevich*, p. 12.

based on the *London Approach* in accordance with their own needs to encourage informal rescue procedures.

"The dead hand of the zombies[509] *is casting a shadow over the economy."*[510]

One of the detriments of facilitating the imminent rescue of distressed companies as opposed to letting them fail is the emergence of *zombie companies*, presenting a drag on economic recovery.[511] Those companies hardly generate enough cash to service their debt,[512] let alone invest in new opportunities.[513]

When business failures began to increase in 2009, the Bank of England cut interest rates to a record low to avoid insolvencies and an increase in unemployment.[514] Although the underlying economics of companies had changed, banks continued their lending with tightened credit terms to avoid strains on companies that could have led to financial distress. With the departure of low-cost easily accessible debt, companies needed to quickly adjust to ensure that they could continue to fund the growth of their businesses. The larger the debts owed by a company, the less likely its bankers are to take precipitate action against it. While banks are obliged to make provisions for loans in distress, the rescue approach encourages banks to nurse companies back to financial health.[515] This is not for altruistic reasons but avoids realising further, potentially significant, losses for the bank by recognising the problem in a timely manner.[516] This may be achieved either by extending the companies' credit terms on very

---

509 *Brooke*, The New York Times online, 29.10.2002: the term first emerged in the 1980s and 1990s when U.S. saving and loan associations and Japanese banks "in the land of economic harmony" were supported by the politics of cheap money provided by the central banks. While the term was initially applied to the financial sector, it had a spill-over to businesses. In the UK, this refers to service companies, manufacturers, builders and retailers squeezed by recession and online shopping. See also *Pym*, BBC News online, 13.11.2012: *zombie companies* is not a phrase that bankers and regulators like to use. And indeed, there is neither much research nor much debate on the *zombies* in the UK or anywhere else in Europe.

510 *Pym*, BBC News online, 13.11.2012.

511 *Laryea*, IMF 2010, p. 5.

512 *Ledwith / Watling*, Reuters online, 13.9.2013.

513 *Pym*, BBC News online, 13.11.2012.

514 *Ledwith / Watling*, Reuters online, 13.9.2013.

515 *Keay / Walton*, p. 315.

516 *Buljevich*, p. 14; also *Swain*, CR&I 2008, 4: "cleaning of loan portfolio".

low interest rates to keep their businesses running or by applying forbearance, and instead of crystallising a loss on the loan[517] giving the company a breathing space and avoiding making tough decisions. However, when competition for working capital and liquidity becomes fiercer and banks enforce strong financial discipline in companies, they might be reluctant to engage in new lending if the money is tied up in *zombie companies*.[518] And while the more viable *zombies* may recover, the weaker ones will eventually fail,[519] which in turn leads to higher unemployment.[520]

While insolvencies are picking up,[521] it remains to be seen whether the Bank of England will keep interest rates low to avoid the wave of insolvencies expected or end the time of cheap lending and increase rates.[522] Although the Bank of England as a regulatory body is also focused on reducing the insolvency risk of financial institutions,[523] authorities like the Financial Supervisory Authority have urged banks to build up their capital reserves in order to bear losses when debt becomes distressed.[524] In addition, policy measures such as forbearance on capital adequacy requirements or on loss provisioning have been provided.[525] Thus, the English insolvency system, rather than helping the economy to move towards

517 *Buljevich*, p. 14.

518 *Pym*, BBC News online, 13.11.2012.

519 *Ibid.,* From the estimated 146,000 *zombie businesses* in the UK, a third of these could be doomed to failure if interest rates go up. See also *Ledwith / Watling*, Reuters online, 13.9.2013: the *zombie count* has declined to just over 100.000, however, more than 200.000 UK companies, nearly 8% of the total, are counted to be in financial distress. Recounting the companies with a negative net worth, the number would rise to 227.000, combining a negative net worth of GBP 70 billion.

520 *Ledwith / Watling*, Reuters online, 13.9.2013: 4.4% of the British work force is employed by *zombie businesses*.

521 Britain's Insolvency Service: in Q2/2013, there were an estimated 4,000 insolvencies a month, which was still behind the average rate in 2009-12 but higher than in Q1/2013.

522 *Ledwith / Watling*, Reuters online, 13.9.2013; Lilico, cityam 5.11.2013, p. 24.

523 *Wood*, Philip, The Law and Practice of International Finance, mn. 1-23.

524 *Pym*, BBC News online, 13.11.2012.

525 *Buljevich*, p. 14: policy measures may undermine progress on corporate and financial sector debt restructurings, particularly in those countries with weak insolvency and foreclosure systems. See also *Pym*, BBC News online, 13.11.2012: "forbearance […] has been a matter of concern for regulators".

long-run efficiency, in fact appears to delay the movement of resources to higher value uses, suffocating economic growth.[526]

4.3 Summary

The Bank of England compared to the German Federal Bank took a proactive approach in providing the necessary liquidity to companies in the financial crisis in the late 1970s. While the *London Approach* has supported the attitude towards restructuring as opposed to liquidations and thereby the development of a rescue culture, it has also led to *zombie companies* that may be even a greater threat to a recovering economy than they would have been if there were allowed to fail when their time passed.

Banks are especially prone to these *zombies* as they would need to write-off their debt if those companies would begin to fail. Before the ECB will take over the supervision of systemically important financial institutions around Europe,[527] it will carry out a stress-test and an asset-quality review on banks' balance sheet. It remains to be seen whether these zombies will then see the light of day and eventually disappear, hopefully leaving not only dead corps behind that could initiate another financial crisis.

5 Judicial Infrastructure: Courts and Administrators

The judicial infrastructure, consisting mainly of courts and insolvency administers, should maximise the effectiveness of the insolvency proceeding and be reasonably stable and predictable for creditors and debtors to give them legal certainty in and about the process.[528] One of the prerequisites for a successful restructuring for companies is to file for insolvency as

---

526 *Bloom / Cairns*, ICR 2012, 223.

527 Communication department of the European Commission "Commission proposes new ECB powers for banking supervision as part of a banking union", 12 September 2012, accessed 05.10. 2013. See also *Wymeersch*, ZGR 2011, 443 et seq.

528 *Wood*, Philip, The Law and Practice of International Finance, mn. 1-23.

early as possible rather than wait until the last minute when the train for going concern has already long passed.[529]

5.1 Germany

With ESUG, various provisions regarding the insolvency courts and administrators were amended, especially to encourage an earlier application for insolvency proceedings.[530]

5.1.1 Courts

The decision to open insolvency proceedings is made by the court when the prerequisites are fulfilled. Which power the court exercises depends on insolvency proceeding chosen or required.

In the past, the number of insolvency courts[531] gave particularly rise to criticism.[532] The high number was a reason for the courts' (partial) inexperience and low qualification in dealing with insolvency plan procedure and self-administrations. A reform of the judiciary was perceived to be the required mean to promote effective corporate restructuring. Considerations related to the concentration of insolvency courts[533] in the district court (*Landgericht*)[534] or Court of Appeal (*Oberlandesgericht*)[535].Thus, the necessary experience would be gained, enabled insolvency judges to be specifically trained.[536] At least for corporate insolvencies this should not

529 *Römermann*, GWR2011, 375.

530 *Braun / Heinrich*, NZI 2011, 505, 516; *Piekenbrock*, NZI 2012, 905, 906.

531 There are 187 lower district courts (Amtsgerichte) able to open an insolvency proceeding, see INDat-Insolvenzstatistik (www.indat.info/statistiken.php, accessed 3.8.2013).

532 *Uhlenbruck*, INDat-Report 6/2007, p. 10; *Kranzusch/Icks*, p. 20.

533 *Leutheusser-Schnarrenberger*, ZInsO 2010, 641, 615; *Eidenmüller*, ZIP 2010, 649, 659; *Jaffé / Friedrich*, ZIP 2008, 1849, 1851.

534 There are 116 district courts (*Landgericht*). The governments of the Länder shall be empowered to designate other or additional local courts as insolvency courts (Sec. 2(2) InsO).

535 There are 24 Courts of Appeal (Oberlandesgerichte).

536 *Rendels / Zabel*, INDat-Report 3/2010, 54, 59.

be a problem for some courts.[537] The question was also the division of work between insolvency judges and registrars (*Rechtspfleger*) to allow an efficient procedure.[538] In general, it is a political problem and the legislator has been lacking the willpower to initiate a structural court reform.

The legislature first planned to concentrate the powers of insolvency courts, according to other countries, such as England.[539] There should have just been one insolvency court for each district court.[540] This concentration, however, was abandoned and, in accordance with the principle of subsidiarity, left to the federal state (*Bundesland*)[541]. The expertise of the courts should be encouraged. The insolvency judges must have specific knowledge of insolvency law, corporate and commercial law.[542] For insolvency plan proceedings, in future, only insolvency judges are responsible.[543]

The German judge must adhere to the strict rules of civil procedure.[544] The legal finding in a case is not determined by the judge's individual discretion. The power of discretion is lower. The judge's boundary is the wording of the law, which is exactly composed by the legislature. Only in exceptional cases, the German judge has a discretionary power. For judicial development of the law there is only limited space in Germany. Most judges have been born to the bench, having never gained experience with insolvency proceedings themselves.

---

537 The insolvency court with the most corporate insolvencies in Germany (31.7.2013) is by far Berlin-Charlottenburg, see INDat-Insolvenzstatistik (www.indat.info/statistiken.php, accessed 3.8.2013).

538 *Hingerl*, ZInsO 2009, 759 et seq.; *Erdmann*, ZInsO 2010, 1437 et seq.

539 *Jaffé*, ZGR 2010, 248, 254 et seq.; *Medla*, p. 91 et seq.

540 Sec. (2)(2)(4) RegE-ESUG.

541 BMJ, RegE-EUSG, BT-Drucks. 17/7511, p. 2.

542 *Römermann*, GWR 2011, 375.

543 See Chapter III 7.1.4.4 for further criticism on the role of insolvency judges in opening insolvency procedures in self-administration. See also *Huep*, ZInsO 2012, 405.

544 *Jasper*, p. 135.

5.1.2 Administrator

Insolvency administrators[545] are often the key person in insolvency proceedings[546] as they are the "*keeper of interests of all interests involved in an insolvency proceeding*"[547], the success, especially in insolvency plan proceedings, does not solely depend on the person.[548]

Insolvency administrators balance the various interests and conflict of interests between the parties involved.[549] Their role was, therefore, also a major discussion point in the context of the insolvency law reform.[550] Critical points include the appointment of the insolvency administrator, the qualifications, the high costs and the low motivation to engage in corporate restructurings.[551] Not only have insolvency administrators been accused of not effectively using the legal instruments for corporate restructuring opposed to liquidation provided by the Insolvency Statute due to their lack of qualifications,[552] but with the remuneration practice they would also mainly be serving their own interests.[553]

545 The insolvency monitor has similar duties and rights as the insolvency administrator, see Chapter III 7.1.4.5 on the duties of the insolvency monitor.

546 *Meyer*, Haftung des vorläufigen Insolvenzverwalters; *Kruth*, Auswahl und Bestellung des Insolvenzverwalters; *Graeber*, Kölner Schrift zur InsO, 2009, p. 299 et seq.; *Köhler-Ma*, DZWIR 2006, 228 et seq.; *Frind*, ZInsO 2007, 643et seq.; *Frind*, ZInsO 2008, 655 et seq.; *Frind*, ZInsO 2009, 1638 et seq.; *Stephan*, ZVglRWiss 2009, 273 et seq.; *Schlinker / Henke*, ZInsO 2010, 503 et seq.; *Neubert*, ZInsO 2010, 73 et seq.

547 RegE-InsO, BT-Drucks. 12/2443, p. 80.

548 *Paulus*, ZIP 2005, 2301, 2302.

549 *Kumpan*, KTS 2010, 169 et seq.

550 *Graeber*, Kölner Schrift zur InsO, p. 300.

551 *Jungbluth*, ZEIT 2.4.2009, p.4.

552 *Weber*, SZ online 17.5.2010; *Amann / Balzter*, FAZ 26.5.2009, p. 12.

553 The remuneration of insolvency administrators, settled by the "Insolvenzrechtliche Vergütungsordnung (InVV)", is based on the insolvency mass to be distributed at the end of the proceeding and additional sums for complexity of the proceeding. This provision may accumulate large amounts to be paid to the insolvency administrators.

Appointment of the Insolvency Administrator

A much-discussed aspect in the past was the appointment of the insolvency administrator.[554] The criticism, especially from the Anglo-Saxon financial investors,[555] was directed particularly at the lack of transparency,[556] inadequate administrator selection and the lack of participation of creditors in the selection process of the insolvency administrator.[557] Especially strengthened creditor participation was demanded to reduce the unpredictable risk of appointment and, more importantly because the administrator primarily represents all the creditors' interests in insolvency proceedings.[558]

ESUG reformed in part the appointment of the administrator. It introduced a preliminary creditors' committee,[559] which has an influence in the appointment of the liquidator.[560] The preliminary creditors' committee has to be heard with respect to the administrator if no disadvantages of the financial circumstances of the debtor are expected.[561] This regulation will

554 Among others *Kruth*, Auswahl und Bestellung des Insolvenzverwalters.

555 *Westphal / Janjuah*, ZIP 2008, Beil. 3, p. 8 et seq.

556 *Weber*, SZ online 17.5.2010. There is a list of insolvency administrators in every regional court for the judge to choose from. It is in the judge's discretion who he is selecting for a case.

557 Although the creditors may elect a different person as insolvency administrator at the first creditors' meeting in case the majority (Sec. 76 Abs. 2 InsO) voted for him, in practice the general direction of the insolvency proceeding has been already decided upon so that this rule is rather useless, see *Eidenmüller*, ZIP 2007, 1729, 1733; *Frind*, ZInsO 2010, 1161, 1166; *Westphal / Janjuah*, ZIP 2008, Beil. 3, p. 1, 10; *Willemsen / Rechel*, BB 2010, 2059, 2061.

558 *Jaffé / Friedrich*, ZIP 2008, 1849; *Kumpan*, KTS 2010, 169 et seq.

559 Ss. 21(2)(1)(no.1a), 22a InsO. Critical *Willemsen / Rechel*, BB 2011, 834, 835; *Urlaub*, ZIP 2011, 1040 et seq.; *Pape*, ZInsO 2011, 1033, 1037 et seq.

560 The Green Paper did not provide provisions for the pre-selection of the insolvency administrator. See *Graf-Schlicker*, in INDat-Report 6/2010, p. 28, 30. In addition, see BMJ, Begr. RegE-ESUG, ZIP 2011, Beil.1, 9 et seq. The provisions were further substantiated in the White Paper.

561 Sec. 56a(2) InsO. Critical *Smid*, DZWIR 2010, 397, 399 et seq.: *Frind*, ZInsO 2010, 1473, 1476 et seq.; *Pape*, ZInsO 2010, 1582, 1587 et seq.; *Vallender*, NZI 2010, 838, 843 et seq.: the time to fulfil the formal requirements may have a negative impact on the restructuring by delaying the appropriate measures. See also *Piepenburg*, NZI 2004, 231, 234 et seq. that there are no requirements for coordination between insolvency administrators in group insolvencies, which may even delay the restructuring further and thereby destroy company value.

strengthen the creditors' influence on the appointment of the insolvency administrator.[562]

The proposed change on the neutrality of the administrator did not pass. The administrator should not automatically lose its neutrality by generally informing the debtor about the insolvency plan procedure or supporting the preparation of an insolvency plan. Therefore, the insolvency administrator still cannot be involved in the early creation of an insolvency plan. This is unfortunate. It could have led to the case where the companies would actually get early assistance in the preparation of a restructuring plan and file earlier for insolvency, increasing the chances of a successful restructuring.

Qualification of the Insolvency Administrator

In Germany, most insolvency administrators have a legal background rather than an economic and business background, which was the reason to suggest the application of necessary quality standards to an insolvency administrator.[563] Larger law firms would benefit from these quality standards as they have the manpower to provide them, eventually leading to a consolidation in the market of insolvency administrators.[564]

Most insolvency administrators reject those standards as "*impractical, bureaucratic and ultimately counter-productive*"[565]. To ensure the much needed business qualifications in addition to the legal education of the administrator, a professional association could be established similar to the auditors.[566] A similar system is already in place in England.[567] The ques-

562 *Frind*, ZInsO 2010, 1473, 1474 et seq.; *Pape*, ZInsO 2010, 1582, 1587. The group of "major creditors" was withdrawn as well as the factual binding of the insolvency court on the suggestion of the insolvency administrator by a group of creditors or majority creditor, which was heavily criticised in the legislative process.

563 *Lambrecht*, DZWIR 2010, 22 et seq. See also *Römermann*, GWR 2011, 375: the lack of quality standards "contributed to the disaster of the German insolvency system".

564 *Huep*, ZInsO 2012, 405.

565 *Gravenbrucher Kreis*, ZIP 1992, 658 et seq.

566 *Köster*, RIW 2006, 24, 27; *Vallender*, NZI 2010, 838, 843; *Paulus*, WM 2011, 2205, 2210.

567 *Köster*, RIW 2006, 24, 25 et seq.

tion arises whether the involvement of creditors in the appointment of the insolvency administrator or the qualification of the insolvency administrator could be a sufficient basis for the application of the insolvency plan proceeding.[568]

5.2 England

The English approach to allow for restructuring is rather advanced and carried out professionally by English courts and administrators.

5.2.1 Courts

The participation of courts is dependent on the proceeding.[569] The Bankruptcy and Companies Court is part of the Chancery Division, which itself is part of the High Court of Justice.[570] The High Court has jurisdiction to wind up any company registered in England and Wales.[571] Where the amount of a company's share capital paid up or credited as paid up does not exceed £120,000 then the county court of the district in which the company's registered office is situated has concurrent jurisdiction with the High Court to wind up the company.[572] Every county court having winding-up jurisdiction has all the powers of the High Court.[573] For the purpose of determining which county court has jurisdiction to wind up a company, that company's registered office is the place which has longest been its registered office during the six months immediately preceding the presentation of the winding-up petition.[574] Cases are dealt by six registrars who are the judges who deal with the majority of cases. Appeals from their decisions are to a single judge of the Chancery Division.

The judges in England have a long tradition of playing an active role in insolvency proceedings. Most of them are not only legally but also com-

568 See Chapter III 7.1.4.3.
569 *Müller-Seils*, p. 85.
570 Homepage Justice Department, http://www.judiciary.gov.uk/you-and-the-judiciary/going-to-court/high-court, accessed 15.5.2013.
571 Sec. 117(1) IA 1986.
572 Sec. 117(2)(3) IA 1986. *Müller-Seils*, p. 85, Fn. 404.
573 Sec. 117(5) IA 1986.
574 Sec. 117(6) IA 1986.

mercially trained as they worked as professionals in restructuring and insolvency before being appointed to the court. Due to the fact that they deal with all cases of companies where the company's share capital is larger than £120,000 they have a valuable experience in dealing with restructurings and insolvencies. They deliberate on the facts presented in their court and then decide on whether they are responsible for the case. A claimant has to recognise that the judges have discretionary powers.[575] Even if the precedents have been decided differently, the claimant still has a chance to convince the judge on his arguments to decide in his favour in the specific case. In England, the judges not only apply the law, the make the law by their discretionary decisions. The process is a cornerstone of legal tradition and runs like a red thread through English jurisdiction.[576]

English law is a preferred jurisdiction.[577] The City of London as the financial centre in Europe is also the root of complex financial structures. The court that deals with these issues is the High Court of London, which is the reason why this court has special and qualified knowledge, particularly in insolvencies and restructurings. It is also aware that "*the City of London is vital to the economic well-being of the country*"[578].

5.2.2 Administrators

The insolvency practitioner is the person responsible for the company's affairs once insolvency has been tested,[579] and is differentiated between liquidator[580], administrator or administrative receiver[581] and depends on whether the company is liquidated or restructured.[582] The insolvency practitioners generally tend to consider reorganising a financially distressed

---

575 *Baird / Rasmussen*, 119 Yale L. J. (2009-2010) 648, 698, discussing the academic critique of bankruptcy judges: exercising too much discretion and too quick to depart from the strict letter of law.

576 *Jasper*, p. 135.

577 *Jasper*, p. 21, 26: For other Commonwealth States or former colonies, English law is generally the role model. See also *Milman*, Preface.

578 *Milman*, p. 21: examples of thought processes to underline the awareness of English courts.

579 *Campbell*, p. 11 et seq.

580 Ss. 91(1), 100(1), 143(1) IA 1986. See *Goode*, mn. 5-02 et seq.

581 *Ibid.*, mn. 9-01 et seq.

582 *Kumpan*, KTS 2010, 169, 181 et seq.

company by way of a combination of administration with a company voluntary arrangement in order to rescue the company as a going concern.[583]

The administrator is appointed where the company is presently or in the future unable to pay its debt and where the objective of the administration, restructuring the company, is reasonably likely to be achieved.[584] The administrator has far-reaching powers to carry out his duties.[585] Wide statutory powers[586] enable the administrator to perform all acts necessary or expedient for the management of the affairs, business and property of the company.[587] His duties are carried out in the interest of all creditors.[588] As most administrators and insolvency administrators tend to be accountants with a business and legal expertise,[589] English courts accept their principle economic decisions when they are taken based on adequate information and are reasonable.[590]

The administrator is the one who analyses the company and then makes a decision as to whether rescuing a company as a going concern is reasonably practicable or not. If a company is facing a short term cash flow problem and the major creditors in respect of the company, or any third party, is willing to inject funds for the troubled company to continue trading, then the administrator may conclude a going concern. If there is no prospect of new financing becoming available for the company to continue trading during the moratorium, the practice shows that the administrators rather continue with the sale of the company's assets as a going concern than a piecemeal sale of the assets in liquidation for the benefit of the creditors.

---

583 For the purpose of the thesis, the focus is therefore on the administrator.

584 *DKLL Solicitors v Revenue and Customs Commissioners* [2007] BCC 908.

585 *Müller-Seils*, p. 125 et seq.

586 Sch. 1 IA 1986, Sch. B1 ss. 59(2), 60 IA 1986. See also *Müller-Seils*, p. 126 et seq.

587 Sch. B1 sec. 59(1) IA 1986.

588 Sch. B1 sec. 3(2) IA 1986. See also *Kumpan*, KTS 2010, 169, 181: The administrator is always also an "agent" of the company (Sch. B1 sec. 69 IA 1986) and has fiduciary duties. In addition, see *Keay / Walton*, mn. 7.5.3.2 (administrator); *Mokal / Armour*, ICR 2004, 136, 137.

589 *Moss*, 23 Brook. J. Int'l L. (1997) 115.

590 *DKLL Solicitors v Revenue and Customs Commissioners* [2007] BCC 908: "The court places great reliance on the expertise of impartial insolvency practitioners." See also *Großfeld*, ZVglRWiss 113 (2014) 4, 14: "Lawyers need to understand accounting thoroughly to present a clear road-map for solutions. [...] Only then jurors can make heads and tails on what is going on."

Administrators have also played an active role in European cross-border insolvency cases.[591] One of the reasons why administrators are perceived to be more active is due to the fact that creditors may choose their administrators and discuss with them plans on how to restructure the company early in the process.

5.3 Summary

A developed legal system to deal with restructuring is an important prerequisite to maximise the effectiveness in the proceedings and create legal certainty for all parties involved. Germany has made progress in dealing with restructuring since the last insolvency reform and even more with ESUG, however, due to the lack of specialised court and judges trained in commercial matters, there is still legal uncertainty involved when deciding on a restructuring rather than a liquidation. The involvement of the creditors' committee in appointing the insolvency administrators may increase creditors' trust, however, insolvency administrators have been subject to criticism themselves when they refused to accept specific industry standards on their education.

Industry standards that have been long established in England for administrators, which may also be one of the reasons why judges, as well being commercially and legally trained prior to their appointment to the bench, trust their decisions. Despite that, judges in England play an active role in restructuring, not just for English but also for foreign companies. The question for them in many cases is not whether they have jurisdiction but rather whether they are exercising it. This pro-active approach towards restructuring, providing adequate court capacity and professional practitioners, being able to implement the necessary measures for a successful restructuring, has made the English judicial system a well-established and trusted locations for companies, English and foreign.

591 *Paulus*, RabelsZ Bd. 70 (2006), 458.

6 Financial Markets and Corporate Finance

"Liquidity is the lifeblood of reorganisations."[592]

Another aspect to be taken into consideration in regarding a nation's legal culture and its legal competitiveness is the support of the commercial environment,[593] a developed financial system and efficient markets. These provide not only the access to liquidity but also allow for the ability to value assets and businesses accurately.[594] Corporate finance is essential to allow economies to exploit the gains from trade.[595] The developments in and transformation of corporate finance[596] attributed to the challenges in restructuring. Globalisation of the financial markets and the growth of alternative lender constituencies have caused banks to no longer serve as the leading financiers in the current global economy.[597] Nowadays financial instruments like mezzanine debt, bonds, convertibles, warrants or other securities are an alternative to bank financing. While in the past banks kept their assets on the balance sheet, nowadays, they securitise the debt and sell it on the global capital market for their refinancing.

In many cases, companies do not even know anymore who their creditors are as credit derivatives[598] and lenders' participations have also weakened the relationship between the original lenders and a borrower in financial difficulty.[599] With the transfer of credit risk from the original lender to another institution, the hedged lender has little motivation to find a voluntary restructuring solution since its potential loss may be either limited or otherwise fully or partially transferred to the participant. This

---

592 *Westbrook / Gottlieb*, 27 ABIJ (2009) 10. See also *Munro*, p. 140.

593 *Vriesendorp / Gramatikov*, 19 Int. Insolv. Rev. (2010) 209, 210.

594 *López Gutiérrez et al.*, IRLE 29 (2009) 229 et seq. for empirical influence of bankruptcy law on equity value of financially distressed firms; *Chrystal / Mokal*, ICR 2006, 63-68, 123 et seq. for example of valuation on *Re MyTravel Group Plc* [2005] 1 WLR 2365. Also *Lys / Sivaramakrishnan*, 26 Journal of Accounting Research (1988) 273 et seq.; *Kokkoris*, ICR 2005, 337 et seq., *Eidenmüller*, Unternehmenssanierung, p. 36 et seq.; *Chatterji / Hedges*, p. 19.

595 *Allen / Gale*, p. 25.

596 *Finch*, J.B.L. 2008, 756, 758.

597 *Dakin et al.*, CR&I 2012, 120 et seq.; *Patel / Fennessy*, ICR 2006, 255.

598 *Finch*, J.B.L. 2008, 756, 761 et seq.; *Baird / Rasmussen*, 119 Yale L. J. (2009-2010) 648, 678 et seq.

599 *Buljevich*, p. 10. *Clementi*, Deputy Governor or the Bank of England, Speech 19.7.2001, p. 2.

leads to a high degree of complexity in a restructuring situation and it has become increasingly difficult to reconcile the agendas of different creditors participating in modern debt restructurings. Moreover, distressed debt trading, which became widespread only in the last decade, has introduced a new dimension to the restructuring arena, contributing to either solving or complicating a restructuring process.[600]

While the local bank would like to support the restructuring for relationship purposes, other banks or investors will try to reach a high recovery rate by enforcing their claims. Another reason for involvement in a corporate restructuring also exists when the restructuring is pursued with a high degree of public interest or the restructuring involves a company providing social services.[601]

Corporate finance has been a focus not only in the light of the restructuring of companies in financial distress but in general. This is mainly due to the fact that the financial crisis has led to a further tightening of capital rules for banks. The cost of capital is usually passed on to the credit markets and, therefore, to debtors.[602] Legislation has paid significantly stricter attention to credit risk and the capital requirements of banks in the aftermath of the financial crisis.[603] The corporate rating, measuring the probability of a company defaulting in the next year, provides the basis for the credit terms of the company's credit.[604] In accordance with the capital requirements of banks, higher risk leads to premiums in credit conditions.[605] In addition, the loan portfolio of a bank should not be biased towards specific industries to avoid concentration risks. Higher capital requirements due to the higher capital requirements of banks could particularly affect poorly rated companies or those from riskier sectors, as it makes lending more expensive for additional funding that is desperately needed for a going concern.[606] It may eventually lead to failure of companies not able to afford the terms any longer.[607] The suspicion was, especially in Ger-

600 *Milmann*, in *De Lacy*, p. 415, 417, fn. 14: "vulture funds" or hedge funds specialised in distressed debt play an aggressive role in disrupting proposed rescues by relying upon their strict legal rights.
601 For example *Southern Cross Healthcare Group PLC*, September 2011.
602 *Heinrich*, in FS Greiner, p. 111.
603 *Becker et al.*, KTS 2011, 53, 54 et seq.
604 *Bonfim et al.*, 36 JBF (2012), 2007 et seq.
605 *Machauer / Weber*, 22 JBF (1998), 1355 et seq.
606 *Vriesendorp / Gramatikov*, 19 Int. Insolv. Rev. (2010) 209, 210.
607 *Heinrich*, in FS Greiner, p. 111.

many, that this would lead to a credit crunch,[608] which would have a significant affect not only on companies in financial distress but also on viable companies no longer able to meet their capital requirements for their daily business.[609] This would trigger a downward spiral if the losses eroded equity, and equity investors and creditors were not willing to provide more liquidity to ensure the going concern of the company and return to profitability. In order to avoid over-indebtedness, a debt-equity swap could be implemented.

However, there are provisions to be accounted for when bank engage in debt-equity-swaps.[610] The accounting treatment of a debt-equity-swap has important implications for lenders, revolving around the impact of the swap on their loan-loss provisions and the on-going valuation of the shares acquired. A debt-equity-swap may require additional capital to be allocated to equity holdings. Depending on the threshold, the shareholding in the company may be treated as an associate and adverse capital adequacy requirements may apply.

6.1 Germany

In the historical context of financial markets,[611] Germany's approach is *bank-oriented*[612] with the *Hausbank* system having provided the primary funding for companies for a long time.[613] Based on this long-term relationship in good and in bad times, German banks have been willing to extend their lending in a crisis situation or, in rare cases, to hold equity in non-financial firms[614] rather than selling their position to the highest

608 *Vriesendorp / Gramatikov*, 19 Int. Insolv. Rev (2010) 209, 227; *Becker et al.*, KTS 2011, 53.

609 While in the direct aftermath of the financial crisis, the fear was unsubstantiated (http://www.blicklog.com/2008/11/21/bundesbank-sieht-keinen-credit-crunch-in-deutschland/), the demands for loans was weaker towards the end of 2012 (https://www.kfw.de/KfW-Group/Newsroom/Aktuelles/Pressemitteilungen/Pressemitteilungen-Details_39572.html).

610 *James*, Rev. Fin. Stud. 1995, 1210, 1221 on empirical evidence.

611 *Allen / Gale*, p.36 et seq. for development of the German financial system.

612 *Kunz / Ehnert*, FINANCE Betrieb 7-8/2007, p. 397 for discussing *relationship banking*.

613 *Ibid.*, p. 37. See also *Größl / Levratto*, DEP, p. 26, 33; *Elsas / Krahnen*, 22 JBF (1998) 1283 et seq.; *Harhoff / Timm*, 22 JBF (1998) 1317 et seq.

614 *Allen / Gale*, p. 73.

bidder in the secondary market.[615] However, the importance of banks in the German financial market[616] was also due to the fact that only relatively few companies are publicly traded[617] and most relied for their primary funding on banks.

This has changed over the last ten years now that companies have discovered the potential of funding via capital markets by means of various corporate finance instruments. Nowadays the long-term relationship is not a primary focus anymore.[618] A provision in most loan agreements allows banks to sell companies' loans in the secondary market or for asset securitisation for the banks' own refinancing. Restructuring or insolvency negotiations on debtors' futures was usually agreed upon and settled in small manageable creditors' committees, with mostly banks around the table. Due to the changes in funding and a much more diverse creditor base, restructuring negotiations are now much more difficult and time-consuming than in the past.

Banks in Germany have refrained from acting as entrepreneurs by holding an equity position in a company as a result of a debt-equity-swap. This was not part of their traditional role. With the amendment of the German Insolvency Statute, the question is whether banks will now be more willing to become (at least temporarily) shareholders of companies in financial distress to save their claim. If the company is rescued, banks participate in the success; if not, they have forfeited their interest rights on the principal. The practice in restructuring companies in financial distress in the aftermath of the financial crisis has shown that banks are more likely to consider providing further liquidity (new money) with priority rights rather than implementing a debt-equity-swap. In order to clean up their portfolios, banks would sell their assets with a discount in the secondary market. For companies with a weak balance sheet and/or negative net worth and no viable business model, banks would rather enforce their claims via an insolvency proceeding to recover (at least a portion of) their assets in the liquidation of the company. The market mechanism works whereby companies with no viable business model or no liquidity to service their debt are forced to exit.

---

615 *Jostarndt / Rodt*, in FS Rudolph, 1100, 1103.

616 *Allen / Gale*, p. 71.

617 *Ibid.*, p. 38.

618 *Zheng et al*, JBF 36 (2012), 468 et seq.: national culture influence on the choice of debt maturity.

6.2 England

The *bank-oriented* approach is in contrast to the Anglo-Saxon *stock-market* model,[619] where companies have already acquired financing on the capital markets for decades. An important aspect of this development is that the banking system frequently engages in short-term rather than long-term loans.[620] The stock exchange allows for the active trading of distressed debt positions. It is not for nothing that most distressed investors are located in London[621] or New York, where the infrastructure is accessible.[622] Banks in England are more likely to engage in a debt-equity-swap in order to rescue a company and provide for a debt structure and debt capacity that allows for a going concern of the company despite the capital requirements of Basel.[623] However, there is one (if not the most) important factor that differentiates restructuring negotiations in England from those in Germany and which has been discussed before: the *London Approach*.[624]

6.3 Summary

Financial institutions are one of the most important business partners for companies, providing liquidity for continuing operational business. Therefore, in a crisis situation, they have an even greater role arranging for a restructuring due to the need for new financing. They will, however, only participate in this process if, in a later insolvency, they enjoy the privileges and remedies and avoidance of the agreement can be excluded as far as possible.

Corporate finance has evolved in Germany, and companies have the same opportunities to gain access to liquidity than in England. With the structured finance boom of the mid-2000s, complex transactions with a diverse creditor base have been financed. This leads to the challenge, especially for banks, to steer a restructuring. English banks have been known

619 *Allen / Gale*, p. 30 et seq.
620 *Ibid.*, p. 32.
621 *Ibid.*, p. 31, 59 et seq.
622 *Patel / Fennessy*, ICR 2006, 255.
623 *Becker et al.*, KTS 2011, 53.
624 See Chapter II 4.2.

to take on equity positions as a strategic interest in the business relationship with the debtor on their balance sheet as a consequence of the voluntary restructuring *London Approach*. In contrast, German banks rather refrain from participating in a debt-equity-swap despite fulfilling the same capital requirements and risk regulations and rather enforce their securities and write-off the balance instead of engaging in a restructuring. Although this strategy is criticised, it makes sense from an economic point of view.

Conclusion

This chapter took into account the various factors that affect the restructuring of companies in financial distress.

Legal culture cannot be developed by law but is rather based on a nation's roots, values, beliefs and perceptions. It is also influenced by legal competition and legal harmonisation, which may result in forum shopping if one jurisdiction is perceived to be superior to another jurisdiction. Legal competition may result in a *race to the bottom* or a *race to the top*. Harmonisation of certain areas as transparency of the administrative process and equitable treatment of creditors, among others, may increase the efficient and effective restructurings of companies to the advantage of the internal market. While the German government provided a reform to encourage restructurings rather than liquidations and the German Federal Bank refrained from intervening directly to support companies, England has been more active in the past: the Bank of England actively intervened into the markets to provide liquidity to companies and developed the *London Approach* as informal guidelines to facilitate restructuring. However, this approach has also lead to the detriment of *zombie companies,* which may cripple the economy even more when they begin to fail. In light or despite this fact, Member States and even the European Commission are embracing (or already over-emphasising) corporate rescue as a mean to allow companies in financial distress to restructure for a going concern. This implies not only the financial but furthermore operational and structural changes to the organisation of the company. However, only considering corporate rescue as the *Holy Grail* rather than corporate liquidation is to refuse acceptance that the market process is selecting unviable companies to ultimately fail, releasing resources to a more value-creating use. This is economic reality and contributes to a nation's wealth and prosperity. It is questionable how far market interventions with corporate insolvency laws and processes should reach to allow for corporate rescue rather than liquidation. Whether a company is viable or not will also be tested by the market in the medium to long run.

The judicial framework is very different in Germany and England, not only due to the fact that Germany is a civil law country and England is a common law country but rather how the profession of judges and administrators perceive themselves to play an active part in the restructurings. The commercial background in England is nurturing the active approach towards restructuring. Germany will need to find a way to provide legal certainty for the judicial environment. One important key feature to encourage successful restructuring is the early application for insolvency proceedings.

The commercial environment is important to provide access to liquidity, necessary to fund the restructurings. Although German debtors were dependent on banks due to the historical ties, English creditors are much more diverse, which could also lead to challenges in providing a common approach to restructure the company in financial distress. English creditors are more used to play an active role in restructuring, which refers back to the *London Approach*. In Germany, creditors are still reluctant to take on equity positions, which is also a reason why the German distressed debt market is underdeveloped.

Chapter III Restructuring Companies using Debt-Equity-Swaps

Introduction

This chapter aims to distinguish between the approaches for restructuring in an informal or statutory proceeding and provides a background of the different proceedings in restructuring and insolvency law in Germany and England.

7 Informal versus Statutory Proceedings for Restructuring

Provided there is not already a legal obligation to file for insolvency under German or English law, the question is whether the debtor should pursue an informal proceeding by negotiation or a statutory proceeding in court to agree with the company's creditors on a restructuring and, thereby, on the going concern for a company in financial distress to return to profitability.[625] A profitable company is viable when the going concern may be achieved without any losses and when the income generated can cover the liabilities and costs of the on-going operations. That the company has prospects of returning to profitability without further losses is probably a necessary but not a sufficient condition for creditors to engage in a restructuring from an economic perspective. They will consider this possibility for the case that the going concern value of the company is often, but not necessarily always, greater than its liquidation value.[626] If the parties in insolvency determine autonomously on restructuring or liquidation, a decision to restructure is always also a decision to use the liquidity value of the legal status of their claims.[627] Creditors would engage in a restructuring when their anticipation is to regain a higher recovery rate through the restructuring of the company than that which would materialise from the insolvency quota in liquidation.[628] In addition, in economic terms the

---

625 *Undritz*, Kölner Schrift zur InsO, p. 938.
626 *Hax / Marschdorf*, BFuP 1983, 112, 115; *Gröner*, ORDO 1984, 247, 252.
627 *Gröner*, ORDO 1984, 247, 253 et seq.
628 *Balz*, Sanierung von Unternehmen, p. 20.

capital invested in the restructuring should bring at least the same yield as alternative investments; only then is a restructuring feasible.[629]

In an informal process, the debtor and its creditors agree on a consensual contractual solution outside a given legal framework[630] generally regarding the interests of the company's creditors as a whole.[631] There are several advantages in an informal consensual restructuring proceeding.[632] There is the potential for higher value preservation or recovery[633] due to the private autonomous negotiations.[634] The process provides flexibility in implementing appropriate measures and it allows for an "*early, quickly and quietly*"[635] restructuring, which is usually less complicated and less expensive[636] but more effective.[637] However, the need for lender consent[638], the blocking potential of (minority) stake- and shareholders,[639] the difficulties of acquiring going concern financing or the legal uncertainties *ex post* with regard to risk of remedies[640] or liabilities for directors for fil-

629 *Gröner*, ORDO 1984, 247, 254.

630 *Eidenmüller*, BB 1998, Beil. 10, p. 19; *Belcher*, p. 13 et seq. See also *Howard / Hedger*, mn. 1.6 et seq.: The *London Approach* as the best known informal restructuring procedure, see Chapter II 4.2.

631 *Finch*, J.B.L. 2008, 756, 758.

632 *Uhlenbruck*, BB 2001, 1641 et seq.; *Drukarczyk / Schöntag*, Sec. 3; *Oberle*, in FS Wellensiek, p. 73, 75; *Eidenmüller*, Unternehmenssanierung, p. 331 et seq.

633 *Kranzusch / Icks*, p. 103 et seq.; Eidenmüller, Unternehmenssanierung, p. 332 et seq.; *Jostarndt*, p. 105 et seq.; *Eidenmüller*, ZHR 160 (1996) 343, 348. Contrary *Spliedt*, InsVZ 2010, 27, 29: high advisory costs in the consensual restructuring solution.

634 *Eidenmüller*, ZHR 160 (1996) 343, 349 et seq.; *Drukarczyk / Schöntag*, Sec. 3, mn. 1.

635 *K. Schmidt*, Gutachten D zum 54. DJT, 1982, S.D. 133. See also *Eidenmüller*, ZHR 160 (1996) 343, 349 et seq.; *Uhlenbruck*, BB 2001, 1641, 1644; *Ehlers*, ZInsO 2005, 169, 170; *Drukarczyk / Schöntag,* Sec. 3, mn. 1 et seq.

636 *Eidenmüller*, Unternehmenssanierung, p. 331 et seq. for empirical evidence.

637 *Finch*, J.B.L. 2008, 756, 776; *Howard / Hedger*, mn. 1.17. *Drukarczyk / Schöntag*, Sec. 3 mn. 42; *Uhlenbruck*, BB 2001, 1641, 1644.

638 *Drukarczyk / Schöntag*, Sec. 3 mn. 3; *Eidenmüller*, ZHR 160 (1996) 343, 344 et seq.: The main obstacle is that the plans only have effect on creditors which have agreed upon it in a consensual way.

639 "Akkordstörer" BGHZ 116, 319 II 1.a) b) of the decision, NJW 1992, 967, 968 et seq. = ZIP 1992, 191: From this follows that an agreement negotiated outside of such a proceeding is not binding on creditors who have not agreed to it. See also *Eidenmüller*, ZHR 160 (1996) 343, 346; *Bitter*, ZGR 2010, 147, 167 et seq.

640 *Cranshaw*, ZInsO 2008, 421, 422.

ing late[641] are a trade-off. In addition, the consensual agreement does not have access to the instruments provided in a statutory proceeding.[642] Without supervision of independent mandatory parties, such as the insolvency court or the insolvency administrator,[643] there is the risk for single creditors to be individually disadvantaged,[644] which would not occur in a statutory proceeding.[645] A consensual restructuring should only be initiated when there is a high probability that the restructuring will be successful.[646] The informal approach of rescuing companies has gradually spread and is used in a considerable number of jurisdictions all over the world, particularly in cases where a financial and economic crisis is present.[647]

Although publicly announced statutory proceedings are assumed to be more complex and lasting, costly and value destroying due to the negative effect on the company's reputation,[648] the legal framework provides for a regulated process with an acceptable solution carried by a majority of creditors. The choice of process depends on the company and the state of the financial crisis. Overall, the advantages and disadvantages weigh off,[649] however, all parties involved gain from an agreement to use the more efficient method.[650]

641 *Rattunde*, ZIP 2003, 2103, 2105; *Uhlenbruck*, BB 2001, 1641, 1644; *Cranshaw*, ZInsO 2008, 421, 422; *Ehlers*, ZInsO 2010, 257; *Smid*, Praxishdb. Insolvenzrecht, Sec. 1 mn. 57 et seq.; *Spliedt*, InsVZ 2010, 27, 32 et seq.

642 *Spliedt*, InsVZ 2010, 27, 29 et seq.; *Uhlenbruck*, GmbH in Krise, Sanierung und Insolvenz, p. 144. Examples are the termination of contracts (Ss. 103 et seq. InsO) and redundancy period for employees (Ss. 113 et seq. InsO), a moratorium (Ss. 21(2)(1)(no.3), 89 InsO) or prohibited netting (Sec. 96 InsO). *See also* Euler Hermes, Rettung aus der Insolvenz, p. 10: an important liquidity source is the state funded money for employees in the first three months (Insolvenzgeld).

643 *Drukarczyk / Schöntag*, Sec. 3 mn. 1.

644 *Finch*, J.B.L. 2008, 756, 766 et seq.

645 *Uhlenbruck*, BB 2001, 1641, 1645.

646 *Rattunde*, ZIP 2003, 2103, 2105.

647 *Cárdenas*, in *Buljevich*, xvi.

648 *Hass / Tschauner*, ICR 2005, 93, 94.

649 *Uhlenbruck*, KSI 2010, 125, 126.

650 *Easterbrook*, 27 J Fin. Econ. (1990) 411, 416.

7.1 Germany

Even with the Insolvency Statute, the German insolvency law previously did not offer the opportunity to enforce financial measures against shareholders. It kept the insolvency plan proceeding in the tradition of a rather liquidation than restructuring oriented process, which served to simplify the management of the insolvent debtor.[651] The question is whether this would have been the only reason for the rare application of the insolvency plan procedure as an effective legal restructuring option in practice.

A detriment of the Bankruptcy Act[652] was the rejection of the petition by the insolvency court due to a lack of assets[653]. The insolvency law reform has already improved the openings of proceedings: while in 1998 still 74.6%[654] of the applications for opening were rejected due to a lack of assets, in 2012, 77.7%[655] were opened. For these companies, there is at least a theoretical chance to accomplish a corporate restructuring within the statutory framework of the Insolvency Statute.

In insolvency proceedings for liquidation, the length of a proceeding is, on average, four years[656], thereby generating high legal costs,[657] leading to an average recovery ratio of 3.6%.[658] Even though the procedural costs are also high in an insolvency plan proceeding,[659] better results are obtained[660]: the expected recovery rates are significantly higher with 10%,[661]

651 *Madaus*, p. 590.
652 BMJ, Begr. RegE-InsO 1992, BT-Drucks. 12/2443, p. 72.
653 Sec. 26(1)(1) InsO.
654 Statistisches Bundesamt, Statistisches Jahrbuch 1999, Unternehmen und Arbeitsstätten, p. 138. See also BMJ, Begr. RegE-InsO 1992, BT-Drucks. 12/2443, p. 72.
655 Statistisches Bundesamt, Unternehmen und Arbeitsstätten, Fachserie 2, Reihe 4.1, Dezember und Jahr 2012, p. 5. There is no statistical information on the different proceedings.
656 *Kranzusch / Icks*, p. 24 et seq.
657 *Icks/Kranzusch*, p. 101 et seq. See also Haarmeyer, ZInsO 2007, 169, 171: the majority of costs are consumed by the insolvency administrator.
658 *Icks / Kranzusch*, p. 87 et seq.; *Paffenholz / Kranzusch*, p. 87 et seq.
659 *Paffenholz / Kranzusch*, p. 87 et seq.
660 *Icks / Kranzusch*, p. 110.
661 *Icks / Kranzusch*, p. 94 et seq.; *Paffenholz / Kranzusch*, p. 101; *Haarmeyer*, ZInsO 2007, 169, 171.

and sometimes even over 20%[662] in a much shorter time for proceedings, on average between eight months[663] to 1.5 years[664]. Although initial expectation[665] were set high, the insolvency plan proceedings was rarely applied[666] and tended to be rather side-lined.[667]

The slightly positive perception in the application of the insolvency plan in the insolvency practice is primarily due to the publicity-effective restructuring success of major German companies through insolvency plan proceedings.[668] It also shows, however, that even the most experienced restructuring experts cannot prevent the subsequent liquidation in an insolvency plan proceeding.[669]

In German law, the creditors generally decide how they want to deal with the assets of an insolvent debtor. The creditors' meeting decides whether the debtor's assets should be liquidated or whether the business activity of the debtor has future potential. Especially for companies whose going concern value exceeds the liquidation value,[670] a going concern ensures the best possibility to satisfy creditors.[671] The Insolvency Statute offers several alternatives to creditors to obtain the best possible satisfaction[672] and it provides for a going concern, liquidation and business-asset

---

662 For examples, see *Rattunde*, ZIP 2003, 596, 597 (*Herlitz*); *Fritze*, DZWIR 2007, 89, 90 (*Senator Entertainment).*

663 *Haarmeyer*, ZInsO 2007, 169, 172.

664 *Paffenholz / Kranzusch*, p. 102 et seq.

665 BMJ, Begr. RegE-InsO, BT-Drucks. 12/2443, p. 90 et seq. See also *Uhlenbruck*, NJW 2000, 1386; *Pape*, ZInsO 2009, 1, 5; *Gottwald*, mn. 50 et seq.; *Häsemeyer*, mn. 27.03.

666 *Fröhlich / Sittel*, ZInsO 2009, 858, 860; *Undritz*, ZGR 2010, 201, 208; *Icks / Kranzusch*, p. 41.

667 *Uhlenbruck / Vallender*, NZI 2009, 4; *Gerster*, ZInsO 2008, 437 et seq.

668 *Rattunde*, ZIP 2003, 596, 597 (*Herlitz*); *Fritze*, DZWIR 2007, 89, 90 (*Senator Entertainment*).

669 *Geldmacher*, p. 29: The insolvency plan proceeding was used for restructuring of *Arcandor AG* and concurrent liquidation of *Quelle GmbH.*

670 *Eidenmüller,* in MüKo-InsO, in front of Ss. 217-269 mn. 6.

671 BMJ, Begr. RegE-ESUG, BT-Drucks. 12/2443, p. 195. See *Scheunemann / Hoffmann*, DB 2009, 983; *Rattunde*, ZIP 2003, 2103, 2110; *Eidenmüller,* in MüKo-InsO, in front of Ss. 217-269 mn. 5 et seq.

672 BMJ, Begr. RegE, BT-Drucks. 12/2443, p. 78, 94. All alternatives may be supported by a plan proceeding, see BMJ, Begr. RegE InsO 1992, BT-Drucks. 12/2443, p. 91; *Smid / Rattunde*, Insolvenzplan, 2005, mn. 2.6; *Häsemeyer*, mn. 28.05; *Jaffé*, in FK-InsO, Sec. 217, mn. 6.

deal as equal proceedings.[673] The assets of a debtor can be liquidated in a regular insolvency proceeding[674] or in an insolvency plan proceeding[675]. A going concern of a company may also be achieved by a business-asset deal[676] in a new legal entity or in an insolvency plan proceeding[677]. The Insolvency Statute does not prefer any particular solution. Which method is chosen depends on the economic condition of the debtor and the preferences of the creditors.[678]

Although the Insolvency Statute provides for three conceptual options[679] for the restructuring of a company, debt-equity-swaps usually do not take place (anymore) in liquidation or business-asset sale. The implementation focuses on the insolvency plan proceeding. For this reason, the liquidation and business-asset-sale are only briefly outlined.

7.1.1 Insolvency

The purpose of any insolvency proceeding under German insolvency law is the

---

673 BMJ, Begr. RegE-InsO, BT-Drucks. 12/2443, p. 77 et seq. See *Smid*, Praxishdb. Insolvenzrecht, Sec. 29 mn. 4; *Seagon*, in *Buth / Hermanns*, Sec. 27 mn. 11.

674 *Smid*, Praxishdb. Insolvenzrecht, Ss. 24 et seq.

675 *„liquidation plan"*, see *Picot / Aleth*, p. 255 mn. 792; *Jaffé*, in FK-InsO, Sec. 217 mn. 71 et seq., Sec. 220 mn. 9 et seq.; *Smid / Rattunde*, Der Insolvenzplan, p. 2 mn. 8; Smid, Praxishdb. Insolvenzrecht 2007, Sec. 29 mn. 11; *Warrikoff*, KTS 1997, 527, 539 et seq. However, in practice, a liquidation is hardly ever conducted by a liquidation plan, see *Paffenholz / Kranzusch*, p. 76 et seq.; *Eidenmüller*, in MüKo-InsO, 2008, in front of Ss. 217-269, mn. 9; *Kranzusch*, ZInsO 2007, 804, 805.

676 A business-asset deal may also be done in an insolvency plan proceeding, *„transfer plan"*; *see* BMJ, Begr. RegE, BT-Drucks. 12/2443 p. 94 et seq.; *Picot / Aleth*, p. 255 mn. 794; *Jaffé*, in FK-InsO, Sec. 217 mn. 73 et seq. and Sec. 220 mn. 12 et seq.; *Warrikoff*, KTS 1997, 527, 541 et seq.

677 *„reorganisation plan"*, see BMJ, Begr. RegE, BT-Drucks. 12/2443, p. 195; *Picot / Aleth*, p. 255 mn. 793; *Jaffé*, in FK-InsO, Sec. 217 mn. 78 et seq., Sec. 220 mn. 25 et seq.; *Warrikoff*, KTS 1997, 527, 542 et seq.

678 Begr. RegE, BT-Drucks. 12/2443, p. 76; *Maus*, in *K. Schmidt/Uhlenbruck*, GmbH in Krise, Sanierung und Insolvenz, p. 159 mn. 355; *Fröhlich / Köchling*, ZInsO 2005, 1121, 1125; *Smid*, Praxishdb. Insolvenzrecht, Sec. 29 mn. 3; *Balz*, Sanierung von Unternehmen, p. 18 et seq.

679 *Smid / Rattunde*, Der Insolvenzplan, mn. 0.18; *Sassenrath*, ZIP 2003, 1517, 1518.

> *"collective satisfaction of a debtor's creditors by liquidation of the debtor's assets and by distribution of the proceeds, or by reaching an arrangement in an insolvency plan, particularly in order to maintain the enterprise."*[680]

7.1.2 Opening Insolvency Proceedings

The insolvency proceeding is an application process, which means that the insolvency court will act only at the request of a creditor[681] or the debtor[682]. The debtor must make an application request without culpable delay, at the latest, however, three weeks after the commencement of insolvency or over-indebtedness.[683] The application initiates the opening process. In the opening process, the insolvency court approves whether the application made is valid, whether there is a reason to open a proceeding and whether the debtor's assets are sufficient to cover at least the costs of the insolvency proceedings.[684] The court also decides on any protective measures.[685] Are the prerequisites fulfilled, the insolvency court opens by the opening decision.[686]

7.1.3 Grounds for Insolvency

It requires (a) ground(s)[687] to apply for an insolvency proceeding. Insolvency proceedings are opened on request by the court in case the debtor has reached material insolvency.

---

680 Sec. 1(1) InsO.
681 Sec. 13(1) InsO.
682 Sec. 15(1) InsO.
683 Sec. 15a(1) InsO.
684 Sec. 26 InsO.
685 Sec. 21(1) InsO.
686 Sec. 27 InsO.
687 Sec. 16 InsO.

7.1.3.1 Insolvency (*Zahlungsunfähigkeit*)

Sec 17 InsO regulates that *insolvency shall be the general reason to open insolvency proceedings*[688].The debtor is illiquid when he is unable to pay its debts when they become due.[689] The inability is not temporarily but likely to be permanent[690] when less than 10% of all liabilities due constitute a liquidity gap within a period of up to three weeks.[691]

7.1.3.2 Imminent Insolvency (*Drohende Zahlungsunfähigkeit*)

In case of imminent liquidity, only the debtor and not the creditor will be able to file for insolvency and open a proceeding.[692] The debtor is therefore in the position to avoid the liquidation of assets or enforcement and prepare a restructuring plan.[693] The debtor is imminent insolvent in case where it will likely be that the debtor will not be able to fulfil its payment obligations when they become due.[694] Imminent insolvency does not include future claims and obligations.

7.1.3.3 Over-Indebtedness (*Überschuldung*)

Over-indebtedness is another ground to open insolvency proceedings.[695] Where the debtor is over-indebted, the assets are not sufficient enough to cover the liabilities.[696] Under the "German Financial Markets Stabilisation Act"[697], this ground for insolvency was suspended until 31 December

---

688 Sec. 17(1) InsO.

689 Sec. 17(2) InsO.

690 BGH, Urt. V. 11.10.1961 – VII ZR 113/60, NJW 1962, 102. The difference between temporary and permanent inability is difficult and controversial, see *Kind*, in *Braun*, InsO 2012, Sec. 17 mn. 7 et seq.; *Seagon*, in *Buth / Hermanns*, Sec. 27 mn 25; *Bork*, mn. 8.10.

691 This refers to the obligation to apply for an insolvency proceeding, Sec 15a IS. See also BGH, Urt. v. 24.5.2005 – IX ZR 123/04, DZWiR 2006, 25.

692 Sec. 18(1) InsO.

693 *Seagon*, in *Buth / Hermanns*, Sec. 27 mn. 27.

694 Sec. 18(2) InsO.

695 Sec. 19(1) InsO.

696 Sec. 19(2) InsO.

697 Financial Markets Stabilisation Act, BMJ, BT-Drucks, 16/10600.

2013[698] if the debtor has a positive going concern prognosis (i.e., if the debtor will likely stay liquid during its current and the immediately following financial year),[699] however, has been finally extended unlimited.[700]

7.1.4 Restructuring and Insolvency Proceedings

There is no stand-alone restructuring proceeding outside a formal insolvency in Germany. The Insolvency Statute provides for different proceedings in the case of insolvency aiming at either the liquidation of the company or allowing the restructuring of the company.

7.1.4.1 Liquidation

The liquidation was the sole result of the former Bankruptcy Act and is still the primary proceeding today. The debtor's assets are realised and the proceeds are distributed to priority or secured creditors; the remaining (if any) is distributed pro rata among the unsecured creditors. The process is based on the primary satisfaction of creditors and the decrease of their claims' impairment. There is no consideration of other economic damage done in the process. Without a positive going concern, liquidation is the best possible solution for an insolvent debtor. The problem, however, is there seems to be a general tendency for early liquidation rather than considering and evaluating other alternatives.

---

698 The original suspension was limited until 31.12.2010, and then prolonged until 31.12.2013. For discussion, see *d'Avoine*, in FS Runkel, p. 263 et seq.

699 The change to the concept of indebtedness had the effect that the mere positive forecast of the company could avoid over-indebtedness. Under a *positive* going concern prognosis, a company must be able to service its medium-term payment obligations. See also *Riegger / Spahlinger*, in FS Wellensiek, p. 119 et seq.

700 Beschlussempfehlung des Rechtsausschusses, BT-Drucks. 17/11385, p. 27. See also *Bitter / Hommerich / Reiß*, ZIP 2012, 1201 et seq.; *de Bra*, Blog Handelsblatt-online, 22.11.2013, *Bretz / Gude*, ZInsO 2010, 515 et seq.

7.1.4.2 Business-Asset Sale

In a business-asset deal[701] the company as the insolvent legal entity is separated from its business and assets. The business or assets are then transferred to an existing or newly established legal entity.[702] The transfer usually takes place in the form of an asset deal.[703] The creditors of the insolvent company are than satisfied with the proceeds from the purchase price according to their recovery rate. The insolvent legal entity is then liquidated and ceases to exist.[704] The actual restructuring measures are carried out at the new entity.[705] A business-asset deal is not so much of a primary restructuring but rather the maximisation of the debtor's assets, yet allowing for the continuation of (potential) productive economic units.[706] The business-asset sale is possible both in a consensual restructuring or a statutory proceedings as well as being a part of a regular insolvency proceedings[707] and in an insolvency plan proceeding.[708]

The business-asset sale is a purchase by single succession (*Einzelrechtsnachfolge*) and is conducted by the insolvency administrator.[709] Although there is no comprehensive data for business-asset deals, it is assumed that the business-asset deal is the preferred method to restructure a viable business.[710] A preparation for a restructuring may also be concluded in a pre-

701 *Karsten Schmidt* gave distinction to the term, ZIP 1980, 328, 336 et seq. Also BMJ, Begr. RegE-InsO, BT-Drucks. 12/2443, p. 78 et seq., 83; *Schwalme*, DZWiR 2004, 230; *K. Schmidt*, in Kölner Schrift zur InsO, p. 1212, mn. 27; *Müller*, p. 317 et seq.

702 *K. Schmidt*, ZIP 1980, 328, 336 et seq.; *Wellensiek*, NZI 2002, 233, 234; *Bitter*, ZGR 2010, 147, 152 et seq.; *Undritz*, ZGR 2010, 201, 205 et seq. The reorganisation company (*Fortführungsgesellschaft*) is the acquiring company (*Übernahmegesellschaft*) in accordance to Sec. 260(3) InsO.

703 An alternative is the less relevant "share deal".

704 *K. Schmidt*, ZIP 1998, 1028.

705 *Hagebuch / Oberle*, NZI 2006, 618, 619.

706 *Wellensiek*, NZI 2002, 233, 234; Kluth, ZInsO 2002, 1115, 1122; *Zipperer*, NZI 2008, 206 et seq.; *Undritz*, ZGR 2010, 201, 208.

707 Ss. 160(2)(n.1), 162 et seq. InsO. See *Eidenmüller*, in MüKo-InsO, Sec. 217 mn. 170 for advantages of a business-asset-deal in a plan proceeding.

708 Sec. 260(3) InsO.

709 The restructuring instruments of the Insolvency Statute cannot be used properly since the restructuring is generally conducted after the business has been transferred.

710 *K. Schmidt*, GmbH in der Krise, p. 204; *Smid / Rattunde*, Insolvenzplan, p. 8; *Undritz*, ZGR 2010, 201, 207; *Wellensiek*, NZI 2002, 233; *Bitter*, ZGR 2010,

packed deal.[711] The process is faster and less complex than an insolvency plan proceeding,[712] however, are mostly compensated by the costs for the sales process and the concurrent liquidation of the company.[713] A business-asset deals requires a buyer, willing to acquire (parts of) the business. For companies with non-transferable rights a business-asset deal is not possible.[714] The only alternative is the sale within liquidation. Accumulated losses may be transferred only under certain conditions or even be lost.[715] Other obstacles include Sec. 613a BGB[716] and several threats for appeal and criminal charges.[717]

Whether the purchase price is valued correctly[718] for the protection of creditors of the selling and acquiring legal entities[719] and actually achieves a higher recovery rate for creditors[720] is another point to be considered. The business-asset deal is a valuable and important restructuring method. It cannot, however, compensate for a statutory insolvency proceeding.[721]

147, 155; *Icks / Kranzusch*, p. 63 et seq.; *Frind*, ZInsO 2008, 127, 130: less than 20% of companies applying for insolvency are restructured for going concern.

711 *Piepenburg*, in FS Greiner, p. 271 et seq.

712 *Wellensiek*, NZI 2002, 233, 239; *Icks / Kranzusch*, p. 26.

713 *Stapper*, ZInsO 2009, 2361, 2364; *Undritz*, ZGR 2010, 201, 206.

714 *Bitter / Laspeyres*, ZIP 2010, 1157 et seq.; *Bitter*, ZGR 2010, 147, 157 et seq.

715 *Bitter / Laspeyres*, ZIP 2010, 1157, 1164.

716 *Kranzusch / Icks*, p. 31 et seq.; *K. Schmidt*, GmbH in Krise, Sanierung und Insolvenz, p. 205; Euler Hermes, Rettung aus der Insolvenz, Nr. 418, 2007, p. 17.

717 *K. Schmidt*, GmbH in Krise, Sanierung und Insolvenz, p. 204 et seq.; *Zipperer*, NZI 2008, 206, 208; *Wellensiek*, NZI 2002, 233, 235. There are is no legal framework for the purchase price negotiations. Risks include remedies or appeal for provisions in the transfer process or non-transparent agreements.

718 *Müller-Feldhammer*, ZIP 2003, 2186 et seq.; *Undritz*, ZGR 2010, 201, 207.

719 *K. Schmidt*, ZGR 1982, 178, 198; *Zipperer*, NZI 2008, 206, 208; *Müller*, p. 285.

720 *Icks / Kranzusch*, p. 92, 110 et seq. The little empirical evidence suggests that the results achieved in a statutory insolvency plan proceedings exceed those of a business-asset-sale: creditors receive a higher recovery rate. See also *Paffenholz / Kranzusch*, p. 104: more jobs are saved.

721 BMJ, Begr. RegE-InsO, BT-Drucks. 12/2441 p. 83. This generally leads to problems when the debtor owns specific rights which cannot be transferred to another legal entity, e.g. concessions, licences or losses carried forward, see *Müller*, p. 302 et seq.; *Gravenbrucher Kreis*, ZIP 1989, 468, 471; *Schwalme*, DZWIR 2004, 230. For further examples, see *Braun*, in *Nerlich / Römermann*-InsO, sec. 217 mn. 39; *Eidenmüller*, in MüKo-InsO, before ss. 217-269 mn. 6 with further literature; *Jaffé*, in FK-InsO, before sec. 217 mn. 2.

7.1.4.3 Insolvency Plan Proceeding

For the legislation, the insolvency plan is a "*private autonomous agreement of the parties involved in accordance with the statutory provisions for the realisation of the debtor's assets*"[722]. The insolvency plan proceeding makes it possible to obtain either the legal personality of a debtor company[723] or to realise the assets of a debtor[724]. In the context of an insolvency plan proceeding, the creditors' satisfaction may deviate from solutions provided by the principle provisions of the Insolvency Statute.[725] The different approach may be more flexible and economically more reasonable than the realisation enforcement of the Insolvency Statute.[726] The insolvency plan gives the creditors and the debtor an opportunity to consensually resolve the insolvency.[727] According to the insolvency law, the parties involved in insolvency proceedings should deal with the insolvency mutually.[728]

Establishment of the Plan

An insolvency plan may be submitted to the insolvency court by the insolvency administrator[729] and the debtor[730]. The creditors' assembly does not

---

722 BMJ, Begr. RegE-InsO, BT-Drucks. 12/2443, p. 91.

723 *Jaffé*, in FK-InsO, Sec. 217 mn. 80; *Braun / Frank*, in *Braun*-InsO, before Ss. 217-269 mn. 1.

724 *Braun / Frank*, in *Braun*-InsO 2012, before Ss. 217-269 mn. 1, 10 et seq.

725 Dispensable and indispensable provisions, see *Frege / Keller / Riedel*, mn. 1915 et seq.; *Smid* Praxishdb. Insolvenzrecht 2007, Sec. 29 mn. 2.

726 Sec. 217 InsO. See BMJ, Begr. RegE-InsO, BT-Drucks. 12/2443, p. 90. See also *Frege / Keller / Riedel*, mn. 1909, 1914, 1915 et seq.; *Jaffé*, in FK-InsO, Sec. 217 mn. 54.

727 BMJ, Begr. RegE-InsO, BT-Drucks. 12/2443, p. 90. See also *Frege / Keller / Riedel*, mn. 1910; *Jaffé*, FK-InsO, Sec. 217 mn. 13; *Madaus*, p. 46 et seq. for the advantages and disadvantages of the insolvency plan proceeding.

728 BMJ, Begr. RegE-InsO, BT-Drucks. 12/2443, p. 90.

729 Sec. 218(2)(1) InsO. See *Jaffé*, in FK-InsO, Sec. 218 mn. 27 et seq.; *Eidenmüller*, in MüKo-InsO, Sec. 218 mn. 12 et seq.; *Warrikoff*, KTS 1997, 527, 528 et seq. Controversial *Braun*, in *Nerlich / Römermann*-InsO, Sec. 218 mn. 25 et seq.

730 Sec 218(1)(1) InsO. See *Jaffé*, in FK-InsO, Sec. 218 mn. 6 et seq.; *Braun*, in *Nerlich / Römermann*-InsO, Sec 218 mn. 1 et seq.

have the right to submit an insolvency plan[731] but may request the insolvency administrator to submit an insolvency plan[732]. An insolvency plan may be submitted to the insolvency court until the final creditors' assembly.[733] Generally, insolvency plans may be submitted several times.[734]

An insolvency plan consists of a declaratory part, a constructive part and attachments. The declaratory part describes the measures taken or still to be taken and creates the basis for the creditors' decision.[735] The constructive part determines how the insolvency plan transforms the legal position of the parties involved.[736] In the case that the creditors will be satisfied from the earnings derived from the debtor's business continued by

731 Sec. 218(2) InsO. See *Braun / Frank*, in *Braun*-InsO, Sec. 218 mn. 4; Braun, in *Nerlich / Römermann*-InsO 2009, Sec. 218 mn. 32.

732 Sec. 218(2) InsO. See *Braun*, in *Nerlich/Römermann*-InsO, Sec. 218 mn. 23 et seq.; *Eidenmüller*, in MüKo-InsO, Sec. 218 mn. 14 et seq.; by request of the creditors' committee to submit a plan, the insolvency is granted an appropriate time period to do so, depending on the complexity this may be between two to six months, see *Braun/ Frank*, in *Braun*-InsO, Sec. 218 mn. 5.

733 Sec. 218(1)(3) InsO. See *Frege / Keller / Riedel*, mn. 1926.

734 *Eidenmüller*, in MüKo-InsO, Sec. 218 mn. 118 et seq.; *Frege / Keller / Riedel*, mn. 1926. Re-submitting an insolvency plan by the debtor may be suspended by the court in a case the insolvency administrator (with consent of the creditors' committee) applies for it in court (Sec. 231(2) InsO), see *Frege / Keller / Riedel*, mn. 1957.

735 Ss. 219(1), 220 InsO. *See Braun / Frank*, in *Braun*-InsO 2012, Ss. 219-221 mn. 3; *Jaffé*, in FK-InsO, Sec. 219 mn. 4 et seq.; Sec. 220 mn. 6 et seq. See also *Hess / Weis*, WM 1998, 2349, 2353 et seq.; *Warrikoff*, KTS 1997, 527, 532 et seq.

736 Sec 219(1), 221 InsO. See *Jaffé*, in FK-InsO, Ss. 219 mn. 11 et seq., 221 mn. 10 et seq.; *Braun / Frank*, in *Braun*-InsO 2012, Ss. 219-221 mn. 5 et seq. See also *Hess / Weis*, WM 1998, 2349, 2355 et seq.; *Warrikoff*, KTS 1997, 527, 535 et seq.

the debtor or by a third party[737], the attachments[738] include a survey of assets[739] and an earnings and finance plan[740].[741]

Declaratory Part

The declaratory part of the insolvency plan describes the measures taken or still to be taken[742] after opening the insolvency proceedings in order to create the basis for the envisaged establishment of the rights held by the parties involved.[743] It contains all other information on the basis and effects of the plan which are relevant to the decision of the parties concerned on approval of the plan, and for its approval by the court.[744] The parties concerned and the court must be able to evaluate the proposed plan as an alternative to a regular insolvency proceeding.[745] The plan includes the development of the financial situation and the organisational structure of the debtor.[746] It evaluates the reasons for the financial distress,[747] what measures have to be taken to achieve the turnaround[748] and how the company

737 Sec. 229 InsO. See *Braun / Frank*, in *Braun*-InsO 2012, Sec. 217 mn. 2 et seq.; *Frege / Keller / Riedel*, mn. 2009; *Staufenbiel / Karlstedt*, ZInsO 2010, 2059 et seq.

738 Ss. 219(2), 229 et seq. InsO. See *Jaffé*, in FK-InsO, Ss. 229, 230; *Braun*, in *Nerlich / Römermann*-InsO 2009, Sec. 229 mn. 4 et seq., Sec. 230 mn. 3 et seq.; *Warrikoff*, KTS 1997, 527, 537.

739 Sec. 229(1) InsO.

740 Sec. 229(2) InsO.

741 This separation is mandatory, see BMJ, Begr. RegE-InsO, BT-Drucks. 12/2443, p. 197. See also *Frege / Keller / Riedel*, mn. 1911/ 1929 et seq.: *Jaffé*, in FK-InsO, Sec. 219 mn. 2 et seq.

742 *Frege / Keller / Riedel*, mn. 1930; *Eilenberger*, in MüKo-InsO, Sec. 220 mn. 4 et seq.

743 Sec. 220(1) InsO. See *Eilenberger*, in MüKo-InsO, Sec. 220 mn. 12 et seq.

744 Sec. 220(2) InsO. See *Frege / Keller / Riedel*, 1933 et seq.

745 BMJ, Begr. RegE-InsO, BT-Drucks. 12/2443, p. 197; BT-Drucks. 12/7302, p. 182. See also *Braun*, in *Nerlich / Römermann*-InsO, before Sec. 217 mn. 167 et seq.

746 *Frege / Keller / Riedel*, mn. 1934.

747 *Eilenberger*, in MüKo-InsO, Sec. 220 mn. 7 et seq.; *Frege / Keller / Riedel*, mn. 1934; *Smid* Praxishdb. Insolvenzrecht 2007, Sec. 30 mn. 12; *Smid / Rattunde*, Der Insolvenzplan 2005, p. 113 mn. 5.19.

748 *Eilenberger*, in MüKo-InsO, Sec. 220 mn. 15 et seq.; *Warrikoff*, KTS 1997, 527, 534.

constitutes after the successful completion of the insolvencyplan proceedings.[749]

Constructive Part

The constructive part of the insolvency plan determines how the insolvency plan transforms the legal position of the parties involved.[750] The insolvency plan may stipulate that the insolvency administrator be authorised to take the measures necessary to implement it and to correct any obvious errors it contains.[751] In order to create, modify, transfer or waive the right, any legal declarations necessary from the parties involved may be included in the constructive part of the insolvency plan.[752]

Formation of Groups

For the determination of the rights held by the parties involved, different groups have to be formed[753] according to the differing legal status of parties concerned.[754] A distinction in the formation of groups is made between the separate classes of parties concerned. These include shareholders[755] and creditors, especially for creditors entitled to separate satisfaction if their rights are encroached upon by the plan,[756] non-lower-ranking cred-

749 *Braun*, in *Nerlich / Römermann*-InsO, before Sec. 219 mn. 38; *Jaffé*, in FK-InsO, Sec. 220 mn. 69 et seq.; *Frege / Keller / Riedel*, mn. 1935a.

750 Sec. 221(1) InsO.

751 Sec. 221(2) InsO.

752 Sec. 228 InsO. See Begr. RegE, BT-Drucks. 12/2443, p. 202 et seq.; *Frege / Keller / Riedel*, mn. 1937; *Jaffé*, in FK-InsO, Sec. 228 mn. 4 et seq.

753 *Frege / Keller / Riedel*, mn. 1939. Different groups are only necessary where there are different legal statuses; otherwise no group formation is necessary. Beschlussempfehlung des Rechtsausschusses, BT-Drucks. 12/7302, p. 153/182.

754 Sec. 222(1)(1) InsO. *See* for class definition *Braun*, in: *Nerlich / Römermann*-InsO, Sec. 222 mn. 5 et seq.; *Eidenmüller*, in MüKo-InsO, Sec. 222 mn. 15 et seq.

755 Sec. 222(1)(2)(no.4) InsO.

756 Sec. 222(1)(2)(no.1) InsO. See *Jaffé*, in FK-InsO 2009, Sec. 222 mn. 10.

itors[757], each class of lower-ranking insolvency creditors[758], and employees[759]. Within each group, all parties involved are offered equal rights[760] if nothing else has been agreed upon by all parties concerned and included in the insolvency plan.[761]

The formation of groups is important to achieve the necessary majorities[762] in the subsequent vote on the insolvency plan[763]. Therefore, it is also a strategic decision.[764] The formation of groups is suggested by either the debtor or the insolvency administrator depending on which one submits the insolvency plan to the insolvency court.[765] By clever arrangement of groups, the decision of parties concerned may be influenced.[766] The insolvency court, however, reviews the formation of groups.[767] In the case the formation of groups are not compliant, the court may order correction on the formation of groups[768] or may refuse the insolvency plan *ex officio*[769]. This should counter any manipulation on the formation of

757 Sec. 222(1)(2)(no.2) InsO. See Eidenmüller, in MüKo-InsO, Sec. 222 mn. 58; *Warrikoff*, KTS 1997, 527, 545 et seq.

758 Sec. 222(1)(2)(no. 3) InsO. See *Braun*, in *Nerlich / Römermann*-InsO, Sec. 222 mn. 10. This is not necessary when the subordinated claims have been released in accordance to Sec. 225 InsO (Sec. 222(1)(2)(no.3) InsO), see *Braun / Frank*, in *Braun*-InsO 2012, Sec. 222 mn. 4.

759 Sec. 222(3) InsO. See BMJ; Begr. RegE-InsO, BT-Drucks. 12/2443, p. 200.

760 Sec. 226(1) InsO. See *Jaffé*, in FK-InsO, Sec. 226 mn. 1 et seq. The class composition relies upon the matching of the same claims, otherwise it is illegitimate, see BGH, Beschl. v. 7. 7. 2005 — IX ZB 266/04, BGHZ 163, 344, 347 et seq. = NZI 2005, 619, 620 et seq. = WM 2005, 1852, 1854; *LG Berlin*, Beschl. v. 20. 10. 2004 — 86 T 578/04, NZI 2005, 335, 337. See *Braun / Frank*, in *Braun*-InsO, Sec. 222 mn. 4; *Braun*, in *Nerlich / Römermann*-InsO, Sec. 222 mn. 55.

761 Sec. 226(2),(3) InsO. See BMJ, Begr. RegE-InsO, BT-Drucks. 12/2443, p. 202; *Frege / Keller / Riedel*, mn. 1945.

762 Sec. 244 InsO.

763 Sec. 243 InsO.

764 *Braun*, in *Nerlich/Römermann*-InsO 2009, before Sec. 217 mn. 217 et seq.

765 Sec. 222(1) InsO.

766 *Frege / Keller / Riedel*, mn. 1943; *Jaffé*, in FK-InsO, Sec. 222 mn. 15.

767 Sec. 231(1) InsO.

768 Sec. 231(1)(no. 1)(c.1) InsO.

769 Sec. 231(1) (no. 1) (c.2) InsO.

groups.[770] The groups have to be adequately separated from each other[771] with the criteria of their separation being indicated in the insolvency plan.[772]

Shareholders' Position

With their legal position, the company's shareholders could significantly block the enforcement of measures to restructure the company in the past.[773] Therefore, ways had to be found to circumvent shareholders and their blocking potential. This was usually achieved by a business-asset deal[774] instead of restructuring the company's legal entity with an insolvency plan proceedings.[775]

A debt-equity-swap in the insolvency plan proceedings was only possible with the consent of all parties concerned. The creditors had to consent to acquire company's shares by converting their debt into equity.[776] The shareholders had to agree to the necessary capital measures with a shareholder resolution by a qualified majority.[777] In particular, the strict

---

770 Example BGH, Beschl. v. 7. 7. 2005 — IX ZB 266/04, BGHZ 163, 344, 347 et seq. See *Frind*, NZI 2007, 374 et seq. for limits on manipulating the process by class composition.

771 Sec. 222(2)(2) InsO. See BMJ, Begr. RegE-InsO, BT-Drucks. 12/2443, p. 199 et seq.; *BGH*, Beschl. v. 10. I.2008 — IX ZB 97/07; BGH, Beschl. v. 26. 4. 2007 — IX ZB 5/06, NZI 2007, 521 = ZInsO 2007, 713. See also *Frege / Keller / Riedel*, mn. 1944; *Braun*, in *Nerlich / Römermann*-InsO, Sec. 222 mn. 47 et seq.; *Hingerl*, ZInsO 2007, 1337, 1338 et seq. on group of only one member.

772 Sec. 222(2)(3) InsO. *See* BMJ, Begr. RegE-InsO, BT-Drucks. 12/2443, p. 199 et seq.; *Eidenmüller*, in MüKo-InsO, Sec. 222 mn. 97 et seq.; *Riggert*, WM 1998, 1521, 1522: separation can be based on legal and economic differences. For further examples, see *Frege / Keller / Riedel*, mn. 1944.

773 *Uhlenbruck*, NZI 2008, 201, 203; *Bitter*, ZGR 2010, 147, 150; *Eidenmüller*, ZIP 2007, 1729, 1736; *Eidenmüller*, ZIP 2010, 649, 652.

774 BMJ, Begr. RegE-InsO, BT-Drucks. 12/2443, p. 78 et seq, 83. See *Schwalme*, DZWiR 2004, 230; *Müller*, p. 317 et seq.

775 This may lead to problems where the debtor owns certain rights that legally cannot be transferred to a new legal entity, e.g. certain contracts, licences and accumulated losses, see *Braun*, in *Nerlich / Römermann*-InsO, Sec. 217 mn. 39; *Müller*, p. 302 et seq.; *Gravenbrucher Kreis*, ZIP 1989, 468, 471; *Schwalme*, DZWIR 2004, 230.

776 Sec. 230(2) InsO.

777 Ss. 182(1)(1), 186(3)(2),222(1)(1) AktG.

separation of insolvency law and company law meant that the debt-equity-swap in an insolvency plan proceeding was virtually eliminated.

With the ESUG reform, the shareholders were included in the insolvency plan.[778] The share rights or membership rights of those persons with a participating interest in the debtor may now be included in the insolvency plan.[779] The shareholders have to be expressively included in the insolvency plan. Otherwise, their rights remain unaffected.[780]

In the case the shareholders are included in the insolvency plan, they form their own group.[781] The group is generally invited to discuss the insolvency plan and the voting rights of the parties concerned, subsequently to vote on the plan (discussion and voting meeting)[782] and to receive the documents of the insolvency court on the approval of the insolvency plan.[783] As a separate group, the shareholders vote separately on the insolvency plan.[784] The voting power right of the debtor's shareholders is thereby determined solely by the participating interest in the debtor's subscribed capital or assets.[785] Shareholders, whose rights are not affected by the plan, have no voting rights.[786] Acceptance of the insolvency plan requires shareholders to back the insolvency plan by exceeding half of the sum of claims in their group.[787]

In the voting process on the insolvency plan, shareholders are also prohibited to obstruct.[788] A reasonable participation of shareholders exists if

---

778 BMJ, Begr. RegE-ESUG, BT-Drucks. 127/11, p. 42 et seq.

779 Sec. 217(2) InsO.

780 Sec. 225a(1) InsO.

781 Sec. 222(1)(2)(no.4) InsO.

782 Sec. 235(2)(3) InsO. This does not apply to shareholders or limited liability shareholders in a partnership limited by shares. Sec. 121(4a) AktG shall apply mutatis mutandis to listed companies; they shall publish a summary of the essential contents of the plan on their website.

783 Sec. 252(2)(2),(3) InsO: Listed companies shall publish a summary of the essential contents of the plan on their website.

784 Sec. 243 InsO.

785 Sec. 238a (1) InsO. See *Simon*, CFL 2010, 448, 449: No account shall be taken of any limitations on voting rights, of special or multiple voting rights. See also *Simon / Merkelbach*, NZG 2012, 121, 122.

786 Ss. 238a(2), 237(2) InsO.

787 Sec. 244(3),(1)(no.2) InsO. A majority by number is not necessary in accordance with Sec. 244(1)(no.1) IS. See also BMJ, Begr. RegE-ESUG, BT-Drucks. 127/11, p. 48.

788 Sec. 245(3) InsO.

under the insolvency plan no creditor receives economic benefits exceeding the full amount of his claim,[789] no shareholder who would be equal in rank to the shareholders in the group if no plan were drawn up is better placed than they are,[790] and the majority of the voting groups have backed the insolvency plan with the necessary majorities.[791] If none of the members of a group of shareholders votes at all, the consent of the group is deemed to have been given.[792] Every shareholder may file the request to refuse the insolvency plan[793] when he opposed the insolvency plan in time[794] and he is likely to be placed at a disadvantage by the insolvency plan compared with his situation without a plan.[795] The request has to be rejected if the constructive part provides for funds being made available in the event that a party concerned shows to the satisfaction of the court that he will be placed at a disadvantage.[796] Whether the party concerned is to receive compensation from such funds is not an issue to be clarified by the insolvency proceedings.[797]

The shareholders may file an immediate appeal against the order of the insolvency court approving or refusing to approve the insolvency plan.[798] After the insolvency court approved the insolvency plan,[799] the decisions of the shareholders included in the plan are deemed to have been submitted in the prescribed form.[800] This applies especially to the formal obligations on the company law measures included in the plan to implement a debt-equity-swap.[801] The insolvency administrator is authorised to make the necessary registrations with the competent register court.[802]

789 Sec. 245(3) InsO in connection with Sec. 245(1)(no.2) InsO.
790 Sec. 245(3)(no.1) InsO.
791 Sec. 245(1)(no.3) InsO.
792 Sec. 246a InsO.
793 Sec. 251 InsO.
794 Sec. 251(1)(no.1) InsO.
795 Sec. 251(1)(no.2) InsO.
796 Sec. 251(3)(1) InsO.
797 Sec. 251(3)(2) InsO.
798 Sec. 253(1) InsO.
799 Sec. 248 InsO.
800 Sec. 254a(2) InsO. Summons, announcements and other measures in the preparation of shareholder decisions required under company law shall be deemed to have been effected in the prescribed form.
801 Sec. 254a(3) InsO.
802 Sec. 254a(2)(2) InsO.

Submitting and Comments on the Plan

The insolvency court may refuse the insolvency plan *ex officio*[803] if the person submitting the insolvency plan actually has not the right to submit the insolvency plan,[804] the insolvency submitted by the debtor obviously has no chance of being accepted by the parties concerned or approved by the court,[805] and if the claims provided for the parties under the constructive part of the insolvency plan submitted by the debtor obviously cannot be satisfied.[806] In addition, the insolvency court only scrutinises the insolvency plan if the provisions governing the plan and its contents are complied with.[807] The court does neither assess nor prove the content of the insolvency plan.[808] The insolvency court decides on the order to refuse or approve the insolvency plan within two weeks following the submission of the plan. In the case that the insolvency court approves the insolvency plan,[809] the insolvency plan is forwarded to the parties not having submitted the plan for their comments.[810] Since the disposition and distribution of the insolvency estate would impair the implementation of an insolv-

---

803 Sec. 231 InsO. See *Frege / Keller / Riedel*, mn. 1951.

804 Sec. 231(2)(no.1)(c.1) InsO. See *Frege / Keller / Riedel*, mn. 1953.

805 Sec. 231(1)(no.2) IS. See BMJ, Begr. RegE-InsO, BT-Drucks. 12/2443, p. 204. See also *Frege / Keller / Riedel*, mn. 1955 et seq.

806 Sec. 231(1)(no.3) InsO. *See* BMJ, Begr. RegE-InsO, BT-Drucks. 12/2443, p. 204; BGH, Beschl. v. 6.4. 2006 — IX ZB 289/04, mn. 9. See also *Frege / Keller / Riedel*, mn. 1953; *Jaffé*, in FK-InsO, Sec. 231 mn. 16 et seq., 25 et seq. See also OLG Dresden, Beschl. v. 21. 6. 2000 — 7 W 951/00, NZI 2000, 436, 437 = ZIP 2000, 1303, 1305 that this provision only applies when the debtor submitted the insolvency plan.

807 Sec. 231(1)(no.1)(c.2) InsO. See BMJ, Begr. RegE-InsO, BT-Drucks. 12/2443, p. 204. In addition, see *Jaffé*, in FK-InsO, Sec. 231 mn. 4 et seq. The court grants the person submitting the plan a time period to redraft the plan due to any defects in the plan, see *Jaffé*, in FK-InsO, Sec. 231 mn. 13; *Braun / Frank*, in *Braun*-InsO, Sec. 231 mn. 4. The "and" within this provision is to be understood as an "or", *see* Eidenmüller, in: MüKo-InsO 2002, Sec. 231 mn. 7; *Braun*, in *Nerlich / Römermann*-InsO, Sec. 231 mn. 4; *Braun / Frank*, in *Braun*-InsO, Sec. 231 mn. 3.

808 LG Bielefeld, Beschl. v. 30. 11. 2001 — 23 T 365/01, ZIP 2002, 951, 952.

809 Sec. 231(3) InsO. In the case the court refuses the insolvency plan, the person submitting the plan has the right of immediate appeal, see *Frege / Keller / Riedel*, mn. 1949, 1959; *Braun / Frank*, in *Braun*-InsO, Sec. 231 mn. 8.

810 Sec. 232(1) InsO. See *Frege / Keller / Riedel*, mn. 1962 et seq.; *Jaffé*, in FK-InsO, Sec. 232 mn. 4 et seq.

ency plan, the insolvency court may order suspension of disposition and distribution at the request of debtor or the insolvency administrator.[811]

Plan Discussion and Voting Meeting

The insolvency court orders a meeting to discuss the insolvency plan, the voting rights of the parties concerned and, subsequently, to vote on the plan.[812] The meeting usually takes place within the month following the submission of the insolvency plan.[813] All parties concerned receive individual summons.[814] All parties concerned may comment on the insolvency plan.[815] In the case there are any revisions necessary, the submitting party is entitled to modify the contents of individual provisions of the insolvency plan in accordance with the results of the discussion meeting.[816] A vote may then be taken at the same meeting on the modified plan.

---

811 Sec. 233 InsO. See *Frege / Keller / Riedel*, mn. 1961; *Braun*, in *Nerlich / Römermann*-InsO, Sec. 233 mn. 6 et seq.; *Smid*, Praxishdb. Insolvenzrecht, Sec. 30 mn. 33 et seq.

812 Sec. 235(1) InsO. See *Braun*, in *Nerlich / Römermann*-InsO, Sec. 235 mn. 4 et seq.

813 Ss. 235(1)(1), 236(2), 241(1) InsO. See BMJ, Begr. RegE-InsO, BT-Drucks. 12/2443, p. 206; *Frege / Keller / Riedel*, mn. 1967, 1972. The discussion and voting meeting may not be ordered prior to the verification meeting but both meeting may take place on the same day.

814 Sec. 235(3)(1) InsO. *See* BMJ, Begr. RegE-InsO, BT-Drucks. 12/2443, p. 205 et seq. *See also Frege / Keller / Riedel*, mn. 1967; *Jaffé*, in FK-InsO 2009, Sec. 235 mn. 25 et seq.

815 Begr. RegE, BT-Drucks. 12/2443, p. 205 et seq. See *Frege / Keller / Riedel*, mn. 1969; *Braun*, in *Nerlich / Römermann*-InsO, Sec. 240 mn. 2; *Hess / Weis*, WM 1998, 2349, 2357 et seq.

816 Sec. 240(1) InsO. See *BGH*, Beschl. v. 26.4. 2007 — IX ZB 5/06, NZI 2007, 521 = ZInsO 2007, 713. It is also appropriate to change essential features of the plan, see also *Frege / Keller / Riedel*, Insolvenzrecht, mn. 1969; *Hintzen*, in MüKo-InsO, Sec. 240 mn. 9; *Braun*, in *Nerlich / Römermann*-InsO, Sec. 240 mn. 2. See further BMJ, Begr. RegE-InsO, BT-Drucks. 12/2443, p. 207; Beschlussempfehlung des Rechtsausschusses, BT-Drucks. 12/7302, p. 183 on changes which effect the legal rights of persons not yet involved in the insolvency plan, which are more problematic and have to be invited again when they have not attended the discussion meeting. For this issue, see also *Jaffé*, in FK-InsO, Sec. 240 mn. 10; *Hintzen*, in MüKo-InsO, Sec. 240 mn. 14.

The voting rights of the creditors are determined at the voting meeting.[817] Each group of parties concerned with voting rights votes separately on the insolvency plan.[818] An insolvency plan is accepted by the creditors when each group the majority of creditors with voting rights backs the insolvency plan[819] and the sum of claims held by creditors backing the plan exceeds half of the sum of claims held by the creditors with voting rights.[820] The decision within a group of creditors is, therefore, made by a majority of votes and heads.[821] The groups have to unanimously accept the insolvency plan.[822]

Plan Consent and Plan Approval

The prohibition to obstruct is valid for all other voting groups besides shareholders[823] and the same prerequisites apply for their voting as deemed to have consented.[824] They may file for protection of minorities[825] or immediate appeal[826]. As soon as the creditors and shareholders have

---

817 Ss. 237(1)(1), 77(1)(1),(2),(3)(no.1) InsO in analogy. See *Frege / Keller / Riedel*, mn. 1971; *Braun / Frank*, in *Braun*-InsO 2012, Sec. 237 mn. 3 et seq.

818 Sec. 243 InsO. *See* Jaffé, in: FK-InsO 2009, Sec. 243 mn. 2 et seq.; Smid, Praxishdb. Insolvenzrecht 2007, Sec. 30 mn. 40; *Frege / Keller / Riedel*, mn. 1974; *Braun / Frank*, in *Braun-InsO*, Sec. 243 mn. 1; *Braun*, in *Nerlich / Römermann*-InsO, Sec. 243 mn. 14, Sec. 244 mn. 2.

819 Sec. 244(1)(no.1) InsO. See *Hintzen*, in Mü-Ko InsO, Sec. 244 mn. 9 et seq.; *Braun / Frank*, in: Braun-InsO 2012, Sec. 244 mn. 6; *Braun*, in *Nerlich / Römermann*-InsO, Sec. 244 mn. 4 et seq.

820 Sec. 244(1)(no.2) InsO. See *Hintzen*, in MüKo-InsO, Sec. 244 mn. 13; *Jaffé*, in FK-InsO, Sec. 244 mn. 6, 13.

821 *Braun / Frank*, in *Braun*-InsO 2012, Sec. 244 mn. 5; *Braun*, in *Nerlich / Römermann*-InsO 2009, Sec. 244 mn. 4. In the case no groups have been formed, a simple majority is enough to accept the plan, see *Frege / Keller / Riedel*, mn. 1977.

822 *Frege / Keller / Riedel*, mn. 1976; *Jaffé*, in FK-InsO, Sec. 244 mn. 12.

823 BMJ, Begr. RegE-InsO, BT-Drucks. 12/2443, p. 93 et seq.; *Frege / Keller / Riedel*, mn. 1981.

824 Sec. 245 InsO.

825 Sec. 251 InsO. See *BGH*, Beschl. v. 22. 3. 2007 — IX ZB 10/06, ZInsO 2007, 442, 443; *BGH*, Beschl. v. 29. 3. 2007 — IX ZB 204/05, ZIP 2007, 923 f. = NZI 2007, 409, 410; *LG Neubrandenburg*, Beschl. v. 31.7. 2000 — 4 T 260/00, ZInsO 2000, 628 (Leitsatz); *LG Berlin*, Beschl. v. 29. 10. 2002 — 86 T 534/02, ZInsO 2002, 1191, 1192.

826 Sec. 253 InsO.

consented to the insolvency plan, the debtor also has to consent.[827] An opposing opinion is deemed to be irrelevant if the debtor is likely not to be placed at a disadvantage by the insolvency plan compared with to a regular insolvency proceeding without an insolvency plan[828] and no creditor receives an economic value exceeding the full amount of his claim[829].

After the insolvency plan was approved by the creditors and the debtors or they are deemed to have consented, the insolvency court determines whether the prerequisites for ordering the approval of the plan have been met. These may include conditions in the insolvency plan[830] and provisions governing the contents and the procedural handling of the insolvency plan.[831] In the case the insolvency court is satisfied with the requirements, it may order the approval or refusal of the insolvency plan,[832] which is then announced.[833] As soon as approval of the insolvency plan has become final and unless the insolvency plan provides otherwise, the insolvency court shall decide on termination of the insolvency proceedings.[834] The implementation of the insolvency plan may be scrutinised by

827 Sec. 247(1) InsO. *See* BMJ, Begr. RegE-InsO, BT-Drucks. 12/2443, p. 210; *Jaffé*, in FK-InsO, Sec. 247 mn. 1 et seq.; *Braun / Frank*, in *Braun*-InsO, Sec. 247 mn. 1.

828 Sec. 247(2)(no.1) InsO. See *Braun*, in *Nerlich / Römermann*-InsO 2009, Sec. 247 mn. 3 et seq.; *Jaffé*, in FK-InsO, Sec. 247 mn. 6.

829 Sec. 247(2)(no.2) InsO. See *Jaffé*, in FK-InsO, Sec. 247 mn. 7; *Braun / Frank*, in *Braun*-InsO, Sec. 247 mn. 4, Sec. 245 mn. 7.

830 Sec. 249 InsO. See *Frege / Keller / Riedel*, mn. 1994; *Sinz*, in Mü-Ko-InsO, Sec. 249 mn. 7 et seq.; *Braun*, in *Nerlich / Römermann*-InsO, Sec. 249.

831 Sec. 250 InsO. See BMJ, Begr. RegE-InsO, BT-Drucks. 12/2443, p. 211; *Frege / Keller / Riedel*, mn. 1995 et seq.; *Jaffé*, in FK-InsO, Sec. 250 mn. 5 et seq.

832 Sec. 248 InsO. See *Frege / Keller / Riedel*, mn. 1993; *Jaffé*, in FK-InsO 2009, Sec. 248 mn. 1 et seq.

833 The approval has to be published in accordance with Sec. 252 InsO. See *Braun / Frank*, in *Braun*-InsO, Sec. 252 mn. 3 et seq., 72 et seq. The approval may be subject to immediate appeal in accordance to Sec. 253, see BMJ, Begr. RegE-InsO, BT-Drucks. 12/2443, p. 212; *Frege / Keller / Riedel*, mn. 2003; *Jaffé*, in FK-InsO, Sec. 253; *Smid*, NZI 2005, 613 et seq.

834 *Frege / Keller / Riedel*, mn. 2003; *Braun, in Nerlich / Römermann*-InsO 2009, Sec. 258 mn. 2; by the legally binding court order, all defects of the proceeding are void, see *RG*, Urt. v. 8.7. 1930 — VII 476/29, RGZ 129, 390, 391 et seq., also *Jaffé*, in FK-InsO, Sec. 253 mn. 12.

a filing for an immediate appeal against the order approving or refusing to approve the insolvency plan.[835]

General Effects of the Plan

As soon as the order approving the insolvency plan becomes final its effects under the constructive part shall become binding upon all the parties involved.[836] If the insolvency plan does not provide otherwise, the debtor shall be discharged of his residual obligations held by the insolvency creditors by the satisfaction of such creditors under the constructive part.[837] The declarations of intent of the parties included in the insolvency plan shall be deemed to have been submitted in the prescribed form.[838]

The insolvency plan is binding upon all the parties involved even those insolvency creditors who have not registered their claims and for parties who objected to the insolvency plans.[839]If the claims held by insolvency creditors were deferred or partly waived in the insolvency plan, such suspension or waiver is no longer binding upon a creditor on whose claims the debtor defaults to a considerable extent in performance of the plan.[840] The effectiveness of the plan will not be affected by non-compliance.[841] The default to a considerable extent is construed only if the debtor has not paid the debt due although reminded by the creditor in writing with a grace period of at least two weeks.[842] If a claim has been contested at the verification meeting or if the amount of the remaining claim held by a creditor entitled to separate satisfaction has not yet been determined, default on performing the insolvency plan is not construed if the debtor takes

835 *Frege / Keller / Riedel*, mn. 2003; *Jaffé*, in FK-InsO, Sec. 253 mn. 13; *Heublein*, NZI 2005, 381 et seq.

836 Sec. 254(1)(1) InsO. See *Jaffé*, in FK-InsO, Sec. 254 mn. 1 et seq.

837 Sec. 227 InsO. See *Jaffé*, in FK-InsO, Sec. 227 mn. 1 et seq.; *Braun / Frank*, in *Braun*-InsO, Sec. 227 mn. 1, 4, 6.

838 Sec. 254a(1)(c.2) InsO. See BMJ, Begr. RegE-InsO, BT-Drucks. 12/2443, p. 202 et seq.

839 Ss. 254(1)(1), 254b InsO. See *LAG Rheinland-Pfalz* Urt. v. 12. 10. 2006 — 4 Sa 281/06, mn. 55, Beck, RS 2007, 44876. See also *Jaffé*, in FK-InsO, Sec. 254 mn. 13 et seq.; *Braun*, in *Nerlich / Römermann*-InsO 2009, Sec. 254 mn. 5; *Otte / Wiester*, NZI 2005, 70 et seq.

840 Sec. 255(1)(1) InsO. See *Braun / Frank*, in *Braun*-InsO, Sec. 255 mn. 3.

841 *Bork*, in *Leipold*, p. 54 et seq.

842 Sec. 255(1)(2) InsO. See BMJ, Begr. RegE, BT-Drucks. 12/2443, p. 213.

into account the claim until final determination of its amount to the extent corresponding to the decision of the insolvency court on the voting right of such creditor upon the vote on the plan. If the court has not decided on the voting right, at the request of the debtor or of the creditor it shall subsequently determine the extent to which the debtor has to provisionally take such claim into account.[843] In the case the final determination shows the debtor is falling short in his payments, he pays the arrears. Default in performance of the insolvency plan is only construed if the debtor omits to pay the arrears despite a written reminder by the creditor within a grace period of at least two weeks.[844] If such final determination shows the debtor overpaying, he may claim restitution of the overpaid amount only to the extent exceeding even the immature item of the claim of the creditor under the insolvency plan.[845]

If new insolvency proceedings are opened for the debtor's assets before the plan has been performed to the full, a suspension or waiver shall be no longer binding upon any of the insolvency creditors.[846] The plan may provide otherwise. However, the plan may not derogate from subsection (1) to the detriment of the debtor.[847] Insolvency creditors with determined claims which were not contested by the debtor at the verification meeting may execute their claims under an approved and final insolvency plan.[848] The same applies to execution against a third party who, by a written statement submitted to the insolvency court without reserving the *beneficium excussionis*, has undertaken responsibility together with the debtor for performance of the plan by the latter.[849] In the case of considerable default on the part of the debtor in respect of performance of the insolvency plan, a creditor may invoke his rights. He must show to the satisfaction of

---

843 Sec. 256(1) 1 InsO. See *Braun / Frank*, in *Braun*-InsO 2012, Sec. 256 mn. 3 et seq.; *Jaffé*, in FK-InsO, Sec. 256 mn. 3 et seq.

844 Sec. 256(2) InsO. See *Jaffé*, in FK-InsO, Sec. 256 mn. 10 et seq.

845 Sec. 256(3) InsO. See BGH, Urt. v. 11. 5. 1978 — VII ZR 55/77, BGHZ 71, 309, 312 et seq.; *Braun / Frank*, in *Braun*-InsO, Sec. 256 mn. 9.

846 Sec. 255(2) InsO. See *Braun / Frank*, in *Braun*-InsO, Sec. 255 mn. 8 et seq.

847 Sec. 255(3) InsO. See *Bork*, in Leipold, p. 54. See also BGH, Urt. v. 29. 1. 1964 — Ib ZR 197/62, BGHZ 41, 98 et seq. for how to deal with overpayment to creditors.

848 Sec. 257(1) InsO. See *Braun*, in *Nerlich / Römermann*-InsO, Sec. 257 mn. 2 et seq.

849 Sec. 257(2) InsO. See *Braun*, in *Nerlich / Römermann*-InsO, Sec. 257 mn. 8 et seq.; *Jaffé*, in FK-InsO, Sec. 257 mn. 16.

the court the reminder and the expiry of the period of grace, but must prove no other facts constituting the default on the part of the debtor in order to receive an execution clause for such rights and to initiate such execution.[850]

Termination of the Insolvency Plan Proceedings

As soon as approval of the insolvency plan has become final, the insolvency court decides on termination of the insolvency proceedings.[851] Prior to termination, the administrator shall settle those undisputed due claims on the insolvency estate and provide securities for disputed or undue claims.[852] A financial plan may also be submitted for undue claims on the insolvency estate which shows that their satisfaction is guaranteed.[853] The offices of the insolvency administrator and of the members of the creditors' committee shall expire upon termination of the insolvency proceedings. The right of unhindered disposition of the insolvency estate shall be transferred back to the debtor.[854]

An action brought in the insolvency proceedings to contest the debtor's transactions may be continued by the insolvency administrator even after termination of the proceedings if provided for in the constructive part of the plan.[855] In such a case the action will be carried on for the debtor's ac-

---

850 Sec. 257(3) InsO. See *Jaffé*, in FK-InsO, Sec. 258 mn. 20 et seq.

851 Sec. 258(1) InsO. See BMJ, Begr. RegE-InsO, BT-Drucks. 12/2443, p. 214. Further *Jaffé*, in FK-InsO, Sec. 258 mn. 1 et seq.

852 Sec. 258(2)(c.1) InsO. See RG v. 15. 12. 1899 — 240/99 III, JW 1900, 73; *Jaffé*, in FK-InsO, Sec. 258 mn. 16, 20 et seq.; *Braun / Frank*, in: *Braun*-InsO, Sec. 258 mn. 5 on how to deal with claims originating after the approval of the plan.

853 Sec. 258(2)(c.2) InsO in connection with ss.232 – 240 BGB. See *Braun / Frank*, in *Braun*-InsO, Sec. 258 mn. 6.

854 Sec. 259(1)(1) InsO. See *OLG Celle*, Hinweisbeschl. v. 20. 11. 2006 — 4 U 166/06, ZIP 2006, 2394 et seq. = ZInsO 2006, 1327 et seq. See also *Jaffé*, in FK-InsO, Sec. 259 mn. 4 et seq.; *Braun / Frank*, in: *Braun*-InsO, Sec. 259 mn. 2. Further LG Berlin, Bescheid v. 8. 10. 2004 — 86 T 588/04, NZI 2005, 338 et seq.; *Frege / Keller / Riedel*, mn. 2010: on the remuneration of the administrator (only calculated after terminating the proceeding). See also *Grub*, DZWIR 2004, 317 et seq.

855 Sec. 259(3)(1) InsO. See *BGH*, Urt. v. 6. 10. 2005 — IX ZR 36/02, NZI 2006, 100, 101 et seq. = ZIP 2006, 39 et seq.; *OLG Jena*, Urt. v. 6. 2. 2002 — 2 U

count unless the plan provides otherwise.[856] The insolvency court decides on the termination of monitoring if the claims monitored for satisfaction have been met or their satisfaction is ensured[857], or three years have elapsed since termination of the insolvency proceedings and the opening of new insolvency proceedings has not been requested.[858] The right of unhindered disposition of the insolvency estate shall be transferred back to the debtor.[859]

7.1.4.4 Self-Administration

The reform of the Insolvency Statute introduced the possibility of self-administration.[860] The role model for this proceeding had been the debtor-in-possession provisions of Chapter 11 United States Bankruptcy Code. The rules, which apply to a regular insolvency proceeding also apply to the self-administration proceeding if there is no contrary to Ss. 270 to 285 InsO.[861] Self-administration is permissible for both natural and legal persons.[862]

Prerequisite for the self-administration order is the request for self-administration by the debtor in the insolvency court before the opening of proceedings.[863] The request may be withdrawn until the opening of the

---

1033/01, ZIP 2032, 538, 539 et seq. See also *Jaffé*, in FK-InsO, Sec. 259 mn. 15 et seq.; *Michels*, EWiR 2002, 293 et seq.

856 Sec. 259(3)(2) InsO. See *Jaffé*, in FK-InsO, Sec. 259 mn. 18; *Braun / Frank*, in *Braun*-InsO, Sec. 259 mn. 7.

857 Sec. 268(1)(no.1) InsO. See BMJ, Begr. RegE-InsO, BT-Drucks. 12/2443, p. 217; *Jaffé*, in FK-InsO, Sec. 268 mn. 2; *Braun / Frank*, in *Braun*-InsO 2012, Sec. 268 mn. 4 et seq.

858 Sec. 268(1)(no.2) InsO. See *Braun*, in: *Braun*-InsO, Sec. 268 mn. 6.

859 Sec. 259(1)(2) InsO. See *OLG Celle*, Hinweisbeschl. v. 20.11. 2006 — 4 U 166/06, ZInsO 2006, 1327 et seq. = ZIP 2006, 2394, 2395; *Jaffé*; in FK-InsO, Sec. 259 mn. 7 et seq.

860 Among others *Hofmann*, 2006; Wetzel, Insolvenzplanverfahren in Eigenverwaltung, 2009; Huhn, 2003; Dietrich, Die Eigenverwaltung als Sanierungsweg nach dem neuen Insolvenzrecht, 2002. See also *Braun*, NZI 2003, 588 et seq., *Buchalik*, NZI 2000, 294, 295 et seq.

861 Sec. 270(1) InsO. See *Riggert*, in *Nerlich / Römermann*-InsO, Sec. 270 mn. 4 et seq.

862 *Pape*, in Kölner Schrift zur InsO, p. 773 et seq.mn. 7 et seq.

863 Ss. 270(2)(no.1), 271 InsO. See *Vallender*, WM 1998, 2129, 2130 et seq.; *Eidenmüller*, ZIP 2007, 1729, 1735; *ibid.*, ZIP 2010, 649, 657: creditors have no

proceeding.[864] The debtor's management must be reliable and have business experience and the business itself is still functional.[865]

The insolvency court must approve the request unless specific indications exist that the self-administration has detrimental effects for the creditors[866] or is the self-administration has no prospects[867]. If such evidence exists, however, the insolvency court may reject the debtor's request for self-administration.[868] Rather the court may open a regular insolvency proceeding under the supervision of an insolvency administrator. The insolvency court must order the self-administration when the preliminary creditors' committee unanimously requested it.[869]

In a self-administration the debtor is admitted essentially the same powers as the insolvency administrator.[870] For the protection of creditors' interests[871], an insolvency monitor (*Sachwalter*) is appointed for the supervision[872] of the debtor instead of an insolvency administrator[873]. The

---

right to propose a self-administration, though the proceeding should be opened with min. 25% voting creditors supporting the application.

864 Sec. 272(1)(no.3) InsO. See *Reuter*, INDat-Report 01-2006, p. 8 et seq.: *Grundig AG* withdrew its application for self-administration and, shortly after, applied to open a regular insolvency proceeding.

865 LG Cottbus, Beschl. v. 17. 7. 2001 – 7 T 421/00, ZIP 2001, 2188.

866 Sec. 270(2)(no.2)(no.3) InsO. In the case the debtor acts against creditors' interests, he is as liable as the insolvency administrator (Ss. 60, 61 InsO). See *K. Schmidt*, AG 2006, 597, 602 et seq.; *Vallender*, WM 1998, 2129, 2132 et seq.

867 Sec. 270a(1) InsO.

868 Sec. 270(3) InsO.

869 Ss. 270(2)(no.3), 271, 272 InsO. The creditors' meeting may give the task to initiate an insolvency plan to the debtor or the insolvency monitor. In case the debtor receives the tasks, the insolvency monitor is advising him, Sec. 284(1) InsO, see *Wittig / Tetzlaff*, in MüKo-InsO, Sec. 284 mn. 13 et seq.

870 The debtor has also the initiative for an insolvency plan, see *Riggert*, in *Nerlich / Römermann*-InsO, Sec. 284 mn. 2; *Wittig / Tetzlaff*, in MüKo-InsO, Sec. 284 mn. 12; *Huhn*, p. 359 et seq.; *Warrikoff*, KTS 1997, 527, 532. For self-administration in insolvency plan proceeding, see also *Bales*, NZI 2008, 216, 218 et seq.; *Spies*, ZInsO 2005, 1254, 1256 et seq.; *Friedhoff*, ZIP 2002, 497 et seq.

871 BMJ, RegE-InsO, BT-Drucks. 12/2443, p. 223, 226; *Häsemeyer*, Insolvenzrecht 2003, mn. 8.04, 8.14 et seq.; *Smid*, Praxishdb. Insolvenzrecht 2007, Sec. 34 mn. 7; *Vallender*, WM 1998, 2129, 2135.

872 *Vallender*, WM 1998, 2129, 2134.

873 *Pape*, in Kölner Schrift zur InsO, p. 796 mn. 53 et seq.; *Smid*, Praxishdb. Insolvenzrecht 2007, Sec. 34 mn. 4 et seq.; *Smid*, WM 1998, 2489, 2510; see also OLG Naumburg, Beschl. v. 2. 5. 2000 — 5 W 47/00, ZInsO 2000, 505 et seq.

debtor keeps its administration and control rights[874] with some restrictions. The insolvency monitor receives certain rights and certain legal affairs of the debtor are subject to authorisation by insolvency monitor.[875] On the other hand, the debtor also receives competences beyond its normal scope.[876] Acts of particular legal importance must receive consent from the creditors' committee.[877] Factually the debtor continues to manage its business. In practice, however, the insolvency monitor manages the business. In addition, the management is usually replaced by a known and experienced administrator before the request for self-administration is made.[878]

The self-administration may be repealed or terminated.[879] Should the debtor breach its obligations, the self-administration should be repealed; it may also be repealed by request of the creditors' meeting, or at the request of the creditor or the debtor himself. Self-administration ends with the termination of the insolvency proceeding.

Self-administration was introduced by the Insolvency Statute with the aim of incurring lower costs through a faster process[880] and by promoting an early debtor request.[881] The knowledge and experience of the existing management should be better used to counteract the disadvantage of the training period of the insolvency administrator. The self-administration had, even in combination with the insolvency plan proceeding[882], no success so far.[883] It was even questioned to be "*the unloved child of the Insolv-*

874 Critical *Vallender*, WM 1998, 2129, 2134.

875 Ss. 275 et seq. InsO. See *Vallender*, WM 1998, 2129, 2135.

876 Ss. 279 et seq. InsO. See *Vallender*, WM 1998, 2129, 2135.

877 Sec. 276 InsO. See *Vallender*, WM 1998, 2129, 2136.

878 *Reuter*, INDat-Report 01-2006, p. 9: in preparation for the self-administration, *Klaus Hubert Görg* was appointed to the board of *Philipp Holzmann AG*, *Horst Piepenburg* was appointed to the boards of *Babcock Borsig AG* and *IhrPlatz GmbH & Co.KG*.

879 Sec. 272 InsO. See *Häsemeyer*, Insolvenzrecht 2003, mn. 8.18.

880 The legal proceeding costs are substantially lower in self-administration compared to a regular insolvency proceeding. However, the savings are compensated by the advisors and insolvency administrators on the board to implement a self-administration.

881 BMJ, RegE-InsO, BT-Drucks. 12/2443, p. 85 et seq.; *Hofmann*, p. 29 et seq.

882 *Emmerich / Wieselhuber*, p. 36.

883 *Hofmann*, ZIP 2007, 260; *Spies*, ZInsO 2005, 1254, 1255; *Undritz*, ZGR 2010, 201, 211 et seq.

ency Statute"[884]. In less than 1% of all insolvency proceedings, self-administration has been used.[885] The trend is even declining.[886] A reform of self-administration was required.[887] The need for reform was also recognised by the German legislature,[888] which is still convinced of the benefits[889] of self-administration. Self-administration is believed to allow for effective restructurings. Especially in insolvencies with complex corporate structures and early attendance for planning the restructuring, self-administration has shown its advantages.[890]

Responsible for the lack of success is the distrust of creditors, the inexperience of insolvency judges and legal uncertainty for the debtor, especially since insolvency administrators have greatly criticised the self-administration.[891] The debtor's management has already forfeited much of the given trust,[892] especially when the insolvency application has been filed late. It is therefore questionable whether the trust would still be enough to "*put the fox in charge of the henhouse*"[893] or whether the creditors mistrust the company's management as it is responsible for the insolvency situation.[894] In practice that has not been the case. With the appointment of an experienced insolvency administrator into the company's management there is already a new wind blowing.

---

884 *Reuter*, INDat-Report 01-2006, p. 8.

885 *Icks / Kranzusch*, p. 43, 132; *Leutheusser-Schnarrenberger*, ZInsO 2010, 614, 615.

886 *Icks / Kranzusch*, p. 132.

887 *Eidenmüller*, ZIP 2007, 1729, 1735; *Ibid.,* ZIP 2010, 649, 657; *Körner*, NZI 2007, 270, 275; *Pape*, ZInsO 2010, 1582, 1592 et seq.

888 BMJ, Begr. RegE-ESUG, BR-Drucks. 127/11, p. 27 et seq.

889 *Leutheusser-Schnarrenberger*, ZInsO 2010, 641, 615.

890 *Phillip Holzmann AG* was the first company to apply for self-administration, however, never went through. *Kirch Media AG*, *Babcock Borsig AG*, *Grundig AG*, *IhrPLatz GmbH & Co.KG* and fashion label *SinnLeffers* are further examples. For background on *SinnLeffers*, see *Beissenhirtz / Specovius*, INDat-Report 7/2009, p. 36 et seq.; *Doliwa*, p. 23 et seq.

891 *Hofmann*, p. 31 et seq.; *Grub*, WM 1994, 880 et seq.; *Körner*, NZI 2007, 200, 274; *Gravenbrucher Kreis*, ZIP 1992, 657, 658; *Gravenbrucher Kreis*, ZIP 1994, 585, 586; *Vallender*, WM 1998, 2129, 2139; *Reuter*, INDat-Report 01/2006, p. 8 et seq.

892 *Kranzusch*, ZInsO 2008, 1346, 1351 et seq.; *Buchalik*, NZI 2000, 294, 296.

893 *Graf / Wunsch*, ZIP 2001, 1029, 1033.

894 *Buchalik*, NZI 2000, 294, 295 et seq.; *Smid*, DZWIR 2002, 493; *Leutheusser-Schnarrenberger*, ZInsO 2010, 614, 615.

The inexperience of the respective judges with self-administration reinforced the negative attitude.[895] Since the self-administration is anchored with restrictive provisions in the law, the court has sufficient discretion in the examination criteria.[896] Also, the risk of public liability (*Amtshaftung*)[897] means that, if in doubt, insolvency courts do not approve the self-administration.[898] The majority of requests for self-administration are rejected.[899] The debtor was daunted by the risk that the insolvency court would reject the request despite an early application or even more opens a regular insolvency proceeding due to imminent insolvency.[900] The debtor should, therefore, be allowed to restrict its application only to open a self-administration. This should give him the opportunity to immediate appeal[901] the decision by the court.[902] The creditors' meeting also represents an uncertainty factor. It determines the proceeding[903] and can terminate the self-administration at any time.[904]

With the ESUG the prerequisites for self-administration were modified. Through simplified access requirements[905] and less intervention in the debtor's management,[906] the self-administration should foster restructurings.[907] The debtor is granted the motion in which the court indicates

895 *Kranzusch / Icks*, p. 43; *Uhlenbruck*, KSI 2010, 125, 127.

896 *Undritz*, ZGR 2010, 201, 2011; *Leutheusser-Schnarrenberger*, ZInsO 2010, 614, 615.

897 *Hofmann*, p. 31; *Bales*, NZI 2008, 216, 220.

898 Examples see *Paffenholz / Kranzusch*, p. 138 et seq.

899 In an empirical study, more than half of the requests were rejected, see *Emmerich / Wieselhuber*, p. 36; also *Paffenholz / Kranzusch*, p. 79 et seq.: insolvency courts rejected every third request for self-administration.

900 *Uhlenbruck*, KSI 2010, 125, 127.

901 Sec. 34(2) InsO.

902 *Smid*, Praxishdb. Insolvenzrecht 2007, Sec. 3 mn. 9; *Häsemeyer*, Insolvenzrecht 2003, mn. 8.09.

903 Sec. 157(1) InsO. See *Smid / Rattunde*, Insolvenzplan 2005, p. 91.

904 Sec. 272 InsO.

905 Sec. 270(2)(no.2) InsO.

906 Sec. 270a(1) InsO.

907 *Pape*, ZIP 2013, 2285, 2286: the amount of applications for self-administration in the first year after ESUG increased, however, considering the amount of insolvencies, there is no conclusion whether the self-administration has made progress in becoming the regular insolvency proceeding. See also *Moldenhauer et al.*, März 2013, p. 8.; *Ibid.*; März 2014, p. 3. However, it is clear that regarding the time of process, ESUG has speeded up the self-administration process, *Ibid.*, p. 12.

whether the application should be approved or the debtor should withdraw the request.[908]

In addition to the modified self-administration, ESUG also introduced the protective shield proceeding.

7.1.4.5 Protective Shield Proceeding

The legislature has taken a courageous step[909] with the newly created protective shield proceeding[910]. In the protection of self-administration, the debtor may work out a restructuring plan, subsequently implemented as an insolvency plan for the company's sustainable restructuring. The planning and legal certainty in the protective shield proceeding should simultaneously create an incentive to file for insolvency at an earlier stage, providing the company with the appropriate time to prepare a successful restructuring.[911]

The protective shield proceeding provides the debtor with a time period between the application and the opening of an insolvency proceeding to prepare for restructuring.[912] The debtor has to make his request on account of imminent insolvency or over-indebtedness, the intended restructuring does not manifestly lack the prospect of success and requests self-administration.[913] The request for a protective shield proceeding is illegitimate for an insolvent company.[914] By order of the insolvency court, the debtor receives up to three months[915] to submit an insolvency plan,[916] protected against the enforcement of creditors' claims and under control of an insolv-

---

908 Sec. 270a(2) InsO.
909 *Buchalik*, ZInsO 2012, 349.
910 Sec. 270b InsO.
911 BMJ, RegE-ESUG, BT-Drucks. 17/7511, p. 40.
912 *Braun/Heinrich*, NZI 2011, 505, 511: protective shield proceeding = preparatory proceeding for restructuring. Contrary *Desch*, BB 2011, 841 et seq.: the protective shield proceeding is not an auto-nomous proceeding but rather a preliminary self-administration with special privileges.
913 Sec. 270b(1)(1) InsO.
914 It does not prohibit a protective shield proceeding when a creditor makes a claim due for payment after the request has for a protective shield proceeding has been filed and the debtor is now indeed insolvent.
915 Sec. 270b(1)(3) InsO.
916 Sec. 270b)1)(2) InsO.

ency monitor.[917] The insolvency court takes all measures appearing necessary in order to avoid any detriment to the financial status of the debtor for the creditors until the insolvency court decides on the request of opening the self-administration.[918]

Requirements for Protective Shield Proceeding

The debtor must submit a certificate[919] provided by a tax advisor, accountant or lawyer with experience in insolvency matters or a person with comparable qualifications.[920] The certificate must provide evidence of the imminent insolvency or overindebtedness but that the debtor is not already insolvent[921] and that the intended restructuring does not manifestly lack the prospect of success.[922]

The certificate must include substantive information on the financial and economic situation of the company and analyses the causes of the crisis.[923] As a result, the certificate should evaluate how the company is constituted after restructuring measures have been implemented and whether it will regain competitiveness again for a successful going concern.

---

917 Sec. 270b(2)(1) InsO.

918 Sec. 21(1) InsO.

919 BMJ, RegE-ESUG, BT-Drucks. 17/7511, p. 40. See *Brinkmann / Zipperer*, ZIP 2011, 1337, 1344 et seq., *Buchalik*, ZInsO 2012, 349, 350 et seq.; *Zipperer / Vallender*, NZI 2012, 729 et seq.

920 *Buchalik*, ZInsO 2012, 349, 351 et seq. on qualification of certificate issuer.

921 *Frind*, ZInsO 2010, 1524, 1528: 99 % of requests are made when the company has already reached the state of insolvency.

922 Sec. 270b(1)(3) InsO. In Germany, the restructuring capability (*Sanierungsfähigkeit*) and restructuring worthiness (*Sanierungswürdigkeit*) must be audited. See IDW Anforderungen an die Erstellung Sanierungskonzepten (IDW 6), 2009, WPg Supplement 4/2009, p. 145 et seq.; *Friedrich / Flintrop*, DB 2003, 233 et seq.; IDW, IDW S 6, 2009, p. 20 mn 99 et seq.; *Weber*, ZInsO 2011, 904 et seq., *Undritz*, Kölner Schrift zur InsO 2009, p. 953 et seq. In addition, see IDW Stellungnahme RegE-ESUG, p. 14: the indefinite legal term that "the aimed restructuring has a reasonable chance to be successful" will need further substantiation by case lase, commentary and practice; also *Hirte*, ZInsO 2011, 401, 403; *Prütting*, ZIP 2013, 203 et seq..

923 *Frind*, ZInsO 2011, 2249, 2261.

This should be a sufficient basis for a plausibility check for the insolvency court to make the decision about the debtor's request.[924] The person issuing the certificate ought to be different from the insolvency monitor,[925] proofing the legal and factual independence of the person to the insolvency court and the creditors.[926] The certificate is only useful if the insolvency court audits both the formal and substantive requirements[927] to prevent any abuse and not to put the whole process in question. It remains to be seen how the insolvency court intends to comply with this obligation in practice without obtaining a third party expert's assistance.[928] Regularly, the insolvency court will have neither the resources nor the business knowledge to objectively evaluate the certificate.[929] The audit requirements of the insolvency court will also extend to evaluate the imminent insolvency or insolvency, as well as the targeted the not manifestly lack of prospect of the restructuring process.[930] The court shall revoke the order in the case that the envisaged restructuring no longer has prospects of success.[931]

---

924 *Desch*, BB 2011, 841, *Frind*, ZInsO 2010, 1524, 1528; *Frind*, ZInsO 2011, 2249, 2261.

925 Sec. 270b(2)(1) InsO. This was heavily criticised by the insolvency administrators, see Stellungnahme des Verbands der Insolvenzverwalter Deutschlands e.V. zu BR-Drucks. 127/11. BT-Drucks. 17/7511, p. 50. See also *Frind*, ZInsO 2011, 2249, 2261: the insolvency monitor and the person issuing the certificate should not work in one legal firm.

926 *Hölzle*, ZIP 2012, 158, 161 et seq.: the person issuing the certificate has not been working for the debtor prior to any proceeding and is independent in accordance with Ss. 56, 56a InsO. Contrary *Buchalik*, ZInsO 2012, 349, 351: another independent party does not make sense either under timing and costs aspects nor for the protection of creditors since the court is verifying the certificate. Neither the law itself nor the legislative reasoning for ESUG presumes such aspects.

927 *Obermüller*, ZInsO 2011, 1809, 1818.

928 *Frind*, ZInsO 2011, 2249, 2261; *Desch*, BB 2011, 841. Contrary *Brinkmann / Zipperer*, ZIP 2011, 1337, 1344; *Hirte*, ZInsO 2011, 401, 404; *Buchalik*, ZInsO 2012, 349, 352 et seq.

929 *Buchalik*, ZInsO 2012, 349, 352.

930 *Ibid.* Contrary *Obermüller*, ZInsO 2011, 1809, 1818.

931 Sec. 270b(4)(1)(no.1) InsO.

Appointment of a Provisional Insolvency Monitor

With the insolvency court's decision on the request of the debtor to open a protective shield proceeding, the court does not appoint a provisional insolvency administrator[932] but a provisional insolvency monitor[933]. The provisional insolvency monitor must not be the same person issuing the certification.[934] This establishes a priori trust between the insolvency court and the debtor.[935] The debtor has the right to propose the provisional insolvency monitor. The insolvency court may only dissent on the debtor's proposal if the proposed person is manifestly not suited to taking on the office[936] and needs to provide reasons for its decision.[937]

The provisional insolvency monitor verifies the debtor's economic situation and monitors the management of his business and expenses for his livelihood.[938] The powers of the provisional insolvency monitor are based on the powers of the administrator in the self-administration.[939] His powers of intervention are limited.[940]

Interim Measures and Justification of Mass Liabilities

With the request to open an insolvency proceeding, the court may order provisional measures.[941] These measures should avoid any creditors' enforcement action that could jeopardise the going concern of the company under the protective shield proceeding. In the opening of the protective shield proceeding, the insolvency court allows the debtor to make dispos-

---

932 Ss. 270b(2)(3)(c.1), 270b(2)(1), 270a(1) InsO. See BMJ, RegE-ESUG, BT-Drucks. 17/7511, p. 41; also *Desch*, BB 2011, 841, 842.

933 Ss. 270b(2)(1), 270a(1)(2) InsO. See *Buchalik*, ZInsO 2012, 349, 355: It shows the willingness of the legislator to provide for a restructuring proceeding in Germany, clearly cutting the power of insolvency administrators in self-administration.

934 Sec. 270b(2)(1) InsO.

935 *Desch*, BB 2011, 841, 843.

936 Sec. 270b(2)(2)(c.1) InsO.

937 Sec. 270b(2)(2)(c.2) InsO.

938 Sec. 270b(2)(1) InsO in connection with Ss. 270a(1), 274(2)(1) InsO.

939 BMJ, RegE-ESUG, BT-Drucks. 17/7511, p. 50.

940 Ss. 270b(2)(1), 270a(1)(2), 274(3)(1) InsO.

941 Ss. 270b(2)(3), 21(1),(2)(1)(no.1a)(no.3-5) InsO.

itions[942] or to order that all of the debtor's dispositions are effective only with the consent of a provisional insolvency monitor[943].[944]

A substantial benefit of the protective shield proceeding is the authority of the debtor given by the insolvency court to justify mass liabilities,[945] if the conditions[946] have been met. The debtor has been given a strong restructuring instrument.[947]

Disclosure

It is unclear whether the decision for of the insolvency court should be published. There is no obligation to do so.[948] The non-disclosure, however, does not make much sense and would likely provide individual creditors an unfair information advantage.[949] With regard to the formation of a provisional creditors' committee, the inclusion of key stakeholders and the orders of measures, the insolvency court will be well advised to disclose the decision on the order of the protective shield proceeding immediately.[950]

Establishment of a Preliminary Creditors' Committee

The provisions on the establishment of a preliminary creditors' committee[951] apply also in the protective shield proceeding. It is advisable to propose the composition of the preliminary creditors' committee to the insolvency court and agree and management on the provisional insolvency moni-

942 Sec. 270a(1)(no.1) InsO.
943 Sec. 270a(1)(no.2) InsO.
944 *Obermüller*, ZInsO 2011, 1809, 1818.
945 Ss. 270b(3)(2), 55(2) InsO. See BMJ, RegE-ESUG, BT-Drucks. 17/7511, p. 50; *Frind*, ZInsO 2011, 2249, 2260;.
946 Sec. 270b(3) InsO. See *Frind*, ZInsO 2011, 2249, 2260 for some contradictory points.
947 *Buchalik*, ZInsO 2012, 349, 356.
948 Sec. 23(1) in connection with Sec. 21(2)(1)(no.2) InsO.
949 *Buchalik*, ZInsO 2012, 349, 354.
950 *Desch*, BB 2011, 841, 843.
951 Sec. 22a(1) InsO.

tor.[952] The preliminary creditors' committee provides protection particularly against creditors trying individual enforcement of claims by appealing the order of the insolvency court to order a protective shield proceeding.[953]

The critics of the protective shield proceeding argue that the implementation of the preliminary creditors' committee is one of the many aspects why this proceeding is too complicated to ensure a necessary timely process.[954]

Presentation of Insolvency Plan and Opening Insolvency Proceedings

The debtor must submit an insolvency plan to the insolvency court within a period of three months.[955] The insolvency plan should be made in consultation with the preliminary insolvency monitor. Unlike the preliminary insolvency administrator, the preliminary insolvency monitor may not refuse permission to reimbursement for the creation of the insolvency plan and, thus, de facto prevent it.[956] After completion of the insolvency plan, the debtor may request to open self-administration. The time regularly coincides with the maximum period for pre-financing insolvency money (*Insolvenzgeldvorfinanzierung*).[957]

The protective shield proceeding is intended to replace the process of an ordinary insolvency proceeding as far as possible.[958] The insolvency money[959] is a useful measure to generate liquidation and keep the company going concern through strained times. The protective shield proceeding is only effective when the insolvency proceeding is opened on reasons the parties involved vote on the submitted insolvency plan. Since the

952 *Buchalik*, ZInsO 2012, 349, 355.
953 Sec. 270b(4)(1)(no.3) InsO.
954 *Buchalik*, ZInsO 2012, 349, 355: the fast formation of a preliminary creditors' committee may be difficult to achieve in practice.
955 Sec. 270b(1)(1),(2) InsO. See *Buchalik*, ZInsO 2012, 349, 353: average time to present an insolvency plan with the requirements for a sustainable restructuring should be issued within six weeks.
956 *Desch*, BB 2011, 841, 842.
957 *Buchalik*, ZInsO 2012, 349, 355.
958 *Ibid.*
959 Ss. 183 et seq. SGB III, insolvency money to be paid the case an insolvency proceeding as been opened in accordance with Sec. 183(1)(no.1) SGB III.

insolvency money is only paid after the opening of an insolvency proceeding, a pre-financing for insolvency money is needed.[960]

Revocation of Proceeding

Contrary to the original White Paper,[961] the protective shield proceeding is not necessarily revoked when insolvency occurs after the order of the proceeding.[962] The relevant date for the assessment of solvency is the time of request to open an insolvency proceeding.[963] The creditors' interests are safeguarded by the debtor's insolvency proceeding, providing statutory conditions like the supervision by insolvency court and the provisional insolvency monitor. In addition, creditors can protect their interests through the preliminary creditors' committee, which can reach at the request of a waiver of the protection proceedings by the court.

The court may revoke the order before the deadline expires if the restructuring no longer has prospects of success[964] or the provisional creditors' committee requests that the order should be revoked[965]. If no preliminary creditors' committee has been appointed, the request may be admissible if a creditor entitled to separate satisfaction or a creditor requesting the order and circumstances become known that lead to the expectation that the order will lead to creditors being placed at a disadvantage.[966] The debtor or the provisional insolvency monitor need to immediately notify the insolvency court in the case the debtor becomes insolvent.[967] The insolvency court takes a decision on whether to open insolvency proceedings either after revoking the order or after expiry of the deadline.[968]

---

960 *Buchalik*, ZInsO 2012, 349, 355 et seq.: details of pre-financing insolvency money and the importance for the going concern of the company.

961 BMJ, RegE-ESUG, BT-Drucks. 17/7511, p. 12.

962 *Brinkmann / Zipperer*, ZIP 2011, 1337, 1344.

963 Sec. 270b(1)(1) InsO.

964 Sec. 270b(4)(1)(no.1) InsO. See *Buchalik*, ZInsO 2012, 349, 356, estimating the requirements for revocation are higher than the disposition. Contrary *Desch*, BB 2011, 841, 844.

965 Sec. 270b(4)(1)(no.2) InsO. The court does not require any reason for the request.

966 Sec. 270b(4)(1)(no.3) InsO. BMJ, RegE-ESUG, BT-Drucks. 17/7511, p. 50.

967 Sec. 270b(4)(2) InsO.

968 Sec. 270b(4)(3) InsO.

With the protective shield proceeding, the German legislature has responded to the market's request.[969] The balancing act between the pre-insolvency (extrajudicial) restructuring proceeding and the insolvency proceeding, however, is likely to succeed only partially with the provisions provided.[970] It provides both opportunities and risks. The debtor has the opportunity to sustainably restructure with protection from creditors. In the case, that the restructuring fails, the possibilities for the administrator to rescue the company are still rather limited.[971] Another risk is the considerable scepticism or outright rejection[972] of insolvency courts when the debtor requests a protective shield proceeding and subsequent self-administration. Not integrated creditors in the restructuring plan may considerably harm the success of the proceeding when they terminate contracts or enforce onerous liquidity measures.[973] Any objection that the protective shield proceeding is much too complicated to allow for quick and timely restructuring should the practice clear up quickly and convincingly.[974]

With the protective shield proceeding, German insolvency law now has a restructuring instrument that can give the restructuring in insolvency a completely new direction.[975] In which direction this may go shows the example of the protective shield proceeding of *Suhrkamp*.[976]

7.2 England

7.2.1 Insolvency

Although the term *insolvency* and *insolvent* is applicable to both individuals and companies, the term *bankruptcy* is reserved for individuals. Corporate insolvency law is heavily interlinked with company law in England.

---

969 *Braun / Heinrich*, NZI 2011, 505, 511.
970 *Buchalik*, ZInsO 2012, 349, 357.
971 *Ibid.* 356.
972 *Frind*, ZInsO 2011, 2249, 2260, as an insolvency judge he seems to remain sceptical about the self-administration, see also *Buchalik*, ZInsO 2012, 349, 357.
973 *Braun / Heinrich*, NZI 2011, 505, 511.
974 *Buchalik*, ZInsO 2012, 349, 357.
975 *Ibid.*
976 See Chapter IV.

7.2.2 Opening Insolvency Proceedings

English insolvency law does not recognise a directors' mandatory duty to file for insolvency within a certain period of time. Since there is no corresponding direct liability for a late filing, directors[977] have few incentives to initiate insolvency proceedings.[978] It is easier, however, for creditors to apply for insolvency proceedings.[979]

A director is obliged to "*act in the way he considers, in good faith, would be most likely to promote success of the company for the benefit of its members as a whole*"[980]. Once a company becomes financially distressed, the focus of the directors' attention shifts away from the protection of shareholders[981] to "*consider or act in the interests of the creditors of the company*"[982].

However, in the case where the company is clearly insolvent, directors may be exposed to fraudulent trading[983] or wrongful trading actions.[984]

---

977 Ss. 171-177 CA 2006. Director in this sense are *de jure* directors (formally appointed), *de facto* directors (assume the role of a director without being formally appointed) and *shadow* directors (under whose directors the official directors are accustomed to act, sec. 251 CA 2006.

978 *Jungmann / Thiessen*, ECFR 2/2008, 190.

979 *Steffek*, Gläubigerschutz in der Kapitalgesellschaft, p. 122 et seq.

980 Sec. 172(1) CA 2006.

981 *Howard / Hedger*, mn. 9.12, see also *Re Smith & Fawcett Ltd* [1942] Ch 304, 306; *Multinational Gas & Petrochemical Co v Multinational Gas & Petrochemical Services Ltd* [1983] Ch 258: "there is no duty to creditors present or future when the company is solvent".

982 Sec. 172(3) CA 2006. See also *West Marcia Safetywear Ltd. V Dodd* [1988] BCLC 250, 4 BCC 30, CA; *Kinsella & Am v Russel Kinsella Pty Ltd* [1986] 4 ACLR 215; *Colin Gwyer & Associates ltd v London Wharf (Limehouse) Ltd* [2003] BCC 885.

983 Sec. 213 IA 1986. Fraudulent trading depends on the "real moral blame" attributable to someone, *see Re a Company (No 001418 of 1988)* [1990] BCC 526. See also *Steffek*, Münchner Handbuch des Gesellschaftsrechts, Sec. 41, mn 10-12.; *Schlegel*, MüKo-InsO / Länderbericht, mn. 37.

984 Sec. 214 IA 1986, see *Re Produce Marketing Consortium Ltd (No 2)* [1989] BCLC 520, 5 BCC 569; *Re Brian D Pierson (Contractors) Ltd* [2001] 1 BCLC 275; *Re Purpoint Ltd* [1991] BCLC 491, [1991] BCC 121. See *Howard / Hedger*, mn. 9.41 et seq.; *Steffek*, Münchner Handbuch des Gesellschaftsrechts, Sec. 41, mn 2-9.; *Schlegel*, MüKo-InsO / Länderbericht, mn. 38.

7.2.3 Grounds for Insolvency

In English law, the term *insolvency* refers to the onset of a formal statutory proceeding[985] while the *inability to pay debts* describes the state of material insolvency.[986]

There are two approaches to be taken to determine a company's *inability to pay debts*: either it is based on ascertainable facts[987] or based on more general criteria and divides into the cash flow test[988] and the balance sheet test[989].[990] The different tests also imply a differentiation between the concept of *debt*[991] and *liability*[992]. Even though the two sections stand side by side, there is no sufficient clarification yet on how they interact.[993]

985 Ss. 240(3), 247(1) IA 1986, s 6(2) CDDA 1986. *See* Goode, para. 4-01.

986 Ss. 123, 222-224, Sch. B1, para 11(a). *See* Goode, 4-01; *Steffek*, Münchner Handbuch des Gesellschaftsrechts, Sec. 38 mn. 8.

987 This is the inability to repay business debt when the debt is due. For example, if a trade creditor can demonstrate to a UK court that they are owed more than £750, they have the legal right to petition the court for bankruptcy proceedings against the company. In this example, if the company could not afford to pay this relatively small invoice, it is approaching cash flow insolvency.

988 *Keay / Walton*, p. 16: The cash flow test is also known as the "commercial insolvency test", applying inability to pay debts as they fall due.

989 *Ibid.,* The balance sheet test is known as the "absolute insolvency test", applying shortfall of assets in relation to liabilities.

990 *Goode*, para. 4-03.

991 *Ibid.,* paras. 4-17 et seq.

992 *Ibid.,* paras. 4-25, 4-26.

993 *BNY Corporate Trustee Services Limited v Eurosail-UK 2007-3bl plc and others* [2010] EWCA 2005 (Ch)*; BNY Corporate Trustee Services Limited v Eurosail-UK 2007-3bl plc and others* [2011] EWCA Civ 227: balance sheet insolvency is more complex than the point of no return test and includes a proper assessment of assets and liabilities, a company's statutory balance sheet is different from the balance sheet test of insolvency and as such can only be a starting point for the court's analysis. See also *Keay / Walton*, p. 16, stressing the fact that "in practice businesses usually tend to fail or pass both tests"; *Goode*, para. 4-06: "there is a close link between cash flow insolvency and balance sheet insolvency [...] a company, which is commercially solvent has a much greater chance of satisfying the balance sheet test of insolvency than one which is unable to pay its debts as they fall due.".

7.2.3.1 Cash Flow Test

The cash flow test[994] considers the question of whether "*a company is deemed unable to pay its debts [...] as they fall due*"[995] and is determined on the balance of probabilities[996] of the company's overall liquidity.[997] It is not just a snapshot of the debt due on a certain date. It also requires an element of futurity[998] but only with regard to the reasonably near future, dependent on the company's business and the overall circumstances.[999] Since

> "*once the court has to move beyond the reasonably near future [...] any attempt to apply a cash-flow test will become completely speculative, and a comparison of present assets with present and future liabilities [...] becomes the only sensible test*"[1000],

therefore, it is necessary to regard the balance sheet test as well.

7.2.3.2 Balance Sheet Test

The balance sheet test[1001] requires the court to decide whether "*the value of the company's assets is less than the amount of its liabilities, taking into account its contingent and prospective liabilities*"[1002].

However, assessing the company's assets and liabilities does not mean simply adding them up but also considering if prospective liabilities become present liabilities.[1003] In the twilight period leading up to a formal

---

994 *Goode*, paras. 4-05, 4-15 et seq.

995 Sec. 123(1)(e) IA 1986.

996 *Mallon / Waisman*, para. 5.15.

997 *Steffek*, Münchner Handbuch des Gesellschaftsrechts, Sec. 38 para. 17.

998 *Re Cheyne Finance Plc (No 2) [2007] EWHC 2402 (Ch).* See *Goode*, para. 4-16; *Fisher*, ICR 2008, 141 et seq.

999 *BNY Corporate Trustee Services Limited v Eurosail-UK 2007-3bl plc and others* [2010] EWCA 2005 (Ch); *BNY Corporate Trustee Services Limited v Eurosail-UK 2007-3bl plc and others* [2011] EWCA Civ 227.

1000 *BNY Corporate Trustee Services Limited v Eurosail-UK 2007-3bl plc and others* [2010] EWCA 2005 (Ch), *BNY Corporate Trustee Services Limited v Eurosail-UK 2007-3bl plc and others* [2011] EWCA Civ 227.

1001 *Goode*, paras. 4-06, 4-24 et seq.

1002 Sec. 123(2) IA 1986.

1003 *Re a Company* [1986] BCLC 261.

insolvency proceeding,[1004] the company's statutory balance sheet is different from the balance sheet test where the value of the company's assets is evaluated in the shadow of liquidation rather than on a going concern basis.[1005] The real prospect of the contingency's probability[1006] makes the assessment even more complex[1007] and "*raises the evidential bar*"[1008], especially when the prospective and contingent liabilities fall due further in the future. In this respect it is not enough to show that the value of company's assets are less than the amount of its liabilities at a particular point but that the company has reached the point of no return due to the incurable deficiency in the company's assets.[1009] While neither test is perfect and have some shortcomings,[1010] English courts have developed jurisprudence on the matter.[1011]

7.2.4 Restructuring and Insolvency Proceedings

English law has no less than seven proceedings for restructuring and insolvency. Whether the business has a future or not determines the nature of the application. Liquidation or winding-up deals with the disposal of a company's assets in cases where the company cannot be rescued. Administration, the company voluntary arrangement (CVA) and the scheme of arrangement are proceedings to restore a company to financial strength.

1004 *Mallon / Waisman*, mn. 5.17.

1005 *Goode*, mn. 4-35, p. 142 et seq.

1006 *Ibid.*, p. 118. See also *AA Mutual International Insurance Co Ltd* [2004] EWHC 2430 (Ch): "likely is more probable than not", referring to a probability of default of higher than 50% in the next year.

1007 *Steffek*, Münchner Handbuch des Gesellschaftsrechts, Sec. 38 mn. 29.

1008 Freshfields, Client Briefing March 2011, p. 1, http://www.freshfields.com/uploadedFiles/SiteWide/Knowledge/A%20commercial%20approach%20to%20the%20balance%20sheet%20insolvency%20test.pdf, accessed 12.8.2013.

1009 *BNY Corporate Trustee Services Limited v Eurosail-UK 2007-3bl plc and others* [2010] EWCA 2005 (Ch), *BNY Corporate Trustee Services Limited v Eurosail-UK 2007-3bl plc and others* [2011] EWCA Civ 227.

1010 *Keay / Walton*, p. 16.

1011 *Ibid.*, p. 17 et seq.

7.2.4.1 Winding-Up

Where a corporate rescue is not possible, an insolvent company will be placed into liquidation,[1012] wound up by a liquidator[1013] and, after all assets are sold,[1014] be dissolved as a separate legal personality within the next three months. Liquidation can be divided into *voluntary liquidation* and *compulsory liquidation*. The main distinction between a *voluntary* winding up (by resolution of the company: members of the board) and a *compulsory* liquidation (by order of the court) lies within the entity which has control of the process.[1015]

A company may be voluntarily liquidated without a court order in a *members' voluntary liquidation*, where the company's directors are willing to give a statutory declaration of solvency that the company is able to pay the creditors' debts in full within the next twelve months of commencement of the liquidation. In a *creditors' voluntary liquidation*, the company is insolvent and not in a position to pay its debts as they fall due. It should be noted, however, that the powers and the duties of the liquidator are similar in both categories of voluntary liquidations.[1016] The processes are initiated by either a special resolution or extraordinary resolution of the company's shareholders,[1017] however, they differ in the manner in which they are set in motion and in terms of to whom the liquidator is accountable.

1012 Ss. 73-229 IA 1986. See *Fletcher*, The Law of Insolvency, mn. 17-003 et seq.; *Finch*, p. 22 et seq.

1013 Sec. 86 IA1986, The liquidator assumes the functions and authorities which the directors of the company previously had. The general functions are to wind up the company, to inquire into its affairs, to realise and distribute its assets and pay its debts. A liquidator, in contrast, will be seeking to sell the assets or business of the company, if possible as part of a sale of the business as a going concern, before its dissolution. This may enable a purchaser to acquire at least part of the company's business as a going concern, thereby preserving the underlying business and workforce.

1014 Sec. 91(2) IA 1986.

1015 *Keay / Walton*, p. 229 et seq.

1016 Sec. 107 IA 1986.

1017 Sec. 84 IA 1986.

A *compulsory* liquidation is commenced by order of the court[1018] in response to a petition[1019] that the company is insolvent. The process is carried out by a liquidator appointed by the court.[1020] The liquidation is the most used proceeding in England.[1021] Once a company has entered into liquidation, there is little hope for corporate rescue.

7.2.4.2 Administrative Receivership

The Enterprise Act 2002 (EA 2002) abolished administrative receivership,[1022] a popular restructuring proceeding,[1023] by raising the formal entry requirements.[1024] It continues, however, to apply to floating charges prior the EA 2002.[1025]

In an administrative receivership, floating charge holders[1026] could enforce their security by the appointment of an administrative receiver. Only if the floating charge holder had been fully satisfied could the residual

---

1018 Sec.124(1) IA 1986.

1019 By either the creditors (ss. 123(1)(a), 221(a) IA1986), the company (sec. 282 CA 2006), DTI, receiver or the Secretary of State.

1020 Ss. 139 et seq. IA 1986.

1021 *Meyer-Löwy / Poertzgen / de Vries*, ZInsO 2005, 296.

1022 *Fletcher*, The Law of insolvency, Chapter 14. There have been notable high profile cases where a secured creditor was entitled to appoint an administrative receiver but chose to allow an administration to proceed. An example of this was the administration of the Olympia & York group arising from the failure of the Canary Wharf project, *Re Olympia & York Canary Wharf Ltd (No.1)* [1993] BCC 154.

1023 *Davis*, Insolvency and EA 2002, p. 38; *Müller-Seils*, p. 44. The appointment of the administrative receiver prohibited to initiate an administration proceeding, *Ibid.,* p. 55.

1024 *Müller-Seils*, p. 71 et seq.; *Meyer-Löwy / Poertzgen / de Vries*, ZInsO 2005, 293, 294; *Sealy / Milman*, p. 520.

1025 Sec. 72 B et seq. IA 1986: exceptions apply where floating charges are granted in relation to certain specialized financing arrangements within the capital markets, both private and public partnerships, financial and utility projects and shared landlords.

1026 A floating charge is a statutory restructuring instrument. As opposed to a fixed charge, determining a specific asset, the floating charge usually relates to an alternating asset (e.g. warehouse), which is made available until the event of default (crystallisation) to the debtor. See *Gottwald*, KTS 1981, 17, 33 et seq.; *Fletcher*, EBOR 5 (2004) 119, 149; *Ehricke / Köster / Müller-Seils*, NZI 2003, 409, 410 et seq.

value in the assets be distributed in an additional proceeding to the remaining creditors.[1027] The "*discrimination*" against the remaining creditors was said to be detrimental in the chances of the company surviving as a going concern.[1028] This prompted the legislature to adopt changes.

7.2.4.3 Administration

With the EA 2002, administration[1029] became the main proceeding to facilitate the rescue[1030] and survival of a company as going concern or achieve a better outcome[1031] for the creditors as a whole.[1032] The formal requirements were simplified.[1033] Prerequisite is the company's inability to its debts.[1034] The proceedings may take place via *in court* or *out-of-court route*.[1035]

A company in administration is under the protection of a statutory moratorium,[1036] which provides the company with a "*breathing space*" during which the administrator can reorganise the company's affairs or conduct an orderly realisation of the company's assets. The moratorium restricts the ability of third parties (particularly the company's creditors) to enforce their rights against the company without the prior consent of the

1027 The additional proceeding is usually a liquidation proceeding, see *Finch*, p. 240 et seq.; *Ehricke / Köster / Müller-Seils*, NZI 2003, 409, 411.

1028 *Armour / Mokal*, LMCLQ 2005, 28, 31.

1029 Sec. 8 IA 1986, Sch 1B1 IA 1986, art. 2(1) EA 2002. See *Fletcher*, EBOR 2004, 119, 133 et seq.; *Finch*, p. 380 et seq.

1030 The English legislator clearly stated that the rescue of the company as going concern applies to the legal entity, see *Müller-Seils*, p. 78.

1031 *T&D Industries plc* [2001] 1 BCLC 471: Although the creditors' views may be relevant, this will ultimately be a decision for the administrator, possibly with the court's assistance if there is any doubt although the court will be reluctant to interfere with what is ultimately a commercial decision.

1032 Para. 3(2) Sch. B1 IA 1986: "the administrator must perform his functions in the interests of the company's creditors as a whole".

1033 The proceedings were streamlined, see *Ehricke / Köster / Müller-Seils*, NZI 2003, 409, 412.

1034 Subpara. 11(a), 27(2)(a) Sch. B1 IA 1986 (company unable to pay its debt…); compare para. 111(1) Sch. B1 IA 1986, sec. 123 IA 1986.

1035 *Ehricke / Köster / Müller-Seils*, NZI 2003, 409, 414; *Müller-Seils*, p. 82 et seq.; *Sealy / Milman*, p. 525.

1036 Sec. 8(3) IA 1986, paras. 40 et seq. Sch. B1 IA 1986. See *Müller-Seils*, p. 98 et seq.

administrator or the consent of the court.[1037] The moratorium does not alter the substantive rights of a party against a company in administration, but simply suspends the exercise of those rights during the administration.[1038] The moratorium prevents the commencement of alternative insolvency procedures in respect of the company.

An administrator takes over the control of the company's business and assets from the company's directors[1039] and arranges within a certain timeframe[1040] a restructuring proposal[1041] for the creditors. The administrator calls for a creditors' meeting[1042] without classification where unsecured creditors'[1043] vote on the proposal. Since shareholders and secured creditor's rights are not addressed in administration there is no necessity for them to vote on the proposal. In case the restructuring is supposed to effect shareholders rights,[1044] the administrator may also propose an administration interlinked with a company voluntary arrangement or a scheme of arrangement[1045] without being limited to these two proceedings.[1046] Once the proposal has been accepted by the necessary majorities,[1047] the administrator implements the plan. The administration proceeding is limited to a year[1048] and may only be extended once for six months by the approval of the creditors' meeting[1049] or by court order.[1050]

There are several circumstances in which the administration is brought to an end.[1051] It can be terminated by time, missing approval for the proposals or where the objective is reached or will no longer be reached.[1052]

1037 Para 43, Sch B1 IA 1986.

1038 *Barclays Mercantile Business Finance Limited & Another v Sibec Developments Limited* [1992] 1 WLR 1253.

1039 Paras 1, 5, 10, 12, 64, 59ff Sch B1 IA 1986.

1040 Regularly eight weeks, Sch. B1 para. 49(5)(b) IA 1986.

1041 Rule 2.33, IR 1986.

1042 Sch. B1 para. 52(1) IA 1986.

1043 In rule 2.38, 2.40 IR 1986. See *Armor / Mokal*, LMCLQ 2005, 28, 31.

1044 *Müller-Seils*, p. 113.

1045 *Armour / Mokal*, LMCLQ 2005, 28, 42.

1046 Sch. B1 para. 49(3) IA 1986. See *Müller-Seils*, p. 106.

1047 Rule 2.43 IR 1986.

1048 Para 76 (1) Sch B1 IA 1986.

1049 Para 76 (2)(b) IR 1986.

1050 *Müller-Seils*, p. 115.

1051 Sch. B1 para. 76 et seq. IA 1986.

1052 *Müller-Seils*, p. 114 et seq for an overview of the nine, partly overlapping reasons to terminate an administration.

The practice has shown that the administration proceeding is not the first choice when the corporate rescue includes a debt restructuring. While in the past, the administration was mostly joined by a company voluntary arrangement or scheme of arrangement as an exit strategy from administration, nowadays, the latter are increasingly implemented as a *stand-alone* rescue procedure for a "*strategic insolvency*".[1053]

7.2.4.4 Pre-Pack Administration

In response to the inherent limitations to the classic administration procedure, the pre-pack insolvency sale has developed.[1054] Immediately after his appointment, the administrator completes the pre-arranged sale[1055] without the approval of creditors or the court.[1056] Advantages of a pre-pack are a more flexible and shorter process,[1057] therefore, fewer direct and indirect insolvency costs, reduced employment liabilities and a higher recovery rate for unsecured creditors.[1058] However, pre-pack sales are perceived as disadvantaging creditors since they are undertaken before the initial creditors' meeting, without the consent of creditors[1059] and lack transpar-

1053 *Eidenmüller*, ZIP 2014, 1197, 1199.

1054 *Finch*, Legal Studies 2012, 302, 314 on objectives and values pf pre-packs. See also Elliot, CR&I 2008, 194, 195, stating that pre-packs are not an option for very complex financing structures, therefore, not for implementing debt-equity-swaps. See also *Larkin / Smith*, ICR 2004, 78: pre-packs were mostly used with administrative receivership and administration.

1055 *Finch*, p. 454 et seq.; *Walton*, Int. Insolv. Rev. Vol. 18 (2009) 85 et seq.

1056 *Finch*, p. 470.

1057 *Wells*, BLR 2012, 156, 158.

1058 *Steffek*, Münchner Handbuch für Gesellschaftsrechts, Sec. 38, mn. 98.

1059 The administrator is not required to hold an initial creditors' meeting if he states either that the company has sufficient property to enable every creditor of the company to be paid in full or that the company has insufficient property to enable a distribution to be made to unsecured creditors other than from the statutory prescribed part for unsecured debts.

ency[1060] on how the value of the company has been determined.[1061] Foreign companies have taken advantage of English pre-pack deals.[1062]

7.2.4.5 Company Voluntary Arrangement

A company voluntary arrangement (CVA)[1063] is an informal but legally binding agreement between the company and its (unsecured) creditors[1064] as a means of rescuing the business as a going concern[1065] for rather simple restructuring structures.[1066] A CVA can be proposed by the directors, by an administrator or liquidator where the company is in administration or liquidation but not by creditors themselves. Since a CVA does not provide for a moratorium,[1067] it is regularly been linked with an administra-

1060 In *DKLL Solicitors v Her Majesty's Revenue & Customs* [2007] EWHC 2067 (Ch), the administration order of the court enabled the administrator to immediately sell the insolvent firm's business despite the opposition by the majority creditor to veto the sale at a creditors' meeting in order to save the jobs of approximately 50 employees with the pre-pack sale. The court concluded that the assets of *DKLL* could not be realised in liquidation for a similar sum compared to the purchase price under the pre-pack sale.

1061 Businesses that are sold by way of a pre-pack are usually sold with limited marketing compared to a normal administration to not leak any information about the company's distress. The real asset value generally declines in a sale when market participants become aware of a company's financial difficulties as they try to make a bargain.

1062 *Re Hellas Telecommunications (Luxembourg) II SCA* [2009] EWHC 3199 (Ch), see *Dakin et al.*, CR&I 2012, 120, 125.

1063 Ss. 1-7 IA 1986. See *Weisgard*, GM, Company Voluntary Arrangements, 2003.

1064 This also refers to secured creditors if they are not fully satisfied. See *Müller-Seils*, p. 157.

1065 *Windsor / Müller-Seils / Burg*, NZI 2007, 7 et seq.

1066 *Wallace*, CR&I 2012, 163: "the restructuring market has had something of a love/hate relationship with CVAs where they have been used for complex high-value restructurings [...] typically limited the scope of the restructuring to one company or a handful of key companies in the group".

1067 While IA 1986 did not provide for a statutory moratorium, the IA 2000, Sch 1, para.2(2) introduced a moratorium, however, only available for small companies as defined in sec. 247 CA 1985 for certain eligible companies. A company will not be eligible for a moratorium if it is: an insurance company, a bank or building society, a party to a market contract, money market contract or related contract, or a participant in a settlement system.

tion[1068] to provide the debtor with the protection of the administration moratorium whilst the CVA terms are being drafted, negotiated and finally presented to creditors for voting approval. A CVA may include a moratorium,[1069] a deferral, and a (partial) waiver of debt, a debt-equity-swap or any other capital measures.[1070]

The CVA will be binding on all creditors whether they have participated in the voting process or even had no knowledge about the process[1071] if the relevant majorities[1072] vote in favour of the proposal[1073] at properly convened meetings of creditors and shareholders of the company.[1074] The CVA cannot affect the rights of secured or preferential creditors in the absence of a unanimous agreement. Any proposal or modification that affects the rights of a secured creditor to enforce its security, or affects the rights of a preferential creditor as regards the priority or amount payable, cannot be approved without their consent. Shareholders also need to vote on the proposal in the company meeting. Their consent,

1068 *Baird / Ho*, Insolv. Int. 2007, 124.

1069 This is only valid for a stand-alone CVA; linked to an administration, the moratorium is statutory.

1070 *Windsor / Müller-Seils / Burg*, NZI 2007, 7, 9.

1071 *Fletcher*, EBOR 5 (2004) 119, 132; *Windsor / Müller-Seils / Burg*, NZI 2007, 7, 10.

1072 The mandatory majorities are set out in rule 1.19 IR 1986. Approval of the CVA proposal requires a simple majority vote of the debtors' members and a majority in excess of 75% by value of the unsecured creditors who attend and vote at the meeting of unsecured creditors convened for the purposes of voting (disregarding connected creditors). If these majorities are obtained, the CVA takes effect and becomes binding on all unsecured creditors (for these purposes irrespective of whether their rights have been affected by the proposal). Creditors vote as a single class and their votes are calculated according to the value of their claim at the creditors' meeting. For liquidated debts, voting is straightforward. In calculating majorities at a creditors' meeting, certain votes are left out of account, including where notice of the claim has not been given and where the claim, or part of it, is secured. A separate meeting of members is also held to vote on the proposals. Cram down in CVA requires approval by more than 50% or half in value of shareholders and more than 75% in value of creditors.

1073 The proposal may be suggested by an administrator, a liquidator or the company's directors, however, the last possibility is terminated once the administration or liquidation is opened, sec. 1 para. 1(1), 1(3) IA 1986. The CVA may be applied for by a nominee, same person as the administrator or liquidator.

1074 Ss. 3 – 5 IA 1986.

however, is only declaratory and limited to the extent that they may apply to the court in disagreement with the creditors' committee.[1075]

Provided that statutory formalities are complied with, CVAs can be very flexible and implement a debt-equity-swap without the consent of the shareholders[1076] as long as there is no residual value to their shares.[1077]

7.2.4.6 Scheme of Arrangement

Schemes of arrangements[1078] are rather for larger enterprises with complex corporate structures[1079] and requiring a long-term solution.[1080]

A scheme of arrangementis a statutory procedure where the (solvent or insolvent) company negotiates a compromise or other arrangement[1081] with all creditors or any class of creditors.[1082] The court orders general

1075 Sec. 4(A)(3) IA 1986.

1076 *Weller*, ZGR 2008, 835, 840 et seq.

1077 *Eidenmüller*, ZIP 2007, 1729, 1736.

1078 Part 26, Ss. 895-899 CA 2006. For procedural requirements, see Practice Statement (companies: schemes of arrangement) [2002] 3 All ER 96, [2002] 1 WLR 1345. The New Practise Direction (PD) 49A of the Civil Procedure Rules (CPR) 1998, part 49 para. 7.

1079 For insurance companies, the Financial Services and Markets Act 2000 introduced schemes as an alternative to liquidation for insurance and re-insurance companies, ensuring an orderly run-off of a solvent insurer's liabilities. *Hawk Insurance Company Ltd* [2001] 2 BCLC 67*; Re Equitable Life Assurance Society,* [2002] EWHC 140 (Ch), *Re Sovereign Marine & General Insurance Co Ltd and other companies* [2006] EWHC 1335 (Ch)*; Re Osiris Insurance* [1999] 1 BCLC 182.

1080 *Milmann*, in *De Lacy*, p. 415, 416.

1081 Without the arrangement or compromise, the court cannot sanction the proposal, *see Mercantile Investment and General Trust Co v International Co of Mexico* [1893] 1 Ch 484n, CA. *See Sneath v Valley Gold Ltd.* [1893] 1 Ch. 477: "in a commercial meaning, an arrangement or compromise is a settlement of a dispute"; *Re Guardian Assurance Co* [1917] 1 Ch 431: "an arrangement can be more than a compromise".

1082 *Re Sovereign Life Assurance Company v. Dodd [1892] 2 QB 573*: the composition of each class entitled to vote are "those persons whose rights are not so dissimilar". See *Re Hawk Insurance Co Ltd* [2001] EWCA Civ 241: the scheme was in first instance not sanctioned on the ground that creditor's rights were sufficiently different to require their separation into more than one class. The Court of Appeal in R*e Hawk Insurance Company Ltd* [2001] 2 BCLC 675 held that in case the proposed division of members/creditors into one or more voting classes

meetings[1083] for each class of creditors.[1084] The appropriate majorities[1085] who are entitled to vote must approve the scheme.[1086] When sanctioned by creditors and by the court[1087] as being just and equitable,[1088] and filed with the Registrar of Companies,[1089] the scheme becomes effective.[1090] The scheme will bind 100% of all shareholders and creditors of each class that approved the scheme,[1091] irrespective of whether or how they voted.

---

appear correct, fairness of the scheme will not be considered by the court. However, in *Re British Aviation Insurance Co Ltd* [2005] EWHC 1621 (Ch) the court has held that it has no jurisdiction to sanction a scheme where the classes have been incorrectly constituted. Potential conflicts of interests between classes (bondholders and banks) were considered in *Re Heron International NV* [1994] 1 BCLC 667.

1083 Sec. 307, 307A CA 2006.

1084 The interests of all member and creditors whose interests may be effected will need to be taken into account: *Re Savoy Hotel Ltd* [1981] Ch 351, [1981] 3 All ER 646. In the matter of *Re Bluebroock Ltd and others* [2009] EWHC 2114 (Ch) the court held that a creditor with no genuine economic interest in the distressed company has no standing to challenge the scheme.

1085 Majority in number representing 75% in value of the member or creditors (or each class, as relevant).

1086 *Re Anglo – Continental Supply Co Ltd* [1922] 2 Ch 723: relevant majority in number and value of the appropriate class(es) passed a resolution to approve the scheme.

1087 Sec. 899(1) CA 2006. There is nothing in the legislation that prescribes the matter of the scheme, however, the subject matter will have to be such that the court will approve it, in other words, to be fair, reasonable and to represent a genuine attempt to reach an agreement between the company and its creditors The explanatory statement setting out the effects of the scheme (Sec. 897, CA 2006) includes all information reasonable necessary to enable a reader to decide how to vote. New information dispatched after the explanatory statement must be communicated to members and/or creditors: *Re Jessel Trust Ltd* [1985] BCLC 119. This applies also to information of non-material nature *Re Minister Assets plc* [1985] BCLC 200.

1088 *Re NFU Development Trust Ltd* [1973] 1 ALL ER 153, the scheme alters members and creditors' rights when they participate in the scheme, which compensates for alterations. In accordance with *Re Bluebroock Ltd* [2009] EWHC 2114 (Ch); *Re Uniq plc* [2011] EWHC 749 (Ch), a scheme as a restructuring arrangement constitutes a valid compromise.

1089 Sec. 899(4) CA 2006.

1090 A scheme cannot be altered without returning to the court for further sanctioning, see *Devi v Peoples Bank of Northern India Ltd.* [1938] 4 AER 337.

1091 Sec. 899(3) CA 2006.

It enables a restructuring plan to be forced through by the court even on commercial terms[1092] if a minority of creditors or shareholders opposes it.[1093] A scheme may be used between a company and its creditors to restructure the company's debt and to rescue the company at a pre-insolvency stage.[1094]

A scheme is not subject to a moratorium where it is not initiated or implemented by an administrator or a liquidator as a part of an administration or liquidation (*insolvent scheme*) but by the company's directors or creditors (*solvent scheme*).[1095] However, since schemes of arrangement usually affect the rights of financial creditors only and trade creditors usually continue to be paid (preserving the goodwill value of the debtor), the financial creditors often agree a formal standstill,[1096] or if not, will usually informally agree to hold off from taking enforcement action, having taken a view that their recovery prospects are likely to be improved by the proposed restructuring.

7.3 Summary

Both the German and the English insolvency framework provide various statutory proceedings to allow companies either to be liquidated or to be restructured, depending on the viability of the company in financial distress. However, statutory frameworks also create difficulties in meeting the objectives of minimum costs in a timely manner with legal certainty. Many of the drawbacks of rescuing companies within a statutory framework could be avoided if a company's stakeholders, and in particular its creditors could assess a company's commercial viability and rather agree to an informal restructuring without recourse to court, being a more effective tool for corporate rescues.

The opening of insolvency proceedings is a major difference between the German and English insolvency framework: whereas the German directors have a duty to file for insolvency in German law within a period of three weeks after having established a ground for insolvency, there is

---

1092 *Countrywide PLC and others* [2009] EWHC 1347 (Ch).
1093 *Clowry*, in *Larkin*, p. 38.
1094 *Re Marconi Corp plc* [2003] EWHC 1083 (Ch).
1095 *Bork*, mn. 10.30, p. 142.
1096 *Laier*, GWR 2011, 252, 253.

no obligation to do so for English directors. They may only be liable for fraudulent or wrongful trading, although these liabilities are seldom established.[1097] The lack of duty to file gives the English debtor and its creditors the space and time to discuss whether the likely solution for the company in financial distress is rather liquidation or an informal or statutory restructuring proceeding, carefully weighing the risks and challenges involved and the effectiveness of the alternatives. Due to the time constraints in German law, there is usually not enough time to consider the different routes to solve the debtor's financial distress.[1098]

ESUG may have provided the solution with the opportunity of the debtor to request a protective shield proceeding whereas the company is given a breathing space to consider the alternatives and negotiate an insolvency plan with its creditors to whether the appropriate route to solve the situation could be a restructuring within the framework of an insolvency plan proceeding or self-administration or rather the liquidation of the company for the satisfaction of its creditors. While a debt-equity-swap is regularly implemented within a scheme of arrangement or a CVA in English law, the insolvency plan proceeding is the likely proceeding to implement a debt-equity-swap in Germany.

On a supra-national level, within the EIR, neither the scheme of arrangement nor the protective shield proceeding as a new proceeding introduced by is part of Annex A.[1099] The European Commission has classified these proceedings as pre-insolvency and hybrid proceedings.[1100] It is a pre-insolvency proceeding when the company in financial distress may restructure under the supervision of a court to avoid a regular insolvency proceeding; hybrids are proceedings where the debtor retains some control

---

1097 *Manning*, ICR 2013, 2: this could change as delinquent directors need to be disqualified following an insolvency.

1098 *Eidenmüller*, BB 1998, Beil. 10, p. 19.

1099 Report from the Commission to the European Parliament, the Council and the European Economic and Social Committee on the application of Council Regulation (EC) No 1346/2000 of 29 May 2000 on insolvency proceedings, COM(2012) 743 final, p. 4 et seq., http://ec.europa.eu/justice/civil/files/insolvency-report_en.pdf, accessed 30.6.2014.
Fn. 5 refers to the current situation of the protective shield proceeding to be unclear whether it refers to Article 1(1) EIR as it is a proceeding of the German Insolvency Statute.

1100 *Ibid.*, p. 4, 5.

over its assets albeit being subject to the control of a court or an insolvency practitioner.[1101]

Within the review process of the EIR, the majority of the respondents shared the view that the pre-insolvency and hybrid proceedings should be included in the EIR to ensure their recognition throughout the European Union and provide legal certainty for both debtors and creditors.[1102] While the scheme of arrangement already manifested its place as a pre-insolvency and hybrid proceeding, the protective shield proceeding has still its way to go. With the Commission recommendation on a new approach to business failure and insolvency [1103] to allow for a more rescue-friendly environment, there may be the implied necessity for the German legislator to amend the protective shield proceeding to comply with the Commission's requirements.

8 Debt-Equity-Swaps to Restructure Public Companies

Debt-equity-swaps in corporate restructuring have not been round for long. Only in the early 1990s, the real estate businesses approached their restructuring for a going concern with debt-equity-swaps to avoid a fire sale of assets in a falling market.[1104] Since then, debt-equity-swaps have proved to provide an upside to in difficult economic times and are expected to move "*from being a luxury to a necessity*"[1105]. In a debt-equity-swap, a creditor's debt is converted into equity by receiving shares of the company. The instrument is generally used when the creditors are unwilling to provide additional debt to the company and other restructuring efforts have already failed despite the fact that going concern value is higher than the liquidation value.[1106] Depending on the constellation of the debt-equity-swap, there may be more aspects to consider.[1107]

1101 *Ibid.*, p. 4.

1102 *Ibid.*, p. 6.

1103 Commission Recommendation of 12.3.2014 on a new approach to business failure and insolvency, C(2014) 1500 final, http://ec.europa.eu/justice/civil/files/c_2014_1500_en.pdf, accessed 30.6.2014.

1104 *Elliot*, CR&I 2008, 194.

1105 *Ibid.*, 195.

1106 *Kestler / Striegel / Jesch*, NZI 2005, 417, 418.

1107 *Wood*, Principles of International Insolvency, mn. 21–088 et seq.

Obviously the degree of conversion and the level of ownership in the company will depend on the valuation of the company relative to its entire indebtedness and the need to de-lever the company so that it is competitive and has an appropriate level of gearing and liquidity.[1108] The implementation of a debt-equity-swap requires careful economic and strategic planning, evaluating the different legal implications, differentiating between the advantages and disadvantages for all parties involved and leading to a sustainable restructuring concept. The legal issues and the preparation of the restructuring plan oppose a fast, flexible and reliable implementation of debt-equity-swaps. Especially the debate on legal issues was long postponed in Germany and only revived in the wake of the financial crisis. In view of the successful restructurings with debt-equity-swaps in England the demands for a legal simplification of debt-equity-swaps[1109] in a pre-insolvency or reformed statutory insolvency proceeding became louder.[1110]

8.1 Opportunities and Risks involved in Debt-Equity-Swaps

The change from a creditor to a shareholder position holds both opportunities and risks.[1111]

1108 *Baird / Bernstein*, 116 Yale L. J. (2005-2006) 1930, discussing different valuation procedures.

1109 *Undritz*, Kölner Schrift zur InsO, p. 973 et seq.; *Undritz*, ZGR 2010, 201, 210; *Eidenmüller / Engert*, ZIP 2010, 541 et seq.; *Westphal / Janjuah*, ZIP 2008, Beil. 3, p. 13; *Drouven*, ZIP 2009, 1052; *Spetzler*, KTS 2010, 433, 435 et seq.; *Himmelsbach / Achsnick*, NZI 2006, 561 et seq.; *Priester*, DB 2010, 1445 et seq.; *Redeker*, BB 2007, 673 et seq.; *Paape*, DZWIR 2009, 9 et seq.; *Jaffé*, ZGR, 2010, 248, 258; *Bork*, ZIP 2010, 397, 407.

1110 *Eidenmüller / Engert*, ZIP 2010, 541 et seq.; *Westphal / Janjuah*, ZIP 2008, Beil. 3, p. 13; *Jaffé / Friedrich*, ZIP 2008, 1849, 1854; *Jaffé*, ZGR, 2010, 248, 258; *Undritz*, Kölner Schrift zur InsO, p. 973 et seq.; *Beissenhirtz*, ZInsO 2011, 126 et seq.; *Madaus*, p. 624 et seq.

1111 *Wood*, Principles of International Insolvency, mn. 21–076 et seq.; *Clowry*, in *Larkin*, p. 27 et seq.; *Finch*, p. 321 et seq.; *Knecht / Drescher*, in *Buth/ Hermanns*, Sec. 20 mn. 41 et seq.; *Franke*, p. 54 et seq.; *Wilson* CR&I 2009, 103; *Born*, BB 2009, 1730, 1731; *Paulus*, DZWIR 2008, 6, 7 et seq.

8.1.1 Opportunities

There are three major opportunities in implementing a debt-equity-swap.

Creditors by converting debt to equity have a greater impact on the business operations of the company. They may introduce a restructuring consultant to the management who implements the restructuring plan in close consultation with the creditors.[1112]

The investor brings the much needed restructuring knowledge into the company. The company in financial distress may be restructured in an out-of-court process rather than in an insolvency proceeding.[1113] Thus, by avoiding an application for insolvency, the devaluation of assets and loss of trust by customers and suppliers could be avoided.[1114]

By reducing liabilities, the indebtedness of the company may be eliminated. Although the swap usually does not directly generate liquidity, it leads to reduced principal payments and reduced interest to be paid,[1115] therefore, increasing the cash flow of the company and providing indirectly liquidity to conquer imminent illiquidity.[1116] The swap leads to better equity ratio, which may attract new sources of financing[1117] through a better company rating.[1118] For the remaining creditors, the chances of repayment of the outstanding debt are increased. By avoiding the statutory element of insolvency or inability to pay debt, the liability risk for the directors decreases.

Maintaining the company as a going concern offers the new shareholders the chance to benefit from a higher recovery rate in the prospective increased value of the company instead of a lower recovery rate in liquidation.[1119] The willingness to take the risk is particularly high in cases where creditors have bought the debt on the secondary market at a discounted rate, perhaps even with the objective to engage in a debt-equity-swap.

1112 See Chapter II 3.2.2. for further details on Chief Restructuring Officer.

1113 Public examples where as debt-equity-swap has been implemented include *IhrPlatz GmbH& Co.KG* or *Senator Entertainment AG*, see *Schleusener*, p. 25-26.

1114 *Toth-Feher / Schick*, ZIP 2004, 491, 495.

1115 *Eidenmüller / Engert*, ZIP 2009, 541, 542; *Paulus*, DZWIR 2008, 6, 7.

1116 *Westphal / Janjuah*, ZIP 2008, Beil. 3, p. 1, 14.

1117 *Wittig*, in FS Uhlenbruck, p. 685, 703.

1118 *Paulus*, DZWIR 2008, 6, 7.

1119 *Ehlers*, ZInsO 2009, 320, 322.

8.1.2 Risks

Not only opportunities arise from the implementation of a debt-equity-swap but also risks are involved.

Especially in distressed companies, there is the potential risk that someday the "*skeletons in the closet*" reappear and the creditors register that the potential of the restructured company was not correctly assessed.[1120] This situation usually results in the immediate liquidation of the company to prevent further loss of the investment. Therefore, the investor will proceed to a careful due diligence and invest primarily in those companies where a significant restructuring contribution has already be done by a debt write-off on the balance sheet.[1121]

The conflict of interest between differently ranked creditors is also a perception of their risk-return expectation. The higher the swap ratio is in a debt-equity-swap, the lower the financial risk is for the company but the higher the loss that the lenders have to recognise immediately on their balance sheets in the form of write-offs. However, having to file for insolvency after a debt-equity-swap, creditors are much worse off since they have also converted their priority ranking position in the insolvency pecking order against a subordinated equity and security enforcement position, if any.[1122] The regular principal, possibly secured by collateral, and interest payment would be converted to unsecured dividend, to be decided by the management of the company.

Especially financial institutions only swapping part of their debt into equity encounter challenges in dealing with compliance (*Chinese walls*)[1123] attributed to the different handling of debt and equity and being an entrepreneur rather than a creditor. The business strategies for debt and equity have to be made independently from each other and may include contrary positions as to proceed further with the relationship of the company. Not only is the organisational structure a challenge, especially when only a portion of the debt is swapped into equity and the bank will be an equity holder, and a creditor at the same time, but also the higher capital

---

1120 *Leithaus*, FINANCE-Magazin, Sonderbeilage Mai 2006, p. 13.

1121 *Becker et al.*, KTS 2011, 53, 57.

1122 *Wittig*, in FS Uhlenbruck, p. 685, 701.

1123 *Toth-Feher / Schick*, ZIP 2004, 491, 492 et seq. for the challenges arising when the bank would be selling the debt position into the secondary market to a distressed investor.

requirements for equity positions are likely to discourage the banks from engaging in being entrepreneurs.[1124] This applies in particular to industries in which banks are exposed to a (high) reputational risk

Due to the mostly complex structure of debt with various different creditors and bondholders, debt-equity-swaps may need extensive planning in order to evaluate all risks and implement a structure to achieve the required outcome for the restructured company to be in a good state of returning back to earnings potential. This involves intensive costs and legal planning.[1125]

8.2 Germany

With the amendments made by ESUG, the insolvency plan proceeding now offers comprehensive latitude[1126] for the corporate restructuring of a company, and in particular it increases the feasibility of debt-equity-swaps.[1127] Capital measures and their impact on the legal status of the parties are to be included in the formative part of the insolvency plan.[1128] From a corporate law perspective, there are several ways to implement a debt-equity-swap,[1129] but the usual way is for the claim to be swapped for equity by means of a capital increase against a payment/contribution in

---

1124 *Becker et al.*, KTS 2011, 53, 58.

1125 *Drukarczyk*, ZGR 1979, 553, 558, stating that the legal planning for a capital decrease and capital increase to implement a debt-equity-swap due to the necessary requirements of notarisation and registry may hardly be possible in the three weeks' timeframe to apply for insolvency. With the protective shield proceeding to prepare for an insolvency plan and the measures to implement a debt-equity-swap, a timely management may now be more possible and achievable.

1126 *Simon / Merkelbach*, NZG 2012, 121, 123.

1127 An explicit codification of a debt-equity-swap in German law can only be found in Sec. 9 KredReorgG.

1128 Sec. 225a(2)(1) InsO.

1129 For alternative structures see *Holbein*, p. 267 et seq.; *Westphal*, in *Eilers / Koffka / Mackensen*, III, p. 243; *Schleusener*, p. 120; *Cohen / Maclennan*, CRI 2009, 91; *Windsor / Müller-Seils / Burg*, NZI 2007, 7, 9; *Clowry*, in *Larkin*, p. 34; *Carli / Rieder / Mückl*, ZIP 2010, 1737 et seq.; *Eidenmüller*, ZIP 2007, 1729, 1736, *Knecht / Drescher*, in *Buth / Hermanns*, Sec. 20 mn. 21 et seq.; *Hass / Schreiber / Tschauner*, in *Hommel / Knecht / Wohlenberg*, p. 843, 844, 857 et seq.; *Steffek*, Münchner Handbuch des Gesellschaftsrechts, Sec. 40, mn. 1.; *Oelke / Wöhlert / Degen*, BB 2010, 299 et seq.; *Toth-Feher / Schlick*, ZIP 2004, 491, 494 et seq.

kind[1130] assigning the claim back to the company. By confusion, the claim ceases to exist.

The conversion of a claim against the company into equity with the purpose of restructuring the company is done by a capital cut, which consists of a simplified capital decrease[1131] with a concurrent effective capital increase whereby the claim is assigned to the company by payment in kind.

8.2.1 Capital Decrease

Simplified capital reduction[1132] eliminates the accounting equity deficit on the balance sheet[1133] by adjusting the capital to the current value of assets (book restructuring).[1134] In the case that the company is already over-indebted, a capital reduction to zero equity is possible.[1135] For the purpose of an accounting restructuring of a company,[1136] the protection of creditors is in some regards weakened and made less complicated.[1137]

1130 The German Federal Court of Justice has neglected the swap of debt into equity by payment in cash due to creditors' protection reasons, see BGHZ 110, 47, 52 et seq. For qualification payment in kind, see BGHZ 132, 141, 143 f. = NJW 1996, 1473. See also *Ekkenga,* ZGR 2009, 581, 589.

1131 *Noack*, mn. 382. An effective capital decrease in a current insolvency proceeding is illegitimate due to creditor protection, Sec. 222 AktG. Possible is a capital decrease with a concurrent capital increase or a balance sheet restructuring (*Buchsanierung*) with a simplified capital decrease procedure (*vereinfachte Kapitalherabsetzung*) with no danger for creditors' protection.

1132 Ss. 229 et seq. SCA.

1133 Wirth, DB 1996, 867, 869: an equity deficit is the negative difference between the assets of the company compared to its equity and therefore the equity on the balance sheet no longer corresponds to the nominal capital of the company. This is to be confined from over-indebtedness where the assets of the company no longer cover its liabilities.

1134 *Hüffer*, AktG, Sec. 229 mn. 2. See also *K. Schmidt*, ZGR 1982, 519, 520 et seq.

1135 Sec. 228 AktG. See BGHZ 119, 305, 319 et seq.; BGHZ 142, 167, 169; OLG Koblenz, AG 1998, 429, 430. See also *Achsnick*, p. 104; *Krieger*, ZGR 2000, 885, 897 et seq.

1136 The capital is decreased nominally without generating any liquidity to be (re)distributed to the company.

1137 Ss. 225(1), 229(2) SCA. The creditor protection is achieved by the fact that the accrued capital reserves above 10% have to be capitalised after the capital decrease, this does not apply to hidden / uncapitalised reserves. The liquidity, however, is not to be distributed to shareholders or creditors but remain in the

The resolution for a simplified capital reduction must explicitly include the relevant purpose[1138] and requires a majority of at least 75 % of the votes of the general assembly, unless the articles of association include other provisions[1139].[1140] This required three-quarters majority for the reduction resolution was difficult to achieve in the past as the shareholders had to not only meet the prerequisites for a corporate restructuring but also make a decision entailing the (almost complete) impairment of their own shares.[1141] In the past, the obligation to obtain the consent of the existing shareholders in the event of a necessary restructuring was derived from the shareholders' fiduciary duties.[1142]

The resolution enacting capital reduction also includes the adjusted nominal value of the shares. The reduction of the nominal value of the share capital and the contribution in kind are to be carried out in accordance with their current relationship. An amendment to the articles of association is also permissible in an opened insolvency proceeding as long as the ultimate purpose of the insolvency proceedings is not avoidance of satisfying creditor claims.[1143]

company in accordance with Sec. 230 SCA. Only in the case that the company still carries losses, restructuring instruments may be implemented.

1138 *Noack*, mn. 382, the provision is provided in Sec. 229(1)(2) SCA.

1139 *Lutter*, MüKo AktG, Sec. 229 mn. 6; *Hüffer*, AktG, Sec. 229 mn. 18.

1140 The capital decrease follows the requirements of ss. 179 et seq. AktG with a majority vote by the general assembly, Ss. 229(3), 222(1)(1) AktG.

1141 *Wittig*, in FS Uhlenbruck, p. 685, 699.

1142 *Eidenmüller / Engert*, ZIP 2009, 541, 543; *Redeker*, BB 2007, 673, 675; *Schmidt / Schlitt*, DK 2009, 279, 282. In accordance with the "*Girmes*"-judgement by the German Federal Court of Justice, the shareholders have to refrain from impede a restructuring, including a capital decrease for a debt-equity-swap, for their selfish reasons, see BGHZ 129, 136. See also *K. Schmidt*, ZGR 1982, 519, 525; *Eidenmüller / Engert*, ZIP 2009, 541, 543; *Pleister / Kindler*, ZIP 2010, 503, 510; *Schmidt / Schlitt*, DK 2009, 279, 282; *von Sydow / Beyer*, AG 2005, 635, 640; *Schäfer*, in FS Hommelhoff, p. 939 et seq.; *Weller*, in LA Winter, p. 755 et seq. Contrary *Brinkmann*, WM 2011, 97, 99: there is no ground to apply the fiduciary duties of shareholders to the debt-equity-swap.

1143 Noack, mn. 337. See also *Eidenmüller*, ZGR 2001, 680, 692 et seq.

8.2.2 Capital Increase

In a public limited company, there are three legal ways to implement a capital increase. It may be made from the authorized capital[1144] or from company funds[1145] or from issuing new shares. Since a capital reduction is made below the minimum capital requirement in a debt-equity-swap, the first two possibilities are excluded. The capital increase will therefore regularly be implemented by means of an ordinary capital increase.[1146] In the case that a capital reduction has been made under the minimum share capital requirement, a capital increase in cash has to be made until the minimum share capital requirement is reached again.[1147] Only after reaching the minimum threshold is a capital increase possible by issuing new shares against a contribution in kind.[1148]

The capital increase must be made in the same resolution as the capital reduction and must also include the person contributing the claim and the nominal share value in exchange for the contribution in kind.[1149] The articles of association must also be amended,[1150] including the details of the contribution in kind and the corresponding value. Capital increases by contribution in kind and by contribution in cash both become effective upon entry in the commercial register.[1151]

It is questionable, however, whether the necessary simplified capital reduction and subsequent capital increase in a debt-equity-swap transaction serve a relevant purpose. With the capital reduction, the company's capital is amended to the company's real asset value, and is therefore no longer available for the collective satisfaction of creditors.

In addition, a prerequisite for the restructuring of insolvent companies and the implementation of a debt-equity-swap is that creditors regularly take a haircut (waiver) to contribute to the restructuring.[1152] Thus, the purpose of collective creditor satisfaction would be further thwarted. This ar-

---

1144 Ss. 192, 193 221(1)(3) AktG.
1145 Sec. 207 AktG.
1146 Sec. 182 AktG.
1147 *Wirth*, DB 1996, 867.
1148 Sec. 182(1)(4) AktG.
1149 Sec. 183(1) AktG.
1150 Ss. 183(1), 27(1)(1) AktG.
1151 Sec. 184 AktG.
1152 *Noack*, mn.279. With the haircut, the creditors contribute their share to the capital decrease, however, it will regularly be smaller than the contribution of the

gument could be countered by the view that the capital reduction serves merely to display the company's financial situation. In liquidation, the market value of the assets would materialise in any case, which would not provide the book value to satisfy liability to creditors.

The subsequent capital increase could contribute to the purpose if the capital increase were regularly included[1153] in the insolvency pool,[1154] which would thus contribute to the collective satisfaction of creditors. The claims of the company against the (new) shareholders arise from the decision on the capital measures in the constructive part of the insolvency plan. The effects for and against all parties legally occur only with the confirmation of the insolvency plan,[1155] at which point the insolvency court generally terminates the insolvency proceeding.[1156] The insolvency plan is generally subject to the autonomy of the creditors, and may include alternative provisions. Even if the insolvency plan were conditional on certain actions being implemented prior to its confirmation,[1157] the legal enforcement of the plan would still depend on confirmation by the insolvency court.

From the substantive character of the insolvency plan procedure, one may argue that a capital increase does not directly serve the satisfaction of the creditors in an insolvency procedure as the remedy for the creditors' claim for satisfaction is based on the date when the claim arose, which is regularly before the onset of insolvency. From a procedural law perspective, the company only incurs claims against the new shareholders after the confirmation of the insolvency plan and termination of the insolvency proceedings. In the case that the creditors were satisfied by the insolvency pool being replenished by the capital increase, the restructuring efforts would be doomed to failure: existing shareholders participating in the cap-

---

shareholders to their realisation of liability. See also *Tashiro*, eurofenix, Spring 2013, p. 4.

1153 *Uhlenbruck*, in Kölner Schrift zur InsO, p. 1157, 1174. *Contrary* Noack, mn. 278.

1154 Sec. 35(1) InsO: "The insolvency proceedings shall involve all of the assets owned by the debtor on the date when the proceedings were opened and those acquired by him during the proceedings (insolvency estate)".

1155 Sec. 254(1)(1) InsO.

1156 Sec. 258(1) InsO.

1157 Sec. 249(1) InsO.

ital increase would be liable twice while new shareholders would already be liable for existing liabilities.[1158] This makes no sense for either.

The intention of existing shareholders to participate in the capital increase to implement a debt-equity-swap may well be to achieve a higher satisfaction of their claims from the restructured company than the recovery rate they would be offered in the event of the company's liquidation. In the case that an existing creditor only swapped a portion of his claim, he would become a new shareholder while still remaining a creditor and the contribution in kind would be used to settle his own debt. This effect would regularly lead to a refusal by the old shareholders to participate in the capital increase and torpedo the restructuring from the start. The question is then whether existing creditors would participate in the restructuring if the inclusion of the proceeds from the capital increase increased the insolvency pool and the expected satisfaction rate in a liquidation were then higher than a possible recovery rate in a debt-equity-swap in an insolvency plan proceeding.

8.2.3 Participation of Shareholders and Creditors

Even though shareholders and creditors are now both parties involved in an insolvency proceeding, there is a differentiation between their positions in a debt-equity-swap.[1159] In general, creditors need to be considered in a restructuring in accordance with the ranking order they had in the financial structure of the company that would apply in the case of liquidation of the company. The ranking of creditors outside insolvency is usually not modified in insolvency proceedings.[1160]

Equity and debt are not to be regarded as opposites but as the two poles of funding necessary, giving space for a variety of mixed contributions,[1161] e.g. convertibles or mezzanines. The existing shareholders are involved in the restructuring process as in the liquidation proceedings only in accordance to the value of the debtor's assets if the debtor is not insolvent. In the past, the shareholders of an over-indebted company in general neither had the right to participate nor to remain in the restructured com-

---

1158 *Uhlenbruck*, in Kölner Schrift zur InsO, p. 1157, 1174.
1159 *K. Schmidt*, ZGR 2012, 566, 570.
1160 *Balz*, Sanierung von Unternehmen, p. 10; *Goodison*, ICR 2006, 164, 165 et seq.
1161 *Balz*, Sanierung von Unternehmen, p. 5.

pany.[1162] However, a consensual restructuring early initiated and fastly carried out will generally involve shareholders. Creditors will give them the option to (re-)gain value of their shares in case they are willing to participate in the restructuring with appropriate means.

8.2.3.1 Shareholders

In a capital increase to implement a debt-equity-swap, it is questionable whether the existing shareholders have to be granted a subscription right or if the subscription right may be legally excluded.

Corporate and Insolvency Law

In the past, it was debatable whether existing shareholders had subscription rights in a capital increase in insolvency proceedings. The right could be derived from the fiduciary duty of the shareholders and the principle of equal treatment, or from an analogy with the exclusion of subscription rights in a capital increase.[1163] The prevailing opinion required a justification in individual cases as well as an explicit shareholder resolution.[1164] ESUG provides the justification for the exclusion of subscription rights in the constructive part of the insolvency plan.[1165] From this provision one may conclude that there is a subscription right in favour of the shareholders in the insolvency plan proceeding in general.[1166] The admissibility of excluding subscription rights to the detriment of existing shareholders is assumed.[1167] German law only allows a simplified exclusion of subscription rights in the particular case that the capital increase does not exceed 10% of the share capital and the share's issue price is not significantly be-

1162 *Ibid.*
1163 Sec. 186(3),(4) AktG.
1164 *Scheunemann / Hoffmann*, DB 2009, 983, 984.
1165 Sec. 225a(3)(3) InsO.
1166 *Simon / Merkelbach*, NZG 2012, 121, 125; BMJ, Begr. RegE-ESUG, BR-Drucks. 127/11, p. 45.
1167 *Bauer / Dimmling*, NZI 2011, 517, 518; *Hirte / Knof / Mock*, DB 2011, 632; *Hölzle*, NZI 2011, 124, 128; *Meyer / Degener*, BB 2011, 846, 847 et seq.; *Brinkmann*, WM 2011, 97, 99.

low the stock market price. It is therefore questionable whether the exclusion of subscription rights in ESUG is constitutional and thus permitted.

Constitutional Law

The provision for excluding subscription rights in the insolvency plan procedure does not result from corporate law but from the insolvency provisions.[1168] Substantively, an effective exclusion of subscription rights in the insolvency plan procedure requires an objective justification.[1169] It must be in the interest of the company, suitable, necessary and appropriate.[1170] If the same objective could also be achieved with other milder legal means, interference in the substance of shareholder rights should be omitted to avoid their dilution and thus protect the (minority) shareholder.[1171]

As part of the capital increase for a debt-equity-swap, it should be noted that the creditors do not provide cash but contribute their claims as a contribution in kind to the company. For the exclusion of subscription rights in a contribution in kind transaction, an objective justification has already been discussed for the case that the company has a sufficient interest in the acquisition of that object.[1172] The objective justification could be negated if the necessary liquidity for the repayment of debt could be procured through a capital increase in cash without subscription rights.[1173] This is regularly not the case in a debt-equity-swap. Whether there should be a capital increase in cash parallel to a capital increase with a contribution in kind – in favour of the other shareholders whose subscription rights have been precluded from the capital increase by contribution in kind to protect them against a dilution of their shares[1174] – is somewhat questionable. An

1168 Ss. 237 et seq, 254a(2),(3) InsO.

1169 BGHZ 71, 40, 43 = NJW 1978, 1316; BGHZ 83, 319, 321 = NJW 1982, 2444; BGHZ 136, 133, 139 = NJW 1997, 2815; BGHZ 120, 140, 145 f.; BGHZ 125, 239, 241; *Peifer*, Mü-Ko AktG 2011, Sec. 186 mn. 71 et seq.; *Hüffer*, AktG, Sec. 186 mn. 25; *Schmidt / Schlitt,* DK 2009, 279, 281.

1170 BGHZ 71, 40, 43 = NJW 1978, 1316.

1171 *Ekkenga*, ZGR 2009, 581, 610.

1172 *Peifer*, MüKo AktG 2011, Sec. 186 mn. 90.

1173 *Hüffer*, AktG 2006, Sec. 186 mn. 35; *Redeker*, BB 2007, 673, 675; *Toth-Feher / Schlick*, ZIP 2004, 491, 495; *Westphal*, in *Eilers, Koffka, Mackensen*, III. 2. a) bb) mn. 7.

1174 *Lutter*, ZGR 1979, 401, 406; *Scheunemann / Hoffmann*, DB 2009, 983, 984.

exclusion of subscription rights is justified in principle in the case that a claim is made as a contribution in kind as part of debt-equity-swap[1175] for the purpose of restructuring the company and this would otherwise not be achieved.[1176] This is especially valid when the creditors willing to participate in the restructuring make their commitment dependent on receiving a sufficient stake in the company.[1177] In these cases, the interest of the (old) shareholders in preserving their shareholding is waived in favour of a successful restructuring.[1178]

Despite the clear statement by the legislature regarding the constitutional implications in relation to the constitutional right to property and freedom of association,[1179] it has further been discussed[1180] whether the interference with the shareholder position by the exclusion of subscription rights in the debt-equity-swap is constitutional and thus legal, since the existing shareholders have a legal position protected by the "Basic Federal Law of the Republic of Germany".

Article 14 Grundgesetz: Property, Inheritance, Expropriation

The right to property of shareholders could conflict with the exclusion of subscription rights in a debt-equity-swap transaction.[1181] Shares in public limited companies are part of constitutionally protected property[1182] and the shareholder is legally entitled to subscription rights in a capital increase. Exclusion of subscription rights is therefore an intrusion into his right as it changes his legal position. The intrusion into the shareholder's rights is not an expropriation as it does not constitute any state action [1183]

1175 *Redeker*, BB 2007, 673, 675; *Sydow / Meyer*, AG 2005, 635, 637.

1176 *Hüffer*, AktG 2006, Sec. 186 mn. 35; *Scheunemann / Hoffmann*, DB 2009, 983, 984.

1177 BGHZ 83, 319 = NJW 1982, 2444, 2446; *Seibt*, Der Konzern 2009, 261, 269.

1178 *Seibt*, Der Konzern 2009, 261, 263.

1179 BMJ, RegE-ESUG, BT-Drucks. 17/5712, p. 31.

1180 *Simon / Merkelbach*, NZG 2012, 121, 125. *Madaus*, ZGR 2011, 749 et seq.; *Decher / Voland*, ZIP 2013, 103, 105 et seq.

1181 *Müller*, p. 364 et seq.; *Smid / Rattunde*, Insolvenzplan, mn. 6.24 et seq.; *Kluth*, ZInsO 2002, 258, 262.

1182 Art. 14(1)(1) GG. See also BVerfGE 14, 263, 276 et seq. *Feldmühle*; BVerfGE 25, 371, 407 *Rheinstahl*; BVerfGE 50, 290, 341f.; BVerfGE 102, 197, 211.

1183 Art. 14(3) GG. For detailed discussion, see *Hofman*, in FS Hopt, 2010, p. 833 et seq.

but rather a determination of content[1184] that the legislators allows creditors to intervene in shareholder rights.[1185]

With the adoption of ESUG, the statutory insolvency regime[1186] intrudes directly and immediately into the rights of shareholders.[1187] This provision was particularly made because of the previous lack of enforcement of debt-equity-swaps against the will of shareholders, which was considered one of the key obstacles to restructuring companies in the past.[1188]

The legislature has held that in cases of insolvency with a target of restructuring the company in an insolvency plan proceeding, the ownership interests of the shareholders are equally or less worth protecting than the asset ownership of creditors derived from their claim.[1189] The Insolvency Statute[1190] recognises that the shareholders may obtain any additional value from the company only after the satisfaction of creditors.[1191] The distributive justice between existing shareholders and creditors in insolvency [1192] is therefore preceded by a complete integration of all debt and equity holders, and thus also the liquidation of equity to satisfy the outstanding creditor claims.[1193]

1184 Art. 14(1)(2) GG.

1185 *Eidenmüller / Engert*, ZIP 2009, 541, 545 et seq.; *Decher / Voland*, ZIP 2013, 103, 108 et seq. for discussion.

1186 Sec. 217(2) InsO.

1187 BMJ, RegE-ESUG, BT-Drucks. 17/5712, p. 30. The intrusion was not granted before, see BVerfGE 14, 263, 277; *Sassenrath*, ZIP 2003, 1517, 1523; *Brüning*, p. 271 et seq.; *Eidenmüller*, ZIP 2007, 1729, 1736 et seq.; *Westphal / Janjuah*, ZIP 2008, Beil. 3, p. 15; *Eidenmüller / Engert*, ZIP 2009, 541, 546.

1188 BMJ, RegE-ESUG, BT-Drucks. 17/1512 Introduction. See also *Müller*, p. 308; *Brüning*, p. 62 et seq., 248 et seq.; *Eidenmüller / Engert*, ZIP 2009, 541, 549; *Westphal / Janjuah*, ZIP 2008, Beil. 3, p. 14.

1189 *Sassenrath*, ZIP 2003, 1517, 1523; *Westphal / Janjuah*, ZIP 2008, Beil. 3, p. 15.

1190 Sec. 199 InsO.

1191 BGH ZIP 2010, 1039, 1041. See also *Bitter*, ZGR 2010, 147, 191; *Eidenmüller / Engert*, ZIP 2009, 541, 549 et seq.; *Jaffé / Friedrich*, ZIP 2008, 1849, 1854; *Madaus*, ZGR 2011, 749, 755, is stating that the priority rule of Sec. 199 InsO is only for the distribution in liquidation.

1192 *Simon*, CFL 2010, 448, 455 et seq.; *Eidenmüller / Engert*, ZIP 2009, 541, 543 et seq.; *Verse*, ZGR 2010, 299, 305 et seq. No precise distribution measures have been developed yet.

1193 BMJ, RegE-ESUG, BT-Drucks. 17/5712, p. 30. See *Eidenmüller / Engert*, ZIP 2009, 541, 544 et seq.; *Sassenrath*, ZIP 2003, 1517, 1526. Contrary *Madaus*, ZGR 2011, 749, 757 et seq.; *Müller*, p. 365 et seq.

It is questionable whether a substantive intervention in the ownership position is justified. If only the creditors agree to convert debt into equity for restructuring purposes, the objective justification is regularly met.[1194] Thus, in these cases the prevailing opinion considers an exclusion of subscription rights permissible.[1195] The creditor making his commitment dependent on receiving a majority stake in the company could provide objective justification.[1196]

To prevent an initial improper exclusion of subscription rights or to allow shareholders to avoid dilution, there could be a capital increase in cash combined with a capital increase with contribution in kind.[1197] This is usually designed as an up-to-capital increase.[1198] It can be performed with a double exclusion of subscription rights or a uniform capital increase; in the latter case an exclusion of subscription rights would be unnecessary.

With the ESUG, the existing shareholders are now a party involved in the insolvency proceedings and they vote on the insolvency plan when their rights are actually affected by the plan.[1199] This will regularly be the case in a forced intrusion into shareholder rights. There is a differentiation with respect to a possible compensation. If the shares are economically worthless, there is no compensation.[1200] However, in comparison with a regular insolvency proceeding, in which the shares are forcibly lost when the company is liquidated for the satisfaction of the creditors, the shareholders should not be worse off in an insolvency plan proceeding.[1201] This is because in an insolvency plan process[1202] the existing shareholders could benefit from a residual value in a going concern scenario[1203] and be

---

1194 *Schmidt / Schlitt*, DK 2009, 279, 281.

1195 *Hüffer*, AktG 2006, Sec. 186 mn. 35; *Toth-Feher / Schlick*, ZIP 2004, 491, 495; *Vaupel / Reers*, AG 2010, 93, 95.

1196 This may especially account for institutional investors with an interest in management and stee-ring power over the company.

1197 *Vaupel / Reers*, AG 2010, 93, 95.

1198 *Schmidt / Schlitt*, DK 2009, 279, 281.

1199 *Urlaub*, ZIP 2011, 1040, 1044.

1200 BGH, NJW 2006, 1663, 1664.

1201 *Vallender*, NZI 2007, 129, 136 et seq.See also *Smid / Rattunde*, Insolvenzplan 2005, mn. 6.624 et seq.; *Uhlenbruck*, NZI 2008, 201, 203; *Sassenrath* ZIP 2003, 1517, 1523.

1202 Sec. 199(2) IS.

1203 *Lüer*, in *Uhlenbruck*, InsO, Sec. 217, mn. 18 et seq.: due to the restructuring the shares should be valued as going concern. See also *Ulmer*, ZHR 1985, 541, 556 et seq.

attributed any surplus.[1204] In this case, there has to be an appropriate compensation for the existing shareholders,[1205] although the relevant value for calculating the compensation has to be real economic value of the shares.[1206] The constitutionality of such provisions has already been proven in the comparable constitutional legal framework[1207] of the squeeze-out procedure.[1208]

It is questionable whether the shareholders may participate in a possible increase in value through the restructuring of a company.[1209] This would be the case if creditors also benefitted from an increase in value in accordance with the nominal amount of their claim.[1210] A justification for such a far-reaching interference with shareholder rights would no longer be justified by the protection of the interests of creditors.[1211] Due to the sufficient participation of existing shareholders in an insolvency plan proceeding as a voting group on the plan there is no ground for expropriation. It can be stated that existing shareholders receive little protection from their constitutional property right.[1212]

The question now arises whether the legal validity of the intervention into the shareholders' property rights will similarly apply to the right to freedom of association.

1204 *Verse*, ZGR 2010, 299, 310.

1205 As far as comparable, see also *BVerfG*. Beschl. v. 27.4.1999 – 1 BvR 1613/94, BVerfGE 100, 289, 303 *DAT/Altana*; BVerfG, Beschl. vom 20.8.2000 – 1 BvR 68/95, NJW 2001, 279, 280 *MotoMeter*; *BVerfG* NJW 2007, 828 *Siemens Nixdorf*; BVerfG NJW 2007, 3266, 3267, *Wüstenrot/Württembergische*; BVerfG NJW 2007, 3268, 3270 *Edscha*. See also *Smid / Rattunde*, Insolvenzplan, 2005, mn. 6.24; *Brüning*, p. 277 et seq.

1206 *Eidenmüller / Engert*, ZIP 2009, 541, 546.

1207 Ss. 327a et seq. SCA.

1208 BVerfG ZIP 2007, 1261; BVerfG ZIP 2007, 2121; OLG Düsseldorf, NZG 2004, 328, 329. See also *Westphal / Janjuah*, ZIP 2008, Beil. 3, p. 15 et seq.; *Jaffé / Friedrich*, ZIP 2008, 1849, 1854; *Eidenmüller / Engert*, ZIP 2009, 541, 546; *Hüffer*, AktG 2006, Sec. 327 a, mn.4.

1209 *Lüer*, in *Uhlenbruck*, Sec. 217, mn. 18 et seq., attributing to the shares an increase in value due to future profits and cash flow.

1210 For details, see *Verse* ZGR 2010, 299, 310 et seq.

1211 *Urlaub*, ZIP 2011, 1040, 1044; *Meyer / Degener*, BB 2011, 846, 848.

1212 *Madaus*, ZGR 2011, 749, 761.

Article 9 Grundgesetz: Freedom of Association

As a result of a compensation payment for the shares or, in particular, their worthlessness and the fact that shareholders may be excluded from the company as a consequence of the vote on the insolvency plan, an intervention in the freedom of association may be justified and therefore constitutional.[1213] The scope of freedom of association extends to companies in insolvency,[1214] especially if the purpose pursued is the restructuring and not the liquidation of the company.[1215]It is questionable whether the fact that the value of the shareholders' share in insolvency is (mostly) worthless justifies interference with shareholders' rights.[1216]

With the company being substantively insolvent and the opening of insolvency proceedings, the shareholders could lose their entitlement to the insolvent legal entity.[1217] The shareholders have to be granted protection mechanisms to ensure that they are not subject to any arbitrariness in return for the inclusion of their rights in the plan process, especially in regard to their shares.[1218]

The exclusion of subscription rights for existing shareholders as part of debt-equity-swaps can therefore only be objectively justified if the insolvency plan providing for a capital increase also includes the possibility for existing shareholders to continue to participate in the company.[1219] This is because the subscription right is nothing other than the shareholders' right to participate in the company by subscribing to new shares to contribute to its restructuring and, consequently, to maintain their position as shareholders even after the insolvency proceedings. Accordingly, they participate with a fair share in the (hopeful) success of restructuring the company.[1220]

Although there could be a tendency to prevent or restrict the constitutionally protected private autonomy and the freedom of association of shareholders during efforts to restructure a company, one should consider that creditors only have a right for their claims to be satisfied by the

1213 *Decher / Voland*, ZIP 2013, 103, 112.

1214 *Müller*, p. 364, regarding the problems of Art. 9 GG as more severe than Art. 14 GG.

1215 *Madaus*, ZGR 2011, 749, 756.

1216 *Brinkmann*, WM 2011, 97, 100.

1217 Contrary *Madaus*, ZGR 2011, 749, 762 et seq.; *Müller*, p. 364 et seq.

1218 Sec. 245(3)(no.1) InsO.

1219 *Ekkenga*, ZGR 2009, 581, 613; *Simon / Merkelbach*, NZG 2012, 121, 126.

1220 *Simon / Merkelbach*, NZG 2012, 121, 125.

debtor's assets. Only assets are liable for the collective satisfaction of the creditors in insolvency.[1221]

This right in particular for shareholders to participate in restructuring measures was repeatedly called for previous to the adoption of ESUG.[1222] However, even in the case of an assumed worthlessness of the shares, there is no justification for imposing new shareholders on old shareholders against their will.[1223] The existing shareholders should be allowed to terminate their participation in the company in the event of a debt-equity-swap provided that their rights have already been completely removed.[1224]

In the case shareholders would be allowed to participate in the capital increase in the restructuring and would execute their subscription rights, it is questionable though which ratio or which absolute value would be attributed to existing shareholders in comparison to creditors.[1225]

The question of the exclusion of subscription rights will be of central importance to the practical application of the new insolvency plan proceedings as a restructuring instrument. Reinforcing company restructuring by insolvency plan proceedings and earlier adoption of this process will only occur if existing shareholders are willing to seek a restructuring by means of an insolvency plan voluntarily and at an early stage. However, this will only be the case if they can continue to remain shareholders in the company even after the insolvency plan procedure. On the other hand, over-extensive involvement of existing shareholders may be detrimental to creditors as they may not be able to achieve a sufficiently interesting stake in the company through the debt-equity-swap. In order to avoid any challenges with the shareholders, creditors could decide to continue for the business-asset deal to be the preferred proceeding.

1221 *Balz*, Sanierung von Unternehmen, p. 55; *Madaus*, ZGR 2011, 749,.

1222 *Brinkmann*, WM 2011, 97, 101; *Urlaub*, ZIP 2011, 1040, 1044; *Hölzle*, NZI 2011, 124, 128.

1223 *Brinkmann*, WM 2011, 97, 100.

1224 *Ibid.* 101.

1225 Prior to ESUG, it was discussed as to whether the existing shareholders wanting to participate in the restructuring should be able to keep their initial participation quota, see *Hölzle*, NZI 2011, 124, 128; *Urlaub*, ZIP 2011, 1040, 1044.

European Law

A debt-equity-swap could also infringe European law[1226] as laid out in the "Second Council Directive",[1227] ECJ case law[1228] and/or the "Charter of Fundamental Rights"[1229] for the case that shareholders are *de lege ferenda* ignored in capital measures regularly accompanying a debt-equity-swap in an insolvency plan procedure.

The "Second Council Directive"[1230] requires all capital measures (capital increases or reductions) and the exclusion of subscription rights[1231] to have the approval of the general assembly. Despite possible interpretations, the ECJ has explicitly rejected exceptions to the "Second Council Directive" for capital measures necessary to facilitate a corporate restructuring in crisis situations. It has held that

> *"The directive is intended to ensure that members' and third parties' rights are safeguarded, in particular in operations for setting up companies and increasing and reducing company capital. In order to be effective, that safeguard must be secured for members as long as the company continues to exist with its own structures. Whilst the directive does not preclude the taking of execution measures and, in particular, liquidation measures placing the com-*

1226 *Müller*, p. 365 et seq.; *Eidenmüller / Engert*, ZIP 2009, 541, 547 et seq.; *Drouven*, ZIP 2009, 1052.

1227 Second Council Directive 77/91/EEC of 13 December 1976, OJ L 026, 31.1.1977 p. 0001 – 0013.

1228 ECJ, C-19/90 and C-20/90 *Karella and Karellas* 1991 I-2691, mn. 28 et seq., confirmed in ECJ, C-381/89 *Syndesmos Melon tis Eleftheras Evangelikis Ekklisias* 1992, p. I-2111 mn. 27 et seq.; ECJ, C-441/93 *Panagis Pafitis and Others* 1996, p. I-1347 mn. 38. See also *Bork*, mn. 15.22; *Teichmann*, p. 220 et seq.

1229 Charta of Fundamental Rights of the European Union of 18. December 2000, OJ 30.3.2010, C 83/02, OJ p. 389-403. The Charter of Fundamental Rights of the EU brings together in a single document the fundamental rights protected in the EU. The Charter contains rights and freedoms under six titles: Dignity, Freedoms, Equality, Solidarity, Citizens' Rights, and Justice. Proclaimed in 2000, the Charter has become legally binding on the EU with the entry into force of the Treaty of Lisbon, in December 2009. See http://ec.europa.eu/justice/fundamental-rights/charter/, accessed 14.7.2013.

1230 Art. 25(1), Art. 29(4), Art. 30 Second Council Directive.

1231 Granting subscription right is only required in certain cases under European Law, Art. 29(1) Second Council Directive provides subscription rights only for capital increases in cash; Art. 29(5) Second Council Directive provides for the exclusion of subscription rights in a capital increase by contribution in kind. See also *Eidenmüller / Engert*, ZIP 2009, 541, 547 et seq.

pany under compulsory administration in the interests of safeguarding creditors' rights, it nevertheless continues to apply as long as the company's shareholders and normal bodies have not been divested of their powers. Certainly, this is true where there is a straightforward rejuvenation measure involving public bodies or companies governed by private law where the members' right to the capital and to decision-making power in the company is in question."[1232]

It is therefore clear that for restructuring measures only aiming to liquidate a company and to permanently deprive shareholders and the company's statutory bodies of their rights a shareholder resolution is unnecessary.[1233] However, where is the purpose in performing capital measures in a pure liquidation process,[1234] and especially since a debt-equity-swap in a company restructuring is specifically aimed at maintaining the company as a going concern? Since the ECJ requires a shareholders' resolution for liquidation it is even more likely to find that one is required for a going concern case.[1235]

The restructuring proceeding has the same legal instruments of intervention available as the liquidation procedure. Therefore, the ECJ's decisions could also be interpreted as implying that the necessary capital measures for implementing a debt-equity-swap in insolvency proceedings are to be subsumed under the term "*enforcement action*".[1236] In addition, as a rule in a regular insolvency proceeding, the statutory bodies of the company together with their legal status and rights are removed, making the company cease to exist in its own structures.[1237]

As a teleological interpretation of the ECJ and the "Second Council Directive", one could also assume that the shareholders lose their influence in the case where the only purpose of the assets is to exclusively or

---

1232 ECJ, C-19/90 and C-20/90 *Karella and Karellas* 1991, p. I-2691, mn. 30, *confirmed* in ECJ, C-381/89 *Syndesmos Melon tis Eleftheras Evangelikis Ekklisias* 1992, p. I-2111 mn. 27.

1233 *Drouven*, ZIP 2009, 1052, 1052.

1234 BMJ, DiskE-ESUG, ZIP 2010, Beil. 28, p. 4.

1235 ECJ, C-381/89 *Syndesmos Melon tis Eleftheras Evangelikis Ekklisias* 1992, p. I-2111 mn. 57. See also *Eidenmüller / Engert*, ZIP 2009, 541, 548.

1236 *Eidenmüller / Engert*, ZIP 2009, 541, 547 et seq., *Verse* ZGR 2010, 299, 312 et seq.; *Drouven* ZIP 2009, 1052.

1237 ECJ, C-19/90 and C-20/90 *Karella and Karellas* 1991, p. I-2691, mn. 30, *confirmed* in ECJ, C-381/89 *Syndesmos Melon tis Eleftheras Evangelikis Ekklisias* 1992, p. I-2111 mn. 27.

principally satisfy the company's creditors.[1238] From the moment of substantive insolvency the protection of shareholders is secondary to the satisfaction of creditors. An intervention in shareholder rights in insolvency proceedings would thus most likely not be objectionable under European law.

Insolvency regimes of other European countries with mandatory interventions in corporate competencies do not apparently violate the "Second Council Directive". The fact that the European Commission has not yet initiated infringement proceedings suggests that it does not assume a breach of European law. Overall, it can therefore be assumed that capital measures, including for the purpose of a debt-equity-swap, could be undertaken without a shareholders' resolution in an insolvency plan proceeding aiming at restructuring a company.[1239]

Whether the shareholders could receive protection from the "Charter of Fundamental Rights"[1240], which provides for both the freedom of assembly and of association[1241] and the right to property[1242] or protection under

---

1238 ECJ, C-19/90 and C-20/90 *Karella and Karellas* 1991 I-2691, mn. 30 et seq., *confirmed* in ECJ, C-381/89 *Syndesmos Melon tis Eleftheras Evangelikis Ekklisias* 1992, I-2111 mn. 27. See also *Eidenmüller / Engert*, ZIP 2009, 541, 547 et seq.; *Richter*, ECFR 2009, 358 et seq.; *Verse*, ZGR 2010, 299, 312 et seq..

1239 *Richter*, ECFR 2009, 358, 362 et seq.; *Eidenmüller / Engert*, ZIP 2009, 541, 548.; *Drouven*, ZIP 2009, 1052; *Binder*, ZVglRWiss 112 (2013), 23 et seq. for further discussions.

1240 Charter of Fundamental Rights of the European Union, 2000, C 364/01-22.

1241 Art. 12 Charter of Fundamental Rights. In accordance with the freedom of assembly and association, the Charter constitutes the right of the "freedom of association at all levels, in particular in political, trade union and civic matters, which implies the right of everyone to form and to join trade unions for the protection of his or her interests." The question remains whether a corporate limited liabi-lity company could be subsumed under "civic matters" and whether "the right to form and to join" would also inherit the right not to be forced out of the company with the implementation of a debt-equity-swap in an insolvency proceeding.

1242 Art. 17 Charter of Fundamental Rights. While the Charter also provides for the "right to own […] lawfully acquired possessions", it also states that "[n]o one may be deprived of his or her possessions, except in the public interest and in the cases and under the conditions provided for by law, subject to fair compensation being paid in good time for their loss." As the Insolvency Statute provides appropriate compensation to the shareholders for the loss of their shares, the shareholders will not receive any protection from the Charter in this regard.

the "European Convention for the Protection of Human Rights and Fundamental Freedoms"[1243] due to a possible collision[1244] and relationship of norms[1245] is not further discussed here.

Summary

It must be noted that shareholders derive little protection of their right to property in a debt-equity-swap. The constitutional argument for the freedom of association will continue to prevail with regard to shareholders. The intention of the legislature was to facilitate restructurings and it has therefore deliberately taken the step of weakening the constitutional rights of shareholders. Legal certainty will only be achieved through court proceedings, tested until the last instance.

8.2.3.2 Creditors

A debt-equity-swap is legally pursuable if the creditors agree to acquire the shares of the company in exchange for their claims.[1246] The plan identifies the kind of shares the creditors will receive and clearly indicates the exchange ratio, dependent on the creditors' ranking and any security prior to the insolvency proceedings. In German law, the value of the shares must not exceed the nominal amount of the claim.[1247]

A company in distress generally has several creditors, not all of whom will be interested in participating in a debt-equity-swap as they fear legal risks and the loss of their collateral in such a case. While shareholders can be forced to be part of a debt-equity-swap when their vote has no impact on the confirmation of the plan, in contrast, existing creditors or groups of shareholders cannot be forced to participate and swap their claims.[1248]

1243 European Convention for the Protection of Human Rights and Fundamental Freedoms of 4 November 1950, 1952 II p.686, as amended by Protocols No. 11 and No. 14.

1244 *Lindner*, EuR 2007, 160, 161.

1245 *Jarass*, EuR 2013, 29 et seq.

1246 Sec. 230(2) InsO.

1247 Sec. 195(2)(no.1) SCA.

1248 *Eidenmüller / Engert*, ZIP 2009, 541, 547 et seq., 552 for the discussion on constitutional issues on whether creditors may be forced to exchanged their claims to be justified for the restructuring of the company.

A debt-equity-swap only makes sense from an economic perspective if a significant number of creditors decide to participate in the process. Consequently, creditors unwilling to exchange their claim into equity may impede or prevent the implementation of a debt-equity-swap. If a debt-equity-swap is part of an insolvency plan, it must be confirmed by each creditor or group of creditors that they accept the share rights in the legal entity. Due to this confirmation requirement, the debt-equity-swap is impeded with substantial transaction costs, especially for international debtors refinanced via capital markets, where creditors are not always known. Therefore, the process can be complicated, lengthy and costly, making it almost impossible to implement a debt-equity-swap to facilitate the restructuring of the company into a going concern.[1249] From a practical point of view, the participation of all the creditors is required to avoid any "*windfall profit*"[1250] for creditors not participating by giving their contribution to the restructuring as this makes negotiations difficult to conclude.

8.2.4 Contribution and Valuation of Claim, Differential Liability

The contribution in kind – the claim – is one of the most complicated aspects in a debt-equity-swap.[1251] The following issues need to be considered: whether the claim is capable of being a contribution in kind at all, when the discharge on the balance sheet happens, which valuation standards apply, when the right valuation point is, and how the value certificate is provided.

In the past, assessment of the claim was controversial in terms of whether the contribution of the claim was rather a payment in kind or a payment in cash, and what value the claim had as a contribution.[1252] An identity-preserving conversion of the claim into a share right is not pos-

1249 *Chatterji / Hedges*, p. 205; *Eidenmüller / Engert*, ZIP 2009, 541, 543.

1250 *Eidenmüller / Engert*, ZIP 2009, 541.

1251 Among others, see *Löbbe*, in LA Winter, p. 423 et seq.; *Kleindiek*, in FS Hommelhoff, p. 543 et seq.; *Weber / Schneider*, ZInsO 2012, 374 et seq.; *Labbé / Rudolph*, FINANCE Betrieb 2/2008, p. 97 et seq.; *Wuschek*, ZInsO 2012, 1768 et seq.; *Kunz / Ehnert*, FINANCE Betrieb 7-8/2007, p. 395 et seq.; *Kresser*, ZInsO 2010, 1409 et seq.; *Schmidt*, GWR 2010, 568 et seq.; *Bay / Seeburg / Böhmer*, ZInsO 2011, 1927 et seq.

1252 *Eilers*, GWR 2009, 3; *Redeker*, BB 2007, 673, 674; *Von Sydow / Beyer*, AG 2005, 635, 636; *Ekkenga*, ZGR 2009, 581, 589; *Toth-Feher / Schlick*, ZIP 2004,

sible under corporate law.[1253] Case law and the prevailing opinion evaluate the contribution as one in kind.[1254] Contributions in kind may only be assets whose economic value can be determined[1255] and proven to the commercial registry by a certificate.[1256]

There are different approaches to the evaluation of the value of the claim. The balance sheet approach recognises the conversion of debt into equity as effective relief of the company from the burden of debt[1257] and therefore attributes the fair value of the claim to the company.[1258] The controversy was over whether the claim should contribute its nominal value or fair value. One may argue that the contribution in kind should be valued according to the nominal value of the claim.[1259] The conversion of claims against the company into equity is not just a mere exchange of positions on the balance sheet but also a commitment to the company's business model.[1260] In the context of a debt-equity transaction, the evaluation of a claim[1261] is required neither for the protection of the company's creditors nor of its shareholders.[1262]

However, the opposing position[1263] argues that, in accordance with the principles of capital contribution, the claim should instead be contributed

---

491, 495; *Scheunemann / Hoffmann*, DB 2009, 983, 983; *Schmidt / Schlitt*, DK 2009, 279, 282.

1253 *Ekkenga*, ZGR 2009, 581, 589. Overview on requirements, see *Schleusener*, p. 41 et seq.

1254 BGHZ 132, 141, 143 = NJW 1996, 1473. Contrary as payment in cash, see *Karollus*, ZIP 1994, 589, 595 et seq.; *Meilicke*, DB 1989, 1067 et seq.

1255 Sec. 27(2) AktG.

1256 Sec. 183(3) AktG. See *Schleusener*, p. 56 et seq.

1257 *Ekkenga*, ZGR 2009, 581, 591; *Schleusener*, p. 43 et seq.

1258 The IFRIC 19 "Extinguishing Financial Liabilities with Equity Instruments" apply obligatory requirements for equity, in the case debt is repaid with equity, the difference has to be recognised between the book value and the fair value of the claim, see also *Paulus*, DZWIR 2008, 6, 9; *Pleister / Kindler*, ZIP 2010, 503, 510.

1259 *Cahn / Simon / Theiselmann*, CFL 2010, 238 et seq.; *Cahn / Simon / Theiselmann*, DB 2010, 1629 et seq.; *Cahn / Simon / Theiselmann*, DB 2012, 501 et seq.; *Simon*, CFL 2010, 448, 451 et seq.

1260 *Cahn / Simon / Theiselmann*, CFL 2010, 238, 247.

1261 *Ibid.*, 239 et seq.

1262 *Ibid.*, 244, arguing that the creditors are not misled by the financial situation of the company.

1263 Especially *Priester*, DB 2010, 1445 et seq.

with its fair value in order to be equal to the capital increase.[1264] This has to be proven by the registry.[1265] Regarding the protection of interests, the primary purpose of a proper nominal capital contribution is the protection of creditors and, only secondarily, of shareholders.[1266] While the law itself does not provide any guidance for the evaluation of the debt position to be converted into equity, the reasoning of the law, in contrast, states that the fair value principle is a requirement for (non-cash) contributions and in cases in which this fair value is not present, an impairment of the nominal value to equal the fair value of the respective debt is required.[1267]

The value assessment is generally made at the time when the contribution is made.[1268] It may, however, also include future cash flows made on the debt.[1269] The contribution in kind to the company is only valid in the case that the claim is of fair value, payable and liquid.[1270] It is of fair value when the assets of the company cover its liability. Hence, the company receives the appropriate value when the debt is swapped into equity.[1271] However, especially in insolvency, (unsecured) claims are usually no longer liquid and fair value.[1272] Therefore, a contribution in kind at the nominal value would be virtually impossible due to the requirement of impairment.[1273] The impaired fair value[1274] is regularly well below the nom-

---

1264 *Ibid.*, 1447 et seq.

1265 *Ibid.,* 1446 et seq., discussing the capital requirements in accordance with Sec. 57(3) AktG.

1266 *Ibid.,* 1447.

1267 BMJ, Begr. RegE-ESUG, BT-Drucks. 17/5712, p. 31 et seq.

1268 BGHZ 110, 47, 61. See also *Born*, BB 2009, 1730, 1732; *Scheunemann / Hoffmann*, DB 2009, 983, 984.

1269 *FG Köln*, EFG 2001, 588, mn. 56. See also *Born*, BB 2009, 1730, 1732; *Scheunemann / Hoffmann*, DB 2009, 983, 985.

1270 BGHZ 125, 141; 113, 335; 90, 37; 15, 52; LG Berlin, BB 1977, 213. See also *Toth-Feher / Schick*, ZIP 2004, 491, 496; *Groß*, GmbHR 1983, 290.

1271 *Marsch-Barner*, DB 1995, 1497; *Redeker*, BB 2007, 673, 675.

1272 *Schleusener*, p. 47, stating that the claim may have an intrinsic value attributed to high hidden/uncapitalised reserves (see FG Hamburg, DStR 2002, 193, 194.), the claim is not immediately due but to be amortised by instalments (see *Scheunemann / Hoffmann*, DB 2009, 983, 985), a waiver or security have been negotiated (see *Paulus*, DZWiR 2009, 6, 9). Other indicators for pricing the claim may be the prices paid on the secondary market (see *Redeker*, BB 2007, 673, 675) or the original goodwill over time (see *Priester*, DB 2010, 1445, 1448).

1273 *Simon*, CFL 2010, 448, 451.

1274 *Schmidt / Schlitt,* DK 2009, 279, 282; *Vaupel / Reers*, AG 2010, 93, 99.

inal amount.[1275] The questions still remain as to whether the right approach to valuation is the fair value[1276] and whether to consider the liquidation or going concern value.[1277]

One may consider the price that a third party would pay for the asset or the determination of the value could also be made on the basis of the price the debtor would have to pay in the case of purchasing back the debt.[1278] The prevailing opinion follows the approach of the recovery rate expected in insolvency.[1279]

It is questionable whether the appropriate value would be the liquidation[1280] or going concern[1281] value of the claim, and therefore whether the liquidation of the company is more likely than its going concern should also be taken into account.[1282] The ESUG clearly provides for the liquidation value. This is the obstacle. Regarding the fact that the value of the contribution in kind is made in accordance with the liquidation value, in most cases, especially when considering subordinated claims, the fair value of the claim tends to be zero or at least far below the nominal value, making the conversion of debt into equity rather unattractive.

In the past, differential liability has been one of the biggest risks in debt-equity-swaps.[1283] After the registration of the capital increase in the commercial register the creditors were obliged to pay an additional contribution in cash in case the nominal value of the claim did not match its fair

---

1275 *Toth-Feher / Schick*, ZIP 2004, 491, 496; *Groh*, BB 1997, 2523, 2324; *Lutter / Hommelhoff / Timm*, BB 1980, 737, 740.

1276 OLG Düsseldorf, GmbHR 1992, 112. See also *von Sydow / Beyer*, AG 2005, 635, 637.

1277 For discussion, see *Brinkmann*, WM 2011, 97, 101; *Simon*, CFL 2010, 448, 452 et seq.; *Urlaub* ZIP 2011, 1040, 1044 et seq.

1278 *Groh*, BB 1997, 2523, 2524.

1279 BGHZ 90, 370, 373; BGHZ 125, 141, 145. See also *Paulus*, DZWiR 2008, 6, 9. *Pleister / Kindler*, ZIP 2010, 503, 510.

1280 The claim may still be fully valuable in case that it is covered by security, see *Paulus*, DZWiR 2008, 6, 9; *Hass / Schreiber / Tschauner*, in *Hommel / Knecht / Wohlenberg*, p. 841, 847 et seq.

1281 *Eidenmüller / Engert*, ZIP 2009, 541, 543; *Knecht / Drescher*, in *Buth / Hermanns*, Sec. 20 mn. 48, arguing that in the case that insolvency plan is aiming for the going concern of the company, this factor should be regarded in the valuation of the claim.

1282 *Stadler*, NZI 2003, 579, 584; *Hass / Schreiber / Tschauner*, in *Hommel / Knecht / Wohlenberg*, p. 841, 847.

1283 *Lutter / Hommelhoff / Timm*, BB 1980, 737, 740; *Bauer*, ZInsO 2002, 153, 157.

value.[1284] This was especially the case when the restructuring failed and a subsequent insolvency proceeding was initiated.[1285] Since differential liability is regardless of fault, it could never be legally excluded but only mitigated by providing a value certificate from a certified accountant.

With ESUG, the valuation risks and uncertainties resulting in differential liability are now excluded when the plan has been accepted by the creditors and confirmed by the courts.[1286] The legislature intended to provide legal certainty for creditors participating in a debt-equity-swap despite the fact that the contribution in kind may not have contributed to the value anticipated and may therefore undermine the creditor protection.[1287] The legislature meets this objection by pointing to the involvement of creditors in the final voting process on the adoption of the insolvency plan. Since the creditors are voting on the insolvency plan, they are aware that the capital requirements and capital maintenance provisions may be undermined. However, new creditors are not taken into account and thus bear the risk of an inadequately capitalised debtor. One may argue that from the perspective of new creditors the risk dissolves when the insolvency plan enhances and improves the financial position of the company.[1288] Whether the contradiction of value and the concurrent liability risks for new creditors or the abrogation of the minimum capital requirements are acceptable or not,[1289] and whether the new provision increases incentives for creditors to participate in a debt-equity-swap,[1290] remains to be seen.

8.2.5 Restructuring Privileges

Creditors who are converting their claims into equity benefit from the restructuring privilege[1291] and possibly the small participation privilege.[1292]

1284 *Lutter / Hommelhoff / Timm*, BB 1980, 737, 740; *Schmidt*, ZGR 1982, 519, 522 et seq. For legal consequences, see BGH, NJW 2006, 1736.
1285 *Wittig*, in FS Uhlenbruck, p. 685, 702.
1286 Sec. 254(4)(2) InsO.
1287 *Steffek*, Gläubigerschutz in der Kapitalgesellschaft, for various aspects of creditor protection in corporate and insolvency law.
1288 *Meyer / Degener*, BB 2011, 846, 848; *Wittig*, NZI 1998, 49, 56.
1289 *Brinkmann*, WM 2011, 97, 101; *Hölzle*, NZI 2011, 124, 129.
1290 *Simon / Merkelbach*, NZG 2012, 121, 130.
1291 Sec. 39(4)(2) InsO.
1292 Sec. 39(5) InsO.

In the case that the creditor acquires the shares of a company due to a debt-equity-swap in an insolvency plan proceeding, it may be assumed that they were acquired for the purpose of the sustainable restructuring of the company.[1293] However, it remains unclear when the restructuring privilege ends, and therefore at what point the restructuring can be deemed sustainable.[1294] As this provision is rather new, first the effects now of the strengthened insolvency plan proceeding after ESUG should be evaluated, rather than already clarifying the duration of the restructuring privilege.[1295] It is likely that the restructuring privilege does not already end once the grounds for insolvency have been eliminated but a sustainable restructuring may be deemed to have taken place if the measures taken are successful in making the company a going concern for at least the current year and the entire following year.[1296]

8.3 England

Technically, the debt-equity-swap is a form of capital decrease combined with a capital increase in which the purchase rights of the current shareholders are excluded and the claims of the creditors are changed into equity. It is a standard instrument of restructuring.[1297]

In case of a material insolvency, the shares of the current shareholders are essentially worthless. Only if they carry a residual value, the shareholders may oppose the vote for a debt-equity-swap if the swap puts them in a worse position than they would have been under insolvency proceeding oriented towards liquidation.

1293 BMJ, RegE-ESUG, BT-Drucks. 17/5712, p. 48.
1294 *Hirte / Knof / Mock*, DB 2011, 632, 643.
1295 BMJ, RegE-ESUG, BT-Drucks. 17/5712, p. 26.
1296 *Hirte / Knof / Mock*, DB 2011, 632, 643.
1297 *Bork*, mn. 15.26.

8.3.1 Capital Decrease

For a capital reduction[1298], the company must comply with the company law requirements.[1299] The shareholders need to pass a special resolution with a 75% majority[1300] at a general meeting and apply with the solvency statement of the directors[1301] to the court for confirmation.[1302] This is because the court can only consider a resolution to approve the scheme, such as the reduction of capital and any necessary changes to the articles of association. If the company is a public company, it must apply to court for confirmation of the resolution to reduce its capital,[1303] confirmation takes place at a court hearing that is separate from the court hearing to sanction the scheme. The reduction confirmation hearing often takes place a few days after the scheme sanction hearing to facilitate the exercise between the two hearings, and to maximise the number of shares that are part of the scheme and reduction. The court order must then be filed with the registry for the reduction to become effective.[1304] The capital reduction is rather a technical reduction since all of the existing ordinary shares in the company would be cancelled, however, immediately be replaced by new shares with no consequential reduction in the company's assets. In this case, the court may approve the capital reduction by waiving the requirements[1305] to convene creditors if the position had been fully explained to the shareholders and that there was no prejudice to the creditors.

8.3.2 Capital Increase

The capital increase is authorised by the directors for the allotment of new shares.[1306] The authorisation for the allotment of new shares is acquired by

---

1298 Sec. 41(4)(i) CA 2006.
1299 Ss. 641, 645-653 CA 2006.
1300 Ss. 284 et seq. CA 2006.
1301 Sec. 641(1)(a),(2) CA 2006.
1302 Sec. 641(1)(b) CA 2006. See also *Davies / Worthington*, p. 308 et seq.
1303 Sec. 645 CA 2006.
1304 Sec. 649(3),(5) CA 2006.
1305 Sec. 62(6) CA 2006.
1306 Ss.549 et seq. CA 2006.

the articles of association[1307] or a resolution by the shareholders[1308] with simple majority.[1309] Generally, existing shareholders have pre-emption rights on the new shares.[1310]. However, the rights are subject to some exemptions. Especially for a capital increase made by issue for non-cash consideration[1311] there are no pre-emption rights of existing shareholders.[1312] In addition, the shareholders may exclude pre-emption rights by special resolution.[1313] New shares may be ordinary shares or preference shares.[1314]

In case the new shares only cause a relatively low dilution of the stake of existing shareholders, the new shares could also be non-voting redeemable preference shares.[1315] Often the new shares could also be convertible preference shares, converting into ordinary shares.[1316] Furthermore, the distributions to the new shareholders may be adjusted according to the revenues expected in the future and, therefore, be variable or increasing according to specific outcome factors.[1317] In connection with the capital measures in a restructuring or insolvency proceeding, English law does not recognise any fiduciary duties of shareholders like German law does.

1307 Sec. 550 CA 2006.

1308 Ss. 549 et seq. CA 2006. See *Cohen / Maclennan*, CRI 2009, 91, 92.

1309 Ss. 551, 282 CA 2006. See *Wood*, Principles of International Insolvency, mn. 21–094. In order to avoid subscription rights "cash box structures" could be used, see *Walker,* CR&I 2009, 211 et seq.

1310 Ss. 560 et seq. CA 2006.

1311 Sec. 565 CA 2006.

1312 *Davis / Worthington*, p. 837 et seq.; the exception does not necessarily apply to a debt-equity-swap.

1313 Sec. 571 CA 2006, following the legal definition of special resolution in Sec. 283 CA 2006.

1314 *Wilson*, CRI 2009, 103 et seq.; *Howard / Hedger*, mn. 6.159 et seq.

1315 *Clowry*, in *Larkin*, p. 33 et seq.; *Wilson*, CRI 2009, 103, 104; *Howard / Hedger*, mn. 6.167 et seq.

1316 *Wilson*, CRI 2009, 103; *Howard / Hedger*, mn. 6.164-6.166.

1317 *Clowry*, in *Larkin*, p. 33 et seq.

8.3.3 Participation of Shareholders and Creditors

8.3.3.1 Shareholders

Depending on which process structure is chosen, the original shareholders' participation may be mandatory.[1318] The fact that the approval of the shareholders under certain conditions may not be necessary in the negotiation situation has far-reaching consequences. Since creditors can threaten the existing shareholders with a process path that can eliminate their participation, the shareholders in the UK are regularly more prepared to agree to a consensual solution.

The consequences for the rights of the current shareholders afflicted by a debt-equity-swap have not been subject to any academic or judicial discussion and there do not seem to be any difficulties in practise.[1319] Although it is recognised that the shareholder must approve the swap and that the rules on capital increases and capital decreases have to be respected, the precise procedural integration is discussed neither in the literature nor particularly in case law. If the swap of the claims is integrated into a scheme of arrangement, there are no further difficulties since the scheme permits the shareholders rights to be modified.[1320] For this reason alone, the scheme of arrangement is the instrument preferred by practitioners for implementing a debt-equity-swap. But if massive resistance is expected from the shareholders and it seems less certain that the required 75% majority for the capital reduction will be achieved, an alternative is the founding of a new company, whose shares are distributed among creditors of the debtor company and which receives the assets of the debtor company in an asset deal.

From the perspective of the existing shareholders of a company entering into a debt to equity swap, since there will be a fresh issue of shares (which will only be offered to the lender in exchange for the reduction or elimination of debt) they will see their equity interests diluted down to a greater or lesser extent, depending on the level of debt that the swap is intended to cover. However, whilst this apparent negative may be true, shareholders may view it in a positive light if it means that they continue to hold a stake in a viable entity going forward (with potential for future

1318 *Cohen / Maclennan*, CRI 2009, 91.
1319 *Bork*, mn. 15.27.
1320 Sec. 895(1)(b) CA 2006.

capital growth) rather than in an entity which may otherwise struggle to maintain its financial viability and from which they would presumably be unlikely to receive any return on their shares in an insolvency.

Although the existing shareholders do not have to approve the scheme due their worthless shares in insolvency, they still need to approve the capital measures since those negatively affect their share rights.

8.3.3.2 Creditors

In addition, for bank lenders in particular, there may be certain regulatory issues to consider and address as well as dealing with the cultural shift from being a holder of debt to an equity holder. The situation is further complicated if a company has several bank lenders with competing interests. The consent of all the banks will be necessary in order to affect a debt to equity swap in such circumstances and the process of achieving consensus between the banks on the terms of the swap is not an easy one. It is also likely that a bank lender will want to be issued with preference shares in any debt to equity swap so that it ranks for dividends and (on a liquidation) for capital, ahead of ordinary shareholders. Either in addition to or as an alternative to preference shares, a bank lender may wish to be issued with warrants which can offer many of the advantages of an equity holding including the opportunity to share in any upturn in the company's fortunes. In a restructuring context, although the composition of classes are important, of equal importance is the treatment of out of the money creditors and therefore making the decision of which creditors not to include in the scheme of arrangement.[1321]

8.3.4 Contribution and Valuation of Claim, Differential Liability

The contribution of the claim to receive equity is regularly treated as a cash consideration which means the release of a liability of the company for a liquidated sum.[1322] The exchange of debt into equity is done by receiving new shares against the release of the claim or set-off in the value

---

1321 *Re Bluebroock Ltd and others* [2009] EWHC 2114 (Ch).

1322 Sec. 583(3)(c) CA 2006. See *Truex v Toll* [2009] EWHC 396; *Re A Debtor (No. 64 of 1992)* [1994] 1 WLR 264.

of the purchase price.[1323] The challenges of differential liability caused by the incorrect value assessment of the creditors' claims do not arise under English law. Therefore, English law makes a debt-equity-swap immensely easier since the claim is recognised at its nominal value as a capital contribution.[1324] The rule that a company's shares must not be allotted at a discount[1325] does regularly not cause any problems.[1326]

8.3.5 Restructuring Privileges

Neither English corporate nor English insolvency law recognises any statutory restructuring privileges for creditors' new or existing loans in restructuring and insolvency.[1327]

8.4 Summary

While both Germany and England address the necessary corporate law measures like the capital decrease and consecutive capital increase for a debt-equity-swap, Germany does so with greater attentiveness and care. Most noticeably, English law provides no special rules for company law measures in insolvency. The most convincing explanation is that the leading proceeding to implement the debt-equity-swap, the scheme of arrangement, is not an insolvency proceeding but a proceeding of corporate law and is available in pre-insolvency stages where special rules for curtailing shareholder rights cannot be legitimated. But whereas the German law spends considerable energy on minority protection for current shareholders, this is at most a marginal theme in English law. The debt-equity-swap is perhaps the central example[1328] of this, a construction that is handled in English discussion mainly as a modification of creditor rather than shareholder rights without thereby giving rise to any practical problems.

1323 *Wood*, Principles of International Insolvency, mn. 21–067.

1324 *Davies / Worthington*, mn. 11–14.

1325 Sec. 580(1) CA 2006.

1326 *Steffek*, Münchner Handbuch des Gesellschaftsrechts, Sec. 40 mn. 28.

1327 There may be, however, contractual privileges in accordance to the inter-creditor agreements.

1328 *Bork*, mn. 15.30.

In the past, the lack of the possibility in German law to execute a debt-equity-swap, especially against the vote of the existing shareholders, was seen as one of the main obstacles to restructuring a company.[1329] As a restructuring instrument, the debt-equity-swap was perceived as violating elementary constitutional and European laws.[1330] This has changed with ESUG, as the legislature has lifted the strict separation between insolvency law and corporate law and thereby enacted, *inter alia*, a basis for making restructurings in an insolvency plan proceeding more attractive and implementing a debt-equity-swap even against the vote of the existing shareholders. The existing shareholders no longer have obstruction potential as their shares are generally considered worthless so their rights will regularly expire.

It is still unclear whether existing shareholders are entitled by their constitutionally guaranteed freedom of association to continue to participate in the company with restructu-ring contributions to the company in the case that their shares are worthless, and whether the insolvency plan has to provide for these subscription rights in the event of a capital increase. It should be kept in mind that a successful restructuring will always depend on the joint approach of all parties involved to implement the appropriate measure in a timely manner. Ultimately the parties involved have the private autonomy to decide on whether and how to structure the insolvency plan. With concessions made by the creditors (in particular accepting a haircut of their claims), an improvement of the economic situation and the financial structure of the company is achieved. It needs to be ensured that the shareholders will not only benefit from the contribution by the creditors by taking an impairment of their claims but the creditors will rather require that the existing shareholders contribute their share to the financial restructuring of the company. This would allow for a reduction of capital: the accumulated losses will be permanently assigned to the previous shareholders who hence realise their liability.

1329 BMJ, RegE-ESUG, BT-Drucks. 17/1512 Introduction; *Müller*, p. 308; *Brüning*, p. 62 et seq. 248 et seq.; *Eidenmüller / Engert*, ZIP 2009, 541, 549; *Westphal / Janjuah*, ZIP 2008, Beil. 3, p. 14.

1330 *K. Schmidt*, Gutachten zum 54. DJT, S.D 83; *Müller*, p. 364; *Drouven*, ZIP 2009, 1052.
Contrary and intrusion justifiable: *Eidenmüller / Engert*, ZIP 2009, 541, 545 et seq.; *Sassenrath*, ZIP 2003, 1517, 1523; *Westphal / Janjuah*, ZIP 2008, Beil. 3, 15 et seq.

Conclusion

This chapter distinguished between informal and statutory proceeding and provided a background of the different proceedings in restructuring and insolvency law in Germany and England. It pointed out the differences between the German and English proceedings and the legal challenges when implementing a debt-equity-swap.

The German legislator decided to codify the debt-equity-swap in its insolvency law, thereby ultimately limiting its utilisation. As only the legal measures such as capital decrease/increase are codified in corporate law and there are no hindering constitutional rights in England, the debt-equity-swap is a much more flexible restructuring instrument, and can be tailor-made for its intended purpose.

Chapter IV Legal Competition and Forum Shopping for Debt-Equity-Swaps in Practice

Introduction

This chapter discusses the various cases of recent years with regard to the competition of insolvency law as well as the competition for corporate law. It will show how German companies used the approach of rescue culture in England to restructure their debt for a going concern.

9 Competition of Insolvency Law – Migration for Forum Shopping

The shift of COMI for German companies is a prerequisite for the application of English law in insolvency proceedings; however, in order to implement a debt-equity-swap, the company must also comply with English corporate law.[1331] The requirements for a capital decrease, a concurrent capital increase and the amendments articles of association in English law may be different than in German law. When a company moves its COMI to England, it has to comply with the English rules even though they may not be beneficial.

A German company must change its legal identity from a German to an English company, in order to benefit from the measures provided by English corporate law.[1332] *Deutsche Nickel*, *Schefenacker* and *Brochier* are famous cases, in which German companies have shifted their COMI to England and changed their legal form in order to benefit from English laws to restructure.

1331 A company formed and registered under the Companies Act 2006 or any previous Company Act. See *Jasper*, p. 30: Legal entities may also be founded by the Crown, by single statute or in accordance to specific requirements. Also *Davies / Rickford*, EBOR 2008, 48, 52 et seq.

1332 *Baird / Ho*, Insolv. Int. 2007, 124, 125 et seq.

9.1 Deutsche Nickel

As a subsidiary of *VDN Vereinigte Deutsche Nickel-Werke AG*, *Deutsche Nickel AG* entered into a financial crisis in 2003.[1333] The accumulated debt consisted of bank debt (EUR 24 millions) and a bond (EUR 104 millions), while equity was only EUR 0.2 million. Despite the surfeit of debt, the company still had the ability to be restructured. A comprehensive financial restructuring of the bond with the German Bond Act failed. In migrating into the English legal system, the *Deutsche Nickel AG* made an attempt to restructure under English law. Reasons for this include the restructuring contributions of the creditors and the feasibility of a debt-equity-swap. This action was made possible because the major creditors were supportive of the migration and partially steered the negotiations. The restructuring aimed to create a structure in which the creditors were satisfied by receiving shares in an English company.

DNick Ltd. was a company registered in London. It acquired 100% of shares of *Deutsche Nickel AG*. *Deutsche Nickel AG* was then transformed into *DNick Ltd. & Co. KG*,[1334] a German limited partnership[1335]. The general partner of the limited partnership was *DNick Ltd.*, the limited partner was another subsidiary of *DNick Ltd.* The limited partner subsequently left the partnership.[1336] With only one remaining partner, the limited partnership automatically ceased to exist as a legal entity. *DNick Ltd.* became the legal successor to the partnership's assets and liabilities (including the bonds) by way of accrual (*Anwachsung*)[1337] or collapse merger under the

---

1333 For detailed background, see *Steffek*, Münchner Handbuch des Gesellschaftsrechts, Sec. 42 mn. 17-19; *Hickmott*, BJIBFL 2007, 272-273; *Ringe*, in *Ringe / Gullifer / Théry*, p. 77.

1334 *Klöhn / Schaper*, ZIP 2013, 49 et seq. on implications of cross-border legal entities.

1335 The requirements for the transformation are a shareholders' resolution and the registration with the commercial register. The German limited partnership has one or more general partners and one or more limited partners. One of these partners (preferably one of the general partners) must be an English limited company. See *Klöhn / Schaper*, ZIP 2013, 49 et seq. for the discussion on the cross-border combination of legal entities and the freedom of establishment.

1336 Either by selling their partnership interests to the English partner or by agreeing to withdraw from the limited partnership.

1337 Ss. 161(2), 105(3) HGB; Sec. 738(1)(1) BGB.

German principle of universal succession (*Gesamtrechtsnachfolge*)[1338]. As a result, the German company became an English limited company.

DNick Ltd. then transferred all shares of *Deutsche Nickel AG* to *DNick Holding PLC*, a subsidiary of *DNick Ltd.*, while the assets and liabilities were transferred to another subsidiary, *Deutsche Nickel GmbH.* Key contracts, including employee contracts, were also transferred.[1339] COMI had shifted from Germany to England.

DNick Ltd. filed for administration along with a CVA to obtain a moratorium from creditors.[1340] The CVA included the swap of all the debts of *DNick Ltd.* for shares of *DNick Holdings PLC.* The conversion rate was pro rata to the existing debt. The shares were calculated accordingly. The CVA also provided *DNick Holdings PLC* with the opportunity to issue further shares to satisfy claims from *DNick Ltd.* creditors. The CVA proposed was passed by a 95% creditors' vote. Bond trading was suspended and the shares of *DNick Holding PLC* began trading. This closed the CVA and the administration.

9.2 Schefenacker

A similar strategy was followed in the restructuring of *Schefenacker*. The case drew a great deal of attention and catalysed discussions about improving German restructuring law. In comparison to *Deutsche Nickel* though, the restructuring was a consensual approach taken by the principal creditors of the company. In retrospective, the initiation of the migration at an early stage was one of the key factors for the successful restructuring of

1338 Although universal succession is not a method for passing title under English law, English law will recognise a foreign universal succession as long as it is properly structured.

1339 Due to the succession of *Deutsche Nickel GmbH* to *Deutsche Nickel AG* and *DNick Ltd.*, in accordance with Sec. 613b BGB all employees were transferred.

1340 One needs to remember that the company's directors may propose a CVA to the company and its creditors to satisfy their claims. If the company is in administration or being wound up, the proposal may be made by the administrator or the liquidator, and not by the directors. If the directors propose a voluntary arrangement, a nominee, who must be qualified to act as an insolvency practitioner, must act as trustee or otherwise supervise the implementation of the voluntary arrangement.

Schefenacker. It is also beneficial to include major creditors in the preparation for the migration.

The German auto parts manufacturer *Schefenacker AG* and its subsidiaries made up a multinational corporation.[1341] The debt consisted of senior secured loans (EUR 205 million) and a senior subordinated bond debt (EUR 200 million), held by a large variety of international investors. An indenture was in force for the bond holders with a U.S. bank acting as a trustee.

In 2006, decreasing profitability in its operations led the company to initiate a restructuring plan as well as negotiations with its senior creditors, an ad-hoc committee of bondholders, stakeholders and the sole shareholder. The term sheet included immediate liquidity for the company and, as an alternative, the restructuring of the company within an English CVA. The CVA option was chosen due to the diversity of the investor base and the risk of not achieving a unanimous vote for restructuring in Germany. A CVA requires a 75% majority vote. Another factor was the involvement of a number of English or American lenders as the German banks had already withdrawn their financing.

After the senior secured lenders had agreed to the migration, *Schefenacker PLC* was registered in Portchester (Hampshire, England). The bondholders agreed by a simple majority to the amendment of the indenture as did the sole shareholder and the relevant stakeholders. *Schefenacker AG* was then transformed into the *Schefenacker GmbH & CO. KG*. The general partner was *Schefenacker PLC* and the limited partner was *Schefenacker GmbH*. *Schefenacker GmbH* exited the limited liability partnership and by way of an accrual all assets and liabilities were transferred to *Schefenacker PLC* and *Schefenacker GmbH & Co. KG* ceased to exist. COMI was thus transferred to England.[1342]

A consensual agreement with the senior secured lenders allowed the bank debt to be refinanced. In addition, the banks would receive 69.6% of ordinary shares of *Schefenacker PLC* for parts of their debt. The sole shareholder received 25.4% of shares for contributing a mezzanine finance facility and a shareholder loan. A CVA was proposed only to the unsecured bondholders since secured and / or preferential creditors were not

1341 For detailed background information, see *Steffek*, Münchner Handbuch des Gesellschaftsrechts, Sec. 42 mn. 17-19; *Rutstein / Bloomberg*, CR&I 2010, 157; *Ringe*, in *Ringe / Gullifer / Théry*, p. 75-76.

1342 Compare critical remarks *Griffiths / Hellmig,* NZI 2008, 418, 419 et seq.

entitled to vote. The first proposal was rejected in the creditors' meeting. The proposal was then amended, giving the bondholders 5% of the equity in *Schefenacker PLC,* a cash payment and certain warrants to receive further shares. This proposal was approved by the majority of bondholders.[1343]

A report to the court was made. There was then 28 days during which dissenting creditors could object on the basis of unfair prejudice or material irregularity. No claims were made. A condition of the implementation of the CVA was its recognition as a foreign main proceeding not only in Europe in accordance with the EIR but also in the United States in accordance with Chapter 15 U.S. Bankruptcy Code.[1344] Any claims made in courts in the U.S. or Europe court would have therefore been rejected on the basis that the proper court for these claims was the English court.

9.3 Brochier

While *Deutsche Nickel* and *Schefenacker* successfully migrated to England, *Brochier*[1345] is an example of failed COMI migration.[1346]

Hans Brochier GmbH & Co. KG was a construction company, registered in Nuremberg. In order to receive favourable benefits from English law, the company's assets and liabilities were transferred to the English company *Hans Brochier Holdings Ltd.* registered in London. *Deutsche Nickel* and *Schefenacker* served as a role model for the process.

1343 *Schefenacker* received 75.9% by value and 56.5% by number creditors' vote, confirming the CVA. While there is usually no class voting in a CVA, *Schefenacker* obtained majority voting to avoid any later appeal, see *Prudential Assurance Co Ltd v PRG Powerhouse* Ltd [2007] EWHC 1002 (Ch). In addition, see also *Baird / Ho*, Ins. Int. 2007, 124, 126.

1344 Sec. 1517(b)(1) Bankruptcy Code.

1345 *Hans Brochier Holdings Ltd v Exner* [2006] EWHC 2594 (Ch), [2007] BCC 127 (Ch) = NZI 2006, 186 = NZI 2007, 187. Detailed information, see also *Steffek*, Münchner Handbuch des Gesellschaftsrechts, Sec. 42 mn. 17-19; *Geva*, EBOR (4) 2008, 605, 610 et seq.; *Ballmann*, BB 2007, 1121; *Andres / Grund*, NZI 2007, 137 et seq.; *Rutstein / Bloomberg*, CR&I 2010, 157; *Ringe*, in *Ringe / Gullifer / Théry*, p. 78-79.

1346 *Hickmott*, BJIBFL 2007, 273 noting that the Brochier tried to follow "the magic recipe [...however] it left something important behind: its COMI". See also *Eidenmüller*, ECFR 2009, 1, 9.

There was then an unintentional "*race to court*".[1347] The company's English directors appointed administrators,[1348] claiming the company's COMI to be in England where the registered office was located. Due to time constraints, the administrators did not make their own evaluation about the company's COMI but trusted the information provided by the company's directors.[1349]

Only 45 minutes later in Germany, employees applied to the Nuremberg court and a preliminary insolvency administrator was appointed.[1350] Unaware of the previous English court order, the Nuremberg court declared that the company's COMI was in Germany. Although both courts opened a main insolvency proceeding, due to the previous filing, the main proceeding was only opened in England. The English administrators, however, doubted that the company's COMI was actually located in England and applied to the court.[1351] The court agreed with that view and determined that the company's COMI had indeed remained in Germany.[1352] The court held that although the registered office of the company was located in London,[1353] the head-office functions were still in Nuremberg.[1354] The company had no permanent economic activity in England and for third parties; on an objective and ascertainable basis, the company's COMI was located in Germany. The court reasoned that the company had no branches in England, the company's trading activities were carried out from Nuremberg with contracts governed by German law.[1355] Financing was provided by German banks: the principal creditors were located in Germany and they perceived *Brochier* to be a German company; in addition, all employees were employed in Germany under German employment law.[1356] The court was unwilling to sanction a COMI migration pri-

---

1347 *Ballmann*, BB 2007, 1121; *Andres / Grund*, NZI 2007, 137, 142.

1348 Sch B1 para. 22 IA 1986.

1349 *Hans Brochier Holdings Ltd v Exner* [2006] EWHC 2594 (Ch), para. 9.

1350 *Ibid.*, para. 21.

1351 *Ibid.*, para. 23 et seq.

1352 *Ibid.*, para. 28.

1353 *Ibid.*, para. 2. Compare AG Köln NZI 2008, 257, 259; *Eidenmüller*, KTS 2009, 137, 149, 151: The fact that the business transfer to London had been just before the opening of proceedings would have not precluded the jurisdiction of the High Court in London.

1354 *Hans Brochier Holdings Ltd v Exner* [2006] EWHC 2594 (Ch), para. 30.

1355 *Ibid.*, para. 26.

1356 *Ibid.*

marily on the grounds of forum shopping. Both courts agreed that the company's COMI was Nuremberg.[1357]

With the main insolvency proceedings opened in England, the Nuremberg proceeding could only be a secondary insolvency proceedings in accordance with the EIR. This meant that the Nuremberg court had to have either terminate the proceeding or opened a secondary proceeding.[1358] The Nuremberg court, however, did not recognise the administration and made reference to the *ordre public*.[1359]

State-funded employee payment is only paid in a German insolvency proceeding. It provides the company with liquidity, necessary for the going concern.[1360] The preliminary insolvency administrator, therefore, tried to convince the administrators that the COMI was indeed Germany. The same conclusion was reached. COMI was, therefore, established in Germany and the administration became ineffective. The court left open whether the ineffective proceeding was *ex tunc* or *ex nunc* with regard to the liabilities of directors.[1361]

The directors did not agree with the ruling, arguing that there was an establishment in England[1362] and, therefore, secondary proceedings could be opened[1363] for the assets in England, being carved out from the German proceeding. The German insolvency administrator objected, reasoning that the facts were not enough to define an establishment. The court agreed, regarded the appointment of the administrators as void, therefore, no main proceeding was opened in London and the administration was terminated.[1364] *Brochier* clearly showed that stakeholders could sabotage a company's restructuring by opening main or secondary insolvency proceedings in another member state. Especially companies from a foreign jurisdiction may be the victim of such misuse.[1365]

1357 *Ibid.* See also *Geva,* EBOR 2007, 605, 610 et seq.
1358 *Ringe*, EBOR 2008, 579, 588 with link to Art. 16 (1) EIR.
1359 *Hans Brochier Holdings Ltd v Exner* [2007] BCC 127, 133 et seq.
1360 *Goetker / Quenby*, IFLR 2007, 48; *Ballmann*, BB 2007, 1121.
1361 *Hans Brochier Holdings Ltd v Exner* [2007] BCC 127, 133 et seq.
1362 Art. 3 (2) EIR.
1363 Art. 3 (3) EIR.
1364 *Hans Brochier Holdings Ltd v Exner* [2006] EWHC 2594 (Ch), paras. 33, 35.
1365 *Andres / Grund*, NZI 2007, 137, 142.

9.4 Migration is the Past – Negotiation is the Future?

Although companies may continue to seek to migrate their COMIs to take advantage of a particular insolvency regime, the flow of cases appear to be decreasing[1366] since the onset of the current financial crisis. The strategic shift of COMI may serve as an effective threat to dissenting creditors to agree to a consensual restructuring rather than litigate through the courts.[1367] There are, however, also many associated risks[1368] and also costs that are accumulating for such a transformation.[1369]

As long as there are different insolvency regimes (those lacking processes for rescue finance, not permitting debt-equity-swaps, or not having mechanisms to achieve a 'cram down' of dissenting creditors) certain jurisdictions will remain more attractive than others.[1370] For as long as the concept of COMI depends on a debtor's factual circumstances, and there remains a misalignment between the commercial reality of corporate groups and the strict legal requirement to recognise single legal entities on insolvency, forum shopping through COMI migration remains on the agenda. Although COMI migration may be criticised for its lack of certainty and artificiality, its flexibility arguably offers the best solution available to debtors or debtor groups wishing to take advantage of the insolvency regime of a particular jurisdiction. It has been shown that this can, in many cases, lead to the rescue of a company or a higher return for creditors, however, only if the process is well-planned and professionally executed.[1371]

1366 Contrary *Hickmott*, BJIBFL 2007, 274: "unlikely to be the final chapter in this particular story".

1367 *Schelo*, in Becker, BZ 2007, p. 2.

1368 *Ballmann*, BB 2007, 1121, 1125.

1369 *Andres / Grund*, NZI 137, 138: *Schefenacker*'s estimated costs: EUR 40 million.

1370 *Tashiro / Beissenhirtz*, ICR 2007, 171–175, arguing that the detour through England was not necessary to achieve the same results as the German proceedings could have provided the same results.

1371 *Tashiro / Beissenhirtz*, ICR 2007, 171, 174.

10 Competition of Company Law – Negotiation for Forum Shopping

Companies have found an alternative to initiating a restructuring under English law without a COMI migration to England. COMI migration is out. Scheme of arrangement is in![1372]

10.1 Tele Columbus

With the application of a scheme of arrangement, *Tele Columbus* followed the trend as the first German company to apply an English scheme of arrangement to restructure its balance sheet without actually transferring its COMI from Germany to England. The scheme of arrangement has already been tested successfully for other European companies,[1373] e.g. the Spanish company *La Seda di Barcelona*[1374] or the Luxembourg company *Hellas Telecommunications*[1375].

Tele Columbus is a telecommunication and cable operator company. In 2010, the company experienced financial difficulties despite having a viable business. The company aimed for a consensual restructuring since it was not yet insolvent as a matter of German law. For more than a year, though, it was not possible to resolve the conflict among more than 100 different creditors, including several hedge funds, which hindered the financial restructuring considerably. It was ultimately not possible to achieve unanimous creditors' approval for such a restructuring, which is a prerequisite under German law. Therefore, *Tele Columbus* decided to propose a scheme of arrangement to its creditors, where at least 75% of voting creditors is sufficient to bind the others. A German insolvency proceeding could thereby be avoided. The scheme sought to amend the terms

---

1372 *Paulus*, ZIP 2011, 1077; *Eidenmüller / Frobenius*, 1210, 1219; *Hertz / MacLennan / Benett*, BJIBFL 2011, 405.

1373 *Rutstein*, CRI 2011, 125, 126 et seq.; *Westphal / Knapp*, ZIP 2011, 2033, 2041, 2044; *Pilkington / Hovering*, CRI 2011, 89.

1374 *Re La Seda De Barcelona SA* [2010] EWHC 1364 (Ch). See also *Gila / Tett / Gilley*, in *Asimacopoulus / Bickle*, p. 103 et seq. for background and transaction structure.

1375 *Re Hellas Telecommunications (Luxembourg) II SCA* [2009] EWHC 3199 (Ch); see *Davies / Glengarry*, in *Asimacopoulus/Bickle*, p. 163 et seq. for background and transaction structure.

of the company's credit agreements to allow for a restructuring. The financial documents were governed by English law.

Due to the different classes of creditors, four schemes were proposed.[1376] The schemes included the restructuring of the company's debt with a partial debt-equity-swap, amendments to the terms of the senior, second lien and mezzanine debt, and the raising of new funds.[1377] The debt-equity-swap would reduce the debt from EUR 947 million to EUR 623 million.[1378] At the same time, shareholders' equity would increase by EUR 35 million. The respective classes approved the schemes.

Before the High Court could approve the schemes, it had to answer the questions about whether the English court would have jurisdiction over a German company, *Tele Columbus* fulfilled the prerequisites for a scheme of arrangement, and the court should sanction the schemes of arrangement.

10.1.1 Jurisdiction by an English court over a German company?

The question is if English law may also apply to proceedings for companies registered or creditors based outside of England.[1379]

The CA 2006 refers to "*any company liable to be wound up under the IA 1986*"[1380]. The IA 1986 confers powers to the court to wind up both registered[1381] and unregistered[1382] companies "*if the court is of opinion that it is just and equitable that the company should be wound up*"[1383]. There are no jurisdictional restrictions referable to the company's place of incorporation, COMI or establishment.[1384] In addition, the company must

1376 *Schümann-Kleber*, IILR 2011, 447.

1377 *Witt*, Bloomberg, 16.9.2010.

1378 *Witt*, Bloomberg, 16.9.2010: The deal leaves *Tele Columbus* with EUR 530 million senior loans (interest either cash or Payment in Kind (PIK)), EUR 30 million junior-ranking second-lien loans (interest PIK), EUR 28 million mezzanine notes, EUR 35 million super-senior Revolving Credit Facility (RCF) (interest cash).

1379 *Seelinger / Daehnert*, ICR 2012, 243 et seq.

1380 Sec. 895(2)(b) CA 2006.

1381 Sec. 220 IA 1986.

1382 Sec. 221 IA 1986.

1383 *Re Rodenstock GmbH* [2011] EWHC 1104 (Ch), para.18.

1384 *Ibid.*, para. 19.

have a sufficiently close connection with England.[1385] A "*sufficient connection*" is established when the company has assets in England or when a significant number of claims affected by the scheme are subject to English law or English law has been agreed upon.[1386] If this condition is satisfied, the scheme of arrangement may also apply to foreign companies. The *Tele Columbus'* schemes applied to loan agreements that were subject to English law and in which England was chosen as the exclusive jurisdiction.

10.1.2 Prerequisites for a Scheme of Arrangement Fulfilled?

Tele Columbus had fulfilled the prerequisites for a scheme of arrangement in the case that 75% of voting creditors would have approved the scheme at the creditors' meetings of each class.

The necessary majorities[1387] indeed approved the *Tele Columbus* schemes.

10.1.3 English Court to Sanction the Scheme?

On the question of whether the English court should sanction the schemes, it is important to note that the sanctioned schemes would also be recognised in Germany since German courts are generally responsible for international lawsuits and claims against insolvent companies with a COMI located in Germany.[1388]

The court argued that the German courts would recognise the schemes as long as they were just and equitable and consistent with the fundamental principles of the German legal system.[1389] The schemes were an amendment to the existing loan agreements, governed by English law.

1385 *Ibid.*, para. 20(i).

1386 *Pilkington / Heverin*, ICR 2011, 89.

1387 *Trimast Holding Sarl – and – Tele Columbus GmbH* [2010] EWHC 1944 (Ch), para. 23(e): "87% of Senior Lenders, 94% of Mezzanine Lenders and 99% of the Second Lien Lenders".

1388 Art. 2, 60 EuGVVO, Art. 3 III EIR. See also *Maier*, NZI 2011, 305, 306.

1389 This does not only refer to the *ordre public* but also many other constellations, see *Maier*, NZI 2011, 305, 306. On the grounds for *ordre public* in European and German private international law; also *Mankowski*, KTS 2011, 185 et seq; *Knof*, ZInsO 2007, 629 et seq.

Thus, a German court would be bound to recognise the schemes as a matter of German private international law[1390].

10.2 Rodenstock

Rodenstock GmbH is a company that specialised in the production and distribution of lenses and frames as well as barometers, precision scales and measuring instruments.[1391] In 2007, the *Rodenstock* family resigned from the company. The company shares were held by *Permira* Beteiligungsberatung (85%), Beteiligungsgesellschaft *Bridgepoint* (10%) and the *Rodenstock* management held 5%. *Bridgepoint* funded the purchase price of its shares by a leveraged-buyout deal. The debt amounted to EUR 305 million (senior debt).[1392] The senior facility agreement included a choice-of-law clause. In an event of default, English law and jurisdiction exclusively would apply.

In 2008, the stagnation of sales and the burden of debt led the company into financial difficulties. In the second quarter of 2009, the company breached its financial covenants under the Senior Facility Agreement. The senior lenders issued various waivers. They also took control over 49% of the company's shares and provided a EUR 40 million restructuring loan. Bridgepoint remained the majority shareholder. The waivers gave the company a breathing space until April 2011.[1393] After that point, the maturity of the loan would have led to the insolvency of the company.[1394]

The senior creditors did not agree unanimously to a method of restructuring the company. In December 2010, they were advised on the four restructuring options[1395] in the event that the scheme of arrangement was not accepted. A group of senior lenders agreed to a restructuring, implemented through a scheme of arrangement.[1396] The prerequisite was that there was no material adverse change in the company's financial pos-

1390 *Maier*, NZI 2011, 305, 306.
1391 *Bruder et all*, in *Asimacopoulus/Bickle*, p. 187; Steffek Münchner Handbuch des Gesellschaftsrechts, Sec. 42, mn. 48 et seq.
1392 *Re Rodenstock GmbH* [2011] EWHC 1104 (Ch), para. 12.
1393 *Ibid.*, para. 8.
1394 *Ibid.*, para. 2.
1395 *Ibid.*, para. 10.
1396 *Ibid.*, para. 11.

ition.[1397] The restructuring agreement allowed for other creditors to join once the restructuring was completed. The scheme provided for amendments the terms of the loan agreement between *Rodenstock* and the senior lenders as well as the inter-creditor agreement.

The creditors agreed to a new super senior loan, the adjustment of interest payments and covenants to prevent over-indebtedness in Germany.[1398] *Rodenstock* granted the senior creditors options to receive 44% of the company's shares in a debt-equity-swap.[1399] Exercising all options, 44% of the shares would be held by senior creditors, 46% by current majority shareholder (*Bridgepoint*) and 10% by management.

After requesting the formal opening of the proceedings, the court ordered the creditors' meeting for the senior lenders. The scheme was approved by the lenders' voting 88.6% by number and 93.36% by value of the receivables. The creditors, who voted against the scheme, had previously submitted an alternative restructuring proposal.[1400] However, the proposal was neither approved by the majority of creditors nor the company's directors.[1401]

The creditors rejecting the scheme announced objections against jurisdiction, the discretion of the court and the usefulness of the scheme.[1402] The request was withdrawn before the court heard the reasons and sanctioned the scheme. The judge took the objections raised as an opportunity to comment on jurisdiction and discretion.[1403] He did this by his own admission because the ECJ may soon preside over these issues.[1404] In addition, he wanted to provide guidance for future applications.[1405]

The court recognised that *Rodenstock GmbH* had its COMI in Munich. The company had a turnover of ~ EUR 258 million.[1406] *Rodenstock* generated sales of ~EUR 4 million with seven customers in the UK.[1407] The re-

1397 *Ibid.*, para. 11.
1398 *Ibid.*, paras. 12, 13.
1399 *Ibid.*, para. 14.
1400 *Ibid.*, para. 16.
1401 *Ibid.*
1402 *Ibid.*
1403 *Ibid.*
1404 *Ibid.*, paras. 3, 75.
1405 *Ibid.*, para. 3.
1406 *Ibid.*, para. 4.
1407 *Ibid.*, para.7.

structuring should only affect the senior lenders, of which 56.5% were based in England.[1408] *Rodenstock* had no physical assets in England.

10.2.1 Recognition of the Scheme of Arrangement?

The arguments on the jurisdiction and the discretion of the court had already been discussed in *Tele Columbus*.[1409] The company must have a sufficiently close connection with England. It is not necessary that these are assets in England. There must, however, be a reasonable possibility of benefits to the creditors by the confirmation of the court and one or more persons, interested in the distribution of assets, must be subject to English jurisdiction.[1410]

The court acknowledged in its judgement that such an understanding of founding jurisdiction was "*prima facie exorbitant*"[1411]. The court will, however, not use this as a "*carte blanche*"[1412] for allowing foreign companies with just any connection to England to find jurisdiction before an English court.

It is questionable whether the EIR and the Judgement Regulation have limited the jurisdiction of the English court to approve schemes of arrangement for foreign companies.[1413] The High Court has already taken a position on this.[1414] In its view, the international jurisdiction of the English courts has changed significantly for the winding-up of companies. As long as a solvent or insolvent company has both its headquarters and its COMI in Germany and no establishment in England, no English court is responsible for its winding-up, unless public interests are affected.[1415] The judge pointed out that due to broader reasons, neither the EIR nor the Brussels I Regulation are a restriction on jurisdiction for a scheme.[1416] The international jurisdiction in *Rodenstock* was already determined by the

1408 *Ibid.*, para. 6.
1409 *Ibid.*, paras. 65 et seq.
1410 *Ibid.*, paras. 21 et seq.
1411 *Ibid.*, para. 21.
1412 *Ibid.*, para. 20.
1413 *Ibid.*, paras. 25 et seq. See also *Schümann-Kleber*, IILR 2011, 447, 449 et seq.; *Mankowski*, WM 2011, 1201, 1202 et seq.
1414 *Sovereign Marine & General Insurance Co. Ltd.* [2006] EWHC 1335 (Ch).
1415 *Re Rodenstock GmbH* [2011] EWHC 1104 (Ch), para. 40.
1416 *Ibid.*

choice-of-law and jurisdiction clause in the senior facility agreement. The vast majority of creditors were based in England.[1417]

The question remains as to whether a scheme under English law is recognised by the German courts, so that the dissenting creditors may pursue their original rights in a German court. In the first judgement on a scheme, the District Court Potsdam refused to recognise the scheme.[1418] The court was missing the clause for exclusive English jurisdiction.

The Regional Court in Rottweil recognised a scheme of an insurance company as a matter of insolvency law in analogy to a Chapter 11-proceedings pursuant to § 343 InsO.[1419] The question was whether it is a solvent or insolvent scheme. The question of application of the EIR did not arise since the debtor was an insurance company to which the EIR does not apply.[1420]

The judge referred in his reasons to the judgement by the Celle Court of Appeal.[1421] The case involved a German customer and the British life insurance company *Equitable Life*. This court refused to recognise the scheme and the contract claims' restriction for German customers.[1422] The judgement was appealed.[1423] The German Federal Court upheld the decision of the Celle Court of Appeal.[1424]

1417 *Ibid.*

1418 LG Potsdam, 22.10.2008 – 2 O 501/07.

1419 LG Rottweil 17. 5. 2010 – 3 O 2/08, ZInsO 2010, 1854, 1855. See also *BGH*, NZI 2009, 859.

1420 Art. 1(2) EIR.

1421 *Re Rodenstock GmbH* [2011] EWHC 1104 (Ch), paras. 50, 74 with reference to OLG Celle, Urt. v. 8. 9. 2009 – 8 U 46/09, ZIP 2009, 1968, 1971.

1422 Art. 32 Judgement Regulation.

1423 OLG Celle, ZIP 2009, 1968.

1424 The confirmation of the appeal was already assumed in the *Rodenstock* judgement, see *Re Rodenstock GmbH* [2011] EWHC 1104 (Ch), paras. 74, 75. See BGH, ZIP 2012, 740: The German Federal Court decided that the scheme in *Equitable Life* was neither an "insolvency proceeding" and could therefore not be recognised as a foreign insolvency proceeding under those German law nor a "judgement" under the Brussels I Regulation due to the specific requirements for insurance companies. An insurance company must bring insurance litigation against a policyholder in the jurisdiction where the policyholder has its COMI. The court added that an English Court order sanctioning a scheme could be classified as a "judgement" for the purposes of the Judgement Regulation. It argued that a "judgement" under the Brussels I Regulation.is open for interpretation. In addition, a scheme process involves adversarial characteristics supporting the classification of a court order sanctioning the scheme as a "judgement". See *Ho*,

10.2.2 Comparable Proceeding in German Law?

The question is whether there is a similar form of proceeding available in Germany with regard to a solvent scheme of arrangement.

Although there have been discussions about a pre-insolvency proceeding for restructurings in German law, there is no equivalent to a solvent scheme outside a statutory proceeding in Germany. The statutory proceedings in German law provide provisions to be used for restructurings and liquidations. The introduction of the protective shield proceeding marks an opportunity for the debtor to arrange a restructuring with its creditors through an insolvency plan. An insolvency plan may also be used to initiate a self-administration to restructure the company. However, in any of these cases, the debtor must file for insolvency and the insolvency court has to open the appropriate statutory proceeding.

Consensual agreements among the parties involved are governed by the private autonomy of contract law. However, there is no possibility of a 'cram down' of dissenting creditors since an informal proceeding requires unanimous creditor consent. Only in limited cases under German law may a decision be made by a voting majority to be forced upon a minority.[1425]

In discussing as to whether and how a scheme should be recognised in Germany, two main approaches are applicable.[1426]

10.2.2.1 Recognition of Foreign Judgement or Procedural Law Approach?

The scheme must be automatically recognised when the decision of the English court on sanctioning the scheme was the equivalent to a judge-

CRI 2009, 3 on the applicability of a scheme of arrangement on an insolvent insurer in Europe with regard to the Insurers Regulation (implementation of the "Insurers Directive 2001/17/EC on the reorganisation and winding-up of insurance undertakings"). In addition, see *Bork*, ZEuP 2013, 132 et seq.

1425 Restructuring bonds is one example.

1426 *Gebler*, NZI 2010, 665, 668 et seq.

ment[1427] in a proceeding.[1428] Decisions by a court in one member state must be recognised in another member state without further formality.[1429] For the automatic recognition, the scheme must be a *proceeding* and the court order, sanctioning the scheme, a *judgement*.

Some argue that the scheme is not an inquisitorial proceeding, including a dispute element between two parties in which the court has any discretion in sanctioning the scheme.[1430] This argument is not convincing.[1431] In a scheme hearing, the judge reasons whether the court has jurisdiction over the company and whether the formal requirements to implement the scheme are fulfilled. If the judge is satisfied on these accounts, he can determine as to whether to sanction the scheme.[1432] The court order in sanctioning the scheme could be said to be a judgement.[1433] It could therefore be recognised as a foreign judgement in a German court.[1434]

1427 Art. 1(d) Judgement Regulation: "Any decision, however described (judgement, order and the like), given by a court in a civil or commercial matter, and includes an award in proceedings on an arbitration if the award has become enforceable in the territory of origin in the same manner as a judgement given by a court in that territory".

1428 *Mankowski*, WM 2011, 1201, 1204.

1429 Art. 32 et seq. Judgement Regulation.

1430 *OLG Celle*, ZIP 2009, 1968, 1971. See also *Gebler*, NZI 2010, 665, 668; *Schnepp / Janzen*, VW 2007, 1057, 1058 et seq.

1431 *Schaloske*, VersR 2009, 23, 27.

1432 *Re Hawk Insurance Company Limited* [2001] 2 BCLC 450, CA: even if the scheme has been agreed upon unanimously, the court may decide to exercise discretion and not sanction the scheme. See *Pilkington / Schorling / Davies*, ICR 2010, 239, 240; *Schaloske* VersR 2009, 23, 27.

1433 *Ho*, A new Byword for Cross-Border Restructuring: Scheme of Arrangement as Judgement, Case Review on R*e Cavell Insurance Company 21.2.2005, Ontario Supreme Court (unreported)*. See also *Paulus*, ZIP 2011, 1077, 1080; *Mankowski*, WM 2011, 1201, 1204; *Schaloske*, VersR 2009, 23, 27.

1434 Art. 33 Judgement Regulation. Confirmative *LG Potsdam* 22.10.2008 – Case 2 O 501/07 (unreported). See also *Schaloske* VersR 2009, 23, 27; *Petrovic*, ZInsO 2010, 665, 668. Refusing *OLG Celle*, ZIP 2009, 1968, 1971; *Gebler*, NZI 2010, 665, 668.

If a scheme is recognised as a foreign judgement, there are also grounds for refusing recognition,[1435] especially on grounds of public policy[1436] or unfair trial[1437].

10.2.2.2 Recognition of Foreign Insolvency Proceeding or Substantive Law Approach?

The scheme must be automatically recognised in Germany when it falls within the scope of the EIR.[1438]

The scheme on a stand-alone basis is not an insolvency proceeding and a matter of insolvency law but it is governed by corporate law. It is not listed as an insolvency proceeding of the United Kingdom in the EIR, Annex A and, therefore, the EIR and automatic recognition would not apply.[1439] English courts have already confirmed this view in similar cases regarding companies in other European jurisdictions.[1440] The ECJ has not been asked for its opinion on any of these cases.

A scheme may also be recognised in Germany in accordance with § 343 InsO.[1441] This provision provides for recognition of foreign insolvency proceedings or, at least, a similar proceeding pursuing the same objectives.[1442] "*The insolvency proceedings shall serve the purpose of collective*

1435 Art. 34, 35(1) Judgement Regulation.

1436 Art. 34 Nr. 1 Judgement Regulation. Especially the breach of any constitutional rights, see *Schaloske*, VersR 2009, 23, 28; *von der Fecht*, NZI 2011, 557, 565: The private autonomy is a constitutional right; BGHZ 54, 247 = NJW 1970, 2019.

1437 Art. 34 Nr. 2 Judgement Regulation. See *Schaloske*, VersR 2009, 23, 28: in a strict sense, the provision applies to an inquisitory proceeding. However, since the judgement is recognised in Art. 32, 33 Brussels I Regulation, Art. 34 No. 2 Judgement Regulation applies accordingly.

1438 Art. 16 EIR, with exception to public policy under Art. 26 EIR. *See also* Schümann-Kleber, IILR 2011, 447, 452 et seq.

1439 Art. 1(1), 2(a) EIR. See *Schaloske*, VersR 2009, 23, 27; *Petrovic*, ZInsO 2010, 265, 267; *Gebler*, NZI 2010, 665, 668.

1440 *Re DAP Holding NV* [2005] EWHC 2092 (Ch); *Re La Seda de Barcelona SA* [2010] EWHC 1364 (Ch), *Re Hellas Telecommunications (Luxembourg) II SCA* [2009] EWHC 3199 (Ch); *Re Heron International NV* [1994] 1 BCLC 667.

1441 *Gebler*, NZI 2010, 665, 668.

1442 BGH, Urt. v. 13. Oktober 2009 – X ZR 79/06, WM 2009, 2330, mn. 8. See also *Gebler*, NZI 2010, 665, 668.

satisfaction of a debtor's creditors by liquidation of the debtor's assets and by distribution of the proceeds, or by reaching an arrangement in an insolvency plan, particularly in order to maintain the enterprise."[1443]

It should include "*collective insolvency proceedings which entail the partial or total divestment of a debtor and the appointment of a liquidator.*"[1444]

A scheme is not a collective proceeding. It does not include all the debtor's creditors for collective satisfaction or for implementation of a restructuring;[1445] nor does it involve the partial or total divestment of a debtor or the appointment of a liquidator. A scheme is also not a (procedural) arrangement in accordance with Art. 58 Judgement Regulation since it is not binding on all creditors and the approval of the scheme is not unanimous.[1446]

The judgement shows that the line between procedural law and substantive law is blurred.[1447] There is no legal clarity for creditors about the effect of a scheme in a German court and the uncertainties should be evaluated cautiously before regarding a scheme as an instrument for a restructuring.[1448]

The court was satisfied on the evidence that the formal requirements for the making of an order sanctioning the scheme had been met, and that the contrary had not been suggested. The scheme meeting was properly convened, it was properly constituted on the basis of a single class and the requisite majorities were obtained in support.[1449] On the question of whether the court should sanction the scheme in its discretion, it reasoned that the scheme has been voted for by creditors acting *bona fide* in their interests and without coercion of the minority.[1450] In addition, intelligent and honest creditors acting in their own interests would reasonably and objectively approve the scheme. The judge was, therefore, satisfied that the scheme met the substantive requirements.[1451]

1443 Sec. 1 InsO.
1444 Art. 1(1) EIR.
1445 OLG Celle, ZIP 2009, 1968, 1971. Also *Gebler*, NZI 2010, 665, 668.
1446 *Von der Fecht*, NZI 2011, 557, 567.
1447 *Ibid.*, 567.
1448 *Pilkington / Schorling / Ben*, ICR 2010, 239, 241.
1449 *Re Rodenstock GmbH* [2011] EWHC 1104 (Ch), para. 78.
1450 *Ibid.*, para. 79.
1451 *Ibid.*, para. 78; for reasons *ibid.*, para. 80 et seq.

One major aspect was left unresolved in *Rodenstock*: it was left "*to another day [...] in which a scheme is sought to be sanctioned in England where all affected members or creditors are domiciled in member states other than the UK.*"[1452]

10.3 PrimaCom

The aspect was soon to be considered. Whether the court would have jurisdiction or deny it, would have a crucial impact on the viability of schemes for foreign companies as it would severely limit its application.

PrimaCom Holding GmbH[1453] is part a group, providing cable television and telecommunication products to customers in Germany.[1454] The company's COMI was located in Germany. Since 2007, *PrimaCom* had tried unsuccessfully to restructure.[1455] Further financial difficulties led the company to propose several schemes[1456] to its creditors in December 2011.[1457] The schemes were to approve a restructuring of the company's finance facilities and provide further working capital.[1458] The outcome of the schemes were valued as more beneficial than an insolvency proceeding.[1459] The company was not technically insolvent at this stage. The company was, however, in an urgent need of liquidity.[1460] The failure to sanction the scheme and implement the restructuring would have eventually led the company to file for insolvency in Germany.[1461] At the application hearing in December 2011, the question rose again on whether an English

---

1452 *Ibid.,* para. 62.

1453 *PrimaCom Holding GmbH and others v Credit Agricole and others* [2011] EWHC 3746 (Ch), para. 21: *PrimaCom Holding GmbH* was originally a wholly-owned corporate subsidiary of *PrimaCom AG*, a listed German company.

1454 *Ibid.,* para. 21.

1455 *Ibid.,* paras. 3, 10, 21, on the shareholder structure and the changes after formal insolvency proceedings were opened in June 2010.

1456 *Ibid.,* paras. 1, 17: The application for a scheme of arrangement was seeking an order to convene four meetings of scheme creditors, on the constitution of classes, paras. 17, 19 et seq.; for approval, para. 72.

1457 *Ibid.,* para. 1.

1458 *Ibid.,* paras. 4, 42.

1459 *Ibid.,* para. 8.

1460 *Ibid.,* para. 6, 22 et seq.

1461 *Ibid.,* para. 27.

court had jurisdiction to approve and sanction a scheme that will be recognised in a German court.

The court established that *PrimaCom* had its COMI in Germany[1462] and that its creditors were also located in Germany. Persons domiciled in a member state shall, regardless of their nationality, be sued in the courts of that member state.[1463] The responsible jurisdiction for *PrimaCom*'s creditors would have been a German court.

The court evaluated whether *PrimaCom* had sufficient connection. The financing agreements as well as the inter-creditor agreement, subject to restructuring, were exclusively governed by English law.[1464] Therefore, the court was satisfied with the test.[1465] The question was then raised of whether the scheme would be recognised in a German court since the scheme was not a conventional form of an adversarial proceeding to be recognised under German law. Following the reasoning of the court in *Rodenstock*, the court concluded that the Brussels I Regulation was applicable.[1466]

The scheme creditors had recognised the jurisdiction of the English courts by effectively agreeing on English jurisdiction.[1467] They also submitted to the English court's jurisdiction by appearing at the hearings and agreed to the convening of creditors' meetings. The judge concluded that even when the defendants are not domiciled in a member state, each member state could continue to apply its own private international law in order to recognise the scheme.[1468] Since the defendants had submitted to English jurisdiction, the court would have jurisdiction to sanction the scheme.[1469] In the hearing on approving and sanctioning or denying the scheme in January 2012,[1470] the judge stated that the schemes were approved by a majority creditors' vote by 96.8% by number and 98.4% by

1462 *Ibid.,* para. 63.
1463 Art. 2 Brussels I Regulation.
1464 *PrimaCom Holding GmbH and others v Credit Agricole and others* [2011] EWHC 3746 (Ch), para. 18.
1465 *Ibid.,* para. 64.
1466 *Ibid.,* para. 66.
1467 Art. 23, 24 Brussels I Regulation.
1468 Art. 4 Brussels I Regulation.
1469 *PrimaCom Holding GmbH and others v Credit Agricole and others* [2011] EWHC 3746 (Ch), para. 67.
1470 *Primacom Holding GmbH and others v Credit Agricole and others* [2012] EWHC 164 (Ch).

value.[1471] The judge clarified specifically the "*conundrum*"[1472] as all of *PrimaCom*'s creditors were located in Germany.

The judge also reviewed the potential complications of *Equitable Life*. The Celle Court of Appeal here ruled that a scheme would not be recognised in a German court.[1473] Schemes, especially solvent schemes, are not an insolvency proceedings recognised under Annex A, EIR. The court order to sanction the scheme does not constitute a judgement that could be given automatic effect as it lacks the requisite dispute element due to the majority support of the scheme from creditors. The judge cited that the difference between the cases in *Re Rodenstock* and *Re PrimaCom* compared to *Equitable Life* was that the claims in *Rodenstock* and *PrimaCom* involved claims governed by English law while the claims in *Equitable Life*'s were governed by German law.[1474] The judge was, therefore, persuaded that there was a reasonable prospect of the German courts accepting the court order sanctioning the scheme.[1475] He thus approved and sanctioned the scheme.[1476]

10.4 APCOA Parking

APCOA Parking[1477] carries out its operations in the UK, Austria, Denmark, Germany, Norway and Belgium.[1478] As the group would have been unable to repay its debt[1479] due to mature on 25 April 2014 and the restructuring process would not be finished until that date, the decision was taken to implement schemes of arrangement for the respective borrowers under the facilities agreement to extend the maturity date by three months with a mechanism to further extend the date to no later than 25 October

---

1471 *Ibid.*, para. 2.
1472 *Ibid.*, para. 9.
1473 *Pilkington / Schorling / Davies*, ICR 2010, 239, 240 et seq; *Tett / Knapp*, ICR 2012, 346 et seq.
1474 *Primacom Holding GmbH and others v Credit Agricole and others* [2012] EWHC 164 (Ch), para. 18.
1475 *Ibid.*, para. 19.
1476 *Ibid.*, para. 20.
1477 *Re APCOA Parking (UK) Ltd & Ors* [2014] EWHC 997 (Ch).
1478 *Ibid.*, para. 2.
1479 *Ibid*, para 5: amounting EUR 660 million (priority senior+second lien) and GBP 33.83 million (priority senior).

2014.[1480] Under the terms of the facility agreement, the extension of maturity would have required unanimous approval. This was not likely to happen and the company would have had to file for insolvency in Germany.[1481] A scheme of arrangement, on the other hand, would allow for extension with the consent of majority in number of the lenders under the facilities agreement.

The novelty in this case compared to previous cases was that the facilities agreement was originally governed by German law and subject to the jurisdiction of the German courts. There was no material connection to English law or to English jurisdiction[1482] to satisfy the English court to establish a sufficient connection for the company with England in order to sanction the scheme. The financial documents did, however, allow for an amendment in governing law[1483] with the requisite majority lender consent (66.6%), which was duly obtained by formal amendment.

The question then arose whether the change to English law and to English courts were valid and thereby created a sufficient connection for the purposes of the proposed schemes. The judge questioned that recognition of the change of governing law in all relevant jurisdictions[1484], in particular, in the jurisdiction originally incorporated into the contract, and the creditors' awareness of the consequences the change of governing law would have: e.g. the implementation of a scheme of arrangement under English law and deferral of the termination date[1485] He was given expert found evidence that the creditors explicitly agreed on the change of governing law and found no obvious reason why the amendment of the financing contract would not be valid.[1486] Assuming the validity of the alteration of the governing law and the jurisdiction clause to English law and the English court, he was satisfied with the sufficient connection and established that the court would have jurisdiction.[1487] Although this route to finding jurisdiction is novel, the arguments of the court are consistent with the existing and established principles.

1480 *Ibid.*, para. 19.
1481 *Ibid.*, para. 4.
1482 *Ibid.*, para. 20.
1483 *Ibid.*, para. 21.
1484 *Ibid.*, para. 35.
1485 *Ibid.*, para. 36.
1486 *Ibid.*, para. 37.
1487 *Ibid.*, para. 39.

The creditors must vote on a scheme. Generally, each class of creditors will have a separate vote due to their different interests[1488], distinctions among different tranches may not be made by the English court.[1489] This also applied to *APCOA Parking* where the priority senior lenders and second lien lenders voted together in one class despite their different ranking in the intercreditor agreement.[1490] The judge argued that the nature of compromise proposed in the schemes affected both types of lender rights against the company equally; therefore, they may discuss the matter with a view to their common interest.[1491] He added that in case the proposed schemes would fail and result in a German insolvency proceeding there would be no difference in ranking for creditors, leading to an equal result for all creditors.[1492] The creditors did not oppose the class composition[1493] and voted in the respective majority for the scheme, which was sanctioned by the court on 14 April 2014.[1494]

The restructuring of *APCOA Parking* by means of scheme of arrangement shows the flexibility of English law in general and the proceeding in particular. While most terms in the facilities agreement require unanimous lender consent (the extension of maturity dates, payment terms or collateral amendments), governing law and jurisdiction clauses generally require majority lender consent by two thirds.[1495] The amendment to English law governing the contract and jurisdiction clause to English courts allow for a scheme of arrangement that does not require unanimous lender consent, thereby, avoiding waiver request and any postponing consequences hindering the implementation of a financial restructuring. *APCOA*

1488 Companies Act 2006, section 899(1); *see also Re Hawk Insurance Company Limited* [2001] 2 BCLC 675.

1489 Example given the separation of creditors in senior secured debt even where such tranches have different orders of priority, maturities, and interest rates, *see Primacom Holding GmbH and others v Credit Agricole and others* [2011] EWHC 3746 (Ch), [2012] EWHC 164 (Ch), and *APCOA Parking (UK) Ltd & Ors* [2014] EWHC 997 (Ch).

1490 *APCOA Parking (UK) Ltd & Ors* [2014] EWHC 997 (Ch), para. 29.

1491 *Ibid.*, para. 29-31; *Re APCOA Parking Holdings GmbH & Ors* [2014] EWHC 1867 (Ch), para. 8.

1492 *APCOA Parking (UK) Ltd & Ors* [2014] EWHC 997 (Ch), para. 32.

1493 *Ibid.*, para. 42-43 despite some challenges by creditors made.

1494 *Re APCOA Parking Holdings GmbH & Ors* [2014] EWHC 1867 (Ch).

1495 The decision in *APCOA Parking* could also have significant impact in the bond market, where a bare majority of bond holders can approve a change of governing law and jurisdiction.

Parking even proves that a scheme of arrangement is an appropriate mechanism to allow groups of companies with subsidiaries in different jurisdictions to be restructured.

10.5 Conclusion

The four cases show that a scheme of arrangement is a powerful tool for complex financial restructurings in an English court, having already established an viable track record for flexible solutions for both English and foreign companies. Especially for companies having accumulated their debt burden in the leveraged-buyout years before 2008, most financing documents already include an English choice-of-law-clause and exclusive English jurisdiction. For other cases, creditors willing to support the restructuring may just change the choice-of-law clause for the purpose of financial restructuring, giving them predictability and certainty about the law applicable to the financial restructuring.

11 Rescue Culture or Mean to an End?

With the introduction of ESUG, the debtor has the possibility to request a protective shield proceeding to develop a restructuring concept within three months while being protected from any enforcement of its creditors and still continue trading. While several well-known names requesting this proceeding[1496] to terminate their grounds for insolvency, *Suhrkamp Verlag GmbH & Co. KG*, a German publishing house, took a more active approach to use insolvency law to solve a corporate law issue: a struggle between a majority and a minority shareholder. The restructuring of has already been labelled "*one of the most spectacular restructuring proceed-*

1496 *Centrotherm* and *IVG Immobilien* are among those that have completed a protective shield proceeding and where the insolvency proceeding was then terminated after the creditors accepted the insolvency plan for restructuring.
A constitutional complaint was also files for the shareholders of *IVG Immobilien* against their expropriation within the protective shield proceeding, which was filed on 20 August 2013 by *IVG Immobilien* after the informal restructuring has failed despite the viable underlying business. The company negotiated an insolvency plan for a restructuring, which included a capital decrease and within the subsequent capital increase the old shareholders were excluded.

ings in German corporate history"[1497]. The company was, in the public eye, attempting to exploit opportunities under new legislation[1498] by using an insolvency plan proceeding in self-administration for a corporate restructuring – and to settle a dispute between the shareholders.[1499] The legislature may have provided the solution of insolvency law issues having in mind the implementation of a debt-equity-swap or prohibiting the obstruction of shareholders rather than to solve corporate law issues.

11.1 Background Suhrkamp

The corporate disputes between the media entrepreneur *Hans Barlach* and the family trust managed by *Ulla Unseld-Berkéwicz* go back to the year 2006, when *Barlach* bought 39% of the shares of the publishing house with special participation and information rights against the will of the trust, which held the remaining 61%. After a further deterioration of the relationship,[1500] and with both partners wanting to take over the shares of the other side,[1501] the dispute climaxed before the District Court in Berlin on 10 December 2012. *Barlach* made a claim for damages[1502] against *Unseld-Berkéwicz* and demanded the dismissal of the management.[1503] *Unseld-Berkéwicz* was dismissed as manager of *Suhrkamp* by court order.[1504] She appealed against the judgement as she would have not been able to steer the proceeding further.

At the same time, the dissolution of the company was requested before the District Court in Frankfurt.[1505] In this trial, both parties tried to obtain the exclusion of the other from the company. The proceeding was repeatedly postponed to give the parties the opportunity to settle the matter out

1497 *Heide*, HB 9.8.2013 online.
1498 *Möhlenkamp*, BB 2013, 2828.
1499 *Madaus*, ZIP 2014, 160.
1500 *Kegel*, FAZ 5.12.2013 online.
1501 *Zielke*, SZ 13.5.2013 online. There is also disagreement about the value of *Barlach*'s shares between EUR 8 million (trust) and EUR 30 million (*Barlach*).
1502 LG Berlin, Urt. v. 10.12.2012, 99 O 79/11 = KG 23 U 186/12.
1503 LG Berlin, Urt. v. 10.12.2012, 99 O 118/11 = KG 14 U 124/12.
1504 In addition to the company's management to pay damages of EUR 282,486.40 to the company.
1505 LG Frankfurt,/M., Urt. v. 13.11.2013 – 3-13 O 72/12.

of court[1506] and it was recommended that a mediator be appointed. *Barlach* refused at first, and then insisted on the condition that the trust retreated from the company and thus *Unseld-Berkéwicz* from the management. *Unseld-Berkéwicz* declined.

On 20 March 2013, the Frankfurt District Court found proof that the management had incorrectly decided on the distribution of *Suhrkamp*'s annual profit for 2010, due to the inappropriate participation of the minority shareholder.[1507] It ordered the trust to make an immediate payment of EUR 2.2 million to *Barlach*.[1508] This ruling meant that all claims of the shareholders to the company for the amount of 8.2 million EUR would have to be accounted for, if the shareholders would not agree to a waiver or a deferral of payment until 2014.[1509] In that case, the company would be over-indebted and would therefore no longer have a sufficient going concern forecast.[1510] In May 2013, *Unseld-Berkéwicz* tried to terminate the shareholders' agreement ordinary and extraordinary; *Barlach* opposed and received approval by the District Court in Berlin.[1511]

Despite the fact that there were discussions of subordinating the claims by both parties,[1512] the management of the company requested the opening of an insolvency plan proceeding in self-administration at the Lower District Court Charlottenburg on 27 May 2013.[1513] With the insolvency plan and the decision to initiate the proceeding pending, a protective shield protection proceeding was opened to prohibit the enforcement of the judgement of the Frankfurt District Court and the distribution of profits to *Barlach*.[1514] The provisional administrator[1515] was appointed, taking over important management decisions from the disputing shareholders. *Barlach*

1506 *Müller*, Die Welt 24.9.2013 online.

1507 LG Frankfurt,/M., Urt. v. 20.3.2013 – 3-13 O 119/12, ZIP 2013, 1280.

1508 LG Frankfurt,/M., Urt. v. 13.8.2013 – 03-9 O 78/13, para. 7.

1509 *Ibid.*, para. 10.

1510 *Kegel*, FAZ online 27.5.2013.

1511 LG Berlin, Urt. v. 16.6.2014 – 95 O 52/13.

1512 LG Frankfurt,/M., Urt. v. 13.8.2013 – 03-9O 78/13, para. 13.

1513 AG Charlottenburg, 36s IN 2196/13, 36i IN 2311/13. See *Brinkmann*, ZIP 2014, 197 et seq. for discussion on the "strategic" application for insolvency and the legal misuse; *Schäfer*, ZIP 2013, 2237, 2243 et seq.

1514 *Kegel*, FAZ online 27.5.2013.

1515 *Rolf Rattunde* was appointed as provisional administrator.

claimed the "*indebtedness scenario [was]...designed as an abuse of law.*"[1516]

It only later became public that on 7 May 2013 *Barlach* had been ordered by the Commercial Court in Zurich to pay SFR 5 million for the shares plus costs and annualised interest. *Barlach* appealed.[1517]

The preliminary creditors' committee approved the insolvency plan and the insolvency proceeding in self-administration on 19 June 2013.[1518] *Barlach* explained that the subordination of his profit claim, which meant that he voluntarily ranked his claim behind those of the creditors, was "*in the interest of the survival of the company*"[1519]. Furthermore, he filed a motion for a preliminary injunction, according to which the trust had to make the same commitment to defer its claims until 2014 with the subordination of its claims against the company.[1520] The over-indebtedness of *Suhrkamp* and the reason for the application to open an insolvency proceeding would have thus been eliminated. This request was granted on 19 July 2013 by the Frankfurt District Court.[1521] As justification, the Court referred to the fiduciary duties of the shareholder, which it saw breached by the trust's recent request to make the profits payable.[1522] That request obviously served other purposes, mainly the disempowerment of the minority shareholder.[1523]

Barlach filed a request for an urgent injunction from the Berlin District Court for the management of the company to be immediately dismissed to still prevent the insolvency proceedings; he failed.[1524]

On 6 August 2013, the *Suhrkamp* insolvency proceeding in self-administration was opened at the Lower District Court in Charlottenburg. The

1516 *Ibid.*

1517 *Kegel*, FAZ online 3.6.2013. The judge found that *Barlach* had paid SFR 10.8 million for his shares, a great discrepancy compared to the estimated company value of EUR 80 million. *Barlach* appealed against the judgement on the basis of a lack of information about the conflict potential in the publishing company.

1518 *Kegel*, FAZ 7.8.2013 online.

1519 *Kegel*, FAZ 20.6.2013 online.

1520 *Ibid.*

1521 LG Frankfurt,/M., Urt. v. 13.8.2013 – 03-9O 78/13, para. 18.

1522 *Kegel*, FAZ online 22.7.2013.

1523 LG Frankfurt,/M., Urt. V. 13.8.2013 – 03-9O 78/13, para. 56, 57.

1524 *Zielcke*, SZ 8.8.2013 online; as a reason for the dismissal request it was especially mentioned that the management had not prevented the insolvency of the company; *Kegel*, FAZ 8.8.2013 online.

administrator was appointed[1525] and confirmed that *Suhrkamp* fulfilled two prerequisites for insolvency: over-indebtedness and insolvency.[1526] The previous management remained in office with the approval of the creditors' meeting.[1527] The insolvency plan submitted included converting the legal form of the company from a limited partnership into a public limited company[1528] by means of a simple majority vote of the creditors and the approval of the court.[1529] The shareholders had to renounce their profit claims, totalling EUR 7 million, in order to lay the foundations for the restructuring.[1530]

This change of legal form would not affect the position of the company's shareholders as such. Their participation and information rights, however, would in future be dealt with according to company law provisions. Thus, *Barlach*'s special rights included in the shareholders' agreement of 2009 would be eliminated. However, the insolvency plan offered a settlement for the shareholders who no longer wanted to remain in the company.[1531] The trust was accused of benefitting from the protection proceedings and the self-administration to eliminate the minority shareholder by urging him out of the company against his will.[1532] *Barlach* filed a constitutional complaint with the German Federal Constitutional Court.[1533]

The company only confirmed that by changing the legal form the insolvency triggered by the shareholders' dispute would no longer affect the op-

1525 *Rolf Rattunde* was appointed as administrator.

1526 *Zielcke*, SZ online 7.8.2013.

1527 *Ibid.*

1528 *Madaus*, ZIP 2012, 2133 et seq. on conversion in insolvency plan proceedings.

1529 *Zielcke*, SZ online 7.8.2013, comparing the different rights of influence in the Kommanditgesellschaft to the Aktiengesellschaft.

1530 *Rüsche*, Focus Online 10.11.2013.

1531 *Kegel*, FAZ online 7.8.2013: the shareholders would be able to trade their shares against a settlement with the other shareholders or – with the agreement of the company, as the shares have restricted transferability – transfer them to a third party. See also *Clausen / Müller*, Die Welt 18.8.2013 online: *Barlach* was offered a settlement of EUR 925.000, which was only a "cold expropriation" as he has invested a minimum of EUR 12 million in the company so far. See also *Müller*, Welt online 24.9.2013: the average value of the company would be EUR 20 million, which would allocate EUR 12.2 million to the trust and EUR 7.8 million to *Barlach*.

1532 *Jahn*, FAZ online 12.8.2013.

1533 BVerfG, Beschl. v. 17.10.2013 – 2 BvR 1978/13. See Rechtslupe online 12.11.2013.

erations.[1534] This "*brilliant Machiavellian manoeuvre*"[1535] would, at last, "*smash the Gordian knot*"[1536] of the irreconcilable and hostile shareholder relationship.[1537]

On 13 August 2013, the Frankfurt District Court decided that the trust would have to declare their claims subordinate, as *Barlach* had already done, in order to perform its fiduciary duties.[1538] The company would therefore no longer be over-indebted, but merely insolvent, and the insolvency proceeding would be void.[1539] The Court found proof that the insolvency expert opinion and the insolvency plan specifically aimed only to weaken and undermine *Barlach*'s legal position.[1540] In particular, the insolvency plan would reduce *Barlach* to a minimum level of corporate law influence, although for a period of seven years he would be bound to the company in order to keep the book values and silent reserves, and therefore the tax benefits,[1541] from the change of legal form in the books. Otherwise they would have to be revealed.[1542] The Court did not account for breaches of fiduciary duties.[1543] All the orders by the Court were appealed by the trust.[1544]

1534 Reference to Pressemitteilung Suhrkamp, 7.8.2013, http://www.boersenblatt.net/632291/, accessed 18.8.2013.

1535 *Bayer / Hammelehle*, Spiegel online, 28. 05. 2013.

1536 *Kegel*, FAZ online 7.8.2013.

1537 *Zielcke*, SZ online 8.8.2013.

1538 LG Frankfurt,/M., Urt. v. 13.8.2013 – 03-9 O 78/13, ZInsO 2013, 1793. See also *Kegel*, FAZ 13.8.2013 online.

1539 *Kegel*, FAZ 13.8.2013 online.

1540 *Kegel*, FAZ 13.8.2013 online. In addition *Rattunde*, in *Kegel*, FAZ 16.8.2013 online, explaining that the shareholder issues were not part of the review process. Further *Rattunde*, in *Heide*, HB 9.8.2013, remarking that he did not have any connection to Suhrkamp yet as the independence of the administrator is an important prerequisite for such a process.

1541 *Clausen / Müller*, Die Welt 18.8.2013 online: the legal opinion on tax issues on converting a limited partnership into a public limited company has as a prerequisite that the shareholders and their shares are located within the European Union. However, *Barlach*'s shares are held by his media holding company in Switzerland.

1542 LG Frankfurt,/M., Urt. V. 13.8.2013 – 03-9 O 78/13, para. 57 et seq.

1543 LG Frankfurt,/M., Urt. V. 13.8.2013 – 03-9 O 78/13, para. 64 et seq.

1544 *Kegel*, FAZ 4.9.2013 online.

Barlach still declined to sell his shares.[1545] He himself had only paid only half of the purchase price for its shares.[1546] With the remaining lien of the former shareholder, the shareholder disputes could have been resolved.[1547] His appeal against the immediate payment of the shares to the former shareholder was rejected at the Federal Court in Switzerland on 26 August 2013.[1548] On 4 September 2013, the Lower District Court Charlottenburg confirmed the insolvency plan and sent it to the parties.[1549] Three weeks later, the Court set a meeting for the creditors to vote on the plan.[1550]

On 9 September 2013, the Frankfurt District Court issued, again at the request of Barlach, a preliminary injunction prohibiting *Unseld-Berkéwicz* from voting on the insolvency plan at the shareholders' meeting.[1551] The injunction was made on grounds of breaching fiduciary duties and the excessiveness of another EUR 2 million payment for each shareholder if the legal form of the company changed into a public limited company.[1552] The trust appealed again. The enforcement proceedings were adjourned by the Frankfurt Court of Appeal on 1 October 2013,[1553] as it would "*probably not endure*"[1554]. In particular, the Court noted that any disputes between the shareholders may only be resolved in the insolvency proceedings.[1555] Thus, the trust could approve the insolvency plan and convert the limited partnership into a public limited company.

The majority of the creditors voted and approved the insolvency plan on 22 October 2013[1556] after the German Federal Constitutional Court had

1545 *Kegel*, FAZ online 13.8.2013: The official highest bit was EUR 10m.
1546 *Zielcke*, SZ 8.8.2013 online. A lack of liquidity could also be a reason why *Barlach* took another mortgage of EUR 2.8 million.
1547 *Zielcke*, SZ online 8.8.2013.
1548 *Zielcke*, SZ online 4.9.2013.
1549 *Kegel*, FAZ online 4.9.2013. The delay of a two-week period proposed by the law was due to the fact that the judge wanted the final and not just interim nominees for the supervisory board of the new company.
1550 Rechtslupe online 12.11.2013.
1551 *Zielcke*, Süddeutsche online 10.9.2013, calling this process a "perfect setting for alienated parties", wanting to know what the new insolvency law has to offer. Also *Kegel*, FAZ online 10.9.2013.
1552 *Gerhart / Meyer*, Welt online 5.9.2013.
1553 OLG Frankfurt, Beschl. v. 1.10.2013, 5 U 145/13.
1554 *Kegel*, FAZ online 3.10.2013.
1555 *Kegel*, FAZ online 2.10.2013.
1556 *Freund*, Die Welt online 9.10.2013.

rejected a request by *Barlach* to adjourn the shareholder meeting until a decision was made on the constitutional issues raised.[1557] *Barlach* voted against the plan; he did not ask for minority protection though and declared that he would not proceed any further against the decision of the creditors' meeting: one reason could be the legal enforcement of the Swiss court's judgement.[1558]. With the adoption of the insolvency plan, "*a pretty spectacular attempt of a hostile takeover of a company has come to an unspectacular end*"[1559].

On 13 November 2013, the District Court in Frankfurt rejected the requests of the mutual claims of the two shareholders against each other from December 2012.[1560] The Court noted that both sides had committed serious violations of their fiduciary duties.[1561] Each party could be excluded from the company on these grounds. Since both parties had violated the interests of the company alike, the exclusion of one party would not be eligible;[1562] the company could only be resolved by both parties.[1563]

The insolvency plan was confirmed by the Lower District Court Charlottenburg on 15 January 2014. As a result of the insolvency plan, *Suhrkamp* will be converted into a public limited company. All special rights under the shareholders' limited partnership agreement expire. At the same time, to raise capital, a third partner will be introduced the company, purchasing a maximum of one-third of the company, according to the insolvency plan. The result of the capital increase will be a dilution of the shares to 40.66% for the trust and 26% for *Barlach*. The remaining 33.3% of the shares will be attributed to the new shareholder.[1564] With more than 25% of the shares, *Barlach* will still hold a blocking minority in the company in accordance with company law, which is required for particularly extensive decisions about the company; however, he will no longer have influence over the operation of the business.

1557 Rechtslupe online 12.11.2013. See also *Plath*, Stuttgarter Zeitung online 22.10.2013.

1558 *Ibid.*

1559 *Schmidt*, ZEIT ONLINE 23.10.2013, questioning the behaviour and the intentions of *Barlach* in this proceeding.

1560 OLG Frankfurt, Urt. v. 13.11.2013, 3-03 O 72/12.

1561 *Ibid.*, para 35 et seq.

1562 *Ibid.*, para. 55.

1563 *Ibid.*, para 72.

1564 *Clausen*, Die Welt online 23.10.2013.

Barlach was not ready to settle into his new shareholder role. He appealed the insolvency plan immediately. His appeal was rejected by the Court on 4 April 2014. Subsequently, *Barlach* appealed at the German Federal Court of Justice, which confirmed his position on 17 July 2014.[1565]

On 20 October 2014, the Regional District Court Berlin denied the *Barlach*'s appeal.[1566] With this decision, the Lower District Court Charlottenburg finally repealed the insolvency proceeding, confirmed by the German Federal Court of Justice and *Suhrkamp* may implement out the change of legal entity in the spring of 2015.[1567]

11.2 Discussion Suhrkamp

With the ESUG coming into force, shareholder rights have changed and are changeable in an insolvency proceeding.[1568]The conversion of a limited partnership into a public limited corporation is possible; in particular, the "*insolvency plan may set out any rule permissible under company law, in particular regarding the continuation of a dissolved enterprise or the transfer of share rights and membership rights.*"[1569] This also entails a conversion of the company's legal form.[1570] The issue that has engaged the courts in Frankfurt is whether this is a new way to deal with shareholders and to resolve shareholder disputes.[1571]

The events around the *Suhrkamp* case have aroused concerns about the rights of minority shareholders, even though the legislature aimed with the ESUG to ensure that the obstruction potential of minority shareholders

---

1565 BGH, Beschl. v. 17.7.2014 – IX ZB 13/14, see discussion below.

1566 dpa, FAZ online 24.10.2014.

1567 *Kegel*, FAZ online 20.12.2014. Barlach could not convince the BGH judges that he was directly affected in his rights by the change of legal entity. If the company would not carry out the change of legal entity, insolvency would be the indispensable result. The judgement has not been published yet.

1568 *Meyer*, ZInsO 2013, 2361, 2368: corporate legal norms will be partly replaces by special legal insolvency norms after the opening of an insolvency proceeding.

1569 Sec. 225a III InsO.

1570 *Haas*, NZG 2012, 961, 965; *Simon / Merkelbach*, NZG 2012, 121, 128; *Madaus*, ZIP 2012, 2133, 2134.

1571 *Herweg* (Kanzlei Hogan Lovells), in *Kegel*, FAZ online 7.8.2013.

would not hinder the restructuring of a viable company. The case was mainly about questions concerning the relationship between insolvency law and corporate law, and also the fiduciary duties of shareholders.[1572]

With ESUG, the role of the shareholder has changed in insolvency. While formerly shareholders were not part of the insolvency plan proceeding, their position has changed and they now form their own group. Creditor rights and shareholder rights are treated equally and shareholders have now become involved parties in the proceeding.[1573] The legislature has thus deliberately wanted to interfere with shareholders' rights.[1574] The exclusion of a minority shareholder could still be better than the insolvency and liquidation of a company. This does, however, also increase the potential for abuse[1575] when the majority shareholder forces the company into insolvency only to then remove an unloved shareholder.[1576]

The legal position of the shareholder worth protecting is limited to the residual value of his shares in an insolvency proceeding, despite the fact that the insolvency proceeding could be a process of restructuring the company. The liquidation value at the initiation of the insolvency proceeding has been chosen as the appropriate measure. The situation in *Suhrkamp* differs, however, since the shares of the minority shareholder were not withdrawn but converted.[1577] Therefore, no constitutional issues arise as to the case where a shareholder loses his share rights as well as his participation rights.[1578] *Suhrkamp* confirms the new primacy of insolvency law over corporate law.[1579]

However, this case gives grounds to differentiate, especially regarding the initiation of insolvency or how it could be solved. With an agreement between the shareholders on the waiver and subordination of the share-

1572 *Thole*, ZIP 2013, 1937; *Meyer*, ZInsO 2013, 2361; *Möhlenkamp*, BB 2013, 2828; *Spliedt*, ZInsO 2013, 2155; *Hölzle*, EWIR 2013, 589; *von Falkenhausen*, EWIR 2013, 581.

1573 BMJ, RegE-ESUG, BT-Drucks. 17/5712, p. 18; *Thole*, ZInsO 2013, 1937, 1945.

1574 *Möhlenkamp*, BB 2013, 2828, 2829.

1575 *Hölzle*, EWIR 2013, 589, 590; *Haarmeyer*, ZInsO 2013, 2345; *Bitter*, in *Jahn*, FAZ 12.8.2013 online.

1576 *Schmidt*, ZIP 2012, 2085, 2086.

1577 *Möhlenkamp*, BB 2013, 2828, 2830.

1578 Critical see *Madaus*, ZIP 2014, 500, 504 et seq.

1579 OLG Frankfurt, Beschl. v. 1.10.2013 – 5 U 145/13, ZInsO 2013, 2112. OLG Frankfurt, Beschl. v. 7.10.2013 – 5 U 135/13, ZInsO 2013, 2162. In detail *Thole*, ZIP 2013, 1937, 1943.

holders' claims, the over-indebtedness and insolvency conditions could have been resolved. This was the allegation of *Barlach*, attacking *Unseld-Berkéwicz*, that by violating her fiduciary duties as a shareholder in not waiving and subordinating the profit claim pay-out, she would contribute to the insolvency of the company.[1580] It is questionable whose interests would outweigh when balancing interests. The aim of the shareholders' fiduciary duties is particularly to promote the interests and purpose of the company, thus restraining the shareholders' own interests. However, the interests of other shareholders receive less consideration.[1581]

In this case, the interests of the shareholders only have the aim of fostering the insolvency of the company,[1582] which could be a breach of a shareholders' fiduciary duty.[1583] It is questionable, however, whether a shareholder must contribute to eliminating grounds for the company's insolvency.[1584] This contrasts with a decision by the German Federal Court of Justice that a shareholder's fiduciary duty is not to prevent the company's insolvency if the situation of the company is hopeless and a quick liquidation is objectively in the interests of all the parties involved.[1585]

An application to open insolvency proceedings and, later, the opening of such a proceeding could be a violation of a shareholder's fiduciary duty as it changes the purpose of the company, which is now to satisfy the creditors' interests[1586] by realising the company's liability in insolvency.[1587] However, the opening of insolvency proceedings could be in the interest of the creditors when the going concern value is higher than the liquidation value and the shareholder dispute would destroy value. In order to allow for a going concern of the company and in the interest of creditors, *Unseld-Berkéwicz* applied for an insolvency proceeding early in order to increase the chances of a successful restructuring in an insolvency process. The fact that the proceeding was used to solve the shareholder dispute is in

---

1580 LG Frankfurt, Urt. v. 10.9.2013 – 3/9 O 96/13.
1581 *Thole*, ZIP 2013, 1937, 1938, 1941.
1582 On corporate fiduciary duties before insolvency, *Meyer*, ZInsO 2013, 2361, 2364 et seq.
1583 LG Frankfurt 13.8.2013, commentary *von Falkenhausen*, EWIR 2013, 581, 582 with reference to OLG Bamberg, NZG 2005, 808.
1584 *Spliedt*, ZInsO 2013, 2155.
1585 *Thole*, ZIP 2013, 1937, 1939.
1586 *Thole*, ZIP 2013, 1937, 1941.
1587 *Möhlenkamp*, BB 2013, 2828, 2829.

effect the legislator allowing an insolvency to overcome the obstruction potential of shareholders.[1588]

While the fiduciary duties of the shareholders are already established in an out-of-court process, they are not yet settled in insolvency proceedings.[1589] It is therefore questionable whether the fiduciary duties of shareholders remain after the insolvency proceedings have been opened, which is what led *Barlach* to prevent *Unseld-Berkéwicz* from voting on the insolvency plan in the creditors' meeting. In addition, one may ask whether the applications for preliminary injunctions by Barlach himself were not a breach of fiduciary duty because they clearly hindered an orderly insolvency process.[1590]

A shareholder's fiduciary duty as an instrument to overcome the obstruction potential of shareholders was previously only discussed for pre-insolvency restructuring measures. It was even considered not just a duty towards the company but even towards the shareholders. This could also justify fiduciary duties in insolvency since the legislator could – by promoting restructurings in insolvency – also extend the pre-insolvency fiduciary duties to restructurings in insolvency.[1591] There is a need to further discuss the fiduciary duties of shareholders in insolvency as compared to pre-insolvency, and whether the insolvency court should consider these fiduciary duties.[1592]

Whether the minority shareholder is worth off or not and the prerequisites for such a case were decided by the German Federal Court of Justice Court. In its decision on 17 July 2014, it strengthens the rights of the minority shareholder *Barlach*. The court confirmed that, in the proceedings of an insolvency plan, a shareholder may proceed with an immediate complaint against the plan confirmed by the insolvency court. This is regard-

1588 *Hölzle*, EWIR 2013, 589, 590. Contrary *Spliedt*, ZInsO 2013, 2155, 2158, arguing that fiduciary duties do not provide any ground to initiate an insolvency proceeding when the reason for the insolvency is a dispute between shareholders.

1589 *Thole*, ZIP 2013, 1937, 1939.

1590 *Ibid.*, 1941, 1945; *Meyer*, ZInsO 2013, 2361, 2366.

1591 Contrary *Thole*, ZIP 2013, 1937, 1939, also OLG Frankfurt, Beschl. v. 1.10.2013 – 5 U 145/13, *Hölzle*, ZIP 2013, 1846, 1847. Agreeing *Madaus*, ZGR 2011, 749, 770; *Simon / Merkelbach*, NZG 2012, 121, 125, who argue that the participation right is not part of the insolvency mass to be distributed to creditors. See also *Spliedt*, ZInsO 2013, 2155, 2158.

1592 *Spliedt*, ZInsO 2013, 2155, 2156.

less of whether the shareholder has already applied for minority protection in the process of confirming the plan at the creditors' meeting. The court pointed out that the possibilities of the new insolvency law should not be used to thwart minority rights and found that the conversion of the *Suhrkamp* Kommanditgesellschaft in an *Aktiengesellschaft* would carry with it three circumstances, which would "*considerably reduce the value of [Barlach*'s*] participation*"[1593]:

- The conversion to an *Aktiengesellschaft* would mean an end to the substantial participation rights, which *Barlach* previously had as a shareholder;
- The option provided in the insolvency plan for a capital increase leads to a dilution of *Barlach*'s participation;
- *Barlach* would only be allowed to sell his shares with the approval of the converted *Aktiengesellschaft,* because of the known restrictions on transferability of the shares.

In these circumstances it is obvious that *Barlach* is likely to suffer a loss of more than ten percent of the shares' value despite the compensation provided. The court further stated that "*[a]ccording to the content of the insolvency plan all insolvency creditors would be fully satisfied without the need for further restructuring measures. Against this background [the Suhrkamp KG] could have continued its business in its present legal entity or be sold through a business-asset sale.*"[1594] This would allow *Barlach* to sell his minority participation to any buyer at full, free market value.[1595]

With the protective shield proceeding and the subsequent insolvency in self-administration, *Suhrkamp* started a voyage through uncharted waters. It comes as no surprise that the previously little-tested instruments of the reformed insolvency law have their pitfalls. Whether the District Court in Berlin will follow the reasons of the German Federal Court of Justice in its examination of the case remains to be seen. The Court in Berlin has, however, the unmistakable order by the German Federal Court of Justice to deal with the content of the insolvency plan as only its substantive assessment can determine whether a "*less favourable treatment*" of *Barlach* has occurred. If this were the result, the District Court in Berlin would have to refuse the approval of the insolvency plan, despite it having been confirmed by the creditors' meeting, thus, the insolvency plan would fail. The

1593 BGH, Beschl. v. 17.7.2014 – IX ZB 13/14, 42.
1594 BGH, Beschl. v. 17.7.2014 – IX ZB 13/14, 2, 41.
1595 BGH, Beschl. v. 17.7.2014 – IX ZB 13/14, 41.

German Federal Court of Justice clearly rejected the view that an immediate appeal towards the insolvency plan may only be permitted if the person concerned had previously applied for minority protection at the insolvency court. The legal protection of minority protection and appeal are alternative options. *Barlach* can rely on its guaranteed legal protection and the District Court in Berlin will have to examine the merits of the instant appeal. The District Court in Berlin found that *Barlach* did not receive a less favourable treatment and opened the way for the Lower Distrcit Court in Charlottenburg to finalize the insolvency proceeding.

Even if this is, at first glance, only a purely procedural question, the case opened up questions on the proportion of corporate law and insolvency law in the context of restructurings under ESUG. This time it was to the benefit of a shareholder, who is now in a better position to defend its entitlement in an insolvency plan proceeding. Although the minority protection request first appears as the lighter and more effective means to adopt against an insolvency plan, because the person concerned must provide credible proof of being made worse off by the insolvency plan (and be the disadvantage however small), than in regular insolvency proceedings. The actual existence of a substantial deprivation is then the subject of the merits test, which – while it is running – slows down the implementation of the insolvency plan. In future, the parties will have to consider, as early as the preparation phase of an insolvency plan, that disadvantaged shareholders can significantly interfere with the implementation of the plan, if not even prevent it – and that would mean that, despite ESUG and the amendments to the insolvency plan in a protective shield proceeding or self-administration, shareholders will still be able to significantly interfere with the restructuring of a company.

11.3 Summary / Conclusion Suhrkamp

The *Suhrkamp* proceeding shows that the legislator, with his desire to prevent the obstruction potential of (minority) shareholders in order to promote the promising restructuring of companies, has set incentives to test the waters of the legislation in practice. Considering the reasoning by the German Federal Court of Justice, the District Court in Berlin has a task that will has great impact on the success of protective shield proceedings in Germany going forward.

The possibility of the protective shield proceeding was now tested to solve a corporate law issue rather than an insolvency law problem – despite the fact that the legislator provided for the intrusion into shareholder rights and the avoidance of shareholders to obstruct any restructuring. The German Federal Court of Justice has returned the question on the fact of being worth off in the implementation in an insolvency plan back to the District Court in Berlin, which has found that no unfavourable treatment has occurred. Its judgement will have an impact on the insolvency culture in Germany and whether the instruments of insolvency law are a mean to an end to solve a corporate law matter. The question about whether the weakening of the constitutional position of shareholders by ESUG was rather a tragic choice will be answered soon. In addition, the legislator will review the experiences and effectiveness of ESUG in achieving its aims for a more rescue-friendly environment, providing a report in 2017.

Conclusion

This chapter discussed the cases of recent years when German companies forum shopped for English law to implement a restructuring for a going concern approach. Though the initial restructuring may have been successfull, it has not ensured that these companies have faced again financial difficulties soon after and even had to initiate an insolvency proceeding, the very purpose they tried to avoid when moving abroad. Companies have to realise whether they have a real chance for a going concern because they have a viable business model or whether a restructuring in a foreign jurisdiction only postpones the inevitable: a failure due to an unviable business model.

It also reviewed the case of a German company intending to solve a corporate law matter with insolvency law. It was a bold approach to change the company's legal entity to avoid further disputes between the shareholders. These disputes between the shareholders almost cost the company its solvency. It remains to be seen how business develops when matters have settled. Only time will tell whether the case will serve as a blueprint for other companies.

Chapter V Summary and Conclusion

12 Summary

The Introduction and Background in Chapter I set the stage to understand the current environment of challenges that companies in financial distress face. The Chapter evaluates the background of insolvency law and the insolvency theories to provide an understanding on the importance of such law. Insolvency law is important for the selection process in a functioning market economy, in which some companies fail and others survive as long as they have a viable business model for a going concern. Both Germany and England inherit aspects of the creditors' bargain theory in their legal framework with the collective proceedings in favour and for the satisfaction of their creditors. German insolvency law inherits market conformity, however, with the discussion on the constitutional issues the question remains whether insolvency law can be in accordance with market conformity when it is not constitutionally valid. Taking into account the perception of *rescue culture*, insolvency proceedings no longer serve for the liquidation of insolvent companies, but, especially in the aftermath of the financial crisis, provide a framework for restructuring viable companies in financial distress to avert further damage to an already crippling economy.

Due to the fact that several German companies were restructured under English law, perceived to have a well-established *rescue culture*, the question was asked of whether and why there is a lack of such a culture to facilitate the efficient restructuring of companies in financial distress in Germany, which paved the way for Chapter II and the evaluation of other factors that affect the effectiveness to restructure companies. The aspects of legislative, judicial and commercial environments are among the most important. The rescue culture is influenced by legal competition, legal harmonisation and forum shopping. Despite the discussions in Germany, there is no evidence though what should be rescued in a restructuring: the company's business or the company's legal entity. There is no evidence in England on this aspect, the perception, however, is that a new corporate structure is generally provided to allow for a fresh start.

The legal competition has led to various reforms of insolvency laws in recent years. The judicial framework accounts for the biggest differences in German and English approaches towards restructurings. While in Germany, insolvency courts and their judges as well as insolvency administrators have been subject to criticism and are made responsible for the lack of flexible, timely, legally certain and effective proceedings, their English counterparties play an active role in restructurings – one of the reasons why England is perceived to have a better established a *rescue culture*.

While some Member States and even the European Commission are embracing (or already over-emphasising) corporate rescue as a mean to allow companies in financial distress to restructure for a going concern rather than to be liquidated, there are detriments to this approach: *zombie companies,* which may cripple the economy even more when they begin to fail; resources that are not allocated to their most effective use when bound in unviable businesses, destroying value and hindering the accruement of a nation's wealth and prosperity. Corporate rescue should not be made the holy grail and the only mean for a distressed business but careful consideration and (market) selection is appropriate to decide whether to restructure or to liquidate a company in accordance to its viable business model – although that will be ultimately tested by the market in the medium to long run.

Chapter III then proceeded to the legal framework itself, for insolvency proceedings that are fit for their purpose, either providing for liquidation or restructuring unviable or viable companies respectively in an informal or statutory proceeding. With ESUG, the legislature intended to initiate a shift in the German insolvency law towards improving the restructuring opportunities for distressed companies, being an aspect for a future rescue culture. The protective shield proceeding as well as the amendments to the insolvency plan proceeding and the self-administration were a response to the shortcomings of the last insolvency law reform and were supposed to pave the grounds for a more effective use of the proceedings.

Particularly the implementation of a debt-equity-swap in an insolvency plan proceedings ought to encourage restructurings. Germany has taken the approach to codify the debt-equity-swap in insolvency law, thereby finally abandoning the separation of corporate law and insolvency law by anchoring the intervention into shareholder rights in an insolvency plan proceeding. Despite the fact that the reasons for ESUG clearly provide guidance that there are no longer constitutional challenges, which were particular defended in the last reform, it seems that this only accounts for the right to property and less so for the freedom of association, however, the critics still challenge the freedom of association as a constitutional reason to prevent enforcement into shareholder rights. Although it is argued to exclude the private autonomy and the freedom of association after the insolvency process has been opened for the benefit to restructure the company, one has to keep in mind that creditors by virtue of their claim only have the right to enforce into the debtor's assets but not into the specific organisational structure and, therefore, the legal action or omission of the shareholders. Subject to liability in insolvency and hence for collective liability realisation for the satisfaction of the creditors is always only the company's assets. One may also regard the intrusion into shareholder rights as a tragic choice whereas Germany accepts some neglecting of constitutional rights to provide for a restructuring instrument it has seen to work so well in England.

In England, there is neither a constitutional protection for shareholders nor a codification for debt-equity-swaps in insolvency law but all measures are a matter of corporate law. Due to the lack of protection, existing shareholders generally engage early with their creditors to engage in a restructuring or, in the case of insolvency, hand over the company to the creditors. There is no narrow legal framework limiting the possibilities to implement a debt-equity-swap for the purpose of restructuring a company as a going concern, the practice has established precedents, which have increased transaction security over the years. The implementation of debt-equity-swaps leads to a new corporate structure, leaving the old legal entity behind for a fresh start. The management is open to receive external counsel to secure the support of their creditors for the restructuring and respectively additional liquidity to fund the ongoing operations. Despite the fact that the *rescue culture* was officially implemented with the EA 2002 and the provision of the administration proceeding, it has evolved and matured over the last 40 years since the Bank of England engaged into informal proceedings to rescue companies in the late 1970s. The perception of an effective *rescue culture* was further nurtured by the fact that foreign companies engaged in forum shopping to apply English law to their restructurings.

The case law then discussed in Chapter IV shows how German companies have engaged in forum shopping to benefit from English law. While previously this was initiated with companies moving their COMI to England, it is nowadays enough to establish English jurisdiction – *ex ante* or *ex post* to the restructuring – by having legal documents being subject to English law. The forum shopping was one of the reasons why Germany has initiated reforms with ESUG for German law to compete with English law. The case of *Suhrkamp* shows how the new measures of German insolvency law have been used to unsuccessfully solve a corporate law rather than an insolvency law issue.

13 Conclusion

The intention of ESUG was to allow for debt-equity-swaps in particular for the restructuring of the company's legal entity in an insolvency plan proceeding. The remaining legal uncertainties will, however, continue to prevent debt-equity-swaps from becoming a standard model for over-indebted companies in Germany and a real alternative alongside traditional restructurings until the all aspects in question have been tested through courts or the debt-equity-swap may be implemented prior to insolvency proceedings. Otherwise, companies will be restructured more likely by a business-asset deal than an insolvency plan proceeding, having the legal entity liquidated while the business will be restructured within a new legal entity.

The implementation of a debt-equity-swap in an English scheme of arrangement may serve as a model for further legal developments in German insolvency law whereas the simplicity of the proceeding opens room for individual solutions that the protective shield proceeding and the self-administration are still lacking.

Whether Germany needs a *rescue* versus an *insolvency culture* or whether such a culture to facilitate the restructurings of companies has already been established is rather a play on words. Such a culture cannot solely evolve from the law itself. It is necessary that the legal framework is supported by other factors to allow for the effective restructuring of companies. An important aspect is the perception of market participants towards insolvency, especially if the focus of the insolvency proceeding is to restructure the company, therefore, not being perceived a stain but rather a second chance for the company. ESUG has provided provisions to facilitate restructurings. The requests of well-known companies to apply for a protective shield proceeding will contribute to an improved, less-stigmatised perception of restructuring in insolvency, especially if the restructuring of viable businesses is carried out in a timely and effective manner to preserve or better create value for their creditors.

Progress has been made in Germany to offer the prerequisites to make the cultural shift towards more effective restructurings. The discussion about earlier applications for insolvency proceedings, the active role of insolvency administrators and insolvency courts in proceedings, or a pre-insolvency proceeding for an adequate use of all measures possible to initiate the restructuring process earlier, including a debt-equity-swap, will continue to engage practitioners and academics alike.

The recommendation of the European Commission on a new approach to business failure and insolvency could further lead the German legislator to amend the protective shield proceeding to comply with the approach towards a European *rescue culture* – and towards progress of a bolder utilisation of debt-equity-swaps in a pre-insolvency stage in Germany and across Europe.

The debt-equity-swap was not used sufficiently in practice to provide for a push towards an established *rescue culture* in Germany. As this has taken England forty years with less legal constraints and challenges to evolve, Germany has just started its journey of progress – and its success and the attractiveness of German insolvency proceedings in general and the debt-equity-swap in particular depend on legal certainty and effective restructurings of companies in financial distress in practice.

"*The only limit to our realization of tomorrow will be our doubts of today. Let us move forward with strong and active faith.*"
— Franklin D. Roosevelt

Bibliography

Achsnick, Jan: Options-Modelle im Insolvenzplanverfahren, Duncker & Humblot GmbH, 2002.

Allen, H. Franklin / Gale, Douglas: Comparing Financial Systems, MIT Press, 2001.

Altman Edward: Corporate Financial Distress and Bankruptcy, Wiley, New York, 1983.

Altmeppen, Holger: Zur Rechtsstellung der Gläubiger im Konkurs gestern und heute, in Festschrift für Peter Hommelhoff zum 70. Geburtstag (FS Hommelhoff), *Erle, Bernd / Goette, Wulf / Kleindiek, Detlef et al.* (eds.), Dr. Otto Schmidt Verlag, Köln 2012, p. 1–20.

Amann, Melanie / Balzter, Sebastian: Unternehmen in Not – Die Insolvenz ist nicht das Ende, FAZ 26.5.2009, p. 12.

Andres, Dirk / Grund, Andreas: Die Flucht vor deutschen Insolvenzgerichten nach England, Die Entscheidungen in dem Insolvenzverfahren Hans Brochier Holdings Ltd., NZI 2007, 137–143.

Armour, John H. / Cumming, Douglas: Bankruptcy Law and Entrepreneurship, ALER 2008, 305–350.

Armour, John H. / Deakin, Simon: Norms in Private Insolvency: The "London Approach" to the Resolution of Financial Distress, JCLS 2001, 21–52.

Armour, John / Hsu, Audrey / Walters, Adrian: Corporate Insolvency in the United Kingdom: The Impact of the Enterprise Act 2002, ECFR 2008, 148–171.

Armour, John / Mokal, Rizwaan Jameel: The New UK Corporate Rescue Procedure – The Administrator's Duty to Act Rationally, ICR 2004, 136–142.

Armour, John / Mokal, Rizwaan Jameel: Reforming the Governance of Corporate Rescue: The Enterprise Act 2002, LMCLQ 2005, 28–64.

Asimacopoulus, Kon / Bickle, Justin (eds.): European Debt Restructuring Handbook, Globe Business Publishing Ltd, 2013.

Bachner, Thomas: The Battle over Jurisdiction in European Insolvency Law, ECFR 2006, 311–329.

Baird, Douglas G.: The Future of Law and Economics: Looking Forward, 64 U. Chi. L. Rev. (1997) 1129–1165.

——: Loss Distribution, Forum Shopping, and Bankruptcy: A Reply to Warren, 54 U. Chi. L. Rev. (1987) 815–834.

Baird, Douglas G. / Bernstein, Donald S.: Absolute Priority, Valuation Uncertainty, and the Reorganization Bargain, 116 Yale. L. J. (2005-2006) 1930–1970.

Baird, Douglas G. / Jackson, Thomas H.: Corporate Reorganizations and the Treatment of Diverse Ownership Interests: A Comment on Adequate Protection of Secured Creditors in Bankruptcy, 51 U. Chi. L. Rev. (1984) 97–130.

Baird, Douglas G. / Rasmussen, Robert K.: Antibankruptcy, 119 Yale L. J. (2010) 650–699.

Bales, Klaus: Insolvenzplan und Eigenverwaltung – Chancen für einen Neustart im Rahmen der Sanierung und Insolvenz, NZI 2008, 216–221.

Balz, Manfred: Market conformity of Insolvency Proceedings: Policy Issues of the German Insolvency Law, 23 Brook. J. Int'l L. (1997) 167–179.

——: Die Ziele des Reformentwurfs, in: Neuordnung des Insolvenzrechts; Kübler, Bruno. M. (eds), Köln, 1989, p. 1–14.

——: Aufgaben und Struktur eines künftigen einheitlichen Insolvenzverfahrens, ZIP 1988, 273–294.

——: Sanierung von Unternehmen oder Unternehmensträgern? RWS Verlag, Köln, 1986.

——: Bericht über die Diskussion, ZGR 1986, 211–218.

Basedow, Jürgen: Theorie der Rechtswahl oder Parteiautonomie als Grundlage des Internationalen Privatrechts, RabelsZ Bd. 75 (2011) 32–59.

——: Rechtskultur – zwischen Mythos und europäischem Ideal, ZEuP 2006, 379–381.

Bauer, Andreas / Dimmling, Andreas: Endlich im Gesetz(entwurf): Der Debt-Equity-Swap, NZI 2011, 517–521.

Bay, Karl-Christian / Seeburg, Dirk / Böhmer, Martin: Debt-Equity-Swap nach § 225a Abs. 2 Satz 1 des geplanten Gesetzes zur weiteren Erleichterung der Sanierung von Unternehmen (ESUG) – Überblick über gesetzgeberische Ziele, Voraussetzungen und Verfassungsmäßigkeit nach Art. 14 GG, ZInsO 2011, 1927–1941.

Bayer, Felix / Hammelehle, Sebastian: Suhrkamp-Insolvenzverfahren: Entmachtung des Querulanten, Spiegel online 28.5.2013, http://www.spiegel.de/kultur/literatur/suhrkamp-schutzschirm-insolvenzverfahren-nach-streit-mit-barlach-a-902345.html, accessed 23.11.2013.

Bebchuk, Lucian Arye: A New Approach to Corporate Reorganisations, 101 Harv. L. Rev. (1988) 775–804.

Becker, Bernhard / Böttger, Peter / Müller, Stefan / Reinke, Jens: Der Debt Equity Swap als Instrument der Unternehmenssanierung, KSI 2011, 53–59.

Beissenhirtz, Volker: Plädoyer für ein Gesetz zur vorinsolvenzlichen Sanierung von Unternehmen, ZInsO 2011, 57–71.

——: Gläubigerautonomie in der Insolvenz, in Unternehmenskrisen – Der Jurist als Notarzt, in Festschrift für Eberhard Braun zum 60. Geburtstag (FS Braun), *Kind, Thomas (editor)*, Beck, München, 2007.

Beissenhirtz, Volker / Specovius, Detlef: Restrukturierung einer Einzelhandelskette – Praxisbeispiel SinnLeffers, INDat-Report 07/2009, p. 36–39.

Belcher, Alice: Corporate Rescue, Sweet&Maxwell, London, 1997.

Berges, August Maria: „Große" oder „kleine" Insolvenzrechtsreform, KTS 1955, 49–55.

Besau, Sascha Heinz-Josef: Chancen und Risiken bei der Rettung von Unternehmen durch übertragende Sanierung, Gestaltungsaspekte vor und nach Stellung des Insolvenzantrags, KSI 2011, 202–213.

Bigus, Jochen / Eger, Thomas: Insolvenzrecht zwischen privatautonomer Gestaltung und öffentlicher Regulierung, 5 (2) Perspektiven der Wirtschaftspolitik (2004) 193–209.

Binder, Heinrich: Dogmatik des Aktionärsschutzes in der Krise – die Zweite gesellschaftsrechtliche Richtlinie im Wandel?, ZVglRWiss 112 (2013) 23–44.

Bitter Georg: Sanierung in der Insolvenz – Der Beitrag von Treue- und Aufopferungspflichten zum Sanierungserfolg, ZGR 2010, 147–200.

Bitter, Georg / Hommerich, Christoph / Reiß, Nicole: Die Zukunft des Überschuldungsbegriffs, ZIP 2012. 1201–1210.

Bitter, Georg / Laspeyres, Anne: Rechtsträgerspezifische Berechtigungen als Hindernis übertragender Sanierung, ZIP 2010, 1157–1165.

Blair, Margaret M. / Stout, Lynn A.: A Team Production Theory of Corporate Law, 85 Va. L. Rev. (1999) 247–328.

Bloom, Alan / Cairns, Ben: Failure Isn't Working, Vol. 9, Iss. 4, ICR 2012, 223–226.

Bonfim, Diana / Dias, Daniel A. / Richmond, Christine: What happens after corporate default? Styliued facts on access to credit, 36 JBF (2012), 2007–2025.

Bork, Reinhard: Keine Anerkennung eines gerichtlich genehmigten Vergleichsplan nach englischem Gesellschaftsrecht ("Scheme of Arrangement"), der eine Lebensversicherung betrifft, ZEuP 2013, 132–146.

——: Creditors' Committees: An Anglo-German Comparative Study, Int. Insolv. Rev. 2012, 127–141.

——: Grundfragen des Restrukturierungsrecht, ZIP 2010, 397–413.

——: Pflichten der Geschäftsführung in Krise und Sanierung, ZIP 2011, 101–109.

——: Die Wirkungen des Insolvenzplans nach §§ 290 bis 305 RefE, in *Leipold, Dieter* (eds), Insolvenzrecht im Umbruch, Heymanns, Köln/Berlin/Bonn/München, 1991, p. 51–65.

Born, Alexander: Aktuelle Steuerfragen im Zusammenhang mit Debt-Equity-Swap-Transaktionen, BB 2009, 1730–1735.

Bowie, Norman E.: Business Ethics: A Kantian Perspective, Business Ethics Quarterly, Vol. 11, No. 1 (2001), 225–231.

Brand, Oliver: Conceptual comparisons: Towards a coherent methodology of legal studies, 32 Brookl. J. Int'l. L. (2007) 411–466.

Braun, Eberhard: Zwei Insolvenzverwalter in der Eigenverwaltung, NZI 2003, 588–590.

Braun, Eberhard / Frank, Achim: in Insolvenzordnung, *Braun, Eberhard* (eds), 5. Auflage, Beck Verlag, München 2012.

Braun, Eberhard / Uhlenbruck, Wilhelm: Unternehmensinsolvenz, Grundlagen, Gestaltungsmöglichkeiten, Sanierung mit der Insolvenzordnung, Düsseldorf, 1997.

Braun, Eberhard / Heinrich, Jens: Auf dem Weg zu einer (neuen) Insolvenzplankultur in Deutschland – Ein Beitrag zu dem Regierungsentwurf für ein Gesetz zur wieteren Erleichterung der Sanierung von Unternehmen, NZI 2011, 505–517.

Bretz, Michael / Gude, Hardy: Beurteilung des neuen Überschuldungsbegriffs in der InsO anhand von Bilanzinformationen, ZInsO 2010, 515–517.

Bridge, Catherine: Insolvency – A second chance? Why modern insolvency laws seek to promote business rescue, in: Law in transition 2013, EBRD, London, 2013, p. 28–41.

Brinkmann, Moritz: Der strategische Eigenantrag – Missbrauch oder kunstgerechte Handhabung des Insolvenzverfahrens?, ZIP 2014, 197–207.

——: Wege aus der Insolvenz eines Unternehmens – oder: Die Gesellschafter als Sanierungshindernis, WM 2011, 97–103.

Brinkmann, Moritz / Zipperer, Helmut: Die Eigenverwaltung nach dem ESUG aus Sicht von Wissenschaft und Praxis, ZIP 2011, 1337–1347.

Brooke, James: They're Alive! They're Alive! Not!; Japan Hesitates to Put an End to Its 'Zombie' Businesses, New York Times online, 29.10. 2002, http://www.nytimes.com/2002/10/29/business/they-re-alive-they-re-alive-not-japan-hesitates-put-end-its-zombie-businesses.html?pagewanted=all&src=pm, accessed 23.8.2013.

Brüning, Marc: Insolvenzplan und Gesellschafter, Gesellschafter und Insolvenzplan: Eine Untersuchung ihrer Stellung in der Reorganisation insolventer Gesellschaften im Insolvenzplanverfahren (§§ 217 ff. InsO), Verlag Dr. Kovac, 2006.

Buchalik, Robert: Das Schutzschirmverfahren nach § 270b InsO (incl. Musteranträge), Ein überzeugender Schritt des Gesetzgebers, der Sanierung durch Insolvenz nachhaltig zum Durchbruch zu verhelfen, ZInsO 2012, 349–363.

——: Faktoren einer erfolgreichen Eigenverwaltung, NZI 2000, 294–301.

Bufford, Samuel L.: Revision of the European Union Regulation on Insolvency Proceedings, IILR 2012, 341–375.

Buljevich Esteban C. (ed.), Cross Border Debt Restructuring: Innovative Approaches for Creditors, Euromoney Institutional Investor PLC, 2005.

Burkert, Michael: Der Debt-to-Equity Swap im Spannungsverhältnis von Gesellschafts- und Insolvenzrecht, Nomos, Baden-Baden, 2014.

Buth, Andrea K. / Hermanns, Michael (eds): Restrukturierung, Sanierung, Insolvenz, 2. Auflage, München 2004.

Decher, Christian E. / Voland, Thomas: Kapitalschnitt und Bezugsrechtsausschluss im Insolvenzplan – Kalte Enteignung oder Konsequenz des ESUG?, ZIP 2013, 103–114.

Cahn, Andreas / Simon, Stefan / Theiselmann, Rüdiger, Debt Equity Swap zum Nennwert!, DB 2010, 1629–1632.

——: Nennwertanrechung bei Debt Equity Swap!, DB 2012, 501–504.

——: Forderungen gegen die Gesellschaft als Sacheinlage? – Zum Erfordernis der Forderungsbewertung beim Debt-Equity Swap, CFL 2010, 238–250.

Campbell, Clare: Corporate insolvency in practice: an analytical approach, SAGE Publishing Inc, 1991.

Carli, Winfried M. / Rieder, Markus S. / Mückl, Norbert: Debt-to-Equity-Swaps in der Transaktionspraxis, ZIP 2010, 1737–1743.

Carlson, David Gray: Philosophy in Bankruptcy, 85 Mich. L. Rev. (1987) 1341–1389.

Chatterji, Subhrendu / Hedges, Paul: Loan workouts and debt for equity swaps: a framework for successful corporate rescues, John Wiley & Sons, Finance, 2001.

Crystal, Michael / Mokal, Rizwaan Jameel: The Valuation of Distressed Companies: A Conceptual Framework, Part I, ICR 2006, 63–68.

——: The Valuation of Distressed Companies: A Conceptual Framework, Part II, ICR 2006, 123–131.

Claussen, Carsten Peter: Kapitalersetzende Darlehen und Sanierungen durch Kreditinstitute, ZHR 174 (1983) 195–219.

Clausen, Sven: Verlage – Hans Barlach dreht im Suhrkamp-Streit bei, Die Welt online 23.10.2013, http://www.welt.de/kultur/literarischewelt/article121147250/Hans-Barlach-dreht-im-Suhrkamp-Streit-bei.html, accessed 23.11.2013.

Clausen, Sven / Müller, Uwe: Suhrkamp-Insolvenz – Was passiert, wenn Ulla Berkéwiczs Plan aufgeht?, Die Welt online, 18.8.2013, http://www.welt.de/kultur/literarischewelt/article119142989/Was-passiert-wenn-Ulla-Berkewiczs-Plan-aufgeht.html, accessed 23.11.2013.

Clementi, David: Maintaining financial stability in a rapidly changing world – some threats and opportunities, Deputy Governor of the Bank of England, at the launch of the Oxford Centre for Computational Finance, University of Oxford, 10 October 2001, p. 1–4, http://www.bis.org/review/r011012c.pdf, accessed 26.11.2012.

Coase, Ronald H.: The Problem of Social Cost, 3 J. Law & Econ. (1960) 1–44.

——: The Nature of the Firm", Economica 4 (1937), 386–405.

Copp, Stephen: Company Law Reform and Economic Analysis: Establishing Boundaries, JCLS Vol. 1 June 2001, 1–19.

Cork, Sir Kenneth / Graham, David: Insolvenzrechtsreform in England – Erläuterungen zum Cork- Report, ZIP 1982, 1275–1285.

Cohen, Adrian / Maclennan, John: Ultimate turnaround: debt to equity swaps, CR&I 2009, 91–93.

Cranshaw, Friedrich L.: Sanierungsunterstützende Maßnahmen des Kreditgebers außerhalb der "klassischen" Kreditgewährung, ZInsO 2008, 421–432.

Dakin, Micheal / Diminch Fabio / Hertz, Philip / Ruiz, Gabrielle: Getting into bed with bondholders, CR&I 2012, 120–128.

Davies, Paul / Rickford, Jonathan: An Introduction to the New UK Companies Act, ECFR 2008, 48–71.

Davies, Paul / Worthington, Sarah (eds.): Gower & Davies: Principles of Modern Company Law, 9th edition, Sweet & Maxwell, 2012.

Davis, Stephen: Insolvency and EA 2002, Jordans, 2003.

d'Avoine, Marc: Finanzmarktstabilisierungsgesetz und Verhältnismäßigkeitsgrundsatz – befristete Anpassung des Überschuldungsbegriffes § 19 Abs. 2 InsO, in Festschrift für Hans Peter Runkel (FS Runkel), *Weber, Norbert / Schmidt, Jens M.* (eds.), Köln, 2009, p. 263–283.

de Bra, Peter: Entfristung des insolvenzrechtlichen Überschuldungsbegriffes, Handelsblatt-online, 22.11.2013, http://blog.handelsblatt.com/rechtsboard/2012/11/22/entfristung-des-insolvenzrechtlichen-uberschuldungsbegriffes/#more-5180, accessed 1.12.2013.

Deacock, Adam: Re Collins & Aikman Corporation Group, ICR 2006, 88–89.

dpa: Genehmigter Sanierungsplan soll Ruhe bringen, FAZ online, 24.10.2014, http://www.faz.net/aktuell/rhein-main/suhrkamp-verlag-sanierungsplan-soll-ruhe-bringen-13228058.html, accessed 28.10.2014.

Del Mar, Maksymilian / Bankowski, Zenon: Law as an Institutional Normative Order, Edinburgh/Glasgow Law and Society Series, 2009.

Desch, Wolfram: Schutzschirmverfahren nach dem RegE-ESUG in der Praxis, BB 2011, 841–846.

Dickinson, Andrew: Legal Certainty and the Brussels Convention – Too Much of a Good Thing?, in: de Vareilles-Sommières, Pascal, Forum Shopping in the European Judicial Area, Studies of the Oxford Institute of European and Comparative Law, 2007, Oxford and Portland, Oregon.

Dietrich, Martin: Die Eigenverwaltung als Sanierungsweg nach dem neuen Insolvenzrecht, Akademischer Verlag, München, 2002.

Dodd, Merrick E.: For whom are Corporate Managers Trustees?, 45 Harv. L. Rev. (1932) 1145–1163.

Doliwa, Cornelia, J.: Die geplante Insolvenz, Nomos, 2012.

Drinhausen, Florian / Gesell, Harald: Gesellschaftsrechtliche Gestaltungsmöglichkeiten grenzüberschreitender Mobilität von Unternehmen in Europa, BB 2006, Beil. 6, p. 3–17.

Drouven, Ralph: Neue Wege: „Reverse Debt-to-Equity-Swap", ZIP 2009, 1052–1053.

Drukarczyk, Jochen: Bilanzielle Überschuldungsmessung, ZGR 1979, 553–582.

Drukarczyk, Jochen / Schöntag, Stefanie: § 3 Außergerichtliche Sanierungsentscheidungen, in Gottwald, Insolvenzrechts-Handbuch, 4. Auflage, Beck Verlag, 2010.

DTI, Insolvency, A Second Chance – The Insolvency Service, Department for Trade and Industry, Productivity and Enterprise, https://www.gov.uk/government/uploads/system/uploads/attachment_data/file/263523/5234.pdf, accessed 23.7.2013.

Easterbrook, Frank H.: Is Corporate Bankruptcy Efficient?, 27 J. Fin. Econ. (1990) 411–417.

Easterbrook, Frank H. / Fischel, Daniel R.: The Economic Structure of Corporate Law, Harvard University Press, 1996.

Ehlers, Harald: Sanierung mit oder ohne Insolvenz, ZInsO 2010, 257–272.

——: Der Eröffnungsgrund der drohenden Zahlungsunfähigkeit – auch ein Haftungsproblem, ZInsO 2005, 169–176.

——: Noch eine Reform – § 224 Abs. 2 – 5, ZInsO 2009, 320–325.

Ehricke, Ulrich: Die neue Europäische Insolvenzverordnung und grenzüberschreitende Konzerninsolvenzen, EWS 2002, 101–107.

Ehricke, Ulrich / Köster, Malte / Müller-Seils, Carsten O.: Neuerungen im englischen Unternehmensinsolvenzrecht durch den Enterprise Act 2002, NZI 2003, 409–416.

Eidenmüller, Horst: Strategische Insolvenzen, ZIP 2014, 1197–1205.

——: Reformperspektiven im Restrukturierungsrecht ZIP 2010, 649–660.

——: Finanzkrise, Wirtschaftskrise und das deutsche Insolvenzrecht, de Gruyter Recht, Berlin, 2009.

——: Abuse of Law in the Context of European Insolvency Law, ECFR 2009, 1–28.

——: Privatisierung der Insolvenzabwicklung: Workouts, Covenants, Mediation – Modelle für den Insolvenzstandort Deutschland?", ZZP 2008, 273–293.

——: Leveraged Buyouts und die Effizienz des deutschen Restrukturierungsrechts, ZIP 2007, 1729–1737.

——: Die GmbH im Wettbewerb der Rechtsformen, ZGR 2007, 168–211.

——: Gesellschafterstellung und Insolvenzplan, ZGR 2001, 680–711.

——: Wettbewerb der Insolvenzrechte? ZGR 2006, 467–488.

——: Unternehmenssanierung zwischen Markt und Gesetz, Schmidt Otto Verlag, 1999.

——: Mediationstechniken bei Unternehmenssanierungen, BB 1998, Beil. 10, p. 19–25.

——: Die Banken im Gefangenendilemma: Kooperationspflichten Akkordstörungsverbot im Sanierungsrecht, ZHR 160 (1996) 343–373.

Eidenmüller, Horst / Frobenius, Tilmann: Die internationale Reichweite eines englischen Scheme of Arrangement, WM 2011, 1210–1219.

Eidenmüller, Horst / Frobenius, Tilmann / Prusko, Wolfram: Regulierungswettbewerb Unternehmensinsolvenzrecht: Ergebnisse einer empirischen Untersuchung, NZI 2010, 545–550.

Eidenmüller Horst / Engert, Andreas: Reformperspektiven einer Umwandlung von Fremd- in Eigenkapital (Debt-Equity-Swap) im Insolvenzplanverfahren, ZIP 2009, 541–554.

Eilers, Stephan: Der Debt Equity Swap – Eine Sanierungsmaßnahme für unternehmerische Krisensituationen, GWR 2009, 3–4.

Ekkenga, Jens: Sachkapitalerhöhung gegen Schuldbefreiung, ZGR 2009, 581–622.

Elliot, Christine: Debt-for-Equity: To thine to own self be true?, CR&I 2008, 194–195.

Elsas, Ralf / Krahnen, Jan Pieter: Is relationship lending special? Evidence from credit-file data in Germany, 22 JBF (1998) 1283–1316.

Emmerich, Volkhard: Insolvenzen in Deutschland – Insolvenzursachen und Erfolgsfaktoren einer Sanierung aus der Insolvenz, Studie der Dr. Wieselhuber&Partner GmbH, München, 2003.

Engelhard, Hans A.: Politische Akzente einer Insolvenzrechtsreform, ZIP 1986, 1287–1291.

Erdmann, Lutz: Rechtspflegerzuständigkeit für das Insolvenzplanverfahren, ZInsO 2010, 1437–1440.

Euler Hermes, Rettung aus der Insolvenz, Nr. 418, 2007, http://www.wirtschaft-konkret.de/de/dokumente/418-rettung-aus-der-insolvenz.pdf/418-rettung-aus-der-insolvenz.pdf, accessed 15.2.2013.

Evans, Rachel: Mind over matter, IFLR 2008, 56–60.

Ewald, William: Comparative Jurisprudence (I): What Was it Like to Try a Rat?, 143 U. Penn. L. Rev. (1995) 1889–2149.

——: Comparative Jurisprudence (II): The Logic of Legal Transplants, 43 Am. J. Comp. L. (1995). 489–510.

Nigel, Feetham / Jones, Grant: Protected Cell Companies: A Guide to Their Implementation and Use, Spiramus Press Ltd., 2010.

Finch, Vanessa: Corporate Insolvency Law, Cambridge, 2009.

——: Corporate Rescue in a World of Debt, J.B.L. 2008, 756–777.

——: Corporate rescue processes: the search for quality and the capacity to resolve, J.B.L. 2010, 502–521.

——: Corporate rescue: who is interested?, J.B.L. 2012, 190–212.

——: Doctoring in the shadow of insolvency, J.B.L. 2005, 690–708.

——: Re-invigorating corporate rescue, J.B.L. 2003, 527–557.

——: Corporate rescue: a game of three halves, Legal Studies Vol. 32 No. 2 June 2012, 302–324.

——: The Measures of Insolvency Law, OJLS 1997, 227–251.

Fink, Steven: Crisis Management. Planning for the Inevitable, Blackinprint.com, 1986.

Fisher, Richard: *Re Cheyne Finance plc* and Commercial Insolvency, ICR 2008, 141–146.

Fleischer, Holger: Europäische Methodenlehre: Stand und Perspektiven, RabelsZ Bd. 75 (2011), 700–729.

Flessner, Axel: Philosophies of Business Bankruptcy Law, in: Ziegel, Jacob S., Current Developments in International and Comparative Corporate Insolvency Law, 1994, Oxford University Press, p. 19–28.

——: Sanierung von Unternehmen, ZRP 1982, 244–249.

——: Sanierung und Reorganisation, Mohr Siebeck, Tübingen, 1982.

Fletcher, Ian F., UK Corporate Rescue: Recent Developments – Changes to Administrative Receivership, Administration, and Company Voluntary Arrangements – The Insolvency Act 2000, The White Paper 2001, and the Enterprise Act 2002, EBOR (5) 2004, 119–151.

——: The Law of Insolvency, 3rd ed.(edited), Sweet&Maxwell, London, 2002.

——: Insolvency in Private International Law – National and International Approaches, Clarendon Press, Oxford, 1999.

Franke, Peter: Debt Equity Swaps – Finanzielle Sanierung von börsennotierten Aktiengesellschaften, Universitätsschriften Nomos, 2011.

Franken, Sefa: Creditor- and Debtor-Oriented Corporate Bankruptcy Regimes, EBOR 5 (2004) 645–676.

Freeman, Ronald E.: A Stakeholder Theory of Modern Corporation, in L.P. Hartmann (editor), Perspectives in Business Ethics, 3rd edition, New York, 2005, p. 112–122.

Freund, Wieland: In der Cause Suhrkamp gibt es keine Sieger mehr, Die Welt online 9.10.2013, http://www.welt.de/kultur/literarischewelt/article121135371/In-der-Causa-Suhrkamp-gibt-es-keine-Sieger-mehr.html, accessed 23.11.2013.

Frege, Michael C. / Keller, Ulrich / Riedel, Ernst: Insolvenzrecht, 7. Auflage, Beck-Verlag, München, 2008.

Friedhoff, Heinrich C.: Sanierung einer Firma durch Eigenverwaltung und Insolvenzplan, ZIP 2002, 497–500.

Friedrich, Marc G. / Flintrop, Bernhard: Sanierungsprüfung — Herausforderung für Unternehmensführung und Gutachter, DB 2003, 223–229.

Friedman, Milton: The Social Responsibility of Business is to Increase its Profits, The New York Times Magazine, September 13, 1970, http://www.umich.edu/~thecore/doc/Friedman.pdf, accessed 17.11.2013.

Frind, Frank: Die Praxis fragt, „ESUG" antwortet nicht, ZInsO 2011, 2249–2261.

——: Zum Diskussionsentwurf für ein "Gesetz zur weiteren Erleichterung der Sanierung von Unternehmen" (Teil 2: Die Regelungen zum Insolvenzplanverfahren, Eigenverwaltung, Insolvenzstatistikgesetz etc.), ZInsO 2010, 1524–1532.

——: Zum Diskussionsentwurf für ein "Gesetz zur weiteren Erleichterung der Sanierung von Unternehmen", ZInsO 2010, 1473–1482.

——: Sechs Maßnahmen um die Sanierungsfunktion der InsO zu stärken, ZInsO 2010, 1161–1169.

——: Verwalterauswahl: Ermessen des Insolvenzrichters im Mittelpunkt, ZInsO 2009, 1638–1639.

——: 25 Fragen und Antworten zur Praxis der Verwalter-Vorauswahl, ZInsO 2008, 655–662.

——: Gerichtserhobene Verfahrenskennzahlen als Mittel und Möglichkeit gerichtlicher Bewertung des Insolvenzverwaltererfolgs und gesteigerter Aufsicht im Insolvenzverfahren ZInsO 2008, 126–131.

——: Die Grenze zwischen Gestaltung und Manipulation im Insolvenzplanverfahren, NZI 2007, 374–378.

——: Der Einfluss von Gläubigern bei der Auswahl des und der Aufsicht über den Insolvenzverwalter, ZInsO 2007, 643–649.

Frisby, Sandra: The Effect of the Enterprise Act 2002: Empirical Research into Corporate Insolvency, in *Ringe, Wolf-Georg / Gullifer, Louise / Théry, Philippe:* Current Issues in European Financial and Insolvency Law – Perspectives from France and the UK, Hart Publishing, Oxford, 2009, p. 45–66.

Fritze, Marc: Sanierung von Groß- und Konzernunternehmen durch Insolvenzpläne – Der Fall der Senator Entertainment AG, DZWIR 2007, 89–93.

Fröhlich, Andreas / Bächstädt, Christian Nicolas: 8 Monate ESUG – Beobachtungen eines betriebswirtschaftlichen Sanierungs- und M&A-Beraters, ZInsO 2012, 2044–2046.

Fröhlich, Andreas / Köchling, Marcel: Verkauf eines insolventen Unternehmens – Bestandsaufnahme und Handleitfaden zur Realisierung übertragenden Sanierungen, ZInsO 2005, 1121–1130.

Fröhlich, Andreas / Sittel, Thomas C.: Game over? Auswirkungen der Finanzmarktkrise auf die übertragende Sanierung, ZInsO 2009, 858–863.

Frost, Christopher W.: Bankruptcy Redistributive Policies and the Limits of the Judicial Process, 74 N. C. L. Rev. (1995) 75–139.

Gebler, Olaf: Ausländische Insolvenzverfahren zur Sanierung deutscher Unternehmen, NZI 2010, 665-669.

Geldmacher, Christoph: Das präventive Sanierungsverfahren als Teil eines reformierten Insolvenz- und Sanierungsrechts in Deutschland, KTS Schriften Band 43, Carl Heymanns Verlag, 2012.

——: BMWi/BMJ-Kolloquium: Sanierung im Vorfeld von Insolvenzverfahren; Ausgestaltung eines rechtlich strukturierten Sanierungsverfahrens?, ZInsO 2010, 1178–1179.

Gerhart, Matthias / Maier, Thomas: Urteil am Dienstag – Barlach will Suhrkamp AG verhindern, Die Welt online 5.9.2013, http://www.welt.de/regionales/frankfurt/article119755118/Barlach-will-Suhrkamp-AG-verhindern.html, accessed 23.11.2013.

Gerster, Erwin, Insolvenzplan, „Das unbekannte. Wesen" oder „Maßanzug des Insolvenzrechts"?, ZInsO 2008, 437–445.

Geva, Eyal Z.: National Policy Objectives from an EU Perspective: UK Corporate Rescue and the European Insolvency Regulation, EBOR (4) 2007, 605–619.

Gilsen, Stuart C. / John, Kose / Lang, Larry H.P.: Troubled Debt Restructurings, 27 J. Fin. Econ. (1990), 315–353.

Gless, Sven-Erik: Unternehmenssanierung: Grundlagen – Strategien – Maßnahmen, Deutscher Universitätsverlag, 1996.

Goode, Roy: Principles of Corporate Insolvency Law, Sweet&Maxwell, 2011.

Goodison, Eric: Second Lien Loan Workouts – What Can Be Expected if the Credit Cycle Turns?, Vol. 3, Iss. 3, ICR 2006, 164–167.

Gottwald, Peter: Aspekte der Unternehmensinsolvenz im englischen Recht, KTS 1981, 17–45.

Graf, Ulrich / Wunsch, Irene: Eigenverwaltung und Insolvenzplan – gangbarer Weg in der Insolvenz von Freiberuflern und Handwerkern?, ZIP 2001, 1029–1040.

Gravenbrucher Kreis: ESUG – Erfahrungen, Probleme, Änderungsnotwendigkeiten, ZIP 2014, 1262–1265.

——: Appell gegen die Verabschiedung der Insolvenzrechtsreform, ZIP 1994, 585–587.

——: „Große" oder „kleine" Insolvenzrechtsreform, ZIP 1992, 657–661.

——: Stellungnahme zum Diskussionsentwurf eines Insolvenzrechtsreformgesetzes, ZIP 1989, 468–475.

Graveson, Ronald H.: Philosophy and function in comparative Law, 7 ICLQ (1958), 649–658.

Griffiths, David A. H. / Hellmig, Nina: Insolvenzkulturen – Kampf oder Harmonisierung? – Eine angelsächsische Perspektive, NZI 2008, 418–420.

Gröner, Helmut: Marktsystem, Unternehmenskontrollen und Insolvenzen: Volkswirtschaftliche Überlegungen zur Reform des Insolvenzrechts, ORDO 1984, 247–267.

Größl, Ingrid / Levratto, Nadine: International Similarities in Bank Lending Practices and Varieties of Insolvency Laws: a Comparative Analysis of France and Germany, DEP (Socioeconomics) Discussion Papers, Macroeconomics and Finance Series, 3/2012.

Grohmann, Uwe: Grenzüberschreitende Mobilität von Gesellschaften nach der Rechtsprechung des EuGH – von Daily Mail bis Cartesio, DZWIR 2009, 322–329.

Groß, Paul J.: Die Umwandlung von Forderungen gegen eine notleidende GmbH in Gesellschaftskapital, GmbHR 1983, 290–297.

Großfeld, Bernhard: Global Financial Challenges: Global Corporations and Legal Education, ZVglRWiss 113 (2014) 4–14.

Grub, Volker: Zur Beendigung des Insolvenzverfahrens bei Insolvenzplan, DZWIR 2004, 317–319.

——: Überjustitialisierung und Eigenverwaltung des Pleitiers, WM 1994, 880–881.

Haarmeyer, Hans: Missbrauch der Eigenverwaltung? – Nicht der Gesetzgeber, sondern Gerichte, Verwalter und Berater sind gefordert, ZInsO 2013, 2345–2347.

——: Die "gute" Insolvenzverwaltung, ZInsO 2007, 169–173.

Häsemeyer, Ludwig: Insolvenzrecht, 3. Auflage, Köln, 2003.

Hagebuch, Alfred / Oberle, Thomas: Gläubigerbefriedigung durch Unternehmenssanierung: die übertragende Sanierung – Eine Bestandsaufnahme vor dem Hintergrund jüngster InsO-Reformen, NZI 2006, 618–622.

Hagemann, Sebastian: Debt Equity Swaps nach englischem und deutschem Recht unter besonderer Berücksichtigung des ESUG, Schriften zum Insolvenzrecht, Nomos, 2014.

Harding, Andrew / Örücü, Esin (eds.): Comparative Law, The Hague: Kluwer Law International, 2002.

Harhoff, Dietmar / Körting, Timm: Lending relationships in Germany – Empirical evidence from survey data, 22 JBF (1998) 1317–1353.

Hass, Detlef / Tschauner, Heiko: Debt-for-Equity Swap as a restructuring Tool under German Law, ICR 2005, 93–101.

Haviv-Segal, Irit: Bankruptcy Law and Inefficient Entitlements, 2 Berkley Bus. L.J. (2005) 355–398.

Hax, Herbert / Marschdorf, Hans-Joachim: Anforderungen an ein Insolvenzrecht aus betriebswirtschaftlicher Sicht, BFuP 1983, 112–130.

Heide, Dana: Suhrkamp-Sachverwalter – Das Problem sind die Streitereien der Gesellschafter, Handelsblatt online, 9.8.2013, http://www.handelsblatt.com/unternehmen/mittelstand/suhrkamp-sachwalter-das-problem-sind-die-streitereien-der-gesellschafter/8613396.html, accessed 23.11.2013.

——: Insolvenzverfahren – Schöner Scheitern, Handelsblatt online, 9.8.2013, http://www.handelsblatt.com/unternehmen/mittelstand/insolvenzrecht-schoener-scheitern-seite-all/8606460-all.html, accessed 23.11.2013.

Heneweer, Jens Christoph Rainer: Das forum shopping einer GmbH unter der deutschen Insolvenzordnung und der Europäischen Insolvenzverordnung, Peter Lang, 2010.

Hertz, Philip / MacLennan, John / Bennett, Tim: Wish you were here? English court becomes the restructuring destination for foreign companies, BJIBFL 2011, 405–409.

Hess, Harald / Weis, Michaela: Der Insolvenzplan, WM 1998, 2349–2362.

Heublein, Gerrit: Die sofortige Beschwerde gegen die Insolvenzplanbestätigung – „Superobstruktion" durch die Hintertür? (Erwiderung auf Smid – NZI 2005, 296), NZI 2005, 381–382.

Himmelsbach, Rainer / Achsnick, Jan: Investments in Krisenunternehmen im Wege sanierungsprivilegierter debt-equity-swaps, NZI 2006, 561–564.

Hingerl, Josef: Richterliche Begleitung des Insolvenzplans, ZInsO 2009, 759–760.

——: Entwicklungen, Erfahrungen, Chancen, ZInsO 2008, 404–411.

Hirte, Heribert: Anmerkungen zum von § 270b RegE-InsO ESUG vorgeschlagenen "Schutzschirm", ZInsO 2011, 401–405.

Hirte, Heribert / Knof, Béla / Mock, Sebastian: Das Gesetz zur weiteren Erleichterung der Sanierung von Unternehmen (Teil I), Der Betrieb 2011, 632–643.

Hölzle, Gerrit: Der Insolvenzantrag als Sanierungsoption – auch gegen den Willen von Gesellschaftern?, ZIP 2013, 1846–1851.

——: LG Frankfurt/M. EWiR § 225 a InsO 1/13, 589–590.

——: Eigenverwaltung im Insolvenzverfahren nach ESUG – Herausforderungen für die Praxis, ZIP 2012, 158–164.

——: Die „erleichterte Sanierung von Unternehmen" in der Nomenklatur der InsO – ein hehres Regelungsziel des RegE-ESUG, NZI 2011, 124–131.

——: Die Sanierung von Unternehmen im Spiegel des Wettbewerbs der Rechtsordnungen, KTS 2011, 291–341.

——: Sanierende Übertragung – Besonderheiten des Unternehmenskaufs in Krise und Insolvenz, DStR 2004, 1433–1438.

Hofman, Christian: Gesellschaftsrecht und Art. 14 GG, in Festschrift Klaus Hopt (FS Hopt) zum 70. Geburtstag am 24. August 2010: Unternehmen, Markt und Verantwortung, *Grundmann, Stefan / Haar, Brigitte / Merkt, Hanno et al (eds.)*, De Gruyter 2010, p. 833–848.

Hofmann, Matthias: Die Eigenverwaltung insolventer Kapitalgesellschaften im Konflikt zwischen Gesetzeszweck und Insolvenzpraxis, ZIP 2007, 260–264.

——: Die Eigenverwaltung in der Insolvenz, Peter Lang, 2006.

Holbein, Carmen: Sanierung insolventer Unternehmen durch Private Equity, Jenaer Wissenschaftliche Verlagsgesellschaft, 2010.

Holzer, Johannes: Krisenerkennung bei insolvenzgefährdeten Unternehmen aus Sicht der gerichtlichen Praxis, NZI 2005, 308–315.

Hommel, Ulrich / Knecht, Thomas / Wohlenberg, Holger: Handbuch Unternehmensrestrukturierung, Springer Gabler, 2006.

Horstkotte, Martin / Martini, Torsten: Die Einbeziehung der Anteilseigner in den Insolvenzplan nach ESUG, ZInsO 2012, 557–581.

Howard, Chris / Hedger, Bob: Restructuring Law and Practise, LexisNexis, 2008.

Huep, Tobias: Auswirkungen des ESUG auf das Tätigkeitsfeld Insolvenzverwaltung – Vorstellung der Ergebnisse einer empirischen Studie, ZInsO 2012, 403–408.

Hüffer, Uwe: Aktiengesetz, Kommentar, Beck Verlag, München, 2006.

Huhn, Christoph: Die Eigenverwaltung im Insolvenzverfahren, Rws Kommunikationsforum, 2003.

Hunter, Muir: The Nature and Functions of a Rescue Culture, J.B.L. 1999, 491–520.

Icks, Annette / Kranzusch, Peter: Sanierungen in Insolvenzverfahren – übertragende Sanierungen und insolvenzplanbasierte Eigensanierungen in NRW, in: Institut für Mittelstandsforschung Bonn (eds.), IfM-Materialien Nr. 195, 2010.

INDat-Report 6/2010, ZIP-Kolloquium zu, Diskussionsentwurf ESUG, 31.8.2010, http://www.rws-verlag.de/fileadmin/res/pdfs/Tagungsbericht_ZIP-Kolloquium.pdf, accessed 3.8.2013.

INDat-Insolvenzstatistik, www.indat.info/statistiken.php, accessed 3.8.2013.

IDW, Anforderungen an die Erstellung Sanierungskonzepten (IDW 6), 2009, WPg Supplement 4/2009, p. 145, http://www.idw.de/idw/portal/d302226, accessed 15.10.2012.

Jackson, Thomas H.: The Logic and Limits of Bankruptcy Law, Cambridge, Harvard Press, 1986.

——: Bankruptcy, Non-Bankruptcy Entitlements, and the Creditors' Bargain, 105 Yale L. J. (1982) 857–907.

——: Avoiding Powers in Bankruptcy, 36 Stan. L. Rev. (1984) 725–787.

——: Of Liquidation, Continuation, and Delay: An Analysis of bankruptcy Policy and Nonbankruptcy Rules, 60 Am. Bankr. L. J. (1986) 399–428.

Jackson, Thomas H. / Scott, Robert E.: On the Nature of Bankruptcy: An Essay on Bankruptcy Sharing and the Creditors' Bargain, 75 Va. L. Rev. (1989) 155–204.

Jacobsen, Lenz: Insolvenzrecht: "Die Politik hat den eigenen Gesetzen nicht vertraut", ZEIT ONLINE, 30.5.2009, http://www.zeit.de/online/2009/23/insolvenzrecht-opel-haarmeyer, accessed 15.8.2013.

Jacoby, Florian: Vorinsolvenzliches Sanierungsverfahren, ZGR 2010, 359–384.

Jaffé, Michael: Restrukturierung nach der InsO: Gesetzesplan, Fehlstellen und Reformansätze innerhalb einer umfassenden InsO-Novellierung aus Sicht des Insolvenzpraktikers, ZGR 2010, 248–263.

——: in FK-InsO – Frankfurter Kommentar zur Insolvenzordnung, Klaus Wimmer (eds), 6. Auflage 2010.

——: Drei Jahre Insolvenzplan, ZIP 2001, 2302–2304.

Jaffé, Michael / Friedrich, Andreas: Verbesserung der Wettbewerbsfähigkeit des Insolvenzstandorts Deutschlands, ZIP 2008, 1849–1858.

Jahn, Joachim: Wirtschaftsrecht – In der Insolvenz wird es für Minderheitseigner schwer, FAZ online 12.8.2013, http://www.faz.net/aktuell/wirtschaft/wirtschaftsrecht-in-der-insolvenz-wird-es-fuer-minderheitseigner-schwer-12528804.html, accessed 23.11.2013.

Jayme, Erik: Die kulturelle Dimension des Rechts – ihre Bedeutung für das Internationale Privatrecht und die Rechtsvergleichung, RabelsZ Bd. 67 (2003) 211–230.

James, Christopher: When Do Banks Take Equity in Debt Restructurings?, Rev. Fin. Stud. Vol. 8, No. 4 (1995) 1209–1234.

Jasper, Dieter: Forum Shopping in England und Deutschland, Duncker & Humblot, 1990.

Jarass, Hans D.: Zum Verhältnis von Grundrechtecharta und sonstigem Recht, EuR 2013, 29–45.

Jeffrey, Anna: Ask the chief restructuring officer, LexisNexis Restructuring and Insolvency, Autumn 2014, p. 6–7.

Jensen, Michael C. / Meckling, William H.: Theory of the Firm: Managerial Behavior, Agency Costs and Ownership Structure, J. Fin. Econ Vol. 3, No. 4 (1976) 305–360.

Jolls, Christine / Sunstein, Cass R. / Thaler, Richard: A Behavioral Approach to Law and Economic, 50 Stan. L. Rev. (1997–1998) 1471–1550.

Jostarndt, Philipp: Financial Distress, Corporate Restructuring and Firm Survival, Beiträge zur betriebswirtschaftlichen Forschung, Deutscher Universitätsverlag, 2007.

Jostarndt, Philipp / Rodt, Marc: Debt Man Walking: Zum Erwerb von Distressed Debt durch Finanzinvestoren, in Risikomanagement und kapitalmarktorientierte Unternehmensfinanzierung – Festschrift für Bernd Rudolph (FS Rudolph), *Schäfer, Klaus / Burghof, Hans-Peter / Johanning, Lutz / Wagner von Knapp, Hannes F. (eds.)*, Knapp Verlag 2009, p. 1100-1112.

Jungbluth, Rüdiger: Insolvenzen: Mehr Masse als Klasse, ZEIT 2.4.2009, p. 4.

Jungmann, Carsten: Solvenztest- versus Kapitalschutzregeln –- Zwei Systeme im Spannungsfeld von Gläubigerschutz und Finanzierungsfreiheit der Kapitalgesellschaft", ZGR 2006, 638–682.

Jungmann, Carsten / Thiessen, Jan: Discussion Report: Restructuring Insolvent Companies in the UK and in the US, ECFR 2008, 189–192.

Kahlert, Günter: Insolvenzrecht und Steuerrecht – Gemeinsam für ein wettbewerbsfähiges Insolvenzrecht, ZIP 2014, 1101–1112.

Kaufmann, Matthias: Recht ohne Regel?, Die philosophischen Prinzipien in Carl Schmitts Staats- und Rechtslehre, Verlag Karl Alber GmbH, Freising/München, 1988.

Karollus Martin: Die Umwandlung von Geldkrediten in Grundkapital – eine verdeckte Sacheinlage?, ZIP 1994, 589–599.

Keay, Andrew R. / Walton, Peter: Insolvency Law Insolvency Law: Corporate and Personal, Jordans Publishing Limited, 2008.

Kegel, Sandra: Von Richtern und Denkern – Vorentscheid im Fall Suhrkamp, FAZ, online 20.12.2014 http://www.faz.net/aktuell/feuilleton/buecher/suhrkamp/vorentscheid-im-fall-suhrkamp-von-richtern-und-denkern-13331600.html, accessed 23.12.2014.

——: Trauerspiel Suhrkamp, FAZ, Freitag, 25. Juli 2014, Nr. 170/30 D 1.

——: Gerichtssache Suhrkamp -Wie bei einer Flucht in Ketten, FAZ, online 5.12.2012 http://www.faz.net/aktuell/feuilleton/gerichtssache-suhrkamp-wie-bei-einer-flucht-in-ketten-11983179.html, accessed 23.11.2013.

——: Suhrkamp auf dem Weg zur AG – Das Gläubiger-Drama von Charlottenburg, FAZ 22.10.2013 online, http://www.faz.net/aktuell/feuilleton/buecher/suhrkamp-auf-dem-weg-zur-ag-das-glaeubiger-drama-von-charlottenburg-12629004.html, accessed 23.11.2013.

——: Streit um Suhrkamp – Endspiel, FAZ 3.10.2013 online, http://www.faz.net/aktuell/feuilleton/streit-um-suhrkamp-endspiel-12601970.html, accessed 23.11.2013.

——: Suhrkamp, Familienstiftung darf doch über Insolvenzplan abstimmen, FAZ 2.10.2013 online, http://www.faz.net/aktuell/feuilleton/buecher/suhrkamp/suhrkamp-familienstiftung-darf-doch-ueber-insolvenzplan-abstimmen-12601309.html, accessed 23.12.2013.

——: Urteil zur Suhrkamp AG – Etappensieg für Barlach, FAZ 10.9.2013 online, http://www.faz.net/aktuell/urteil-zur-suhrkamp-ag-etappensieg-fuer-barlach-12567766.html, accessed 23.11.2013.

——: Suhrkamp-Verfahren – Frankfurt gegen Berlin, FAZ 13.8.2013 online, http://www.faz.net/aktuell/feuilleton/suhrkamp-verfahren-frankfurt-gegen-berlin-12530438.html, accessed 23.11.2013.

——: Geschäftsführung bestärkt – Suhrkamp in Siegerlaune, FAZ 8.8.2013 online, http://www.faz.net/aktuell/feuilleton/buecher/suhrkamp/geschaefts-fuehrungbestaerkt-suhrkamp-in-siegerlaune-12452334.html, accessed 23.11.2013.

——: Fall Suhrkamp – Ausbruch aus der Feindschaft, FAZ 7.8.2013 online, http://www.faz.net/aktuell/feuilleton/fall-suhrkamp-ausbruch-aus-der-feindschaft-12427238.html, accessed 23.11.2013.

——: Suhrkamp – Terra juristica, FAZ online 20.6.2013, http://www.faz.net/aktuell/feuilleton/suhrkamp-terra-juristica-12238096.html, accessed 23.11.2013.

——: Schutzgeschirmter Verlag – Suhrkamp sucht die saubere Lösung, FAZ online 3.6.2013, http://www.faz.net/aktuell/feuilleton/buecher/suhrkamp/schutz-geschirmterverlag-suhrkamp-sucht-die-saubere-loesung-12205382.html, 23.11.2013.

Kestler, Matthias / Striegel, Andreas / Jesch, Thomas A., Distressed Debt Investments – Insolvenzrechtliche Instrumentarien der Unternehmenssanierung über Fremdkapital, NZI 2005, 417–424.

——: Distressed Debt Investments, Rws Kommunikationsforum, 2006.

Kilger, Joachim: Grundzüge eines Reorganisationsverfahrens, ZIP 1982, 779–787.

Kleindiek, Detlef: Debt-Equity-Swap im Insolvenzplanverfahren, in Festschrift für Peter Hommelhoff zum 70. Geburtstag (FS Hommelhoff), *Erle, Bernd /Goette, Wulf / Kleindiek, Detlef et al. (eds.)*, Dr. Otto Schmidt Verlag, Köln 2012, p. 543–563.

Klöhn, Lars / Schaper, Martin: Grenzüberschreitende Kombination von Gesellschaftsformen, ZIP 2013, 49–56.

Kluth, Thomas: Auf der Suche nach dem verlorenen Partner – die merkwürdige Unternehmensveräußerung im Insolvenzplan, ZInsO 2002, 1115–1122.

——: Die „wertlosen Gesellschaftsanteile" – der Stein des Anstoßes im Sanierungs-Insolvenzplan, ZInsO 2002, 258–264.

Knof, Béla: Der Ordrepublic-Vorbehalt nach Art. 26 EuInsVO – eine Allzweckwaffe gegen forum shopping im europäischen Insolvenzrecht?, ZInsO 2007, 629–637.

Knop, Jan: Die Wegzugsfreiheit nach dem Cartesio-Urteil des EuGH, DZWIR 2009, 147–152.

Köhler-Ma, Christian: Deutsches Insolvenzrecht = unflexibel?, DZWIR 2007, 410–413.

Kölner Kommentar zum Aktiengesetz, Kommentar, Carl Heymanns Verlag, 1993.

Kölner Schrift zur Insolvenzordnung. 3. Auflage, Köln, 2009.

Kokkoris, Ioannis: Weak-Form Tests of Market Efficiency in Corporate Debt Restructurings, Vol. 2, Iss. 6, ICR 2005, 337–343

Konecny, Andreas: Europäische Insolvenzkultur(en) – Kampf oder Harmonisierung, NZI 2008, 416–417.

Körner, Martin: Die Eigenverwaltung in der Insolvenz als bestes Abwicklungsverfahren?, NZI 2007, 270–276.

——: Unternehmens-Turnaround durch Eigenverwaltung in der Insolvenz. Insolvenz – Eine Chance zum Neuanfang?, Sierke Verlag, 2006.

Köster, Malte: Der englische insolvency practitioner – Berufsbild und Berufszugang, RIW 2006, 24–28.

Kötzle, Alfred / Zirener: Erfolgreiche Sanierung in der Insolvenz aus Sicht des Schuldnerunternehmens, ZP 2006, 73–98.

Korobkin, Donald R.: The Role of Normative Theory in Bankruptcy Debates, 82 Iowa L. Rev. (1996) 75–126.

——: Rehabilitating Values: A Jurisprudence of Bankruptcy, 91 Colum. L. Rev. (1991) 717–789.

Kraakman, Reinier R. / Davies, Paul / Hansmann, Henry et al.: The Anatomy of Corporate Law: A Functional and Comparative Analysis, Oxford University Press, 2004.

Kranzusch, Peter: Die Eigenverwaltung im Insolvenzverfahren – Anwendung und Hindernisse, ZInsO 2008, 1346–1354.

——: Sanierungen insolventer Unternehmen mittels Insolvenzplanverfahren, ZInsO 2007, 804–807.

Kranzusch, Peter / Icks, Annette: Wann werden die Gläubiger ausgezahlt? – Dauer von Unternehmensinsolvenzverfahren im regionalen Vergleich, in: Institut für Mittelstandsforschung Bonn (Hrsg.): IfM-Materialien Nr. 193, Bonn.

Kraus, Karl-J. / Knecht, Thomas: Notwendigkeit eines ganzheitlichen Konzepts für die Unternehmensrestrukturierung, in Festschrift für Jobst Wellensiek zum 80. Geburtstag (FS Wellensiek), *Flitsch, Michael / Hagebusch, Alfred / Oberle, Thomas*, Beck, München, 2011, p. 55–71.

Kresser, Matthias: Debt-equity-swaps im Insolvenzplanverfahren de lege ferenda, ZInsO 2010, 1409–1418.

Krieger, Gerd: Beschlußkontrolle bei Kapitalherabsetzungen – Besprechung der Entscheidungen BGHZ 138, 71 – Sachsenmilch und BGH ZIP 1999, 1444 – Hilgers –ZGR 2000, 885–907.

Kruth, Claus-Peter: Auswahl und Bestellung des Insolvenzverwalters, 2006. Heymanns, 2006.

Kumpan, Christoph: Der Insolvenzverwalter als Interessenwahrer, KTS 2010, 169–194.

Kunz, Hartmut / Ehnert, Thoralf: Debt for Equity Swaps – Turnaround Investment in Deutschland, Finanz Betrieb 2007, 7-8, 395–406.

Labbé, Marcus / Rudolph, Jens: Debt-Equity-Transaktionen im Insolvenzplanverfahren: Eine unterschätzte Sanierungschance, Finanz Betrieb, 2/2008, 97–102.

Lambrecht, Martin: „Sie können nicht einmal Bilanzen lesen“ – Zur Bestellung von Juristen als Insolvenzverwalter, DZWIR 2010, 22–28.

Larkin, Ben: Restructuring and Workouts: Strategies for Maximising Value, Global View Publishing Ltd., London, 2008, 51–58.

Larkin, Ben / Smith, Alexandra: Pre-Packaged Business Sales Following the Introduction of the Enterprise Act 2002, ICR 2004, 78–84.

Laryea, Thomas: Approaches to Corporate Debt Restructuring in the Wake of Financial Crises, International Monetary Fund, Legal Department, SPN/10/06, January 26, 2010.

Lechner, Roland: Waking from the jurisdictional nightmare of multinational default: the European Council Regulation on Insolvency Proceedings, AJICL 2002, 975–1024.

Ledwith, Sara / Watling, Jack: UK recovery may be kiss of death for some 'zombie' firms, Reuters online, 13.9.2013, http://uk.reuters.com/article/2013/09/13/uk-britain-zombies-idUKBRE98C04S20130913, accessed 25.9.2013.

Leithaus, Rolf: FINANCE-Magazin, Sonderbeilage Mai 2006, p.13.

Leutheusser-Schnarrenberger, Sabine: Rede der Bundesministerin der Justiz beim 7. Deutschen Insolvenzrechtstag am 18. März 2010 in Berlin, ZInsO 2010, 614–617.

——: Rede der Bundesministerin der Justiz beim Deutschen Insolvenzverwalterkongress 2011 am 28. Oktober 2011 in Berlin, ZInsO 2010, 2078–2081.

Lieder, Solveig: Grenzüberschreitende Unternehmenssanierung im Lichte der EuIns-VO, De Gruyter, 2007.

Lilico, Andrew: This ist he eye of the financial storm: UK banks are far from being healthy, cityam 5.11.2013, p. 24.

Lindner, Josef Franz: Grundrechtsschutz in Europa – System einer Kollisionsdogmatik, EuR 2007 Heft 2, 160–194.

Löbbe, Marc: Gesellschaftsrechtliche Gestaltungsmöglichkeiten des Debt Equity Swap, in Liber amicorum für Martin Winter (LA Winter), *Hoffmann-Becking, Michael / Hüffer, Uwe / Reichert Jochem et al.* (eds.), Schmidt Verlag, Köln, 2011, p. 423–446.

Löffler, Gunter / Maurer, Alina: Incorporating the dynamics of leverage into default prediction, 35 JBF (2011) 3351–3361.

López Gutiérrez, Carlos / García Olalla, Myriam / Torre Olmo, Begona: The influence of bankruptcy law on equity value of financially distressed firms: A European comparative analysis, IRLE 29 (2009) 229–243.

LoPucki, Lynn M.: A Team Production Theory of Bankruptcy Reorganization, 57 Vand. L. Rev. (2004) 741–779.

Lutter, Marcus / Hommelhoff, Peter / Timm, Wolfram: Finanzierungsmaßnahmen zur Krisenabwehr der Aktiengesellschaft, BB 1980, 737–750.

Lutter, Marcus: Materielle und förmliche Erfordernisse eines Bezugsrechtsausschlusses – Besprechung der Entscheidung BGHZ 71, 40 (Kali + Salz) –ZGR 1979, 401–418.

Lys, Thomas / Sivaramakrishnan, Konduru: Earning Expectations and Capital Restructuring: The Case of Equity-for-Debt Swaps, Journal of Accounting Research, Vol. 26, No. 2 (Autumn 1988) 273–299.

MacCormick, Neil: Institutions of law: an essay in legal theory, Oxford University Press, Oxford, 2007.

Machauer, Achim / Weber, Martin: Bank behaviour based on internal credit ratings of borrowers, 22 JBF (1998) 1355–1383.

Madaus, Stephan: Schutzschirme für streitende Gesellschafter? Lehren aus dem Suhrkamp-Verfahren für die Auslegung des neuen Insolvenzrechts, ZIP 2014, 500–508.

——: Die Bewältigung von Masseschäden über ein Planverfahren – Möglichkeiten und Grenzen des neuen Insolvenzrechts, ZIP 2014, 160–163.

——: Keine Reorganisation ohne die Gesellschafter, ZGR 2011, 749–775.

——: Der Insolvenzplan, Tübingen, 2011.

Maier, Daniel: Die praktische Wirksamkeit des Schemes of Arrangement in Bezug auf englischrechtliche Finanzierungen, NZI 2011, 305–310.

Mallon, Christopher / Waisman, Shai Y.: The Law and Practise of Restructuring in the UK and US, Oxford University Press, 2011.

Mankowski, Peter: Der ordre public im europäischen und im deutschen Internationalen Insolvenzrecht, KTS 2011, 185–218.

——: Die Anerkennung englischer Solvent Schemes of Arrangements in Deutschland, WM 2011, 1201–1210.

——: Rechtskultur JZ 2009, 321–331.

——: Klärung von Grundfragen des europäischen Internationalen Insolvenzrechts durch die Eurofood-Entscheidung? Centre of Main Interest (COMI), Anerkennung, ordre public, vorläufige Insolvenzverwaltung, BB 2006, 1753–1759.

Manning, Lee: Review of the Insolvency and Restructuring Landscape in the UK, Vol. 9, Iss. 1, ICR 2013, 2–3.

Marks, David: EC Insolvency Regulation: Is it Reform Time?, Vol. 9, Iss. 4, ICR 2012, 227–235.

Marsch-Barner, Reinhard: Nochmals: Umgehung der Sacheinlagevorschriften durch Wandelschuldverschreibungen und Wandelgenussrechte, DB 1995, 1497.

May, Hartmut: „Wo Du nicht bist, da ist das Glück" – Die Konkurs-Wanderungen entbehrlich machen, ZInsO 2012, 165–169.

McCormack, Gerard: Time to Revise the Insolvency Regulation, IILR 2011, 121–130.

——: Reconstructing European insolvency law – putting in a place a new paradigm, Legal Studies, Vol. 30 No. 1, March 2010, 126–146.

——: Corporate Rescue Law – An Anglo-American Perspective, Edward Elgar Publishing Ltd, 2008.

——: Apples and Oranges? Corporate Rescue and the Functional Convergence in the US and UK, Int. Insolv. Rev., Vol. 18 (2009) 109–134.

——: Super-priority new financing and corporate rescue, J.B.L. 2007, 701–732.

Medla, Natalia Alexandra: Präventive Unternehmenssanierung im deutschen und im französischen Recht, Nomos, 2008.

Meilicke, Wienand: Die Kapitalaufbringungsvorschriften als Sanierungsbremse – Ist die deutsche Interpretation des § 27 II AktG richtlinienkonform?, DB 1989, 1067–1075.

Meyer, Heinrich / Degener, Jan-Moritz: Debt-Equity-Swap nach dem RegE-ESUG, BB 2011, 846–851.

Meyer, Stefan: Die Haftung des vorläufigen Insolvenzverwalters, Heymanns, 2003.

Meyer, Susanne: Vorrang des Insolvenzrechts vor dem Gesellschaftsrecht? – Überlegungen zur Position des Minderheitsgesellschafts im Schutzschirmverfahren, ZInsO 2013, 2361–2369.

Meyer-Löwy, Bernd / Poertzgen, Christoph / de Vries, Christoph: Einführung in das englische Insolvenzrecht, ZInsO 2005, 293–298.

Michelman, Frank I.: A Comment on Some Uses and Abuses of Economics in Law, 46 U. Ch. L. Rev. (1979) 307–315.

Michels, Stephan: OLG Jena § 259 InsO, EWiR 2002, 293.

Milman, David: National Corporate Law in a Globalised Market: The UK Experience in Perspective, Edgar Elgar Publishing Ltd, 2009.

Milman, David: Reforming Corporate Rescue Mechanism, in *De Lacy, John*, The Reform of United Kingdom Company Law, Cavendish Publishing Limited, 2002, p. 415–438.

Möhlenkamp, Andreas: Flucht nach vorn in die Insolvenz, funktioniert Suhrkamp?, BB 2013, 2828–2831.

Moldenhauer, Ralf / Herrmann, Wolfgang / Wolf, Rüdiger / Drescher, Frederik: Zwei Jahre ESUG – Hype weicht Realität, BCG / WBDat. INDat-Report, März 2014.

——: Die ersten 1 ½ Jahre ESUG – Zögerliche Schritte zu einer neuen Sanierungskultur, BCG / WBDat. INDat-Report, September 2013.

——: Das erste Jahr ESUG – Zögerliche Schritte zu einer Sanierungskultur, BCG / WBDat. INDat-Report, März 2013.

Moss, Gabriel: Comparative Bankruptcy Law Cultures: Rescue or Liquidation, Comparison of Trends in National Law – England, 23 Brook. J. Int'l L. (1997) 115–138.

Moss, Gabriel / Fletcher, Ian F. / Isaacs, Stuart: The EC Regulation on Insolvency Proceedings, 2nd edition, Oxford, 2009.

Mucciarelli, Federico M.: Not just Efficiency: Insolvency Law in the EU and its political dimension, EBOR 14 (2013) 175–200.

Müller-Feldhammer, Ralf: Die übertragende Sanierung – ein ungelöstes Problem der Insolvenzrechtsreform, ZIP 2003, 2186–2193.

Müller, Hans-Friedrich: Verband in der Insolvenz, Heymanns, 2002.

Müller, Uwe: Suhrkamp-Prozess – Gewinnt Barlach die wichtige Schlacht? Die Welt online 24.9.2013, http://www.welt.de/kultur/literarischewelt/article 120337423/ Gewinnt-Barlach-die-wichtige-Schlacht.html, accessed 23.11.2013.

Müller-Seils, Carsten O.: Rescue Culture und Unternehmenssanierung in England und Wales nach dem Enterprise Act 2002, Nomos, Baden Baden, 2006.

Münchener Kommentar zur Insolvenzordnung: InsO, Kommentar, Gesamtwerk in 3 Bänden, 2002.

Münchener Kommentar zum Aktiengesetz, Kommentar, 2011.

Munro, Heike: Non-performing loans (especially corporate restructuring): status and exit strategies, in Performing and Non-performing Loan Transactions Across the World – A Practical Guide, *Gottlieb Griser / Simon, Wulfken, Jörg* (ed.), Euromoney Books, 2009, p. 128–147.

Nerlich, Jörg / Römermann, Volker: Insolvenzordnung, Beck Verlag, München, 2009.

Neubert, Klaus: Das Hannoveraner Modell zur Verwalterauswahl, ZInsO 2010, 73–78.

Nietsch, Michael: Die Stellung des Aktionärs im europäischen Gesellschaftsrecht – vom Mitglied zum Anleger und wieder zurück?, ZVglRWiss 112 (2013) 45–69.

Noack, Ulrich: Gesellschaftsrecht, Sonderband I zu Kübler, Bruno/Prütting, Hanns (eds), Kommentar zur Insolvenzordnung, Köln, 1999.

Oberle, Thomas: Außergerichtliche Sanierung oder Sanierung in der Insolvenz? – Ansätze für eine Vergleichsrechnung, in Festschrift für Jobst Wellensiek zum 80. Geburtstag (FS Wellensiek), *Flitsch, Michael / Hagebusch, Alfred / Oberle, Thomas*, Beck, München, 2011, p. 73–89.

Obermüller, Manfred: Das ESUG und seine Auswirkungen auf das Bankgeschäft, ZInsO 2011, 1809–1821.

Oelke, Herbert / Wöhlert, Helge-Torsten / Degen, Stephan: Debt Mezzanine Swap – Königsweg für die Restrukturierungsfinanzierung?, BB 2010, 299–303.

Ofek, Eli: Capital structure and firm response to poor performance, 34 J. Fin. Econ. (1993) 3–30.

Omar, Paul J.: Four models for rescue: convergence or divergence in European insolvency law? Part 1, 18 (4) I.C.C.L.R. (2007), 127–135.

——: The rule of *Interedil* and the Concept of Establishment, ICR 2012, 349–354.

——: The wider European Framework for insolvency, IL&P 2001, 135–138.

Örücü, Esin / Nelken, David (eds.): Comparative Law: A Handbook, Hart Publishing Oxford, 2007.

Otte, Karsten / Wiester, Roland: Nachmeldungen im Planverfahren, NZI 2005, 70–77.

Paape, Anna Lena: Die Regeln des Eigenkapitalersatzes beim Debt-Equity-Swap, DZWIR 2009, 9–14.

Pape, Gerhard: Entwicklungstendenzen bei der Eigenverwaltung, ZIP 2013, 2285–2294.

——: Gesetz zur weiteren Erleichterung der Sanierung von Unternehmen, ZInsO 2011, 1033–1041.

——: Erleichterung der Sanierung von Unternehmen durch Stärkung der Eigenverwaltung, ZInsO 2010, 1582–1596.

——: 10 Jahre Insolvenzordnung, ZInsO 2009, 1–5.

——: Von der „Perle der Reichsjustizgesetze" zur Abbruchhalde, ZInsO 2005, 842–844.

Patel, Swati / Fennessy, Mark: The Changing Nature of Stakeholders in Restructurings, Editorial, ICR 2006, 255–256.

Patterson, Dennis (editor): A Companion to Philosophy of Law and Legal Theory, 2nd Edition, Wiley-Blackwell, 2010.

Paulus, Christoph: EuInsVO: Änderungen am Horizont und ihre Auswirkungen, NZI 2012, 297–336.

——: Deutschlands langer Weg in die insolvenzrechtliche Moderne – Auf der Suche nach einer Sanierungskultur (Rescue Culture), WM 2011, 2205–2210.

——: Das englische Scheme of Arrangement – ein neues Angebot auf dem europäischen Markt für außergerichtliche Restrukturierungen, ZIP 2011, 1077–1083.

——: Ist das Insolvenzrecht wirklich eine Schlüsselmaterie für die Wirtschafts- und Finanzstabilität eines Landes?, in Sanierung und Insolvenz: Festschrift für Klaus Hubert Görg zum 70. Geburtstag (FS Görg), *Dahl, Michael / Jauch, Hans-Gerd H. / Wolf, Christian* (eds.), Beck Verlag, München, 2010, p. 361–370.

——: Ein Kaleidoskop aus der Geschichte des Insolvenzrechts, JZ 2009, 1148–1155.

——: Die ersten Jahre mit der Europäischen Insolvenzverordnung, RabelsZ, Bd. 70 (2006), 458–473

——: Die Insolvenz als Sanierungschance – ein Plädoyer, ZGR 2005, 309–326.

——: Notwendige Änderungen im Insolvenzrecht?, ZIP 2005, 2301–2302.

——: Ein Spannungsfeld in der Praxis: Sanierung und Insolvenzanfechtung, BB 2001, 425–430.

Paulus, Christoph / Berberich, Matthias: National Report for Germany, in Commencement of Insolvency Proceedings, *Faber, Niels E.D. / Vermunt, Niels / Kilborn, Jason J. / Richter, Tómas*, Oxford international and comparative insolvency law series, Oxford University Press, 2012, p. 313–364.

Paulus, Roman: Die ausländische Sanierung über einen Debt-Equity-Swap als Angriff auf das deutsche Insolvenzrecht?, DZWIR 2008, 6–14.

Peters, Katharina: Von Holzmann zu Opel: Chefsache Firmenrettung, Spiegel online, 18.11.2008, http://www.spiegel.de/politik/deutschland/von-holzmann-zu-opel-chefsache-firmenrettung-a-590864.html, accessed 13.8.2013.

Petrovic, Radmila: Die rechtliche Anerkennung des Scheme of Arrangements in Deutschland – eine Chance für die Restrukturierungspraxis, ZInsO 2010, 265–272.

Paffenholz, Guido / Kranzusch, Peter:,Insolvenzplanverfahren – Sanierungsoption für mittelständische Unternehmen, in: Institut für Mittelstandsforschung Bonn (eds.): Schriften zur Mittelstandsforschung Nr. 114 NF, Wiesbaden.

Piekenbrock, Andreas: Das ESUG – fit für Europa?, NZI 2012, 905–912.

Piepenburg, Horst: Unternehmenskauf in Krise und Insolvenz, in Festschrift für Günter Greiner zum 70. Geburtstag am 19. März 2005 (FS Greiner), *Piepenburg, Horst (editor)*, Carl Heymanns Verlag, Köln/Berlin/München, 2005, p. 271–284.

——: Faktisches Konzerninsolvenzrecht am Beispiel *Babcock Borsig*, NZI 2004, 231–238.

Pilkington, Christian / Schorling, Tom / Davies, Ben: UK Schemes of Arrangement: A Risk of Non-Recognition in Germany?, ICR 2010, 239–241.

Pilkington, Christian / Heverin, Kevin: Schemes of Arrangement in Cross-Border Restructurings – Issues of Jurisdiction and Recognition, ICR 2010, 89–92.

Pinfield, Scott: European Turnarounds and the Chief Restructuring Officer: Delivering Value for Investors through Strategic Execution, ICR 2006, 111–113.

Plath, Jörg: Suhrkamp Verlag – Suhrkamp auf dem Weg zur AG, Stuttgarter Zeitung online 22.10.2013, http://www.stuttgarter-zeitung.de/inhalt.suhrkamp-verlag-suhrkamp-auf-dem-weg-zur-ag.bf0f1fa2-b2ae-4b61-bce8-651bf2aca2f3.html, accessed 23.11.2013.

Platsas, Antonios Emmanuel: The Functional and the Dysfunctional in the Comparative Method of Law: Some Critical Remarks, vol. 12.3 Electronic Journal of Comparative Law, (December 2008), 1-15, http://www.ejcl.org/123/art123-3.pdf, accessed 9.7.2013.

Pleister, Christian / Kinder, Steffi: Kapitalmaßnahmen in der Insolvenz börsennotierter Gesellschaften, ZIP 2010, 503–512.

Picot, Gerhard / Aleth, Franz: Unternehmenskrise und Insolvenz, München 1999.

Pieck, Sarah: Die Kritik an der funktionalen Rechtsvergleichung, ZEuP 2013, 60–87.

Posner, Richard A., Economic Approach to Law, 53 Tex. L. Rev. (1975) 757–782.

——: Some Uses and Abuses of Economics in Law, 46 U. Ch. L. Rev. (1979) 281–306.

Priebe, Klaus: Der misslungene Sanierungsversuch im Spiegel der Insolvenzanfechtung: Sanierungskultur versus Insolvenzkultur?, ZInsO 2012, 1589–1601.

Priester, Hans-Joachim: Debt-Equity-Swap zum Nennwert?, DB 2010, 1445–1450.

Prütting, Hanns: Der neue IDW-Standard zur Erstellung von Sanierungskonzepten (IDW S 6) in der rechtlichen Beurteilung, ZIP 2013, 203–209.

Pym, Hugh: Zombie' companies eating away at economic growth, BBC News online, 13.11.2012, http://www.bbc.co.uk/news/business-20262282, accessed 13.5.2013.

Raiser, Thomas: Einige methodische und kritische Nachbemerkungen, ZGR 2006, 494–498.

Rajak, Harry: Company Rescue and Liquidations, 2nd ed., Sweet&Maxwell, London, 2005.

Rajan, Bob / Dettbarn, Jan / Kroner, Steffen: The ABCs of the CRO, eurofenix, Summer 2014, 24–27.

Rasmussen, Robert L.: Behavioral Economics, the Economic Analysis of Bankruptcy Law and the Pricing of Credit, 51 Vand. L. Rev. (1998) 1679–1703.

——: Debtor's Choice: A Menu Approach to Corporate Bankruptcy, 71 Tex. L. Rev. (1992) 51–121.

Rasmussen, Robert K. / Skeel, David A.: The Economic Analysis of Corporate. Bankruptcy Law, 3 Am. Bankr. Inst. L. Rev. (1995) 85–116.

Rasmussen, Robert K. / Thomas, Randall S.: Timing Matters: Promoting Forum Shopping by Insolvent Corporations, 94 Nw. U. L. Rev. (1999–2000) 1357–1408.

Rattunde, Rolf: Fachberater für Sanierung und Insolvenzverwaltung, (DStV e. V.), 2. Auflage, Berlin, 2012.

——: Sanierung durch Insolvenz, ZIP 2003, 2103–2110.

——: Sanierung von Großunternehmen durch Insolvenzpläne – Der Fall Herlitz, ZIP 2003, 596–600.

Rechtslupe, Rechtsschutz des Minderheitsgesellschafters gegen ein Insolvenzplanverfahren – der Fall Suhrkamp, 12. 11.2013, http://www.rechtslupe.de/zivilrecht/rechtsschutz-des-minderheitsgesellschafters-gegen-ein-insolvenzplanverfahren-der-fall-suhrkamp-368366, accessed 23.11.2013.

Redeker, Rouven: Kontrollerwerb an Krisengesellschaften: Chancen und Risiken des Debt-Equity-Swap, BB 2007, 673–680.

Reinhart, Stefan: Die Überarbeitung der EuInsVO, NZI 2012, 304–311.

Reitz, John C., A Life in the Craft of Comparative Law, 100 Mich. L. Rev. (2002) 1453–1469.

Reuss, Philipp M.: „Forum Shopping" in der Insolvenz, Mohr Siebeck, 2013.

Reuter, Peter: Eigenverwaltung – Das ungeliebte Kind der InsO?, INDat-Report 01/2006, p. 8–13.

Reuter, Peter: Erste Prüfung für ESUG, INDat-Report 6/2010, p. 28–35.

Richter, Nicolas: Möglichkeiten und Grenzen des Distressed Debt Investing in Deutschland: Am Beispiel von Unternehmensverbindlichkeiten (Schriften zum europäischen Management), Deutscher Universitätsverlag, 2006.

Richter Tomáš: Reconciling the European Registered Capital Regime with Modern Corporate Reorganization Law: Experience from the Czech Insolvency Law Reform, ECFR 2009, 358–369.

Riegger, Bodo / Spahlinger, Andreas: Die insolvenzrechtliche Fortführungsprognose – notwendige Klarstellungen für die Praxis, in Festschrift für Jobst Wellensiek zum 80. Geburtstag (FS Wellensiek), *Flitsch, Michael / Hagebusch, Alfred / Oberle, Thomas*, Beck, München, 2001, p. 119–131.

Riggert, Rainer: Das Insolvenzplanverfahren – Strategische Probleme aus der Sicht absonderungsberechtigter Banken, WM 1998, 1521–1525.

Ringe, Wolf-Georg: Forum Shopping under the EU Insolvency Regulation, EBOR 2008, 9(4), 579–620.

Ringe, Wolf-Georg / Gullifer, Louise / Théry, Philippe: Current Issues in European Financial and Insolvency Law – Perspectives from France and the UK, Hart Publishing, Oxford, 2009.

Römermann, Volker: Neues Sanierungsrecht ab 2012: Der Regierungsentwurf des ESUG, GWR 2011, 375.

Rüsche, Alexander: Barlach-Anwalt: Suhrkamp-Chefin verzögert Insolvenzplan, Focus online 10.11.2013, http://www.focus.de/kultur/buecher/verlage-barlach-anwalt-suhrkamp-chefin-verzoegert-insolvenzplan_aid_1154109.html, accessed 23.11.2013.

Rutstein, Michael / Bloomberg, Linton: A wind blows through an English brothel, CR&I 2010, 156–158.

Sassenrath, Gerd: Der Eingriff in die Anteilseignerrechte durch den Insolvenzplan: Ein Beitrag zur Reform des Insolvenzrechts, ZIP 2003, 1517–1530.

Schäfer, Carsten: Insolvenzplan als Lösungsmittel für Mehrheits-/Minderheitskonflikte? – Lehren aus dem Fall Suhrkamp, ZIP 2013, 2237–2093.

——: „Girmes“ wiedergelesen: Zur Treuepflicht des Aktionärs im Sanierungsfall, in Festschrift für Peter Hommelhoff zum 70. Geburtstag (FS Hommelhoff), *Erle, Bernd / Goette, Wulf / Kleindiek, Detlef et al. (eds.)*, Dr. Otto Schmidt Verlag, Köln 2012, p. 939–959.

Schaloske, Henning: Abwicklung von Versicherungsbeständen durch Solvent Schemes of Arrangement, VersR 2009, 23–30.

Schelo, Sven: Der neue § 270b InsO – Wie stabil ist das Schutzschirmverfahren in der Praxis? Oder: Schutzschirmverfahren versus vorläufige Eigenverwaltung, ZIP 2012, 712–715.

——: Flucht aus Deutschland oder der Wettbewerb der Insolvenzordnungen, Gastkommentar, NZI 2006, VII-VIII.

Scheunemann, Marc / Hoffmann, Guido: Debt-Equity-Swap, DB 2009, 983–986.

Schlegel, Ursula: Länderbericht England und Wales, in Münchner Kommentar zur Insolvenzordnung, 2. Auflage, Band III, München, 2008.

Schleusener, Ann-Kathrin: Der Debt-Equity-Swap, Peter Lang, 2012.

Schlinker, Steffen / Henke, Johannes: Kontrolle des Unternehmensinsolvenzverwalters und Mechanismusdesign, ZInsO 2010, 503–507.

Schmerbach, Ulrich / Staufenbiel Peter: Die übertragende Sanierung im Insolvenzverfahren, ZInsO 2009, 458–467.

Schmidt, Jens: Der Debt Equity Swap als Sanierungsinstrument im Fokus des Gesetzgebers, GWR 2010, 568.

Schmidt, Karsten: Debt-to-Equity-Swap bei der (GmbH & Co.-)Kommanditgesellschaft – ESUG, „Sanieren oder Ausscheiden“ und vor allem: Fragen über Fragen!, ZGR 2010, 566–584.

——: Aktienrecht und Insolvenzrecht – Organisationsprobleme bei insolventen Gesellschaften, AG 2006, 597–605.

——: Wege zu einem Insolvenzrecht der Unternehmen, Kommunikationsforum, 1990.

——: Die sanierende Kapitalerhöhung im Recht der Aktiengesellschaft, GmbH und Personengesellschaft, ZGR 1982, 519–538.

——: Gutachten D zum 54. DJT, 1982, S.D. 133.

——: Organverantwortlichkeit und Sanierung im Insolvenzrecht der Unternehmen, ZIP 1980, 328–337.

Schmidt, Karsten / Uhlenbruck, Wilhelm: Die GmbH in Krise, Sanierung und Insolvenz, Schmidt Verlag, 2009.

Schmidt, Mario / Schlitt, Michael: Debt Equity Swap – Eine attraktive Form der Restrukturierung?, DK 2009, 279–290.

Schmidt, Thomas E.: Suhrkamp Verlag: Es ist vorbei, ZEIT ONLINE 23.10.2013, http://www.zeit.de/2013/44/suhrkamp-verlag-ende-machtkampf, accessed 23.11.2013.

Schümann-Kleber, Kirsten: Recognition of English solvent schemes of arrangements affecting dissenting creditors of German Companies, IILR 447–459.

Schuppe, Walter: A survival guide for a successful turnaround, ABIJ 2005, 52–53.

Schwalme, Sebastian: Die Stellung des Anteilseigners in der Unternehmensinsolvenz, DZWIR 2004, 230–233.

Scott, Robert E.: Through Bankruptcy with the Creditors' Bargain Heuristic, Cases, Problems, and Materials on Bankruptcy by Douglas G. Baird; Thomas H. Jackson, 53 U. Chi. L. Rev. (1986) 690–708.

Sealy, Len / Milman, David: Volume 2: Annotated Guide to Insolvency Legislation 2011, Sweet&Maxwell, 2011.

Seibt, Christoph H.: Sanierungskapitalerhöhungen: Dogmatische Überlegungen und Praxisgestaltungen, Der Konzern 2009, 261–272.

Seelinger, Jan / Daehnert, Alexander: International Jurisdiction for Schemes of Arrangement, Vol. 9, Iss. 4, ICR 2012, 243–248.

Skeel, David A.: Markets, Courts, and the Brave New World of Bankruptcy Theory, 1993 Wis. L. Rev., 465–521.

Skouris, Vassilios: Towards a European Legal Culture, ZEuP 2012, 1-6.

Siehr, Kurt: Forum Shopping" im internationalen Rechtsverkehr, ZfRV 25 (1984), 124–144.

Simon, Marcus: Das Recht im Wettbewerb, Newsletter 04/2008, LMU München, http://www.uni-muenchen.de/aktuelles/publikationen/einsichten/084/0845.pdf, accessed 16.8.2013.

Simon, Stefan: Der Debt Equity Swap nach dem Gesetz zur weiteren Erleichterung der Sanierung von Unternehmen (ESUG), Corporate Finance law 2010, 448–459.

Simon, Stefan / Merkelbach, Matthias: Gesellschaftsrechtliche Strukturmaßnahmen im Insolvenzplanverfahren nach dem ESUG NZG 2012, 121–129.

Smid, Stefan: Rechtsmittelverfahren bei Anfechtung des Bestätigungsbeschlusses nach § 248 InsO, NZI 2005, 613-616.

——: 10 Jahre Insolvenzordnung – (k)ein trauriger Rückblick aus Sicht der Kreditinstitute(!)?, DZWiR 2009, 397–404.

——: Praxishandbuch Insolvenzrecht, de Gruyter, 2007.

——: Zu einigen Fragen der Eigenverwaltung, DZWIR 2002, 493–500.

——: Sanierungsverfahren nach neuem Insolvenzrecht, WM 1998, 2489–2515.

Smid, Stefan / Rattunde, Rolf: Der Insolvenzplan, Kohlhammer, 2005.

Smith, Adam: Wealth of Nations (1776), Prometheus Books, 1991.

Spetzler, Sophie: Insolvenzrechtsreform und Bankenreorganisation, KTS 2010, 433–461.

Spies, Jörg: Insolvenzplan und Eigenverwaltung – Sanierungsansatz zur Krisenbewältigung bei Unternehmen mittlerer Größe, ZInsO 2005, 1254–1259.

Spindler, Gerald: Finanzmarktkrise und Wirtschaftsrecht, AG 2010, 601–617.

Spliedt, Jürgen D.: Insolvenz der Gesellschaft ohne Recht der Gesellschaft, ZInsO 2013, 2155–2158.

——: Ist die außergerichtliche Sanierung pleite? – Ein Vergleich zur Sanierung im Insolvenzverfahren, InsVZ 2010, 27–39.

Stadler, Markus: Die Sanierung von Aktiengesellschaften unter Einsatz von Wandelgenussrechten, NZI 2003, 579–588.

Stapper, Florian: Die Praxis der Arbeit mit Insolvenzplänen oder die Insuffizienz des Insolvenzplans: Diagnose und Therapie, ZInsO 2009, 2361–2376.

Staufenbiel, Peter / Karlstedt, Thomas: Der Liquiditätsplan im Insolvenzverfahren ZInsO 2010, 2059–2068.

Stephan, Guido: Die Praxis der Auswahl des Insolvenzverwalters – ein Sanierungshindernis?, ZVglRWiss 2009, 273-286.

Steffek, Felix: Gläubigerschutz in der Kapitalgesellschaft, Mohr Siebeck, 2011.

——: Münchener Handbuch des Gesellschaftsrechts, Teil 2. Internationales Insolvenzrecht, Kapitel 2 Insolvenz und Sanierung deutscher Unternehmen in England, § 37–42, Beck Verlag, 2013.

Stiglitz, Joseph E.: Economics, Norton & Company, 1993.

Stürner, Rolf: Möglichkeiten der Sanierung von Unternehmen durch Maßnahmen im Unternehmens- und Insolvenzrecht, ZIP 1982, 761–772.

——: Aktuelle Probleme des Konkursrechts, ZZP 1981, 263–310.

Sullivan, Teresa A. / Warren, Elizabeth / Westbrook, Jay Lawrence: Less Stigma or More Financial Distress: An Empirical Analysis of the Extraordinary Increase in Bankruptcy Filings, 59 Stan. L. Rev. (2006-2007) 213–256.

Tashiro, Annerose: The legitimacy of a haircur, eurofenix, Spring 2013, p. 4.

——: Bankruptcy Tourism, Recovery winter 2009, 22–23.

Tashiro, Annerose / Beissenhirtz, Volker: German Companies heading towards England for their Rescue, ICR 2007, 171–177.

Teichmann, Christoph: Binnenmarktkonformes Gesellschaftsrecht, de Gruyter Rechtswissenschafts-Verlag Berlin, 2006.

Tett, Richard / Knapp, Marvin: German Federal Court Rules on the Equitable Life Scheme of Arrangement, Vol. 9, Iss. 6, ICR 2012, 346–348.

The Economist, Shareholder v stakeholder – a new idolatry?, 22.4.2010, http://www.economist.com/node/15954434, accessed 22.11.2013.

Thole, Christoph: Treuepflicht-Torpedo? Die gesellschaftliche Treuepflicht im Insolvenzverfahren, ZIP 2013, 1937–1945.

Teubner, Gunther: Unternehmensinteresse – das gesellschaftliche Interesse des Unternehmens „an sich“?, ZHR 148 (1984) 470–488.

Thierhoff, Michael / Müller, Renate / Illy, Thomas / Liebscher, Marc: Unternehmenssanierung, C.F. Müller Wirtschaftsrecht, 2011.

Toth-Feher, Geza M. / Schick, Olaf: Distressed Opportunities – Rechtliche Probleme beim Erwerb notleidender Forderungen von Banken, ZIP 2004, 491–497.

Uhlenbruck, Wilhelm: Risiken vorinsolvenzlicher übertragender Sanierung und Anschlussinsolvenzverfahren, ZInsO 2013, 2033–2039.

——: Modernisierung oder Zersplitterung des deutschen Insolvenzrechts?: kritische Anmerkungen zu den Änderungsplänen des BMJ, KSI 2010, 125–128.

——: Insolvenzordnung: InsO, Kommentar, Beck Verlag, München, 2010.

——: Von der Notwendigkeit eines eigenständigen Sanierungsgesetzes, NZI 2008, 201–206.

——: Eine Schicksalsfrage Not leidender Unternehmen, BB 2001, 1641–1648.

——: Die Insolvenzordnung – ein Jahrhundertgesetz? NJW 2000, 1386.

——: Sanierung und Organisation als drittes Insolvenzverfahren in einem zukünftigen Recht?, KTS 1981, 513–575

Uhlenbruck, Wilhelm / Vallender, Heinz: Zehn Jahre Insolvenzordnung – eine kritische Zwischenbilanz, NZI 2009, 1–11.

Ulmer, Peter: Die gesellschaftsrechtlichen Regelungsvorschläge der Kommission für Insolvenzrecht, ZHR 149 (1985), 541–574.

Undritz, Sven-Holger: Restrukturierung in der Insolvenz, ZGR 2010, 201–217.

United Nations Centre on Transnational Corporation, Debt Equity Conversions, A Guide for Decision-makers, 1990, http://unctc.unctad.org/data/stctc104a.pdf, accessed, 13.7.2013.

Urlaub, Jasmin: Notwendige Änderungen im Gesetz zur weiteren Erleichterung der Sanierung von Unternehmen (ESUG) zur Verhinderung von Missbräuchen, ZIP 2011, 1040–1045.

Vallender, Heinz: Insolvenzkultur gestern, heute und morgen, NZI 2010, 838–844.

——: Gefahren für den Insolvenzstandort Deutschland, NZI 2007, 129–137.

——: Eigenverwaltung zwischen Gläubiger und Schuldnerautonomie, WM 1998, 2129–2139.

Vaupel, Christoph / Reers Ulrich: Kapitalerhöhungen bei börsennotierten Aktiengesellschaften in der Krise, AG 2010, 93–105.

Verse, Dirk A.: Anteilseigner im Insolvenzverfahren. Überlegungen zur Reform des Insolvenzplanverfahrens aus gesellschaftsrechtlicher Sicht, ZGR 2010, 299–324.

Vickers, Tom: In search of a rescue regime: considering 'encouraging company rescue – a consultation', CRI 2009, 262–263.

Vriesendrop, Reinout D. / Grmatikov, Martin A.: Funding Corporate Rescue: the Impact of the Financial Crisis, 19 Int. Insolv. Rev. Vol. (2010) 209–237.

Von Bogdandy, Armin / Schill, Stephan: Die Achtung der nationalen Identität unter dem reformierten Unionsvertrag – Zur unionsrechtlichen Rolle des nationales Verfassungsrechts und zur Überwindung des absoluten Vorrangs, ZaöRV 70 (2010), 701–734.

Von der Fecht, Wolf-Rüdiger: High Court of Justice: Internationale Zuständigkeit Englands für Bestätigung von Schemes of Arrangement bei hinreichender Verbindung zu England, NZI 2011, 557–567.

Von Falkenhausen, Joachim Freiherr: LG Frankfurt/M. EWiR § 169 HGB 2/13, 581–582.

Von Lovenberg, Felicitas: Suhrkamp-Verfahren – Insolvent sein oder nicht, FAZ 22.7.2013, http://www.faz.net/aktuell/feuilleton/buecher/suhrkamp/suhrkamp-verfahren-insolvent-sein-oder-nicht-12291401.html, accessed 23.11.2013.

Von Münch, Ingo: Rechtspolitik und Rechtskultur, Berliner Wissenschafts-Verlag, Berlin, 2011.

Von Sydow, Christian / Beyer, Oliver: Erwerb von notleidenden Krediten und anschließende Kapitalerhöhung mit Sacheinlage, AG 2005, 635–644.

Wallace, Ian: CVAs: easy as ABS?, CR&I 2012, 163–165.

Walters, Adrian / Smith, Anton: ‚Bankruptcy Tourism' under the EC Regulation on Insolvency Proceedings: A View from England and Wales, 19 Int. Insolv. Rev. (2010) 181–208.

Walton, Peter: Pre-packin' in the UK, Int. Insolv. Rev. Vol. 18 (2009) 85–108.

Warren, Elizabeth: Bankruptcy Policy making in an Imperfect World, 92 Mich. L. Rev. (1993) 336–387.

——: Bankruptcy Policy, 54 U. Chi. L. Rev. (1987) 775–814.

Warrikoff, Alexander: Gestaltungsmöglichkeiten im Insolvenzplan, KTS 1997, 527–546.

Watson, Alan: Legal Transplants, First edition, Edinburgh, 1974.

——: Legal Change: Sources of Law and Legal Culture, 131 U. Penn. L. Rev. (1983) 1121–1157.

——: Society and Legal Change, 1977.

Watson, Adam: Comparative Law and Legal Change, 37 Cambridge L. J. (1978) 313–336.

Weber, Jens: Anforderungen an den Inhalt von Sanierungskonzepten nach der Rechtsprechung insbesondere des Bundesgerichtshofes, ZInsO 2011, 904–908.

Weber, Jens / Schneider, Petra: Die nach dem Gesetz zur weiteren Erleichterung der Sanierung von Unternehmen (ESUG) vorgesehene Umwandlung von Forderungen in Anteils- bzw. Mitgliedschaftsrechte (Debt-Equity-Swap), ZInsO 2012, 374–385.

Weber, Stefan: Sieben auf einen Streich, SZ online 9.12.2010, http://www.sueddeutsche.de/wirtschaft/karstadt-insolvenzverwalter-goerg-sieben-auf-einen-streich-1.1033784, accessed 13.5.2013.

——: Karstadt: Insolvenzverwalter Görg Es ist Zahltag – in eigener Sache, SZ online 7.10.2010, http://www.sueddeutsche.de/wirtschaft/karstadt-insolvenzverwalter-goerg-es-ist-zahltag-in-eigener-sache-1.1009404, accessed, 13.5.2013.

——: Insolvenz – die selten genutzte Chance, SZ online 17.5.2010, http://www.sueddeutsche.de/wirtschaft/sz-serie-mittelstand-insolvenz-die-selten-genutzte-chance-1.484575, accessed 13.5.2013.

Weiland, Severin: Forderung nach Opel-Insolvenz: Guttenberg gibt den einsamen Kämpfer, Spiegel online, 30.5.2009, http://www.spiegel.de/wirtschaft/forderung-nach-opel-insolvenz-guttenberg-gibt-den-einsamen-kaempfer-a-627791.html, accessed 13.8.2013.

Wellensiek, Jobst: Übertragende Sanierung, NZI 2002, 233–239.

——: Probleme bei der Betriebsveräußerung aus der Insolvenz, NZI 2005, 603–606.

Wellensiek, Jobst / Krispenz, Sabina: Die börsennotierte Aktiengesellschaft in der Insolvenz, in Sanierung und Insolvenz: Festschrift für Klaus Hubert Görg zum 70. Geburtstag (FS Görg), *Dahl, Michael / Jauch, Hans-Gerd H. / Wolf, Christian (eds.)*, Beck Verlag, München, 2010, p. 867–370.

Weller, Marc-Philippe: Die Klagbarkeit gesellschaftsrechtlicher Treuepflichten, in: Liber amicorum für Martin Winter (LA Winter), Hoffmann-Becking, Michael/ Hüffer, Uwe/Reichert Jochem et al. (eds.), Schmidt Verlag, Köln, 2011, p. 755–773.

——: Die Verlegung des Center of Main Interest von Deutschland nach England, ZGR 2008, 835–866.

Wells, Alan: Insolvency – Is the UK Suited to Chaper 11?, BLR 2012, 156–159.

Werlauff, Eric: Relocating a Company within the EU, ECL Vol. 5, Iss. 3 (2008) 136–139.

Wessels, Bob: Harmonizing of Insolvency Law in Europa, ECL 2011, 27–31.

——: European Union Regulation on Insolvency Proceedings, ABIJ, November 2001, 24–31.

Westbrook, Jay Lawrence / Gottlieb, Lawrence C.: Reorganizations, Exemption of Financial Assets, 27 ABIJ 2009, 10.

Westphal, Lars: Debt-Equity-Swap, in: Eilers, Stephan / Koffka, Matthias/Mackensen, Marcus (eds.), Private Equity – Unternehmenskauf, Finanzierung, Restrukturierung, Exitstrategien, München 2009.

Westphal, Lars / Janjuah, Riaz K.: Zur Modernisierung des deutschen Sanierungsrechts – Ein Beitrag zur aktuellen Diskussion über die Reformbedürftigkeit des deutschen Insolvenzrechts, BB 2008, Beil. 3, 1–28.

Westphal, Lars / Knapp, Marvin: Die Sanierung deutscher Gesellschaften über ein englisches Scheme of Arrangement, ZIP 2011, 2033–1083.

Wetzel, Dennis: Das Insolvenzplanverfahren in Eigenverwaltung, Avm Akademische Verlagsgemeinschaft, 2009.

White, Michelle J.: The Corporate Bankruptcy Decision, J. Econ. Persp., Vol. 3, No. 2. (Spring, 1989) 129–151.

Willcock, John: Dutch propose ‚lean and mean' Scheme of Arrangement

Willemsen, Reinhard / Rechel, Janine: Die Reform des Insolvenzplanverfahrens – Ein Zwischenstandsbericht: Anmerkungen zu den vorgeschlagenen Änderungen, BB 2010, 2059–2068.

Wilson, Charles: Debt equity swaps: an alternative form of corporate rescue, CR&I 2009, 103–104.

Windsor, Jo / Müller-Seils, Carsten O. / Burg, Michael: Unternehmenssanierungen nach englischem Recht – Das Company Voluntary Arrangement, NZI 2007, 7–12.

Wirth, Gerhard: Vereinfachte Kapitalherabsetzung zur Unternehmenssanierung, DB 1996, 867–872.

Witt, Karl-Heinz: Modernisierung der Gesellschaftsrechte in Europa, ZGR 2009, 872–930.

Wittig, Arne: Übernahme der Gesellschafterstellung in Krisenunternehmen als Sanierungsbeitrag der finanzierenden Institute, in Insolvenzrecht in Wissenschaft und Praxis: Festschrift für Wilhelm Uhlenbruck zum 70. Geburtstag (FS Uhlenbruck), *Prütting, Hans / Vallender, Heinz*, Otto Verlag Köln, 2000, p. 685–722.

——: Beseitigung der Insolvenzgründe mit Bankenbeiträgen als Voraussetzung der freien Unternehmenssanierung, NZI 1998, 49–57.

Wolf, Annika: Cross-Border Insolvency Proceedings of Multinational Corporations – Parmalat – A European and American Perspective, http://www.iiiglobal.org/component/jdownloads/finish/337/4050.html, accessed 18.2.2013.

Wood, Philip: The Law and Practice of International Finance, Sweet&Maxwell, London, 2008.

——: Principles of International Insolvency, Sweet&Maxwell, London, 2007.

Wruck, Karen Hopper: Financial Distress, reorganization, and organizational efficiency, 27 J. Fin. Econ. (1990) 419–444.

Wuschek, Thomas: Debt-Equity-Swap – Gestaltung von Anteilsrechten im Insolvenzplanverfahren, ZInsO 2012, 1768–1772.

Wymeersch, Eddy: Das neue europäische Finanzmarktregulierungs- und Aufsichtssystem, ZGR 2011, 443–470.

Zheng, Xiaolan/El Ghoul, Sadok/Guedhami, Omrane/Kwok, Chuck C.Y.: National culture and corporate debt maturity, 36 JBF (2012) 468–488.

Zielcke, Andreas: Konflikt im Suhrkamp Verlag – Wenn Trennung die einzige Lösung ist, Süddeutsche online 13.2.2013, http://www.sueddeutsche.de/kultur/konflikt-um-suhrkamp-verlag-wenn-trennung-die-einzige-loesung-ist-1.1599570, accessed 23.11.2013.

——: Konflikt um Suhrkamp – Feinde, die es ganz genau wissen wollen, Süddeutsche online 10.10.2013, http://www.sueddeutsche.de/kultur/konflikt-um-suhrkamp-feind e-die-es-ganz-genau-wissen-wollen-1.1767634, accessed 23.11.2013.

——: Konflikt um Suhrkamp – Drama in Akten, Süddeutsche online 4.9.2013, http://www.sueddeutsche.de/kultur/konflikt-um-suhrkamp-drama-in-akten-1.1762829, accessed 23.11.2013.

Zipperer, Helmut: „Übertragende Sanierung" – Sanierung ohne Grenzen oder erlaubtes Risiko?, NZI 2008, 206–210.

Zipperer, Helmut / Vallender, Heinz: Die Anforderungen an die Bescheinigung für das Schutzschirmverfahren, NZI 2012, 729–735.

Zypries, Brigitte: Ein Rechtssystem mit Qualitätssiegel, FAZ Nr. 251, 27.10.2008, p. 10.